The Theology of Deuteronomy

BIBAL Collected Essays 2

The Theology of Deuteronomy

Collected Essays of Georg Braulik, O.S.B.

translated by

Ulrika Lindblad

BIBAL Press
Publishing agency of BIBAL Corporation
Berkeley Institute of Biblical Archaeology & Literature

The Theology of Deuteronomy: Collected Essays of Georg Braulik, O.S.B.

Library of Congress Cataloging-in-Publication Data

Braulik, Georg.
The theology of Deuteronomy : collected essays of Georg Braulik / translated by Ulrika Lindblad.
p. cm. -- (BIBAL collected essays : vol. 2)
Includes bibliographical references (p.).
ISBN 0-941037-30-4
1. Bible. O.T. Deuteronomy--Theology. I. Title. II. Series.
BS1275.2.B725 1994
222'.1506--dc20
94-43980
CIP

Published by BIBAL Press
P.O. Box 821653
N. Richland Hills, TX 76182

Printed by Great Impressions, Dallas, TX

This book is dedicated to my sister

Dr. Irmengard Braulik-Löri

who has for many years devoted herself to making young people familiar with the English language and with English and American literature.

Table of Contents

PREFACE

This collection of articles owes its existence to a suggestion made by Dr. Duane L. Christensen. Dr. Christensen and I are united not only by a friendship of many years' standing, but also by our common interest in and research on the ever-fascinating book of Deuteronomy.

The present volume contains a selection of my articles specially chosen for the American reading public. Several of them have already been given as lectures at various universities in the United States, although in a less developed form. All contributions are concerned with the theological themes of Deuteronomy. I have used the methods of historical and literary-historical research; nevertheless, most of the articles also contain a dialogue with the New Testament and the Church of our times. They are presented in the order in which they were written. As I wrote them, I was simultaneously engaged in writing a commentary on Deuteronomy. This commentary has been published in two volumes in the German *Neue Echter Bibel* and provides further information about the wider context of the texts which are explored in the present volume.

The articles in this volume can also be considered as a preparation for a more extensive commentary which Professor Norbert Lohfink, S.J. and I are preparing for the series *Hermeneia*.

I am grateful, first of all, to Dr. Ulrika Lindblad, the translator of this volume; and also wish to express my gratitude to Dr. Alfred Friedl for preparing the bibliography. I owe Dr. William Scott, Director of BIBAL Press, a particular debt of gratitude for his extensive editorial work and ever-efficient organization.

Georg Braulik, O.S.B.
Vienna, October 1994

1
Wisdom, Divine Presence and Law

Reflections on the Kerygma of Deut 4:5-8

**German title: "Weisheit, Gottesnähe und Gesetz"
(see bibliography)**

Even today, Christian theology is in danger of judging the Torah of Moses in accordance with the New Testament antithesis directed against "legalism." Usually, this must be blamed on some form of retrojection and generalization of the Pauline polemics against "Jewish legalism" or of Jesus' confrontation with the literalism and rigid learning of the scribes. But the responsibility for this state of affairs is shared by a scheme of evolution which is problematic even from the point of view of the history of religion. The following quotation from O. Eissfeldt is typical:

> The most wonderful fruits of religious poetry demonstrate the intimate fusion of Hebrew transcendent belief in God and Canaanite immanent vision of God. But these promising beginnings were interrupted by what appears like a frost in a spring night. There followed the period of which Paul says: "The law got in the way," the period of Judaism. God sat on his throne in the far distance without any connection either with man or with nature. The law stood between him and humanity . . . The law remained the custodian until the arrival of Christ. Those promising beginnings which we discovered in the fusion of the Hebrew and the Canaanite image of God attained its fullest flower in Jesus of Nazareth. In him, we discern a wonderful harmony of yahwism and baalism, of transcendence and immanence. His God is perfect and the task of man is to be perfect as he is perfect. His God is the stern judge who, at the last judgment, judges according to the measure of justice . . . and yet, this very same God who is a stern judge

is also the God of the weary and the exhausted, the poor and the tormented, the God of those who are poor and suffer, of those who hunger and thirst after righteousness.[1]

Scholars have continuously—and with good reason—pointed to the manifold influence of Deuteronomy on postexilic Judaism.[2] This study constitutes an attempt to show, by analyzing a short but seminal deuteronomic text that the gift of "this Torah" (4:8) constitutes a salvific action on the part of YHWH and makes men and women free before God and before themselves. This means that the Torah gives the same image of God as the New Testament does—"in truth, a wonderful harmony between the transcendent and the immanent experience of God."[3]

Translation and Structure of Deut 4:5-8[4]

I 5a See[5]

II I teach[6] you statutes and ordinances
as YHWH, my God,[7] has commanded me
5b in order that you act according[8] to them in the land which you are entering in order to take possession of it.

III 6a You are to observe (them) carefully and to act (according to them).

IV for this is your wisdom and your understanding in the eyes[9] of the peoples
6b who will hear all these statutes and then will say "Indeed,[10] they are a wise and understanding people, this great nation."
7a For what great nation (is there)
that (has) a god[11] (so) near to it
7b as YHWH our God (is to us)
when we call upon him?
8a And what great nation (is there)
that (has) statutes and ordinances (as) righteous
8b as the whole of this Torah
which I set before you today?

Introductory Remarks on Deut 4:5-8

This pericope constitutes a thematically and structurally distinct section of the literary unity Deut 4:1-40,[12] which in late exilic times was inserted before the deuteronomic Torah (chapters 5-28; cf. 4:8)[13] and the Deuteronomic History[14] *as a theological key text.* Verses 5-8[15] together with verses 1-4 function as a prologue, related by thematic and stylistic correspondences to the epilogue formed by verses 32-40. Verses 7-8 speak of the worldwide horizon for Israel's uniqueness, whereas verses 32-39 describe the uniqueness of YHWH within the framework of the history of humankind. In both sections, the affirmations of incomparability take the form of rhetorical questions. There are also some formal resemblances without strictly factual parallels. All these relations will be taken into account in the interpretation.

Nearly all of the parenesis in chapter 4 has borrowed its formal structure from the legal domain. The long period constituted by verses 5-8 is constructed according to a four-part *scheme for legal decisions.* In Deuteronomy as well as in the rest of the Old Testament, legal documents are used as a basis for the text.[16] The basic structure is as follows:

- I the interjection *r^{e}'ēh*:
- II a legal decision
- III imperatives
- IV sometimes a substantiation clause, which is introduced by *kî*[17]

In our verses, the second and especially the fourth element of this basic structure are given an elaborate rhetorical development.[18] As to the third element, injunctives[19] are used to modify[20] its grammatical forms. The entire piece is bracketed by two parts of a formula, *r^{e}'ēh* (verse 5) and *ntn lipnê* (verse 8). In all other parts of Deuteronomy, these expressions are only found together, as a standard formula.[21]

If the structure of verses 5-8 is not merely due to artistic development of ideas, but has taken a juridically significant form, what does establishing the legal character of laws which are not communicated in these verses signify? In any sophisticated legal system, a distinction is made between simply communicating the contents of a law (which can be done privately) and the *formal act of promulgation.* It is only through the act of promulgation that a law comes into effect. A law can be promulgated in many different ways: by the signature of the head of state, by publication in a legal gazette, by being posted in a particular place, by oral proclamation in the course of a special ceremony, and so on. However, the legal atmosphere of the ancient Near East is not comparable to that of a modern state.[22] The views regarding the great legal codifications, especially the Code of Hammurapi, still fluctuate between two extremes: a code of law in the modern sense and a polemic treatise or academic study without legal signification.[23] Yet even here we discern a structure which distinguishes between making known the contents of the law and giving legal force to a code of law. For instance, the prologue and the epilogue on one hand, and the corpus of the law on the other are clearly differentiated. All questions which today would be considered part of the promulgation are treated in the prologue or in the epilogue. The corpus of the law in no way differs from a private collection of laws, such as is constituted by the Middle Assyrian laws. In the Code of Hammurapi, the poetically sonorous introduction and the bold and imaginative ending are not merely contextually differentiated from the legal main part of the code. They also differ widely in language and style and are not joined to the corpus through any stylistic devices.[24]

> The purpose of the "frame" is evidently a twofold one: in the first place to confirm that Hammurapi is the author of the laws, to explain their intention and use, and stress their perpetual validity; in the second place, to portray the legal activity of Hammurapi as a divine mission and integrate it in the great ultramundane event of Marduk being called to be the lord of all nations.[25]

Thus, although both the prologue and the epilogue deal with the function, intent and principles of the laws, they express a way of thinking which is clearly different from our modern conception of the validity of laws.

> The validity Hammurapi hopes that his work will achieve is fundamentally different from the claim to validity possessed by modern codes of law. His so-called laws are exemplary decisions, models of good jurisdiction. His work will have an impact because it is there, because it is of a high quality and because the author is competent and the content exemplary.[26]

With regard to 4:5-8, there is certainly a considerable formal similarity to actual law. Later, this similarity becomes even greater because the contents and formulations of this text resemble those of the Code of Hammurapi. According to the text, Moses proclaims the laws by divine appointment. This time, however, he is not transmitting commandments which have already been communicated by YHWH as is the case in chapter 5. Instead, the legislation here is authorized by Moses himself.[27] This is one reason why it appeared necessary to add to the mere presentation of the contents an act which modern legal thought would define as an act of promulgation. As in the Mesopotamian law codes, the establishment of legal validity need not be an integral part of the legal text itself; the validity can be established in a nearby passage. In the Mesopotamian codes, the prologue and the epilogue constitute eulogies of the legislator and of his work. Deut 4:5-8 similarly attempts to gain acceptance for the deuteronomic law code. Verse 5 even refers to the act of promulgation.

Rival conceptions of this promulgation in Deuteronomy 27 and 31 are to be explained by the way the book of Deuteronomy came into being. There is, therefore, nothing surprising about the fact that chapter 4, a reinterpretation intended for the late exilic period, presents the legislating function of Moses, the process of promulgation, as well as the formal acceptance of the law by the people in a different configuration.

The Claim Made by the Code of Law (Verse 5)

The verb *rᵉʾēh*,[28] which serves to attract the reader's attention, introduces three syntactically and stylistically distinct *legal decisions*.[29] First is the act of promulgation ("I teach you the statutes and ordinances"). Elsewhere in 4:1-40, this is described only in relative clauses. Second is the legal status of this communication of the laws ("as YHWH, my God, has commanded me"). Third is the time at which the laws are to come into force and their range of validity ("that you may act according to them in the land"). The status of these formal declarations and the fact that they were inserted into their context at a later stage suggest that it was the author's intention to define the obligatory character of the entire deuteronomic law (chapters 5-26) in this passage.

The Mosaic proclamation of the commandments appears as *teaching*. In the corpus of the law, *lmd*, which in the Pentateuch occurs only in Deuteronomy, means acquiring a disposition,[30] whereas in the "frame" texts, it is used of learning the law[31] or of learning the Song of Moses.[32] True, the deuteronomic parenesis had a rhetorical-didactic character from the beginning.[33] Nevertheless, in the latest strata of the book, the didactic objectives gain in importance. Even *lmd* appears to have obtained its decisive role only in the context of the new theological orientations.[34] Finally, in chapter 4, *lmd* functions (on five occasions) as a key word in proclaiming the law. YHWH himself explains the intention of the revelation at Horeb: "I will let them hear my words (*d^ebāray*), which (*'^ašer*)[35] they are to learn, in order that they may honor (*l^eyir'â*)[36] me faithfully" (that is, by acting according to these words): "and their children, too, are to learn these words." This means that learning and teaching the words of YHWH—that is, the Decalogue[37]—constitutes the authentic way of honoring YHWH. In verses 1, 5 and 14, the activity of Moses is also described as "teaching." This slight shift in relation to the promulgatory verbs of older texts[38] gives the impression that during that phase of the Babylonian exile, there was a dangerous break in the living transmission of faith and that the text was intended to counteract this.[39]

What Moses legislates and teaches are the "statutes and ordinances." This double expression occurs most frequently in chapter 4—in verses 1, 5, 8 and 14—and illustrates the introductory character of this chapter. Concretely, the expression refers primarily to 4:45 - 26:16.[40] These *ḥuqqîm ûmišpāṭîm* are, in contrast to the Decalogue, only the will of god at one remove, so to speak. However, in the final analysis, the authority behind them is the same. Their proclamation, according to the *retrospective formula* of verse 5a, follows on YHWH's explicit order. This commissioning of Moses also brings YHWH as "my God" into focus.[41] That Moses was commissioned to teach is told in a retrospective view of the events at Horeb, appended to our passage. This retrospective view also throws light on the relation between the Decalogue and the Mosaic law "and (YHWH) revealed his covenant to you and commanded you to keep it: the ten commandments. And he also commanded me to teach you statutes and ordinances that you may keep them in the land which you are entering in order to take possession of it" (verses 13-14). In contrast to 5:31, which distinguishes between the Decalogue and the rest of the law, that is, between the mediated and the unmediated word of YHWH, the whole emphasis is on the existence of the Mosaic law. This law, however:

> . . . is not introduced as a transmission of the words of YHWH at Horeb, but as an interpretation of YHWH's statutes and ordinances (again in contrast to 5:31, the terms have no article!). According to this view the deuteronomic

> law is the authorized interpretation of the Decalogue communicated at Horeb. It is not the reiteration of another law, communicated by YHWH to Moses alone at Horeb, in addition to the Decalogue.[42]

This distinction between the words of YHWH themselves and the interpretation which actualizes them[43] and which is given by Moses or by a prophet, his divinely authorized successor (18:15-18),[44] does not, however, imply any difference of degree in the binding force of the law. There is a difference in the range of validity: the Decalogue and in particular the first commandment remain binding for YHWH's people always and everywhere.[45] This is clear from the unconditional *la'ᵃśôt* in 4:13. The statutes and ordinances, on the other hand, determine Israel's life only after the conquest of the land (4:5, 14).[46] Possibly this was intended to settle a discussion of the exiles in Babylon regarding the problem of whether the law was binding in exile.[47] In any case, it constitutes an expression of the unbroken hope of a new life for all Israel in *the promised land*.[48] For if it is only there that the law can be observed, the possession of the land is vital for Israel. At the same time, the New Testament problem of "law and grace" would have found its solution: in his grace, YHWH gives his people, before they do anything and through no merit of theirs, a blessed space in which Israel can serve him by observing the law.

The Obligation (Verse 6*)

In Deuteronomy, the "keeping" (*šmr*) of the statutes and the "doing" (*'śh*) together make up a formula. The parts of the formula are not experienced as distinct words; they constitute a set expression.[49] This is the only passage in Deuteronomy where these two verbs are found in an absolute sense, that is, without any other legal verbs and without being directly united to any object. It is also the only passage in Deuteronomy where they are found together. In the context of the deuteronomic linguistic world, as well as because of the exceptional brevity of the speeches within a wide rhetorical context, the two injunctives receive a clear stylistic profile: this is the formal pledging of the people to observe the statutes.

The Motivation to Obey the Law

The Wisdom (Verse 6) and Uniqueness (Verses 7-8) of Israel. The Israel which is here primarily addressed is still living as an unimportant people outside Canaan and is striving for a position among those great powers which set the tone in the political, religious and cultural spheres. If the Israelites wanted to rival them, they needed the education and culture the others had, but they also needed a god who was "near to them," that is, a god who was able to help, and they needed a just legislation. The motivation outlined in verses 6-8 fits in very well with the idea of the Moses group coming from the desert and (according to the literary fiction of Deuteronomy) camping on the borders of the promised land. But in fact the motivation was still better adapted to the situation of the people of God in their Babylonian exile. How could the remnant of Israel, scattered among the nations (cf. verse 27), who had had their political existence destroyed and whose religious center, the Temple of Jerusalem, lay in ruins, retain their identity in the dramatic struggle for status among the nations? In order to answer this question, in order that they may recognize their extraordinary position precisely in exile, a position which rests on the fact that they still possess their law, the people of YHWH are reminded of the uniqueness their law gives them, even in their present inferior position. On the one hand, they had to endure the contrast with the past glory of their own history. On the other hand, they needed a means of withstanding the depressing greatness and tempting attractions of the ruling alien institutions.

The golden age of "all Israel" was the Solomonic era. During the period to which verses 6-8 were addressed, comparison with the Davidic-Solomonic empire and other powers was vital for Israel's self-confidence. The terminology of these verses shows evidence of a self-conscious effort to retain specific forms of expression and thus reveals that they constitute a reinterpretation of that portrayal of this ideal period which is to be found in the Deuteronomistic History. The Deuteronomistic History presents this period as a period during which Israel found itself in the limelight of world opinion because of the wisdom of its king (verse 6) and the temple cult on Zion (verse 7).[50] The exiles, however, probably experienced the just laws of the wise King Hammurapi as the highest achievement of any foreign culture. This is why the text of Deuteronomy contains parallels to the prologue and the epilogue of the Code of Hammurapi. These parallels are designed to show that Israel and its laws are superior even to this king and his impressive achievements. Most of the motifs and formulations in verses 6-8 differ from the usual themes and expressions of Deuteronomy. Consequently, they occur seldom or not at all in the rest of the Old Testament.

This allows us to conclude that they are used with a particular purpose in mind. From the methodological point of view, we must find their point of insertion in the Old Testament and in the ancient Near Eastern traditions in order to discover their particular theological message.

Observance of the Commandments as Wisdom (Verse 6). The only way of making an international forum recognize Israel and hence the only way of making Israel discover itself consists in the practice of the entire Mosaic law. For, as the *kî* makes clear, the wisdom and learning of Israel consists precisely in its *observance* of these laws.[51] It is this observance, not simply the fact that they possess the law[52] or their national greatness,[53] which gives rise to the nations' astonished praise of Israel (and not of the law) as "wise and understanding." It is true that only the quality of the deuteronomic law makes the approval we have spoken of possible: This is why this quality is described in more detail in verse 8. But the law itself is not equated with wisdom.[54]

The formula "in the eyes of the peoples" is reminiscent of a legal process intended to prove the truth. It is not (as in Ezekiel and Deutero-Isaiah) a question of glorifying YHWH's name or of recognizing his salvific actions in the course of his history with his people.[55] On the contrary, the judgment of outsiders is to encourage an Israel that has lost confidence in itself to observe and to proclaim "all these statutes." The reference to bearing witness (*l*^e^*'ênê*) and the tone of the entire text suggest that the nations will "come to know"[56] the deuteronomic law promulgated by Moses (*kol haḥuqqîm*)—that is, the parenesis and the individual commandments in chapters 5-26[57]—because of its practical validity.

The topoi *ḥokmâ ûbînâ* and *ḥākām w*^e^*nābôn* are often taken as indications of wisdom language and wisdom thought.[58] However, this method of determining wisdom influence meets with increasing criticism, and justifiably so.[59] As I shall demonstrate below, this striking expression which, apart from the Song of Moses[60] occurs here for the only time in Deuteronomy, does not have its origin in an "intellectual tradition."[61] Instead, the explanation is that the motif has been taken over from narratives which ascribed exceptional "wisdom" to certain rulers.

The words *ḥokmâ* and *bînâ*[62] are used as synonyms in verse 6,[63] just as they are elsewhere in the Old Testament. Only in Isa 11:2 and 29:14 do they occur as a dual expression. According to 11:2, the future ruler will be endowed with "the spirit of wisdom and understanding." In verses 3-5, this endowment is claimed particularly for the judiciary office of the promised descendant of David, who will "judge the poor with justice and defend the humble in the land with equity" (11:4). For "the task of the king is, above all, to be the custodian of divine justice."[64] Wise statesmanship may belong to the ideal image of national leaders; nevertheless, the Old Testament attributes this divinely granted ability only to a few rulers. The "wisdom of the wise and the discernment of the discerning" in Isa 29:14 refers to the competence to which the self-confident ruling class pretended.[65] Apart from Deut 4:6, Isa 29:14 is the only passage in the Old Testament where the abstract terms *ḥokmâ* and *bînâ* are found together with *ḥākām* and *nābôn*.[66]

Apart from our text, the predicate *ḥākām wᵉnābôn* is attributed only to Solomon in 1 Kgs 3:12 and (in reverse order) to Joseph in Gen 41:(33), 39. Deut 1:13 uses it in the plural in reference to the leaders of the people.[67] According to the predeuteronomistic verse[68] 1 Kgs 3:12,[69] the "wise and understanding heart"[70] granted by YHWH is the reason for Solomon's uniqueness in world history. This uniqueness, however, merely implies an immeasurably greater proportion of what other human beings, and particularly rulers, may also receive from God. The "divine wisdom" (*ḥokmat ʾᵉlōhîm*, 3:28) possessed by this king[71] is emphasized in the narrative of the Solomonic judgment (1 Kgs 3:16-27). This pericope, which narrates how Solomon proved himself a wise judge, was inserted at the beginning of a compilation of Solomon narratives which was probably predeuteronomic. Its purpose was to extend this viewpoint to the entire reign of Solomon.[72]

Whereas the figure of Solomon, whose intellectual interests and great riches made him known all over the world (see for instance 5:9-14; 10:1-13), appears as the brilliant prototype of the wise king; the Egyptian Joseph incarnates the ideal courtier as a man of culture.[73] Yet in Gen 41:39 (cf. verse 33),[74] the Elohist characterizes him as incomparably "wise and understanding" (New English Bible = "shrewd and intelligent"), because in contrast to the wisdom which can be taught and learned in the ordinary way, "God has let him know all this." Therefore, only Joseph fulfills all the criteria for the wise minister of agriculture that he himself counseled Pharaoh to appoint (verses 33-36*, E). Hence Joseph becomes second in authority in the state (verse 40). According to the yahwistic verse 38,[75] Pharaoh recognizes Joseph as a man possessing the *rû^{a}ḥ *$^{\prime e}$*lōhîm*, and one who is equaled by none. JE (the so-called "Jehovist") must already have understood the spirit of God as *rû^{a}ḥ ḥokmâ*, since he added verse 39 as an interpretation. This gives us a terminological link with the *rû^{a}ḥ ḥokmâ ûbînâ* of Isa 11:2.

For the rest, verbal affinities between Gen 41:39 and 1 Kgs 3:12—the oldest Old Testament statements about divinely inspired wisdom[76]—also suggest a dependence.[77] As Deut 1:13, 15 bear witness, even subordinate popular leaders must possess adequate qualities of leadership.[78] The domain within which one can compare the wisdom of Solomon and that of Joseph is not limited by religious or national boundaries. Yet one can look for their unequaled qualities only within a homogeneous sphere of life. If these qualities are recognized by someone with the right competence, they count as proven. No king could equal Solomon (1 Kgs 3:13). This is explicitly affirmed by the Queen of Sheba with her great knowledge of riddles and difficult questions (10:6-9). Pharaoh judged Joseph's wisdom to be greater than that of all the ministers in Egypt (Gen 41:39), a country famous for its wisdom (1 Kgs 5:10).

To sum up: The wisdom of Solomon and Joseph is a wisdom which enables them to govern, which eyewitnesses on an international level recognize as unequaled, that is, unsurpassed in its compass because infused by God. This gives us the traditional background against which the allusions and differentiations of Deut 4:6 must be understood.

To begin with, our text does not speak of rulers. Instead, it transfers predicates which are elsewhere reserved for the king or for high officials to the whole people. Such a "democratization" may have seemed obvious in the exilic situation. The same "democratization" occurs when Deutero-Isaiah applies the Davidic promises to the entire people. And Deutero-Isaiah is almost contemporaneous with Deuteronomy 4.[79] Democratization also occurs in the characterization of Israel as a kingdom of priests in Exod 19:6[80] and in the extension of the prophecy of Nathan which we find in 2 Sam 7:23-24, a deuteronomistic interpolation which has affinities with Deuteronomy 4.[81] Jer 4:22 is the only other passage where *ḥākām* and *nābôn* are found together with *'am*. This passage, however, denies that the people possesses any insight (*lō' n^ebônîm hēmmâ*), since they show intelligence only in wrongdoing (*ḥ^akāmîm hēmmâ l^ehāra'*). Furthermore, this (plural) wording does not quite abolish that distance between the individual and the masses which is usually linked to the characterization of certain individuals as wise and understanding. In addition, the statement is negative – grammatically speaking, half negative, in intention wholly negative – and it is always easier to apply the negation of a selective concept to an extended subject.

Deut 32:6 (*'am . . . lō' ḥākām*; cf. Isa 27:11) and 28-29 (where the wording is slightly different) belong to this level. Only in 4:6 is this double expression used in a positive sense and applied to the entire people of Israel.[82] This technique of applying originally selective attributes to the people as a whole, a technique which is found elsewhere in Deuteronomy, distinguishes Israel from all other nations and thus indirectly testifies to its election.[83]

The theological justification for transposing the motif in verse 6 can be found in Proverbs,[84] especially in those passages which are intended to teach true ethical behavior.[85] In spite of this traditional background, there is obviously no direct dependence on the so-called sapiential literature. In view of the particular function of 4:1-40 within the framework of the Deuteronomistic History, the sequence of the adjectives and Solomon's dedication prayer, which probably constitutes the horizon for verse 7, it appears more probable that Deut 4:6 is related to 1 Kgs 3:12. If this is correct, there is a second reinterpretation: wisdom no longer displays itself in the ability to rule, in giving judgment[86] or in political counseling;[87] instead, it has become a *religious and ethical attitude*. According to the deuteronomistic conception of the Solomonic history in 1 Kings, this is ultimately what determines both the greatness and the ruin of Solomon's glory.[88]

When the people is exhorted to observe the law, the reason is not only that such is the will of YHWH (Deut 4:5). The favorable judgment of foreign nations is also stressed. Verse 6 explicitly cites their words as a confirmation that Israel possesses such wisdom.

Verses 7-8 are concerned with Israel's uniqueness, which in the last analysis has its foundation in God. The characterization of the people of God as a "great nation" gives us the level presupposed by the subsequent comparison with other nations. When Israel is described as *gôy gādôl*, this is not merely a way of expressing its exceptional status among the nations. The phrase also refers to a new self-consciousness, discernible in the reinterpretation of the qualification.

Apart from this text, the expression *gôy gādôl*[89] is found only in those Pentateuch texts where Israel is promised many descendants—and, of course, it is also applied to Israel's enemies.[90] However, then the expression does not refer to the number of inhabitants, but to their status and importance. Like the epithet *ḥākām w^e^nābôn*, *gôy gādôl* at first sight reminds us of the Davidic-Solomonic state, where the descendants of Abraham had become a great nation.[91] In contrast to this political greatness, verses 6-8 emphasize Israel's religious and ethical greatness.[92] This greatness constitutes the most profound fulfillment of the promise that Israel would become a *gôy gādôl*.[93] At the time of the exile, there was no risk of a nationalistic-triumphalistic misunderstanding. At the same time, this terminology, which refers back to Gen 12:2-3, suggests a universal preeminence of Israel among the nations even before Deut 4:7-8 affirms its uniqueness.[94] As is proven by 4:31, and implied even by the contiguity of Gen 12:1-3 and Genesis 15, the religious emphasis in no way excludes the hope that the promise Abraham once received of possessing the land and becoming a numerous people should again come true in the near future.

Having lost its political independence and become dispersed among the nations, the people of God is in danger of losing its identity. Now this people is told two things. First, that Israel's standing is not dependent on the respect accorded to it because of the wisdom of its king, but on the wisdom and understanding which characterizes its religious and ethical attitude. Second, it is not the power of the Solomonic empire which represents Israel's real greatness, but the fact that its obedience depends on the nearness of YHWH and on the law he has authorized. Since ultimately it is a question of YHWH, Israel cannot abandon its claim. This is made clear by the triple repetition and the prominent position of the expression *gôy gādôl*. Yet how can this judgment by the nations be justified in the face of the magnificent temple cult and world-famous legislation of Babylon?

The Uniqueness of Israel (Verses 7-8). The rhetorical culmination of the passage has been reached. The speaker makes two parallel *assertions of incomparability*[95] (verses 7 and 8) as a comment on the confession of the nations. These assertions are in the form of rhetorical questions and express the highly emotional content of the declarations of uniqueness with great stylistic skill.[96] To be more specific, they belong to a type of *mî* questions in which the comparative clause is preceded by the description of a state of affairs and an attribution. In such a case, the statement of the relative clause is always in the irreal mood.[97] Israel is being compared with all other nations. And there are no spatial or temporal limits to this comparison. When Israel is compared to the other nations, the incomparability[98] of Israel is always ultimately founded on a gift of grace, as were, for instance, the wisdom of Solomon and of Joseph. It is precisely this which is intended to make the bitterly humiliated people of God aware of the fact that its election remains valid[99] and to encourage it to accept and live in accordance with its exceptional position among the nations,[100] in spite of every temptation to adapt itself to what was practiced everywhere else.

The Nearness of God (Verse 7). In addition to describing the wisdom of King Solomon, the Deuteronomistic History gives an extensive description of the building of the Temple of Jerusalem, carried out under Solomon. The long prayer of dedication (1 Kgs 8:22-53) as well as the consecratory formula (verse 13) and the blessing of the king (verses 54-61) – uniting as they do literary-critically distinct strata – reflect Israel's relationship with God.[101]

The tension inherent in this relationship can be described by the two concepts "presence of God" and "absence of God" (Jer 23:23). Deuteronomy attempts to master this tension in several ways in its various theological outlines. In order to avoid the misconception that YHWH's activity was limited to the sanctuary or that he himself was somehow localized there, Deuteronomy avoids the statement that YHWH resides in his temple. Instead, it speaks of "the place which

YHWH your God will choose as a dwelling for his name" (*l^{e}šakkēn š^{e}mô šām*—e.g., Deut 12:11) or "will choose ... to receive his name" (*lāśûm 'et š^{e}mô šām*—e.g., 12:5). The expressions "dwelling for his name" and "which he will choose to receive his name" must not be understood as ways of spiritualizing the concept of god, but as ways of expressing the fact that YHWH takes possession of the sanctuary.[102] Deuteronomy does not further discuss how the dwelling of YHWH's name in the temple is related to YHWH's dwelling in heaven.

Contrary to this linguistic usage, the older stratum (strata) of the Deuteronomistic History[103] avoid(s) everything which might make the temple appear as the dwelling of God and explicitly speak(s) of heaven as "the place where your throne stands" (*m^{e}kôn šibt^{e}kā* 1 Kgs 8:39, 43, 49; cf. *m^{e}qôm šibt^{e}kā* verse 30). In this way, the notion of the Solomonic temple as YHWH's dwelling-place (*mākôn l^{e}šibt^{e}kā* verse 13) communicated by the consecratory formula is avoided. Over and above that, the temple appears primarily as a place of prayer.

At the same time, the deuteronomic conception excludes the danger of thinking that YHWH's presence in the temple means that he is at the disposal of his people. Simultaneously, this conception implies that YHWH and his salvific actions are accessible to human beings.

Finally, verses 27-30 and 44-51 develop a theology of their own regarding the presence of the divine name. According to these verses, one prays either in the Temple of Jerusalem or turned towards it, for that is where YHWH receives prayers. Yet God himself is not tied to the earthly temple; only his name as a pledge of his salvific will is. God himself is enthroned in heaven, and it is from his heavenly throne that he hears suppliants. This theological notion regarding the name of God may have rendered valuable service during the exilic period: it left the supremacy of God on his heavenly throne intact, even though the temple was in ruins; in addition, the place where the temple had stood could remain the focal point for prayers.[104]

Yet the religious experience of the presence of God was confused by the way in which the active presence of the name of YHWH in (the ruins of) the temple and the intact divine transcendence were rationalized. Even verse 27 qualifies the notion of YHWH dwelling in heaven, thereby demonstrating the inadequacy of the whole theological conception. Then the revision of the prayer of consecration and of the blessing in verses 52-53 and 59-60 effectively breaks up all auxiliary theological constructions. These verses no longer speak of the divine name or of the exiles turning towards the Temple of Jerusalem when praying and of their prayers being heard. Instead, "my words" (the words spoken by Solomon earlier) are to be "present to YHWH, our God night and day (*d^e^bāray . . . q^e^rōbîm 'el YHWH '^e^lōhênû*) in order that he may procure justice for his servant and for his people Israel, as it is needed day by day" (verse 59). Then all nations will realize that YHWH alone is God (verse 60).

The theology in this insertion, as well as some of the motifs and phrases, correspond to Deut 4:7. Indeed, the text was probably written by the author of 4:1-40 or was at least written in close dependence on this passage.[105] In other words, the destruction of the temple made it possible to return to the original simplicity of the *unlimited and immediate access* of human prayers to YHWH (1 Kgs 8:59) and indeed of YHWH's nearness to his people (Deut 4:7).[106] Like Moses, Solomon identifies himself with his people in confessing their common God (YHWH *'^e^lōhênû*).[107] Through the wordplay on the similarity between (*'^e^lōhîm*) *q^e^rōbîm*[108] and *kol qor'ēnû* in verse 7, both expressions are given additional meaning: That God is near is understood to mean that one can appeal to him, that he hears and answers. God is not tied to any particular time or place. No notice is taken of spatial categories, whereas 1 Kgs 8:46-47 still reflects on them. The construction *kol* + *qr'* (infinitive), which occurs only in Deut 4:7 and in 1 Kgs 8:52 abolishes all temporal limits (cf. the different view represented by verse 59). This constitutes a guarantee that YHWH will be near his people *always and everywhere*.

As Solomon is seen as separate from his people only in so far as he intercedes for them, so Moses is separated from his people only in so far as he is their legislator.[109] Both functions, however, are oriented towards Israel.[110] Israel is seen in the context of all nations of the earth (1 Kgs 8:60; Deut 4:6). According to 1 Kgs 8:59, YHWH procures right for his people [111] because the words of Solomon have reached him.[112] In Deut 4:7-8, *the law which Moses teaches in the name of YHWH obviously constitutes the concrete divine presence*[113] as well as *the answer to the appeal of the people*. "Israel was very conscious – in Deuteronomy – of the unique quality of this will for law revealed to her. Through it, she was preferred above all the other nations and these had to recognize in Israel's law the proof of her special nearness to and direct communication with God."[114]

Alliterations call attention to the link between *b^eqereb* (verse 5) and *q^erōbîm* (verse 7). It is true that the Torah comes into effect only in the promised land. But this constitutes no contradiction of the assurance that God is near precisely in the exilic period. The nearness of God does not exclude present suffering; it means help and salvation for those in distress.[115] Incidentally, this is proved by all texts in which *qrb* and *qr'* are related to each other.[116] The expression *qr' 'el YHWH*, which is often used in individual laments,[117] occurs in Deuteronomy—apart from the text we are discussing—in 15:19[118] and 24:15. In both cases, YHWH is called upon to intervene against unjust behavior in a context of social legislation. The emphasis is in accordance with 4:8. In this verse, the Torah is praised as incomparable precisely because of its just laws—and, as will be shown, this means its social laws. By realizing these laws, Israel comes closest[119] to the wisdom Solomon showed as a judge (1 Kgs 3:28).[120]

In the final analysis, Israel could maintain its claim to incomparability in the rivalry between the nations only if *its standards were in fact valid in the ancient world*. The category *gôy gādôl* does not need to be established any further. It is quite evident that there was a common notion of what a "great power" meant, although this notion was politically oriented in the neighboring countries. But do other nations also speak proudly of the nearness of their gods and of their helpful intervention when they are appealed to for help?

The experience of the proximity of a god could be expressed in the naming of a child. In point of fact, it is shown by several Akkadian names that all Old Semitic peoples had in common the (hearing) presence of a god (God). The following names all contain the element *qrb*: *Ana-šasê-qerbet*, "she (the goddess) is close to the call(er),"[121] *Qerbassi*, "she (the goddess) is close to her (who prays),"[122] *Ina-qerbi-tašmanni*, "she was near to me and heard me,"[123] *Ina-qerbi-šiminni*, "be near to me and hear me,"[124] *Ili-iqriba*, "my god has approached me,"[125] *Ilum-qerub*,[126] "God is near."[127]

This linguistic usage does at any rate show a common background. However, we must investigate the issue itself. A process in the religious history of ancient Greece may serve as a starting point. Especially since the Hellenistic era, people felt a need to transfer their religious allegiance from the major gods of the state cultus to "those gods who were near to human beings, who were called gracious and thought to be present, helping and healing gods."[128] Behind this, there is the idea that the great gods dwelling on Olympus were either occupied with more important things or busy enjoying themselves and therefore took little interest in the everyday problems of ordinary human beings.[129] A similar system existed in Mesopotamia as early as the third millennium BCE and later in Asia Minor, Syria and Palestine:[130] that of the "personal guardian."[131]

> While the other gods remain more or less indifferent to the fate of the individual, the personal deity is very near to the individual human being. From this deity, the individual expects life and prosperity, as well as protection against all those powers which threaten his life. He turns to this deity and asks for his intercession before the other gods. Thus the fate of the individual is closely connected with his personal god.[132]

Such a faith certainly safeguards the experience that the god is near. However, not even total obedience towards one's personal deity provides any definite guarantee of divine assistance, although such obedience may ensure the benevolent attitude of the deity. To be on the safe side, people preferred to communicate with their personal god in writing, in a so-called "letter to the god," rather than simply appeal to him orally.

The actual granting of the prayer was further complicated by the fact that the personal guardian deity had to obtain the good offices of the major gods before he could procure advantages for his protégé. Even justice itself cannot be simply demanded. It can only be obtained by perseverance and with the aid of influential friends, that is, through favoritism.[133] In all these notions of mediation between the gods, the experiential knowledge of how distant the gods are is clearly apparent.

In contrast to this complex conception of the nearness of God, our text affirms: What great nation has a God close at hand as YHWH is to us – not *a* god, but the highest God, our god – simultaneously the personal God of every member of the people and directly of the people as such, every time we appeal to him? His helping presence is, as verse 8 explains, at every time embodied in the just laws.[134]

The Social Justice of the Law (verse 8). By means of the legal terms it uses (*kol haḥuqqîm ha'ēlleh*), verse 8 refers back to verse 6. The confession of Israel's uniqueness, formulated as a rhetorical question, however, constitutes a parallel to verse 7. Israel surpasses all nations in that its "statutes and ordinances" are *ṣaddîqim*. This certainly constitutes a claim that the Mosaic law is perfect.[135] Is it then sufficient to render the expression *ṣaddîq* in this context by "appropriate"?[136] Or is this predication a way of expressing that YHWH has proven his fidelity to Israel by revealing these commandments?[137] Is it true that YHWH's commandments were "often praised as *ṣaddîqim*, that is, as beneficial"?[138] Except in this passage, *ṣaddîq* is used only of persons.[139] The use of this word therefore suggests a relation to the personal and the communal. Are the *ḥuqqîm ûmišpāṭîm* characterized as *ṣaddîqim* while they make just and equitable relations within the community possible?[140] The *extrabiblical background* of verse 8 may help us to specify the intention, in spite of the problematic terminology. At the same time, the texts cited below illustrate that combination of wisdom and law which finds such a characteristic reinterpretation in verses 6 and 8.

The corresponding material is directly or indirectly related to the major Mesopotamian legislations. Directly related is the presentation of the "legal ideology" which we find in the *prologue and epilogue of a legal code*; indirectly related are those *kindred royal hymns* in which either the ruler who gave the law or the present ruler is glorified.

The prologue to the laws of Ur-Nammu[141] may be compared with a hymn to the same king in which his righteousness and wisdom in connection with the legal reforms are praised even more clearly than in the prooemium of the law code.[142] In a similar way, the prologue of the laws of Lipit-Ištar[143] is completed by two hymns related to this king.[144] A song to Enlil-Bani of Isin greatly resembles the first of these hymns.[145] In this context, the hymns to Iddin-Dagan of Isin should also be mentioned.[146] In all these hymns, the kings are praised for being endowed by the gods with wisdom and therefore being able to grant justice, usually through a legal reform. The prologue and epilogue of the Code of Hammurapi, which will shortly be discussed, are the most beautiful texts of this kind we possess. These texts also have their parallels among other inscriptions concerning this ruler.[147] In this royal and legal ideology, no rupture can be discerned between the Sumerian and the Akkadian documents.[148] But later inscriptions also permit us to conclude that the royal ideal did not undergo any substantial change after the times of Hammurapi.[149]

That these conceptions, in spite of many changes, were still alive in the first millennium is shown by a copy of the Babylonian "mirror of the prince" from the library of Assurbanipal.[150] It was probably revised for the last time around 710 BCE. The table begins "If the king has not paid attention to justice (*dīnu*)." However, the first paragraph ends with the promise "But if he has paid attention to the teaching of Ea, the great gods will give him insight (*ina šitulti*) and (always) lead him in the paths of justice (*mīšari*, verses 7-8)."

At the very beginning of this study, we found ourselves obliged to refer to the epilogues and prologues of the Mesopotamian law codes in a formal and functional context. Not least because of this, we are justified in instituting a comparison between such prologues and epilogues and Deut 4:5-8.

In addition, the expression *mišpāṭîm ṣaddîqim* probably alludes to the corresponding term *dīnāt mīšarim* in the epilogue to the Code of Hammurapi.[151] It can be rendered "just judgments."[152] The word *dīnu* signifies both the judgment and the legal case, in later usage also the established law.[153] "Righteousness" is signified by *mī/ēšarum*, which also carries a suggestion of "social equalization."[154]

Both in the prologue and in the epilogue, *mī/ēšarum* is also a key word.[155] Even apart from this concept, both texts indicate what is the intention of the law: to protect the weak in society.[156] This social tendency also emerges quite clearly from the legal decisions themselves: numerous paragraphs have the intention of alleviating the distress of the economically weaker groups and especially the evident misery of "widows and orphans."[157] Hammurapi calls himself "king of justice" (*šar mīšarim*).[158]

> Hammurapi hates all arbitrariness, the law is his religion and he enforces it whenever he is appealed to. In this, he feels himself united to the lord of justice, to Shamash. This awareness becomes so strong that he actually identifies himself with the sun god and, like him, "illuminates the land."[159]

Hence the epilogue speaks encouragingly:[160]

> Let any oppressed man who has a cause
> come into the presence of the statue of me, the king of justice

and then read carefully my inscribed stela,
and give heed to my precious words,
and may my stela make the case clear to him, may he understand his cause;
may he set his mind at ease!
"Hammurapi, the lord,
who is a real father to the people,
bestirred himself for the word of Marduk, his lord,
and secured the triumph of Marduk above and below,
thus making glad the heart of Marduk, his lord,
and he also ensured prosperity for the people forever
and led the land aright."

This text, as well as what is said elsewhere about Hammurapi's deeds, about his position and his relationship with the major gods[161] *makes him appear almost like the tutelary God of his people.*[162] Hammurapi praises, not only his own *righteousness,*[163] but also—although much less frequently—the wisdom with which the gods have endowed him for his task and which every wise man must admire.[164] Because of his words and because of his efficiency, he surpasses all other kings,[165] his deeds are *incomparable.*[166] The clearest summary of this is found just before the "blessings and curses" section:

I, Hammurapi, am the king of justice,
to whom Shamash committed law.
My words are choice, my deeds have no equal,
it is only to the fool that they are empty;
to the wise man they stand as an object of wonder.[167]

Although the extensive law of Hammurapi greatly surpasses the level of other ancient Near Eastern law codes,[168] it obviously never attained practical validity anywhere. In spite of that, numerous fragmentary copies bear witness to the great renown attained by this magnificent monument of Old Babylonian legal culture. Its growing *literary fame* must have penetrated the entire ancient Near East. Assurbanipal, the last great Assyrian king, who was a passionate collector of old documents, introduced a copy into his library in Nineveh. This copy bore the title "The Legal Decision of Hammurapi." The founder of the Neo-Babylonian/Chaldean empire, Nabopolassar, imitated the style of his predecessor. Finally, his son Nebuchadnezzar, through his activities and aims, appears like a "Hammurapi redivivus." All these facts are important for our study. It is perfectly possible that Deut 4:5-8 refers to the Code of

Hammurapi[169] while being at the same time preoccupied with acquiring a profile of its own.[170]

In contrast to Mesopotamian legal ideology, which finds its classical expression in the Code of Hammurapi, the praise in the deuteronomic pericope focuses, not on the lawgiver, but on the people which observes this law (verse 6). This ethical attitude is praised for its wisdom and true greatness. When Israel was in distress, it was, like the Babylonian citizen when deprived of justice, referred to a divinely authorized law code. But in this law code, Israel does not simply encounter the figure of a mediator like Hammurapi or Moses; instead it experiences the immediate presence of its God. Israel can experience this presence always and everywhere without having to approach any "image" (verse 7). Finally, Israel's "statutes and ordinances" surpass all similar "legal decisions," not only those of Solomon but in particular those of Hammurapi. Their uniqueness lies in the fact that they are "just" (*ṣaddîqim*, verse 8). As is made clear by the presumed reference to the Code of Hammurapi, and indeed by Deuteronomy itself, the term "just" refers to the *social orientation* of the entire law. It contains a reform of the debt laws and the slave laws.[171] The strangers, widows and orphans[172] are the objects of particular solicitude. Their protection appeared to ancient Near Eastern rulers as the quintessence of their social endeavors. In contrast to the Book of the Covenant, Deuteronomy is not satisfied with ensuring that they are protected, but also makes provisions for their maintenance. "There is hardly any law, whether social or cultic, in which they are not considered."[173] The care for the distressed is not, however, limited to the many ordinances in the corpus of the law. The social aspect is also of great importance in the parenesis as well as in the substantiations of the commandments.[174] Thus Deuteronomy's conception of itself as a collection of social *ḥuqqîm ûmišpāṭîm*, consisting of the parenesis of the major commandments as well as of individual laws, is fully justified by the contents of the book.

> Although there is no lack of humane traits in the Code of Hammurapi, it offers no striking parallels to the humane protection which the law of Israel gives the poor and the humble, the widows, orphans and strangers.[175]

But how can an experience of the presence of God be attributed to this system of social security? After all, this experience was normally restricted to the cult. Yet the linkage between verses 7 and

8 implies such an attribution. What has taken place is an actualization, for the exilic era, of that theology which characterized Deuteronomy even in its early stages. G. von Rad[176] has characterized this theology as follows:

> One of the most striking performances is the almost complete adaptation of the religious and cultic life to the social and ethical responsibilities of the people . . . here, too, we discover the ultimate notion which gives rise to this precious and close-knit union: the deuteronomic notion of the people of god . . . What has been carried out with particular clarity in the legislation about the cult in the main sanctuary can, to a certain extent, be shown to be present in all relevant ordinances.

In point of fact, it is this theological interpretation of the laws which makes Deuteronomy unique—even when it is compared to the world-famous Code of Hammurapi.[177]

It is true that verse 8 offers no further evidence for this affirmation. Indirectly, however, it invites a comparison with "this whole Torah." As is shown by the judgment of the peoples in verse 6, this Torah can be understood even beyond the religious world of Israel and can be discussed according to the criteria of experience. Within Deuteronomy, *tôrâ* here refers principally to the aspect of a compilation of teachings, whereas the older strata use this expression to stress the legal character of the contents and the sanctions through various curses.[178] In the first instance, this follows from the parallelism *ḥuqqîm ûmišpāṭîm*. In verse 5, this dual expression is linked with the promulgatory verb "to teach" (*lmd*). In comparison with other words for "law," it does not merely indicate its extension, but also suggests its parenetic structure (chapters 5-11) and its individual decrees (chapters 12 - 26:16).[179] The "parallelization" of the two legal terms in verse 8 brings these contents to the fore even in connection with the *tôrâ*. This is why translating *tôrâ* by "teaching" brings out the shades of meaning of the deuteronomic self-definition in this passage better than the term "law" does. Nevertheless, Moses must not be characterized as a teacher of wisdom.[180] When he *presents* the *tôrâ* to Israel (*ntn lipnê*), this constitutes a legal act. This formula of transmission is found a second time in Deuteronomy, in 11:32, where it refers to *kol haḥuqqîm wᵉhammišpāṭîm*. Thus the *tôrâ* is once more—apart from the parallelization in the comparative clause in verse 8—linked to this dual expression.

The promulgation of the deuteronomic instruction (teaching) takes place "today" (*hayyôm*). Nothing that is already past becomes present through this act; on the contrary, everything is new. In the context of chapter 4, the tendency towards an existential interpretation of the "actualization" in the life of the individual as well as in that of the people emerges clearly. The exhortation to observe the law which is embedded in the reference to God's intervention in history and which directs the entire life of both the individual and the people towards YHWH can be compared to, though not equated with, the word of God in the New Testament. The comparison is possible because the word of the law is also founded on historical reality and is intended to incorporate the addressees in this reality or to maintain them there. It also aims at existential appropriation, the "pro me" of the salvation founded "extra me."[181]

The Grace of a Fresh Start

The catastrophe of the year 587 BCE meant the end of national autonomy for the people of YHWH and also the end of its temple cult and liturgy. There was no king any more, the temple lay in ruins, the social structure of the people had collapsed. The exiles in Babylon were obliged to watch the imposing symbiosis between throne and altar in the conquering power. How could Israel in exile maintain its identity in spite of the severe blows it had received by divine judgment? How could it continue to proclaim its own election by YHWH in a convincing manner during this period of crisis?

Deut 4:5-8 constitutes – if we abstract from the particular function of this pericope within the framework of the entire book and of the Deuteronomic History – one of those theological efforts which have grown out of the ruins of Jerusalem and of its fundamental political and religious institutions. There are no polemics against possibly petrified institutions or against possible abuses.[182] Instead, the experiences of the exiles are seen as implying the grace of a fresh start, which makes possible a profound reflection on the remaining, and therefore essential, foundations of the faith. This reflection showed that being elected meant committing oneself.[183] It is not, then, simply a question of an encouraging address or dogma implying that one may be free from care. If, on being challenged by a pagan culture rich in traditions and highly successful, Israel wanted to survive, even to surpass the nations, it had to discover its wisdom and its true greatness in the observance of its own "law."

In this law, YHWH was uniquely near to all the afflicted and the social justice of the law was incomparable. This teaching could be surpassed only by the "word" in which God expressed himself perfectly, in which God remains immediately present to us even after the crucifixion of Jesus of Nazareth and in which he grants us perfect justice.

> Immensa divinae largitatis beneficia, exhibita populo christiano, inestimabilem ei conferunt dignitatem. Neque enim est, aut fuit aliquando tam grandis natio, quae habeat deos appropinquantes sibi, sicut adest Deus noster. Unigenitus siquidem Dei Filius, suae divinitatis volens nos esse participes, naturam nostram assumpsit, ut homines deos faceret factus homo. Et hoc insuper, quod de nostro assumpsit, totum nobis contulit ad salutem. Corpus namque suum pro nostra reconciliatione in ara Crucis hostiam obtulit Deo Patri. Sanguinem fudit in pretium simul et lavacrum; ut redempti a miserabili servitute, a peccatis omnibus mundaremur.[184]

> The immense gifts of divine magnificence shown to the Christian people gives it an inestimable dignity. For there is not, and there never has been, a great nation whose gods are so near to it as our God is to us. The only begotten Son of God, wishing us to share in his divinity, took upon himself our nature, that in becoming man, he should make men into gods. And through that which he took upon himself of what belonged to us, he led us to salvation. For he offered his body as a sacrifice to God the Father on the altar of the Cross in order to reconcile us with God. He shed his blood both in order to pay the price and in order to purify us: "that redeemed from a miserable slavery, we should be made free of all sin."

2
The Joy of the Feast

The Conception of the Cult in Deuteronomy
The Oldest Biblical Festival Theory

German title: "Die Freude des Festes"
(see bibliography)

After the liturgical reform of the Second Vatican Council, the renewal of Catholic worship appears to be in a state of crisis. It is not merely a question of transforming ceremonies and replacing texts. The fundamental question of the very structure of church liturgy becomes increasingly important. J. Ratzinger reduces the attempts to find an answer to two diverging conceptions:

> The key concepts of the new liturgical view can be represented by the terms creativity, freedom, feast and community. From this point of view, rites, ties with the past, interiority and the common order of the whole Church appear as negative concepts describing the state of the "ancient" liturgy, a state which ought to be overcome.[1]

The common presupposition of both these conceptions is the conviction that "the essence of the liturgy is its festival character."[2] If it were possible to clarify what makes a feast into a feast, it might also be possible to surmount the present catastrophic state of the discussion.

In collecting "bricks for constructing a theory of the feast,"[3] the first element one discovers is joy. Without this element, there is no feast. John Chrysostom writes, "festivity is joy and nothing but joy."[4] However, joy—even the joy belonging to an authentic feast—presupposes a real reason for rejoicing. It is not enough that there be an objective "authorization to rejoice."[5] The festive occasion must be subjectively recognized as a ground for rejoicing, experienced as meaningful and as a participation in something one loves. According to J. Pieper, "the briefest and most lucid way of describing the inner structure of the feast is John Chrysostom's incomparable sentence: 'Where love rejoices, there is a feast.'"[6] If, finally, "the cultic feast constitutes the highest form of the feast,"[7] the joy belonging to the religious feast must be a topic for theological reflection. Christian reflection, however, has its origins in the biblical tradition. Now there is "hardly a more central word in the Old Testament than the word joy."[8] In the book of Deuteronomy, cultic joy becomes a central part of faith in YHWH. This is a way of withstanding the seductive practices of the world surrounding Israel. According to the reports we find in the Acts of the Apostles, the deuteronomic festival theory may be said to characterize life in the early Church. From this we can draw a line to the "secular divine service" which Cardinal König once in a meditation called "the real test for believers."[9]

> The great secular divine service for men and women ... takes place where there is true love, where authentic values are what people strive for ... A life which contains authentic values is a full and therefore a happy life. For joy is precisely that: a full life.[10]

In the following contribution, I intend to explore the fundamental traits of festal joy as it is described by Deuteronomy and to confront these traits with contemporary theories of the feast.

The Relation to God and Liturgy

The specific characteristic of the experience of God in the Old Testament has found its most typical expression in the so-called "covenant" or "allegiance" formula. With slight variations for different texts, it reads: "I will be your God and you shall be my people."[11] The speaker is YHWH, the God of Israel. He is not addressing individuals or all humanity, he is addressing members of the people of Israel. YHWH and Israel have a unique, very close relationship. This relationship finds its realization in time: it has a history. This is why the covenant formula is often related to the date of the origin of Israel's history, the exodus from Egypt (their being-led-out-of-Egypt). But Israel's relationship with YHWH will continue in the future and find new forms of realization. This is why the covenant formula always occurs together with a reference to the "laws." But in this case, the "laws" are not a collection of individual ordinances. The laws are rather to be understood as concrete formulations of the "principal commandment," arising from the close relationship. This commandment constitutes YHWH's claim that Israel proclaim its allegiance to him alone as its only God. YHWH's exclusive claim is realized most unambiguously in the liturgy when the cult is centralized and concentrated to the Temple of Jerusalem in the late monarchic period.

YHWH's Exclusive Claim and the Deuteronomic Cult Centralization

In the second half of the eighth century, the Southern Kingdom of Judah came increasingly under Assyrian rule. This dependence did not merely imply the obligation to pay tribute; there was also a considerable cultural and religious influence in all spheres of life.[12] At the turn of the eighth and seventh centuries, King Hezekiah attempted to liberate Judah from the Assyrian yoke. However, his rebellion failed. Jerusalem was, certainly, the only town not to be occupied by the Assyrian Sennacherib, which many took as a visible sign of the divine election of this city and its temple. But the independence movement had failed.[13] For decades, Hezekiah's son Manasseh practiced a consistent policy of submission, combined with the promotion of alien cults and the renewal of old Canaanite rites.[14] It was only in the second half of the seventh century, when the Assyrian power was in a state of decline, that King Josiah was gradually able to regain Judah's independence, and even to extend his influence to the former Davidic state of Israel.[15] For over a century, Judah was subjected to strong influences from the superior Assyrian culture. The identity of the small satellite state was deeply affected. The traditional faith in YHWH was no longer socially credible. Simple people were more impressed by military successes, celebrated as victories of the god Assur. True, it seems probable that the new rulers did not oblige their Judean vassals to accept the Assyrian state cultus.[16] Nevertheless, political tactics alone made it desirable to take into account the world view of the new overlords. As early as the eighth century, the Assyrian-Aramaic star cult had obtained a place in the Southern Kingdom.[17]

In the climate of general instability, religious underground movements which up till then had remained repressed were revived. The native fertility rites, for instance, had always exercised a magic fascination on the farming population.[18] These subreligions now superimposed themselves on the official cultus, and the emotional ties with the authentic traditions and its values were weakened or even lost. Judah had suffered a cultural shock. The world had become pluralist.[19] A complex process of defense and adaptation began.[20]

The crisis in the yahwistic world of meaning could be overcome only by making the contemporary world understand the unifying foundation of the various old traditions. In other words, the numerous traditions and liturgical rites had to be systematized in a way which would be meaningful to people living in the contemporary world. This was the beginning of theology. If theology proved itself capable of integrating the categories of thought and patterns of behavior as well as the dominant language of the rival symbolic world without abandoning faith in YHWH, then these theological efforts would produce an interest in things which people had long known and would even make them practice the cult again. Traditions can be preserved only if they are made comprehensible, are actualized and are assimilated into people's minds. In fact, the movement behind Deuteronomy did succeed, at a very critical turn of the history of Israel, in bringing the dominant life view into its theology.

With the aid of a "constructive restoration,"[21] the yahwistic world of faith was made attractive once again. In the seventh century, the Neo-Assyrian empire was kept together mainly by a large number of treaties of various types. Oaths were in fashion. Thus Asharhaddon, the suzerain of Manasseh of Judah, with the aid of his priests, drew up a covenant between the god Assur, himself and the Assyrian people.[22] To a people uncertain of itself and living at the margin of the empire, covenants must have appeared to provide a guarantee of unassailable security. Therefore Deuteronomy accepted the structure of the covenant. It systematized Israel's relation to God after the fashion of covenantal documents. All spheres of life were covered by the treaty with YHWH as the authentic suzerain. Precisely through this way of adjusting to the imposing Neo-Assyrian was of thinking, it became possible to declare the treaties formerly made with foreign rulers invalid.

The exclusive relation between YHWH and Israel finds its concrete form in the so-called parenetic texts in Deuteronomy—particularly in chapters 4-11 and 29-30—as well as in its cult legislation.[23] As the seclusion and integrity of the people had obviously been lost to a great extent, even the earliest deuteronomic stipulations concerning the cult aimed at giving the people a new center in the one cult site. YHWH's relation to Israel, which had formerly been understood in an undifferentiated, holistic manner, was, to begin with, localized. YHWH's exclusive claim, which had been understood in a general way, became particularized by the relation to a specific sanctuary. In the second place, the cult centralization was founded and legitimized through a divine act: YHWH's election of Israel. The exclusive claim, which had not previously been the object of reflection, was dealt with theologically with the aid of the notion of election. Thirdly, the relation to YHWH received a temporal character. According to the literary fiction of Deuteronomy, YHWH will choose the place for the cult only in the future, when Israel has taken possession of the promised land. In fact, however, at the time when Deuteronomy was written, one could look back on a history during which YHWH had already selected a particular sanctuary, the Temple of Jerusalem.

In this way, it became possible to elucidate the reasons for a centuries-long evolution and to systematize the history of Israel within a theological system proper to it.

Probably the oldest testimony of the deuteronomic "liturgical reform" is found in Deut 12:13-19, provided that one abstracts from some later additions:[24]

> See that you do not offer your whole-offerings in any place at random, but offer them only at the place which YHWH will choose in one of your tribes, and there you must do all I command you. On the other hand, you may freely kill for food in all your settlements, as YHWH your God blesses you. Clean and unclean alike may eat it, as they would eat the meat of gazelle or buck. But on no account must you eat the blood; pour it out on the ground like water. In all your settlements you may not eat any of the tithe of your corn and new wine and oil, or any of the first-born of your cattle and sheep, or any of the gifts that you vow or any of your freewill offerings and contributions; but you shall eat it before YHWH your God in the place that YHWH your God will choose—you, your sons and daughters, your male and female slaves, and the Levites in your settlements; so you shall find joy before YHWH your God in all that you undertake. Be careful not to neglect the Levites in your land as long as you live.

In its assertion that an election has taken place, Deuteronomy is on the one hand dependent on tradition, on the other it expresses a theory of its own. The cult centralization gave YHWH's old claim on Israel's exclusive loyalty a new terminolocal focus by introducing the notion of "election." Furthermore, inherited ideas of the divine choice of a particular sanctuary, ideas found not only in Israel but also in Mesopotamia, are taken up and briefly summarized in a formula. Finally, this temple theology probably constituted a systematization of the way in which the entire people had experienced the presence of God. The most recent confirmation of this presence was the preservation of Zion during the Assyrian attack in the reign of King Hezekiah.[25]

The formula expressing YHWH's choice of a sanctuary appears, however, to have been misinterpreted, especially in popular piety. People assumed that one could, so to speak, look for YHWH and find him in this particular place. The consciousness of the presence of God very easily turned into the temptation to reduce YHWH to his presence in the temple and attempt to manipulate him with the aid of rites. This danger grew as Zion consolidated its unique power. The dilemma between the traditional claims of this sanctuary and YHWH's unbounded presence was eliminated "with the aid of a theological distinction between YHWH and his name."[26] Also, the brief centralization formula which speaks of "the place which YHWH your God will choose"[27] is added to at two different times.[28] To begin with, the text adds "... in order to make his name dwell there."[29] This addition was probably made in the heyday of King Josiah; at any rate it was made before the Babylonian exile. The Hebrew phrase originally meant "put his name on." It alluded to the custom of immortalizing one's name on a memorial and thus demonstrating one's possessory right and sovereignty. In consequence of the linguistic evolution, the phrase was later understood to mean "make ... dwell." By introducing the formula "... and put his name there,"[30] it was possible to preserve the original meaning. There are no ancient Near Eastern parallels to the association of these expressions with the assertion of an election.[31] In this context, they consider the purpose and motivation of YHWH's action. At the same time, however, they distinguish between two different forms of his presence in the Jerusalem sanctuary. This means that YHWH himself is not localized in the earthly temple; his name is present there as a guarantee of his salvific will.

The Canaanite religion,[32] on the other hand, was "a popular religion with all its characteristics."[33] Its content was influenced by the interests of the dominant peasant culture, the renewal of vitality and fertility. In such a close union with agriculture, the strictly regulated year and a small community (which was easy to survey at a glance) made the relation to God a comprehensible whole. The Canaanite religion was not, however, simply a nature religion. Transcendence and immanence were combined in the Canaanite pantheon. There was El, who was approached with prayer and adoration, since it was from him that they received their blessings. But besides El, there was Baal, a projection of something man himself is part of and with which he can experience communion. In addition, both these deities were polar beings. Baal, for instance, was the dying and resuscitating vegetation god, with whose death all life on earth died only in order to be renewed as he revived. Local gods with all their particular characteristics were subsumed into the all-encompassing religious system. Ancient features remained in the adoration of trees and stones, mountains and springs, in the magic attitude, in the intoxicating experiences provided by the cultic revels, and in the sexual excesses of sacral intercourse in the service of fertility. In these sometimes rather crude forms, Canaanite religion attempted to build up a relationship of trust between man and nature, to involve man in the ongoing process of creation and to compensate for his dependence on the deity by making him his collaborator. "To this simplicity corresponds an astonishing flexibility, to the originality a great capacity for synthesis."[34] It is hardly surprising that in the Israelite cult it was not always easy to distinguish between a canaanized YHWH cult and a yahwistically influenced Baal cult. Therefore, the deuteronomic reformers were obliged to correct popular views of the presence and availability of YHWH in holy places if they wanted to counteract the syncretistic tendencies. One may ask whether these liturgical theorists did not interfere too much with a practice that was centuries old. Was it possible to continue to offer up sacrifices, bring firstlings and tithes and celebrate festivals although the entire cult had become centralized? Did not such a theological regimentation of spontaneous popular piety bring with it a considerable limitation of genuine religious experience? In this context—where values had become questionable and the world view and the feeling for life had been impaired—Deuteronomy exhorted people to rejoice.

Joy, Not Orgiastic Exultation

A Brief Cult Formula. Deuteronomy understands itself as the treaty document of a covenant between YHWH and his people. According to the structure of ancient Near Eastern treaty formulas, the covenant contains a sequence of curses—the sanctions against the faithless partner in a covenant. They are found (expanded and variegated) in 28:15-68. At the beginning or end of the individual curses, a stipulation or substantiation clause mentions the disobedience of Israel as reason for such punishment.[35] In this way, they provide a new, terse summary of YHWH's exclusive claim. 28:47 explains the coming disaster as due to neglect of the cult celebration which had been laid down by the deuteronomic legislation. As Israel had refused to serve God, it had been obliged instead to serve its enemies. According to verse 48a, the punishment corresponds exactly to the culpable neglect. In 28:47-48a, we read the following threat:[36]

> Because you did not serve YHWH your God with joy and in the goodness of your heart for all your blessings, you shall serve your enemies whom YHWH will send against you, in hunger and thirst, in nakedness and in total destitution.

The ironical play on the word "serve" is striking.[37] The relation to YHWH is contrasted not only with a relation to alien gods,[38] but also with subjugation to enemies. Not only does this provide a key word for the subsequent description of other nations, it also suggests a connection which is typical of the origin and the theology of Deuteronomy: the connection between divine rule and freedom. Israel's loyalty to YHWH, described as "service,"[39] had its origin in the redemption of the people from slavery in Egypt. In the plague narrative, the notion of freedom is combined with the demand that Pharaoh let the people go in order that they may serve their god in the desert.[40]

The decisive verbs, "send out" and "serve," are used only in connection with punishment for Israel. This exodus background makes it possible to associate the cultic and the social aspects of the service of YHWH. Israel demanded freedom in order to be able to bring YHWH a sacrifice and celebrate a feast.

First, however, it must be freed from social and juridical dependence on Pharaoh and become united with YHWH. For the rest, in deuteronomic and deuteronomistic literature, the phrase "to serve YHWH" "as a historico-theological term always refers to the totality of the relations between YHWH and Israel."[41] It is a question not only of the true or the false cult, but of the entire relationship with YHWH and thus of Israel's whole existence. Hence verse 47 characterizes the divine service of Israel both according to its cultic and according to its social and charitable side. The expression which is rendered by "in the goodness of your heart" cannot, as frequently happens, be translated merely by "happiness"[42] and be regarded as a synonym for "joy." In verse 48, the "joy" which Israel refused is replaced by "hunger and thirst," the lack of "goodness of heart" they showed, in spite of all the blessings, is punished by "nakedness and total destitution." According to deuteronomic linguistic usage, we have to do with real antitheses.[43] Cultic joy as understood by Deuteronomy encompasses a festive meal. We shall discuss this more in detail at a later stage. The "goodness of your heart," especially when there is enough of everything (15:7-11),[44] may be demanded by the "brother" in want. The loan without interest which according to deuteronomic legislation should be given to any impoverished Israelite was not intended to enlarge his property but to help him to overcome a state of extreme poverty. "The 'right of the poor' is, in the last analysis, a right to social benefits."[45]

Deut 28:47—in this particular context a way of formulating the first commandment of the covenant with God and a deuteronomic expression for honoring God—shows that "joy" and an attitude of social awareness arising out of gratitude make up the essential elements of the "divine service" in the large sense of the term. They can neither be separated from each other nor can they be measured against each other. What solidarity implies in each particular case is extensively described by the deuteronomic law. What is intended by the "joy" which Deuteronomy requires can be concluded only from the previous history of this concept and from the way it is used in Deuteronomy.

Rejoicing and Exulting. Before Deuteronomy "joy" (*śimḥâ*), "rejoicing" (*śāmaḥ*) and "joyful" (*śāmēᵃḥ*) were not often used in cultic or religious contexts.[46] The only instance in the Pentateuch is the so-called Blessing of Moses, a collection of old tribal sayings which was inserted into Deuteronomy at a late date. Deut 33:18 exhorts Zebulun and Issachar to rejoice. They are to slaughter valid sacrifices (verse 19). This probably refers to the cult on Tabor, characteristic of these two tribes.[47]

The following passages are probably also preexilic. They were all transmitted within the framework of the so-called deuteronomistic history. At the beginning of this history, we find Deuteronomy—in a way, it constitutes a measure for the history of the people as it was presented by the last revision of the books of Joshua, Judges, Samuel and Kings.

Judges 16:23-25 speaks of the triumphant joy of the Philistine lords, who celebrate the capture of Samson by a sacrifice to their god Dagon in Gaza. They sing a song of victory and a taunt against their formerly powerful enemy.

Twice it is the Ark which gives occasion for joy. In 1 Sam 6:13-14, the inhabitants of Beth-Shemesh, delighted at the return of the Ark from the land of the Philistines, offer (two cows as) a whole-offering. David also sacrifices as he, full of joy, brings back the Ark to the City of David. This is recounted in 2 Sam 6:12-15. He dances before the Ark while the procession mounts towards the city with great shouting and blowing of trumpets.

Finally, in four passages, joy is connected with the king. As in 1 Sam 11:15, the entire people invests Saul as king in Gilgal in the presence of YHWH (before YHWH—*lipnê YHWH*), that is, in the sanctuary[48]—they sacrifice shared offerings "before YHWH" and Saul and the men of Israel rejoice greatly. After Solomon had been anointed, the whole people escorted him home with the playing of pipes. The people rejoiced with (so) great a joy that the earth shook with the noise; this is affirmed by 1 Kgs 1:40, 45. According to 2 Kgs 11:20, the people rejoiced over the newly crowned King Joash, whom they greeted with trumpets and hand-clapping.

It is true that there are only four preexilic prophetic texts which use the root *śmḥ* for religious joy.[49] Yet precisely these texts must be considered to constitute the decisive traditio-historical background against which, for the first time, the deuteronomic (which means the Israelite) view of the joy of serving YHWH appears as it really is.[50]

Hence these passages must be analyzed with the greatest care. I propose to analyze them in the order in which they were written. The fulminations of Hos 9:1 struck Israel like a bolt from the blue, just as, full of enthusiastic joy, they rejoiced over the rich harvest when celebrating the great autumn festival:

> Do not rejoice (*'al tiśmaḥ*), Israel.
> Do not exult (*'al tāgēl*) like the nations.
> For you behave like a wanton and forsake your God.

> You love to prostitute yourself on every threshing floor
> heaped with corn.[51]

The prophet turns an obviously customary exhortation around, almost word for word, when he commands Israel not to rejoice.[52] His interdiction is justifiable, for

> the joy has degenerated into Canaanite ecstasy. The uncontrolled rejoicing and shouting come from the "canaanization" of the cult and is a sign that Israel is "behaving like a wanton away from its God." Grotesquely, Israel's joy becomes joy over their apostasy from their own God.[53]

Israel regards the corn on the threshing floor not as a gift from YHWH, but as a gift from her lovers, the baals. True, we cannot conclude from this prophetic word that "rejoicing" (*śāmaḥ*) and "exulting" (*gîl*) "were originally part of the dionysiac features of the Canaanite fertility cults"[54] and had to be condemned on that account. What is rejected is not, in any case, the joy itself,[55] even though the "exulting" (*gîl*) made it into "violent, shrill, wild screaming."[56] Israel's(!) rejoicing and exulting during the practice of its own cult(!) was rejected,

> not because it has its origin in the Canaanite fertility cult, but because it did not constitute a response to what its God had done; hence: "You behave like a wanton away from your God."[57]

As for the linguistic usage of Deuteronomy, we must maintain that the context in which Hos 9:1 speaks of "rejoicing" is the harvest festival and the confrontation of the Yahwistic religion with the baalistic fertility cults. Since it is found in parallel with *gîl*, *śāmaḥ* probably also means "an inarticulate, more or less orgiastic shouting."[58]

Isa 22:13, part of an Isaianic rebuke, regrets the untimely exultation of the population of Jerusalem.[59] The atmosphere in the city is not characterized by grief over King Hezekiah's capitulation before the Assyrian Sennacherib, or by earnest self-examination; instead, there is the "uncontrolled joy of life of those who have escaped disaster once more."[60]

> On that day, the Lord YHWH of the hosts called for weeping and beating the breast, for shaving the head and putting on sackcloth. But instead there was exultation and rejoicing (*śimḥâ*), slaughtering of cattle and killing of sheep, eating of meat and drinking of wine—"Let us eat and drink, for tomorrow we die."

In these verses (12-13), Isaiah used "the language of the cult . . . as a vehicle for his own prophetic call to return to YHWH. One cannot affirm that the prophet is thinking particularly of cultic feasts."[61]

There is no verse in the Old Testament which gives a more intense description of joy than Isa 9:2; this verse constitutes an expression of gratitude because YHWH has saved Israel from the threat posed by the Assyrians.[62]

> You have increased their exultation (*haggîlâ*)
> and made their joy (*haśśimḥâ*) great.
> They rejoiced before you (*śam^{e}ḥû l^{e}pānêkā*)
> as one rejoices at the harvest time (*k^{e}śimḥat haggāsîr*)
> as one exults (*yagîlû*) when sharing out the spoil.

Here the restoration of Davidic Israel under King Josiah is compared to proverbial times of joy with the aid of two elementary but plastic images: the joy of the harvest, when the ever-present danger of famine has disappeared, and the rejoicing when the spoils of war are shared out and one passes from war with all its dangers to a peaceful and more prosperous life. The context as well as the parallelism between "joy" (*śimḥâ*) and "exultation" (*gîla*) do not allow us to infer that there are any differences between the connotations of the two expressions.[63]

There is but little reason to conclude that the phrase "rejoice before YHWH" (*śāmaḥ l^{e}pānêkā*) refers to a particular religious rite, in this case to the enthusiastic acclamations at the enthronement of the king.[64] The "joy before YHWH" is neither a particular action within the sanctuary nor indeed an act at all in the literal sense of the word. Rather, this joy characterizes human behavior as the expression of an inner religious attitude.[65]

The approaching destruction of the Assyrian empire gives rise to singing, music and dancing (Isa 30:29),[66] which are not unlike the rejoicing spoken of in Isa 9:2. The joy is compared to the joy of a festival night and a procession to the temple.

> But for you there shall be songs,
> as on a night of sacred pilgrimage,
> the night that the feast is celebrated,[67]
> your hearts will be glad (*śimḥat lēbāb*)
> as the hearts of those who walk to the sound of the pipe
> on their way to the hill of YHWH, to the rock of Israel.

True, the Old Testament (e.g., Deut 16:6-7)[68] mentions a night celebration only for the Passover. But we cannot conclude from this that the comparison in Isa 30:29 refers to the centralized Passover in

Jerusalem introduced by Josiah.[69] The deuteronomic Passover differs from other feasts in that there is no reference to joy in connection with it. Hence the comparison would hardly seem indicated. One should think rather of the New Year/Autumn Festival, *the* feast of joy, even though it cannot be proven that there was any night celebration.[70] In order to create an image of a joyful feeling, it is quite enough to evoke the atmosphere of the night before a feast. Verse 27 betrays a certain proximity to deuteronomic theology and thereby to the times of King Josiah. This verse proclaims the coming of the "name of YHWH" from afar, that is, from Zion.[71]

"Joy," especially in the cult, is a common religious phenomenon. Strictly speaking, however, none of the predeuteronomic passages mentioned characterizes the ordinary yahwistic cult by *śāmaḥ-śimḥâ-śāmēaḥ*. Hos 9:1 forbids Israel to rejoice. Isa 22:13 describes the atmosphere of a joyous feast, which, however, has degenerated into an uninhibited drinking bout. Isa 9:2 merely speaks of a religious attitude. Isa 30:29, on the other hand, only compares the joy of the people at the coming of YHWH with a joyful procession to Zion on the night preceding a feast. The religious joy mentioned in all the preexilic texts quoted

> does not as a rule mean a state of mind, indeed not a state at all, but a joy which expresses itself in a spontaneous and elementary manner . . . The most elementary expression of joy is a joyous shout or a cry of exultation with hardly any verbal elements.[72]

This exultation gives rise to many kinds of noise and gesticulation, shouting, hand-clapping, music and dancing. It is always proclaimed within a community. "This joy is by its very nature exuberant to the point where one becomes frantic with joy."[73] Whether such "dionysiac exuberance" really "belongs to every festival joy"[74] can only be discussed in connection with the deuteronomic conception of the cult of YHWH.

The Exhortation to Rejoice. Whenever a sacrifice or a gift-offering from the produce of herd or field had to be brought to the central sanctuary in Jerusalem and whenever the people assembled there after the harvest, in order to celebrate the Feast of Weeks or the Feast of Booths, the following words from Deuteronomy applied, "You are to rejoice."[75] In this context, only the verb *śāmaḥ* is used (more often, however, than in any other book of the Old Testament except for the Psalms, which is a collection of widely differing independent songs and hence does not allow us to make any real comparison). When Deuteronomy speaks of human joy,[76] it uses only this root. The authentic place for joy is the Israelite cult. As W. Kasper states,

> The highest joy is only possible when, at least for a moment, we feel ourselves to be part of an extensive pattern of meaning, when the tragic conflicts which are always present and which we are usually unable to resolve suddenly disappear, when, for a moment, we are filled with something like peace. This kind of joy is essentially related to religion.[77]

In Deuteronomy we find, for the first time, a systematic consideration of this phenomenon. "Rejoicing" constitutes the key word in a theory[78] of the "feast."[79]

In calling for joy, Deuteronomy is carrying out a double strategy. On one hand, it confronts the question of adaptation to some very attractive features of the Canaanite fertility cult. In the cult of YHWH, too, one may—indeed one should—rejoice. Those features of the Canaanite cult which are accepted because of their human value[80] and which are, for the first time, introduced into the Israelite cult with a theological explanation must first be freed from all traits which are incompatible with the authentic traditions of faith in YHWH. And so there is, on the other hand, a rejection of rites. This rejection can be concluded from a comparison between the ancient Israelite and the Canaanite (that is, alien) practice with what is stipulated by Deuteronomy—and not only with what is positively determined, but also with those elements of joy which are deliberately not mentioned in Deuteronomy. The joy spoken of in Deuteronomy is by no means a harmless, naively positive attitude. On the contrary, once cannot imagine anything more critical than this joy.[81]

It used to be thought that one could define this type of joy by distinguishing strictly between the root *śmḥ* and *gîl* (with its derivatives).[82] Deuteronomy was thought to have deliberately excluded the ecstatic exultation (*gîl*) from its vocabulary because of its Canaanite origin and its relation to pagan orgies.[83] Against this view, however, there is the fact that the Old Testament (with the exception of Hos 10:5) knows no meaning for *gîl* which could not be applied to *śmḥ* as well.[84] The word groups receive their positive or negative valence from their context.[85] It was not because it denoted a pagan expression of joy that *gîl* was excluded from Deuteronomy, but because "*śmḥ* is an all-encompassing word for 'joy' with a much wider range of meaning"[86] than *gîl*. From a theological point of view, it is important that *gîl* is never found together with *lipnê*, whereas "to rejoice before YHWH" (*śāmaḥ lipnê YHWH*) occurs frequently, particularly in Deuteronomy.[87]

Apart from 27:7 and 28:47, Deuteronomy speaks of joy only in the law code. And in fact these two passages, which do not belong to the law code of chapters 12-26, are no real exceptions. 27:7 is a cultic ordinance which is to be followed on a single occasion, on Mount Gerizim after the crossing of the Jordan. By its very nature, this ordinance has no place in a code of general and atemporal laws. 28:47 again resumes all concrete individual laws in the deuteronomic legislation and thus produces its own formulation of the first commandment. In all passages of Deuteronomy—and with only a few exceptions, this means only in this book in the whole Old Testament—the syntactic function of the verb *śāmaḥ* is that of an injunctive.[88] Thus Deuteronomy speaks of "rejoicing" only in hortatory form.

Obviously this is not self-evident, either from the human or from the divine point of view. It is true that joy cannot be enforced by a commandment, especially since there is no question of any exultation rite or of any other concrete expression for joy which could simply be carried out obediently. But the obligation is intended to provide an incentive for looking for a way to rejoice. For the "joy" to which people are exhorted is "a serious, indeed a stern thing."[89] It is different from the kind of superficial cheerfulness which comes and passes. Nor is this joy an artificially produced, exterior merriness, expressing itself in witticisms and jokes.[90] On the contrary, we are dealing with a highly qualified form of joy, a joy which ultimately has its foundation as well as its limits in the blessing of YHWH.[91] This blessing is limited to earthly life, yet it makes authentic joy possible.[92]

The following command seems to contradict the religious foundation of the joy:

> you shall rejoice in all that your hands have produced (*b^{e}kōl mišlaḥ yādekā*, Deut 12:18).

Both the immediate and the wider contexts in Deuteronomy show that the last phrase is inextricably bound up with the blessing of YHWH.

> You and your families are to rejoice over everything your hands have produced while YHWH, your God, has blessed you (12:7).

For the Feast of Booths, we also find the conditional version:

> If YHWH, your God, has blessed you in everything, in your harvest and in the work of your hands, then you are to rejoice (16:15).

Finally, in connection with the offering of the first fruits (that is, the best fruits), the text explicitly states:

> For you are to rejoice over all the good things that YHWH, your God, has given you and your family (26:11).

Whenever the reference to "the produce of your hands" (*mišlaḥ yādekā/yedkem*) or "the work of your hands" (*maʿaśeh yādekā*) may have originated,[93] the deuteronomic covenant theology subsumes the entire activity of the individual, the family and the people under the active blessing of YHWH.[94]

> The blessing of YHWH is temporal, but it is not worldly. It sounds paradoxical, but very possibly Israel was never more piously prepared to receive gifts straight from the hand of God than they here are to receive material things. Neither in predeuteronomic times nor in subsequent periods do we find such a completely natural acceptance of temporal goods for their own sake. There is no suggestion that they are somehow the fruits of spiritual qualities. They are accepted for their own sake, as undeserved gifts of God.[95]

This is because "the blessing of YHWH, which is concerned with the entire material and physical life of his people is the salvific good κατ' ἐξοχην."[96] However, when Deuteronomy recognizes YHWH so enthusiastically as the giver of all blessings, this is the result of a tremendous struggle.[97] It is YHWH, not Baal, who grants fertility and the success of human endeavor. The commandment to rejoice – the very core of the Israelite cult – is also oriented towards the "first commandment," the "principal commandment."[98]

Deuteronomy understands the current blessed existence of Israel on the one hand as a result of the promise YHWH made on oath to the patriarchs to make their descendants a people and give them the land (e.g. 4:31; 6:10-11; 7:12-13; 26:15). On the other hand, Deuteronomy also derives the present experience of bliss from YHWH's salvific action in favor of the fathers. The "brief historical credo," which was to be recited when the first fruits were offered, declares: He who brought Israel out of slavery in Egypt also brought it to this place where it can thank him for the fruits of the land (26:5-10). The relation of the yahwistic faith to history does not constitute an essential element in the deuteronomic festival theory. Later, however, it seems to have become a decisive criterion in the Israelite cult.[99] The Passover constitutes an exception; it was introduced by King Josiah only after the book of Deuteronomy was discovered in the temple (2 Kgs 23:21-23). The memory of the exodus is, from the theological as well as from the literary point of view, at the very center of the order for celebrating Passover as well as of the stipulations about the Feast of Unleavened Bread (Deut 16:1-8), which the Passover order had assimilated.[100]

Characteristically, the Passover is never called a "feast" (*ḥag*) in the Old Testament (although there are two possible exceptions, Exod 12:14 and 34:25) and is not celebrated as a feast (*ḥāgag*). Its rites do not allow us to assimilate it to the feasts in the strict sense of the word (the Feast of Weeks and the Feast of Booths). Rather, it should be compared to the sacrificial cult. Finally, it is not mentioned among the three pilgrimage feasts (16:16). It is characterized by the "bread of misery" (*leḥem ʿōnî*). According to the festival theory of Deuteronomy, however, joy is the characteristic feature both of the various sacrifices and of the feasts in the strict sense of the word.

Hence Israel does not merely desire the joy which is demanded of it, but is able genuinely to experience it: joy over the fulfillment of YHWH's promise to bless them. The Israelites rejoice because their efforts have attained their goal, the enterprise has paid off, the work has become meaningful. That an enterprise succeeds and that one may rejoice together over this success is not, however, self-evident. Hence the joy demanded by Deuteronomy is gratitude for the success which God has granted, for the material prosperity and for the fulfillment of the meaning of religious existence.[101] As R. Schulte phrases it,

> Every gift, in its very essence, refers back to the giver . . . Hence it is part of the acceptance, the development, and the appreciation of a gift to see, to respect, even to accomplish this relation to the giver . . . In our case: When man understands his significance and life as gifts, they reveal a special "obligation," which cannot be compared to anything else. When he fully understands his experience of himself, he becomes aware of a power, which irresistibly urges him to render thanks. In "delivering" himself up to

> this power, he evolves towards greater freedom: to give thanks, to fulfill the obligation to give thanks makes man happy and joyful and thus allows him to possess himself peacefully.[102]

J. Splett has actually called this "grateful response" the "only possible joy."[103] In this joy, the "acceptance of the world" is experienced, the "acceptance of the world" which, according to Pieper, constitutes the heart of every feast.[104] But this also means that "acceptance of the world implies a celebration of thanks. A feast celebrates the fact that what is accepted is not self-evident."[105]

Deritualization: Feast or Celebration? Everywhere, the succession of the seasons and their effects are celebrated according to a definite cultic scheme. This is obvious from the history of religion.[106] There are rites which symbolize—indeed, magically bring about—on the one hand the withering, on the other hand the renewal of the force of life. The basic pattern contains four essential elements: the mortification of the flesh, symbolizing the dying vegetation; physical and moral purification rites, which are intended to ward off anything that might be detrimental to future fertility; rites of confirmation, intended to give fresh life to the dying vegetation; finally, rites of joy when the new year has begun and life continues. The cosmic crisis is also celebrated with resurrection rites and with a common repast. Seen in relation to these customs expressing grief and joy which shaped the Canaanite fertility religion,[107] the deuteronomic festival theory gains a sharper profile.

Every third year, when the Israelites presented their poor tithes, they had, among other things, to make the following "negative confession"[108] (26:14a).[109]

> I have not eaten any of the tithe while in mourning, nor have I rid myself of it for unclean purposes, nor offered any of it to the/a dead (god).[110]

This confession is probably not simply an assurance of cultic purity while presenting the tithe offering, especially as such ancient sacral stipulations are foreign to the "rational and humanitarian world of Deuteronomy."[111] It seems more probable that the Israelites by these words explained that they had not taken part in any Canaanite harvest rites or brought any sacrifices to the dead Baal. Deuteronomy demythologizes the sacral offerings and adapts them to social and charitable purposes. The offertory ceremonies are replaced by a confession "before YHWH." In this way, people become aware of the process as an act of obedience towards YHWH and his commandments and a rejection of abuse of the cult (verses 12-15). In addition, all Canaanite mourning rites such as gashing one's skin or shaving one's forelock are strictly forbidden. The Israelites are "sons of YHWH" their God (14:1), not of Baal (cf. Jer 3:4, 19 with 2:27). They constitute a "holy people: and this obligates them to refrain from all cultic customs in honor of other gods (Deut 14:2). Thus Deuteronomy has even demythologized the numen of dying and refused both the dead and their graves any kind of sacral status.[112] For Deuteronomy, the *status confessionis* was an issue not only in connection with the cult of the dead, whether human or divine, but also in connection with the liturgies of confirmation and of joy.

Whereas the Canaanite mourning rites render present the death of the vegetation deity, the celebrations of joy represent his resuscitation. Indeed, the joy of the participants in the feast and the sacrificial repast was intended to bring about the joy of the god himself by means of magical equivalence.[113] There is textual evidence for this function of cultic joy from Akkadian to Neo-Assyrian times.[114] Deuteronomy also protests against this. Certainly, for Deuteronomy too, joy is characteristic of all feasts of the peasant culture determined by the rhythm of nature, and of all sacrifices and offerings of natural produce. Joy is even the only element which was taken over from the fourfold yearly rites of the neighboring religions and made part of every cultic performance.

According to the deuteronomic conception, however, this joy is not a joy "for the sake of the god," so to speak, or in his favor, nor is it intended to obtain his favor. It is joy over the favors which YHWH has already granted, a joy which is also gratitude. All ritual details are passed over in silence. Sacrifices and offerings, as well as the feasts are desacralized, and also, the differences between them are, to a large extent, reduced. The only thing that is essential is the "joy before YHWH" and the sharing of this joy with all those who are socially dependent and needy. For those who believe in YHWH, the greatest temptation through the fertility cults came when they brought the first fruits to the temple (26:10). However, in this context, a credo expressing gratitude (26:5-9) makes it clear that the best fruits of the land, which are laid down before YHWH—their nature is not specified—are YHWH's gifts (26:10, 11).[115] On this occasion, God is honored by *proskynesis* – a cultic act prescribed only in this passage of Deuteronomy. As Pieper points out,

> a feast is something which is transmitted in the strongest sense of the word: received as something of superhuman origin, in order to be handed on undiminished, then received and handed on again. It has been said that the vital power of tradition is nowhere as evident as in the history of the feast . . . A "preservation of tradition" which concentrates on the exterior image does not promote but rather hinders a genuine transmission, a living process of mediation between the generations. It is not simply a question of preserving and conserving, but of a continuous creative renewal of that which is authentically celebrated at the feast.[116]

In Deuteronomy, however, this actualization is not only in opposition to the alien fertility cults surrounding Israel. It also desacralizes and deritualizes, rationalizes and humanizes the transmitted yahwistic worship.[117] "Deuteronomy was surrounded by more or less accepted cultic ordinances, priestly laws and general ritual stipulations which – this will not be further discussed – had at an early stage been formulated in casuistic detail. Coming to Deuteronomy after this, one feels as though transferred to another world."[118] The most striking way of studying the liturgical renewal of Deuteronomy is to compare it with the parallel stipulations of the priestly legislation. Certainly the latter are much later,[119] but today they are generally regarded as a typical expression of the Old Testament cult.

For Deuteronomy, sacrifices are, to a large extent, not part of an institutionalized cult, but a personal pious practice with two main objectives: that of expressing gratitude towards YHWH and that of having a festive meal together with one's family, one's servants and those in need.[120] One "vows to YHWH" (*nādar l^{e}YHWH*) choice gifts (12:11; 23:22, 24),[121] yet no sacrifices are "offered to YHWH" (*l^{e}YHWH*).[122] The harvest festivals, on the other hand, are characterized by the fact that they are "kept to YHWH" (16:10, 15).

Nowhere do we find any polemic against bringing sacrifices. But neither do we find any subtle explanations of the kind that were later given in the priestly cult order. As far as the external rites went, there was probably no difference between the sacrifices of Israel and those of the Canaanite religion. But the context gives similar forms different meanings. Furthermore, Deuteronomy always enumerates the various sacrifices systematically in connection with the literary context. Before all individual stipulations, chapter 12 determines the spatial (verses 4-7) and temporal (verses 8-12) limits. This results in a distinction between sacrificial and profane slaughtering (verses 13-19). However, in neither case may the blood be eaten (verses 20-28). The importance of these deuteronomic principles is shown by their position at the beginning of the law code.

Since, according to verses 4-7, all sacrifices are to be brought to the one and only cult site, verse 6 enumerates the sacrifices one by one. This is the most comprehensive list.[123] It begins with the two types of animal sacrifice, distinguished from each other by the method of sacrificing: "burnt offerings," where the meat was entirely consumed on the altar, and "sacrifices" (or "shared offerings"), where only the blood and the fat were sacrificed, while the meat, after part of it had been assigned to the priests (18:3), was consumed at a sacrificial meal at the holy site by the person who had brought the sacrifice and his guests. Then there are five individual types of sacrifice, distinguished according to content and occasion: "tithes"; "heave offerings," probably of vegetable stuffs; "votive offerings," which were not ordained by the law but made in fulfillment of a vow; "freewill offerings," which were brought neither in obedience to the law nor in fulfillment of a vow; finally, "firstlings" of herd and flock (sheep and goats). It is remarkable that there is no reference to sin or guilt offerings.[124] The forms these sacrifices took began to be developed at the beginning of the exile. In the priestly cult legislation, these, together with the burnt offerings, are of crucial importance. It is also striking that there is no special mention of the offering of the first fruits. This offering, however, has been given a very noticeable position at the end of the law code (26:1-11).

According to verses 8-12, the moment at which the laws become valid is as universal as the place where the sacrifices are brought. In the corresponding passage (verse 11), the two last sacrifices in the first list (verse 6), the freewill offerings and the firstlings, are not mentioned, whereas the other sacrifices are enumerated in the same sequence. Firstlings, after all, can only be brought during a brief period of time (cf. 15:20). Leaving out the freewill offerings is probably a way of highlighting the particular emphasis of verse 8:

> You are not to act as we act here today, each of us doing what he pleases.

This interdiction is, so to speak, made up for when verse 11 mentions not simply "votive offerings," but "all the choice gifts that you have vowed to YHWH."

In the third place, the pericope consisting of verses 13-19 contrasts sacrifices in general with profane slaughtering.[125] The terminology is adapted to this. The context never mentions "slaughtering sacrifices," a fact which accentuates the contrast. There is no need for a particular mention of the "slaughtered sacrifices," since all types of sacrifices are in any case mentioned in verse 17. The structure of verses 13-19 did, of course, demand that the sequence differ from the normative lists in verses 6 and 11. The first section (verses 13-14) thematizes the "slaughtering": burnt offerings are to be burnt in the central sanctuary. This obviously presupposes that the animals have just been slaughtered there. But the verb "to slaughter" is deliberately avoided in sacrificial contexts. "Slaughtering," after all, is permitted always and everywhere. The second section (verses 15-19) is concerned with eating. Slaughtering is permitted in all settlements. It is only in this context that the Old Testament—in verse 15 and in the retrospect in verse 21—uses the verb *zābaḥ* for profane slaughtering. However, the blood may not be eaten together with the meat, but must be poured out. The various sacrifices, on the other hand—and this includes nearly all sacrifices except the burnt offerings, which were entirely consumed in smoke on the altar—may not be eaten in the settlements, but only at the central sanctuary.[126]

In the fourth place, verses 20-28 take up and develop the interdiction of eating blood which was briefly mentioned in verse 16. According to verse 26, all "holy gifts" which are to be brought, just as every first-born (cf. 15:19) is to be dedicated to YHWH, as well as the votive gifts which the sacrificer himself has defined as sacrifices, are to be brought to the one valid place for sacrificing. The blood is to be treated differently for burnt offerings and for sacrifices. This distinction, connected with the blood ceremony by using the terms "burnt offerings" and "sacrifices" in verse 27, comprises all animal sacrifices.[127] Only in this passage do we find a description of the rite.

> You must present your burnt offerings, both the flesh and the blood, on the altar of YHWH, your God; but of your shared offerings you shall eat the flesh, while the blood is to be poured on the altar of YHWH, your God.

In comparison with the priestly cult order, it is surprising that Deuteronomy so entirely ignores the stipulation that the fat is also to be consumed in smoke on the altar. After all, the fat, like the blood, is reserved for YHWH and must be sacrificed in the sanctuary.

Outside the four basic paragraphs analyzed above, only individual sacrifices are mentioned and the concrete circumstances are explained.[128] Regulations concerning tithes and firstlings of herd or field are found within the deuteronomic festival theory; votive and freewill offerings, however, are not mentioned here, which gives them a private character. Hence it can be stated of the deuteronomic laws in their entirety (and we should not forget that they are in reality intended as instructions for laypeople) that:

> they are not concerned with the ritual ceremonies of the various sacrifices, which constitutes a sharp contrast to Leviticus 1-7. On the contrary, their intention is to explain the cult regulations to a large audience. The core of their message is the fact that all sacrifices must be brought in one place, as well as the reason for this, *how* it is done is less important in this context.[129]

Until the time of the deuteronomic legislation, any act of slaughtering—apart from the killing of game—seems to have been understood as a ritual act, although it seems improbable that it was always performed at the sanctuary. Deuteronomy (12:15-16, 20-24) refuses to attribute any sacral meaning to this procedure. Thus all meat is equated with game, which cannot be sacrificed. Hence one need not be cultically pure in order to consume such meat. The blood must still be separated. However, it is no longer sprinkled on the altar as a sacrifice; it is poured out on the ground like water (12:16, 24), indeed like any other "profane" stuff (cf. Lev 17:1-16). In spite of this secularization, the act retains a confessional character. It was in consequence of the cult centralization that it became necessary to allow profane slaughtering. It would obviously have been unreasonable to expect people to undertake the journey to Jerusalem every time they wanted to kill an animal. However, when such an emphatic difference is made between slaughtering in order to sacrifice and slaughtering in order to eat, we have not only a rational organization of traditional customs, but also a tendency towards desacralization.

This tendency is also found in connection with the tithes and with the offering of the first fruits. The tithes of the agricultural produce had to be brought to the central sanctuary. Therefore the distance from the one and only cult site made certain practical alleviations necessary. Deuteronomy allows the farmers to sell the produce at their place of residence and then spend the money on a meal in common at the Temple of Jerusalem (14:22-27)—"an astonishing rationalization of cult practice, considering earlier notions about sacrifice!"[130] At the same time, the new regulations implied yet another piece of desacralization.

> At any rate a lack of respect for the direct religious relation to the fields can be discerned in the concession that the fruits of one's own land need not always be offered to the deity; they may be exchanged for money. This breaks the intimate ties between field and cult, in a wider sense between nature and religion. It constitutes a denial of any inherent sanctity in the first fruits. The entire cultic act receives its meaning in the heart of the pious.[131]

The same is true of the firstlings. Deuteronomy explicitly instructs the Israelites to consecrate the first-born among their animals to YHWH (15:19). This is in direct contradiction of the concept of the priestly law, according to which every first-born belongs to YHWH from the beginning (Lev 27:26; Num 18:17).[132] Deuteronomy completely ignores the redemption of the human first-born and the first-born of unclean animals (cf. Exod 34:19-20; 13:2, 12-16).[133]

In Deuteronomy, the Feast of Weeks and the Feast of Booths (16:9-12 and 16:13-15) are not, contrary to priestly cult legislation (Lev 23:15-21 and 23:33-36, 39-43), celebrated according to a determined ritual. The two harvest festivals have many features in common. At the Feast of Weeks, at the end of the approximately seven week long (grain) harvest, a votive offering is to be made as a form of thanksgiving. It is, however, the giver who determines both content and size of the offering (Deut 16:10).[134] As soon as the grain had been brought in from the threshing floor and the wine from the wine press, the end of the agricultural year was celebrated in the Feast of Booths. This name is probably a reminiscence of earlier times, when people spent this period in the vineyards (cf. Judg 21:19-21) and lived in huts as they did during the harvest. However, nothing more is said about that. The Feast of Booths is—like the Feast of Weeks—a feast "for YHWH." But at the same time, it is "your feast" (16:14), simply intended for the farmer and his friends. After the long hard work, everybody enjoys themselves for seven days. It is, quite simply, *the* feast. Only here (verse 15) does

Deuteronomy speak of "celebrating a feast" (*ḥāgag*).[135] Only here do we find—beside the customary exhortation to joy (verse 14)[136]—the explicit final words "You shall only rejoice!" (verse 15).[137] "Nowhere (in the deuteronomic cult legislation) is there any suggestion that the mere performance of cultic acts is significant."[138] Nowhere do we find "any stipulation according to which a breach against an absolutized cultic element in the laws would, as such, be regarded as a sin; even less do we find any law concerning unintentional sins against the cult regulations."[139]

Not least because the manner of the concrete cultic performance is left open, the deuteronomic liturgy for sacrifices, tithes, firstlings, the Feast of Weeks and the Feast of Booths have the character of a "feast" rather than of a "celebration." A celebration usually has historical and biographical origins. Its fully developed ceremonies and symbols are reminiscent of ritual behavior. The performance of a "solemn" act makes the participants into a group. A feast, on the other hand, can express the joy of life and thereby express gratitude even without any exterior occasion. It is closer to creative play and free self-expression. In spite of certain elements fixed by tradition, it is open to spontaneous, creative contributions and unexpected guests. The relationship between a "feast" and a "celebration" are, however, more important than the differences. The concept of "feast" would appear to be more comprehensive and to have a wider range of meaning. This concept includes the alternation between "festive" and "solemn" elements.[140] In any case, such an overall concept of the "feast" appears to do better justice to the deuteronomic concept of the cult than the term "celebration."

This "indifference towards the correct cultic form"[141] is found only in the rigid cult centralization. The Israelites are obliged to bring all sacrifices, firstlings and first fruits, and in one way or another even their tithes to the Temple of Jerusalem. The journey there is seen as a participation in the march of the people from slavery in Egypt to the land of their inheritance, a land flowing with milk and honey (12:8-12 and 26:1-11). Whereas in connection with the sacrifices and offerings, the centralization formula emphasizes the unity of place through the verbs "go," "go up," "take with you" and "offer" (e.g., 12:5, 11, 14; 14:25; 26:2), the feasts emphasize the unity of time. In the old calendar of the Book of the Covenant (Exod 23:14-17), the pilgrimage to a (local) sanctuary is given no date; now the pilgrimages are dated to the Feast of Unleavened Bread, the

Feast of Weeks and the Feast of Booths (16:16-17). In this way, Deuteronomy created the pilgrimage feasts.[142] But what was the reason for this unification which limited the cultic activity of the whole people in such a radical way? It was not the cult site as such which was important.[143] Nothing is said about the sacrality of the sanctuary and its concerns, nor about revering it (cf. Lev 19:30). There are no ordinances intended to protect its altar from ritual desacralization (cf. Exod 29:37; Lev 21:16-23). The particularity of the deuteronomic cult order cannot be understood through a centralization law made absolute. Rather, the centralization is a consequence of Israel's relation to YHWH its God, and it is this relation which constitutes the core of deuteronomic theology.[144]

The unifying framework of one sanctuary and one date, created by the deuteronomic cult centralization for the sake of Israel's relation with God did more than guarantee cultic purity through cultic unity. It also assembled the individual families, professions and classes into a united people. Only then were they able to experience to the fullest the reality of the feast, even though the ideal feast was never fully realized (cf. the redactional change in 16:16 to "three times a year" and "all your males"). A feast is defined by the fact that it assembles everybody, does not allow the isolation of one person from another, and constitutes a community – indeed, represents community in its most perfect form.

Fraternal Community and Social Care

A feast is intended to unite the community. "A feast is a joyful event experienced in common."[145] However, one can experience joy only if one brings others joy.[146] Thus, both joy and feast have a social dimension. "At a 'popular feast,' the class barriers break down. Differences disappear."[147] The deuteronomic cult order, which is otherwise very reticent about stipulations, never tires of enumerating the participants in sacrifices or feasts. The following are mentioned: "you and your family," "you, your son and daughter, your male and female slaves" (the individual expressions are also found in the plural); then "the Levites who live in your settlements" and finally, "the aliens, orphans and widows who live among you." According to Deuteronomy, these groups together form "all Israel." The variations in the enumerations are mainly due to the differences between sacrifices, firstlings, tithes, and feasts.

The group of participants in the sacrifices is the smallest one. Verse 12:7 uses the briefest formula: "you and your families." This phrase did not constitute a deuteronomic innovation, but is found elsewhere in the Pentateuch, as early as in the old Yahwistic History. (It was also used later than Deuteronomy.)[148] Verses 12:12 (in a plural address) and 12:18 (in a singular address) explicate this designation further: "you, your sons and daughters, your male and female slaves." At first sight, it appears that the father in the Israelite extended family[149] is missing. By the term "fathers," Deuteronomy understands the patriarchs as recipients of the divine promise. The same is true of the "brothers" ("brother usually means a member of one's own people) and the "neighbors" (the ties with one's neighbors are those of blood relationship). But brothers, sisters, and neighbors have their own families, which means that the law addresses them directly.

One is particularly struck by the fact that women are not explicitly mentioned[150] Of course, the intention of Deuteronomy was not to make the rest of the family set off for the temple, leaving the wife and mother alone at home.[151] On the contrary, she is not mentioned because the "you" at the beginning of the list is addressed to the free woman as well as to the free man. Deuteronomy desires the equality of the sexes and therefore makes a number of stipulations in favor of the emancipation of women. Furthermore, the detailed enumeration of the members of the family is characteristic of Deuteronomy. It appears to be a self-evident development of the family theme; yet it is socially explosive. The deuteronomic version of the sabbath commandment provides the best proof of how revolutionary the notion of the equal status not only of women and children but also of male and female slaves must have appeared to society in those days. It is not simply that male and females slaves are mentioned among those who have a right as well as a duty to keep the sabbath rest. The crucial point is stressed at the end:

> Your male and female slaves are to rest as you do (5:14).

The existence of slaves is still presupposed. But in fact the authors are on the verge of undermining the slave society. What is eliminated is the division of work and rest between different groups. There is even more to it: there is already a suggestion of the emancipation of slaves."[152]

In Deuteronomy, the sacrifices are expressions of gratitude for the blessings granted by YHWH (12:7; cf. 12:15). The blessing of YHWH is primarily experienced by the individual families and not by the whole people. "A blessing was originally understood to mean the fertility of body, field and cattle and was thus essential to the economy of the family."[153] The framework within which thanks are rendered is thus—with good reason—limited to the (entire) individual family. In sacrificing, however, one also offers God a gift from "the produce of one's hands" (12:7, 18). Thus it is comprehensible that—even apart from the practical difficulties—the poor of Israel are not mentioned. The Levites, however, are to participate in the sacrifices. They are present at all liturgical acts and are, with a single exception, always explicitly mentioned. In the list of participants, they always come after the members of the family and before the group of the needy, "the aliens, orphans and widows." This order corresponds exactly to the position the Levites have in the cult. On the one hand, they are, because of their potential priestly function, associated with the families who perform the sacrifices; on the other, they constitute the first of the "social cases" and are thus "aliens" in the sense of "protected residents" (18:6).

Unlike the other Israelites, the Levites[154] possessed no land of their own, but were to nourish themselves on their part of the sacrifices, the inheritance of YHWH (18:1). Through the deuteronomic cult centralization, those Levites who exercised their priestly functions in the local sanctuaries did not merely become unemployed, they also lost their means of support. Therefore Deuteronomy ensures that the Levites "who live in your settlements" (12:12, 18; 14:26; 16:11, 14) receive their maintenance. In addition, they are given the right to serve in the central sanctuary and receive an "income" from this service (18:6-8). According to 2 Kgs 23:9, the rural Levites did not receive this right at the Josianic reform. It is customary to conclude from this that the Jerusalemite clergy had, out of self-interest, prevented the legal equality intended by Deuteronomy. It seems probable, however, that the claims of the rural Levites were inserted into Deuteronomy at a later stage, although before the end of the exile.[155] The deuteronomic cult stipulations intend the Levites to participate in all liturgical acts, but say nothing about the extent to which they could or should be active. Hence it was possible to reinterpret the stipulations and to bring them to the fore in various ways.[156] Deut 12:7 does not mention the

Levites nor does it list the individual family members. Perhaps the editor has taken up the old abbreviated formula "you and your families"[157] because the primary intent of verses 4-7 was to emphasize that the central sanctuary was the only cult site for Israel.

Who else is mentioned in the list of participants depends entirely on the particular intention of each individual cult stipulation. This intention is mirrored in a symbolic and liturgical way in those members of the festival community who are explicitly mentioned. Verses 8-12, for instance, state the moment at which the deuteronomic cult legislation becomes valid. It is only when Israel is living in the land which YHWH has given them as patrimony (verse 10) that the Israelites are obliged to bring their sacrifices to the Temple of Jerusalem. The Levites are to participate "because they have no holding or patrimony among you" (verse 12). Verses 13-19 draw the conclusion which follows from the institution of a single sanctuary: one must distinguish between sacrifices and profane slaughtering. The Levites are to take part in the sacrificial meal (verse 18). After Israel has crossed the Jordan, they are, according to 27:1-8, to offer whole offerings and shared offerings on Mount Ebal (Gerizim). In this command, "you" means the entire people of Israel.

The tithes and firstlings are counted among the sacrifices (12:6, 11, 17). It was necessary to make further stipulations about them and these stipulations are found in 14:22-29 and 26:1-11. The first-mentioned participants are again "you and your family" (14:26; cf. 26:11). It is not, however, enough that the Levites be allowed to join in the sacrificial meal (from tithe money and firstlings) at the central sanctuary. This is presumably why it is not explicitly demanded by 12:18. Tithes and firstlings are ways of expressing gratitude to YHWH for giving Israel the land and granting it fertility. They are offered "so that you may learn to fear YHWH, your God, as long as you live" (14:23). This attitude, however, must become apparent in social and charitable practice.[158]

> You must not neglect the Levites who live in your settlements; for they have no holding or patrimony among you (verse 27).

This stipulation is directly connected with the yearly offering of gifts at the sanctuary, which—it was not even necessary to mention—was, of course, to be deducted from the tithes and firstlings. As former rural priests, the Levites were connected with the altar. As they do not in principle have any holding or patrimony in Israel, they belong to those groups who are often destitute and who need particular support: the aliens, orphans and widows (verse 29). It was probably only in Deuteronomy that the "aliens" were added in front of the old phrase "orphans and widows"—in the Ancient Orient this was the characteristic expression used for those in need of support[159]—and that the formula was thus expanded to a triad of needy persons.[160] Like these, the Levites enjoy the proceeds of the poor tax in the locality where they reside (verses 28-29). Apart from any theological considerations, it would have been impossible for every family to bring all the needy to Jerusalem and there regale them on a sacrificial or a tithe meal! It was quite enough if a family traveled to the temple for the sacrifice, taking their farm laborers and maids, as well as the Levites with them. In order to prevent the needy from being left with nothing, the tithes of every third year were to remain in the settlements and, without their being regarded as a sacrifice, be given to the Levites, the aliens, the orphans and the widows.[161] Hence, every third year is regarded as the tithe year par excellence (26:12). The prerequisite for any consequent blessing is that the marginal groups have enough to eat (14:29; cf. 26:15).

In 14:22-29 the offering of tithes and firstlings are fixed, but not the offering of first fruits, which (as a defense against the Canaanite fertility cult) is provided with a rite of its own. Anyone who brings the best/first fruits to the Temple of Jerusalem commemorates by a confession the fate Israel had to suffer as an alien (*gwr*, verse 5) without rights in Egypt (verses 5-6). Not only did YHWH see their distress in a situation where they had no rights (verse 7) and save them from it (verse 8), but he also gave Israel "this land, a land flowing with milk and honey" (verse 9). Both facts are expressed symbolically in the liturgy. Not only the family and the Levites,[162] but also, explicitly, "the aliens (*gēr*) among you"[163] are invited (verse 11).[164] It is striking that here, as elsewhere in Deuteronomy, there is no reference to the subjective position of the *gēr*—"the resident aliens, not the authentic foreigners—as a condition for their incorporation. All that Deuteronomy demands—and demands emphatically—is that they be treated as part of the people of God."[165] The next paragraph (verses 12-15) also dissociates the "holy gifts" from Baal through a special confession and associates them with YHWH as the one who grants all blessings.[166] As in the case of the offering of the first fruits, the culmination is a confession. It begins:

> I have rid my house of the tithe that was holy to you and given it to the Levites, to the aliens, the orphans and the widows, according to the commandments which you have laid upon me (26:13).

With such obedience, with such a cult confessing YHWH as lord of history as well as of nature, guaranteeing the poor a human existence and showing them solidarity, Israel could indeed hope that the final prayer would be granted:

> Bless your people Israel and the land which you have given us as you swore to our forefathers, a land flowing with milk and honey (26:15).

Finally, the Feast of Weeks and the Feast of Booths unite all ranks and classes at the one sanctuary and thus render present the unity of the whole people. This implies a decisive extension of the group of participants in comparison with the old festival calendar (Exod 23:16; 34:22). This is not maintained in the later priestly cult legislation. It must be admitted that Deuteronomy does not consider how the entire people is to come to the temple! It is the theological purpose which is essential to Deuteronomy, not any casuistic regulations. Possibly Deuteronomy's enumeration of all those who are to participate in the feast is made in deliberate opposition to the Canaanite religion. For the Canaanite religion "is related to the politically constituted unity of the people, whereas personal experience and the salvation of the individual are of secondary importance."[167] The deuteronomic attempt at integration, on the other hand, resulted in people becoming more aware of personal piety—both in the cult and in everyday life—and experiencing it with greater intensity. Deuteronomy founds the festival community on the families[168] and the individuals, so that the community is structured from below, so to speak, instead of being organized from above. Cult reform and social reforms are closely associated. Thus Israel appears as an overdimensional family whose individual members are brothers and sisters.[169] The people of God is also the family of Deuteronomy (*'am YHWH*).[170]

Even those on the outmost margins of Israelite society are integrated into this fraternity. Thus on one hand, the king is a brother among brothers and sisters, even an exemplary brother; on the other hand, so is the slave.

From king to slave, all Israel gets its living from the common patrimony of the land given them by YHWH.[171] This fraternal relation founded by God and preceding even biological fraternity (cf. 13:7-12) does oppose inequality of one type, but does not prevent the formation of social classes. For "fraternity is not the result of romantic ideas and social formlessness, but of the acceptance and use of social differences and social plurality."[172] Yet the notion of brotherliness characterizes the behavior of the Israelites towards each other since they all exist only because they have been saved and blessed by YHWH. Because YHWH redeemed them from Egypt, the Israelites can regard a slave as a brother (15:12-18); the wealth of the land given by God makes "democratization" a duty, just as it is a duty to let everyone share in the blessing (15:1-11). "In a remarkable way, and with great terminological preciseness, Deuteronomy teaches the Israelites how to behave towards each other, towards their brothers."[173] The notion of fraternity as a structural principle for the whole people also means that this ethos is incorporated in the liturgical life, although at the feasts Israel does not explicitly appear as an assembly of brothers and sisters.[174] This is not the least important of the reasons why the deuteronomic cult regulations appeal to the social conscience of the participants – in opposition to earlier practice, where the cultic meals could even lead to exploitation of the poor (Amos 2:6-8).[175] The theory of Deuteronomy is that the feast liberates people from existential anguish and abolishes class barriers so that all may rejoice before YHWH. "A feast is where love rejoices" (John Chrysostom).

The brotherliness of YHWH's family is not merely proclaimed by Deuteronomy; it is also intended to be experienced. Its most effective symbol is the liturgical meal which follows on the animal sacrifices (12:7, 18; 14:23, 26; 27:7). For "only when the gift is tasted do we realize how precious it is."[176] For the shared offerings, communion with God alone is not sufficient – indeed, it is typical of Deuteronomy not even to mention the part given to God.

> In life, there is union and exchange between people; the sacrificial meal culminates in a meal expressing love. Having received the gift of life from God, people are able to give something to others. And it is only because of this that there is wide-spread, exuberant joy.[177]

In the pericopes expressing the deuteronomic festival theory, the joint meal precedes the rejoicing. The feast is a result of the meal and of the sacrificial communion. What is celebrated is not the mere consumption of the gifts as such,[178] but the community which finds its expression in the sacrifice. Deuteronomy never speaks only of eating the sacrificial meat. On the contrary, this is always described as "eating in the presence of YHWH your God" (*'kl lipnê YHWH 'ᵉlōhêkā*),[179] it is a "sacrament" in the original sense of the word.

Finally, the "deuteronomic book of the law, which represents a peak in the history of the Israelite cultus,"[180] associates the command to "eat before YHWH" with joy. Indeed, it is only in Deuteronomy that joy is mentioned. In a world in which sacrifices were frequent and important, and in which the centralization of the cult to a single sanctuary was therefore experienced as a restriction and an impoverishment, it is now made certain that every meal at this site will be a joyful one. "We may regard this as a basic motif, perhaps as the most important one behind what is said about eating and drinking in the Old Testament. It is expressed in lapidary form and has important consequences."[181] Hence, it is probably significant that the list of participants is not, as one would expect, added to the exhortation to hold a meal in common, but is added to the call to rejoice. It is only in 12:18 that the list is given in connection with the cultic meal which constitutes a central point of this law.

However, if, as Splett demonstrates, "a feast is always a feast of reciprocal giving,"[182] it is surprising that precisely for the feasts in the full sense of the term, that is, the Feast of Weeks and the Feast of Booths, there is at the most an indirect suggestion of a meal. It is true that, at the Feast of Weeks, people are supposed to bring freewill offerings (16:10), or according to another version, they are not to come empty-handed to any of the three pilgrimage feasts, where they come to see the face of YHWH (16:16). To that extent, it is true that "the sacrifice constitutes the heart of the feast."[183] Yet there is no distinct mention of a meal in common. It is, however, impossible to imagine that the Feast of Weeks, the feast of joy par excellence, was kept by a seven day long fast! When, if not at the end of the harvest of corn and wine, would one eat and drink and make merry with one's friends and allow all the impoverished to participate in this abundance? Deuteronomy's obstinate silence on this point has a theological meaning which is impossible to neglect. Precisely because it seems so obvious (judging by common festival customs) that a joyful meal is to be announced, the absence of any such announcement obviously implies a reevaluation of what used to be regarded as customary. The spiritual background to this "error" can be concluded from what is common to all those deuteronomic cult stipulations which do not foresee any cultic meal: the offering of the best fruits in 12:8-12,[184] of the best/first fruits in 26:1-11, and the celebration of the harvest in 16:9-12 and 13-15. The fertility of the soil always constitutes the center of these liturgical acts. When nothing is said about eating, this is a way of marking the difference from the cultic meals of the Canaanite fertility religion.[185] Of course all Israelite feasts could still be—and were!—celebrated with a joint meal at the central sanctuary. Deuteronomy does not prohibit such a meal, but merely divests it of all syncretistic and sacral features.

This type of indirect polemic against the cult of Baal, with Israelite practice nevertheless remaining the same,[186] is even more evident when it comes to "drinking." Again, not a word is said about it, although Israel regards wine as a blessing of the cultivated land (e.g., 28:39) and even considers alcoholic beverages normal for a cultic meal. After all, the Israelites are encouraged to spend their tithe money in Jerusalem on "cattle or sheep, wine or strong drink, or whatever you desire" and then to "consume it with rejoicing . . . in the presence of YHWH your God" (14:26). The satisfaction of human "desires" is to be included in the cultic joy, but cannot be equated with it. What is decisive is the symbolic content of all liturgical acts. They may no longer be interpreted according to the fertility cult. The ancient human customs, however, could be maintained as long as it was within a framework which prevented misunderstanding—the sacrificial meal could be eaten only at the central sanctuary and the joy was to be a joy "before YHWH." "Wine was of crucial importance in secular life, but was excluded from the cult" in the way described.

> In the Canaanite cult, it was obviously part of the ritual that man and god should drink together. Once more, this makes it clear that the identification of human and divine is rejected: Through intoxication—both through sexual and alcoholic intoxication—man experiences the abolition of the distance and thus a union with the god and with nature. In opposition to this, the Israelite cult maintains a sober distance between God and man.[187]

Because of Israel's unique relationship with YHWH, Deuteronomy rejects any "natural-magical way of bringing about a relation to the deity." This was something which occurred "in regrettable ways in the YHWH-Baal cults in their various forms."[188] The "rejoicing before YHWH," however, proves that in spite of this radical demystification, perhaps indeed because of it, it was possible for the whole people to have an intimate relationship with God.

The Experience of the Presence of God and *Koinōnia*

G. Ebeling once expressed the dialogic structure of worship (admittedly, this structure can be correctly understood only as the development of a single process) in the following terms.

> From God, human beings can expect not only gifts but also the presence of God himself. And from human beings, God expects not only gifts but also that they give themselves, their hearts to him . . . Thus the essential event in the cult is God becoming more God and human beings becoming more human, man before God and God before man.[189]

Deuteronomy expresses this fundamental dimension of the liturgy through the "cult formula"[190] (however, the particular accent depends on the context): "before YHWH your God" (*lipnê YHWH ʾelōhêkā/ʾelōhêkem*). In Deuteronomy, for the first time in the Old Testament, this formula occurs (most frequently) in connection with the sacrificial repast (*ʾākal lipnê YHWH ʾelōhêkā/ʾelōhêkem*, 12:7, 18; 14:23, 26),[191] or with cultic joy (*śāmaḥ lipnê YHWH ʾelōhêkā / ʾelōhêkem*, 12:12, 18; 16:11; 27:7).[192] This does not, however, constitute any absolute "either/or," as is shown by 12:18.

Only when the first fruits are brought is the cult formula detached from any reference to joy. Typically the reference to a meal is also missing. Instead, the formula is related to three rites: the proclamation of the "brief historical credo" before YHWH (26:5); after this confession, the basket with the best/first fruits is to be put down before YHWH; finally, one is to prostrate oneself before YHWH (verse 10). It is only in connection with the Feast of Booths that there is no cult formula at all.[193] Yet the Feast of Booths is celebrated "for YHWH" (*ḥāgag leYHWH ʾelōhêkā*, 16:15),[194] just as the Feast of Weeks is to be kept "to YHWH" (*ʿāśâ ḥag leYHWH ʾelōhêkā*, 16:10). It is, however, certain that "what takes place 'before YHWH' in the cult is also performed 'for YHWH.'"[195] In both cases, the emphasis on YHWH is related to his blessing as a measure for the freewill offerings and the joy (16:10, 15).

It is not hard to discover that what is here rejected is the influence of the baalistic syncretistic fertility rites. There was a particular risk of such an influence at the harvest festivals. Yet, despite the fact that faith in YHWH was in danger, Deuteronomy did not give God's claims such an absolute status that human needs were neglected. It is typical that, in the deuteronomic cult legislation the liturgy is never called the "service of YHWH" or "divine service." The key word is not adoration,[196] but human joy before YHWH. Even though there be sacrifice and communion, the exhortation to rejoice is closely connected with the meal. Because of the context, joy as a relationship with YHWH is valid even in the absence of the cult formula. It follows from this that a feast does not simply mean joy about something, but above all joy in communion with others, before God. It is, after all, characteristic of joy that it "feels at home when it is close to the origin."[197] But is this really what Deuteronomy means by "before YHWH"?

However one interprets the historical relations between the transmitted cult formula ("before YHWH") and the centralization formula ("in the place which YHWH has chosen"), they express different things in the context of deuteronomic cult laws. The expression "before YHWH" means neither the immediate area of the temple nor a genuine cultic act; rather, it "expresses an interior religious attitude."[198] Perhaps the cult formula also bears the suggestion of a causal relationship where eating and rejoicing in the personal presence of God are ultimately experienced as having him as their authentic origin.[199] Thus the joint meal and the unity with God in joy are indissolubly amalgamated as the apex of the life in "peace" in the "land which God allots them as patrimony" (cf. 12:9-10), a life which expresses the presence of salvation.[200] The "care for others" has found its deepest cause in an extensive *koinōnia*, communion. Within this framework, but in perfect liberty, the "divinization and humanization" of the world and of human existence, the "participation and activity," the "interiority and expression" of both the individual and the community find their liturgical context.

Only when the cult formula is understood in this way do the desacralization and deritualization of Deuteronomy receive their authentic meaning and true interpretation. Sacrality is detached from objects, performances and persons in their material sense, as well as from their functions; rites are no longer seen as absolute. And thus the personal relationship between YHWH and Israel can become fully effective again.[201]

Thus what Gregory the Great saw as the meaning of the cult for man is also true of the deuteronomic festival theory.

> Ad contemplandum Creatorem homo conditus . . . (est), ut eius speciem semper quaereret, atque in solemnitate illium amoris habitaret.
>
> Human beings are created in order to see their God (that is, in order to live in a personal dialogue with him), in order to search for his face without ceasing (that is, in order to desire continually to taste the joy of divine friendship) and to live in the festal joy of this love (that is, in God's love for human beings and in human love for God).[202]

If, after analyzing the deuteronomic conception of the cult, we now take another look at the "new" conception of the liturgy as described by Ratzinger, we realize that its roots are to be found in Old Testament traditions. However, the festival theory of Deuteronomy refuses to make "creativity, freedom and communion" into alternatives to "interiority, ties with the past, the common order of the Church." On the contrary, Deuteronomy provides a model for the relations between these key words which could be as fruitful for Christian liturgy today as they once were decisive for the life of the early Church.

Festal Joy in the Primitive Christian Community

The concept of joy (*śmḥ*) is presented in clear outline in Deuteronomy. Outside of this book, however, the connotations of the term are less theological. In postexilic literature, *śmḥ* is usually understood as festal joy; in the Psalms, it is seen as spiritual.[203] This cult poetry uses "rejoice" (*śmḥ*) and "exult" (*gîl*) as well as other terms for joy more or less synonymously.[204] The Septuagint[205] usually translates *śāmaḥ/śimḥâ*, especially in Deuteronomy and in the Deuteronomic History, as εὐφραίνειν/εὐφροσύνη, in later Old Testament books—although rarely in a cultic context—also as (συν)χαίρειν/χαρά. Finally, the Septuagint uses ἀγαλλιᾶσθαι/ ἀγαλλίασις although this is mainly a rendering of Israel. However, the boundary lines between εὐφραίνειν and ἀγαλλιᾶσθαι are fleeting. Among these word groups, which are most commonly used to express human joy in the New Testament,[206] εὐφραίνειν / εὐφροσύνη characterizes "the joy of celebrating a feast together,"[207] sometimes in a secular but usually in a religious sense. ἀγαλλιᾶσθαι / ἀγαλλίασις, on the other hand, is found only in biblical and ecclesiastic language. This joy, which is always religious, seizes the entire person. It means not so much an interior feeling of joy as a joy demonstrated by proud exultation and visible action.[208] It becomes

> the characteristic attitude of the New Testament community as well as of the individual Christian. It fills their worship, gives a joyous character to the thanksgiving at the meal of the Lord (the breaking of the bread) ... and it embraces the salvation objectively fulfilled by Christ and personally experienced, as well as the future salvation.[209]

In the New Testament, these two word groups are found most frequently in Luke.[210]

The primitive community as the true Israel[211] leads a life full of joy. According to the narratives of Acts 2:43-47 and 4:32-37, this joy arises from communion with the risen Christ present in the cult as well as in one's brothers and sisters in the faith, who form a socio-religious *koinōnia*.[212] The life of the primitive community is characterized by daily visits to the temple, shared meals in private houses and the praise of God.

> With one mind they kept up their daily attendance at the temple, and breaking bread in private houses, shared their meals with unaffected joy, as they praised God and enjoyed the favor of the whole people (Acts 2:46-47).[213]

Luke transmits a trustworthy old tradition when he speaks of the joyous character of the breaking of the bread, although he is using his own words. At the breaking of the bread, the community assembles at one table and experiences anew the sacrifice of the last supper, although in fact nothing is, in this context, said specifically about a commemoration of the passion and death of Jesus. The community experiences a profound communion and exults over the risen Lord, who is present among them. But there is also such exultant joy when somebody becomes a member of the community of the saved through acceptance of the faith and by baptism. And there, too, is a suggestion that the joy is somehow related to a meal (16:34).[214] To the communion in the cult is added a social communion consisting of joint property and of social care:

> All whose faith had drawn them together held everything in common (ἅπαντα κοινά): they would sell their property and possessions and make a general distribution as the need of each required (Acts 2:44-45).

This fraternal spirit is described as "being united in heart and soul" (4:32). This constitutes a fulfillment of Deuteronomy's notion of a future fraternal community:

> They had never a needy person among them (Acts 4:34).
>
> Indeed, there ought to be no poor among you (Deut 15:4).

How closely this *koinōnia* was related to the breaking of the bread of the first Christians is shown by the following verse:

> They met constantly to hear the apostles teach, and to share the common life (κοινωνία), to break bread and to pray (Acts 2:42).

The teaching and the prayers as oral expressions of communal life are contrasted with the κοινωνία and the breaking of the bread as practical expressions. All these acts are part of the cult.[215] That the Christian common meal and the "daily distribution" (the "service at the tables"), social care, have a fundamental relation to each other is finally demonstrated by Acts 6:1-6. Because of the growing number of members in the community, charity had to be separated from the apostolic service for organizational reasons and entrusted to "deacons." The expression "service at the tables," however, still implies the "fundamental unity of λειτουργία and διακονία.[216] It is in the κοινωνία[217] of liturgy and care that the eucharistic festal joy[218] breaks through. This joy is a work of the Holy Spirit which at Pentecost, that is, at the Feast of Weeks, descended on those assembled in Jerusalem. But "in this case, the joy is not only the result of a messianic miracle, it is also ... a consequence of the stipulation of Deut 16:10-12 to rejoice in the company of one's entire 'house' at the Feast of Weeks."[219] The festal joy of the primitive Christian community has its origin in the Christ event. And that is why it immeasurably exceeds that festal joy which Deuteronomy demands of Israel.

3
Commemoration of Passion and Feast of Joy

Popular Liturgy According to the Festival Calendar of the Book of Deuteronomy (Deut 16:1-17)

German title: "Leidensgedächtnisfeier und Freudenfest" (see bibliography)

The Second Vatican Council's Constitution on the Liturgy defines the divine service of the Church primarily as "celebration" (*celebratio*). According to B. Neunheuser, "celebration" in its full liturgical sense means "the sacred action (*actio sacra*) of the community assembled for divine service, for the commemoration of Christ's salvific act; that is, in order to render this act present, to reenact it with gratitude and praise."[1] Thus, in the reality of Christian faith, what can already be known through the previous history of salvation is brought to its highest fulfillment:

> All the feasts of the people of God in the Old Testament are based on a celebration of the deeds of God, a cultic celebration. One celebrates a sacrifice before YHWH, then one sits down with one's family or with the whole people in order to eat and drink and be merry before the Lord . . . Everybody participates in these feasts; the poor are particularly invited. True, these celebrations are provisional and point towards a final eschatological fulfillment.[2]

This description of the Old Testament cult is found in one of the latest articles on the topic of feasts; yet it simply repeats a widespread—and, as I intend to show—an undifferentiated and thereby false cliché.

Contrary to Neunheuser, who stresses the celebration of God's (historical) deeds by bringing sacrifices for all Old Testament feasts,

H. Haag in the *Lexikon für Theologie und Kirche* characterizes the Old Testament liturgy by affirming: "The aim of the cult is to create a holy people."[3]

In what follows, both theses will be questioned from the point of view of biblical scholarship. The point of departure for this critical sketch is the so-called deuteronomic "festival calendar" (Deut 16:1-17)[4]—the core of the oldest biblical theory of feasts. In Deuteronomy, for the first time in the Old Testament, we find "a consistent theology" which attempts "to encompass the extremely variegated world of the cult and to give it a standardized interpretation."[5] This concept of divine service was modified in later periods by other cult regulations. Nevertheless, its basic structure must be taken into account when one attempts to grasp the biblical understanding of the liturgy.

Remarks Concerning the History of the Deuteronomic Liturgical Reform

The first interpretation of the Israelite cult as a comprehensive phenomenon—as it is set out in the book of Deuteronomy—is rooted in the cult centralization of Hezekiah and Josiah.[6] This deep-reaching new regulation of the two Judean kings must have been motivated by both political[7] and religious considerations.

In the eighth and seventh centuries BCE, the Southern Kingdom was a vassal of the New Assyrian Empire.[8] Its military success and the cultural dominance resulting from its political power caused an extensive crisis of values among the vanquished. Also, the Assyrian-Aramaic astral worship and the indigenous fertility cult estranged people from the traditional faith in YHWH and loosened their emotional ties with the authentic cult. What was needed, then, was not only national liberation, but also a theology and a liturgical reform suited to the terms. But how could Judah rediscover its identity and overcome the cultural shock, if the local sanctuaries remained largely autonomous and exposed in many ways to syncretistic influences? The centralization of the cult, made compulsory in the various stages of deuteronomic legislation and re-effected several times, was an attempt to master both the political and the religious emergency.

Indeed, the team of authors by whom Deuteronomy was probably composed consisted of world-wise court officials with diplomatic training and of tradition-conscious Jerusalemite priests. They systematized Israel's diverse traditions, which many people obviously felt were no longer relevant, into the contemporary legal construction of "covenant" and formulated them in the wordy eloquence of Neo-Assyrian covenantal rhetoric. Thus they were able to make the preaching and practice of their own faith attractive once more. In this, they were aided by the use of the categories of thought, the models of action and the fashionable language of the competing symbolic system.

Individual stipulations must have been composed as early as around 700 BCE under Hezekiah. However, this king's revolt against the Assyrian supremacy failed. His cult centralization, in which the sacrifices in the high places were abolished (2 Kgs 18:4, 22) and the Feast of Unleavened Bread was moved to Jerusalem (2 Chr 30:13, 21),[9] had no lasting success.

It was only King Josiah who managed to free himself gradually from the vassal relationship. He destroyed the local sanctuaries (2 Kgs 23:4-20). The old Book of the Torah, rediscovered in the Temple of Jerusalem, was promulgated as the constitutional law of the country and made the charter of a "covenant." He also swore an oath on the original book of Deuteronomy, an oath to which the whole people gave allegiance (2 Kgs 23:1-3). Josiah was probably reintroducing here an earlier enthronement ceremony of the Judaic kings by which a treaty was sealed between YHWH, the king, and the people; and by which the new "people of YHWH" was repeatedly formed.[10] In the days of King Joash, this ritual had actually been followed by people marching to the temple of Baal and demolishing it (2 Kgs 11:17-18). When the relationship with God was understood as a treaty, the exclusive claim of YHWH could also justify the political independence movement. The treaty with YHWH as Israel's overlord replaced the previously valid treaty with the Assyrian king. The covenant with Assyria had made the Assyrian rule legitimate; now the covenant with YHWH legitimized independence. Josiah's covenant ceremony culminated in a Passover common to the whole people and celebrated in the central sanctuary—as prescribed in the Book of the Covenant. "A Passover such as this had not been celebrated since the days of the judges" (2 Kgs 23:21-23).[11]

This text shows that King Josiah's Passover reform was not understood as a liturgical revolution but as a "constructive restoration."[12] It was intended to recreate the original national unity as the judges had once created it for the political deliverance of Israel. In any case, it is significant that under Hezekiah the cult centralization found its most striking expression in the Feast of Unleavened Bread and under Josiah in the Passover. Even before they were transferred to the sanctuary of Jerusalem, these two rites commemorated the exodus from Egypt (Exod 34:18; 23:15; 13:4-7; and 12:21-23).

The exodus theme appears to suggest yet another political intention. The gradual dissolution of the vassal relationship, pursued by Josiah in view of the decline of the Assyrian empire, was accompanied by the danger of becoming dependent on Egypt. In the second half of the seventh century Egypt had, under Psammetichus I, withdrawn itself from the Assyrian overlordship. The political question was then, "From now on, will Judah be free or a vassal, the 'servant' of Egypt?"[13] Seen against this background, the Passover also implied a rejection of any idea of joining forces with Egypt. (Concerning this tendency in later times, cf. Deut 17:16; 28:68.)[14]

Hence the context of the covenant ceremony and its connection with the exodus event show that the introduction of a Passover celebrated by "the whole people" was primarily a cultic-*political* act. A deuteronomistic redactor later inserted the "reform narrative" about the purification of the YHWH cult from idolatry between the covenant and the Passover (2 Kgs 23:4-20). After the editing, the Passover narrative followed directly on the cult purification report. And now the religious reestablishment of the authentic YHWH cult finds its definitive expression in the Passover. This notion was taken up in the postexilic period. Each time the temple cult was renewed, it was with a Passover celebration (Ezra 6:19-22; 2 Chronicles 30 and 35; Num 9:1-5; and Exod 40:2, 17).

Now rural life is fashioned mainly by the natural cycle of seasons. And thus, from the very beginning of Israel's history as a people, the Canaanite fertility cults held considerable fascination for Israel's pious. Beyond this, there were certain strata of the population which, although politically incorporated into Israel, constituted a kind of religious underground movement. The deuteronomic "festival theory" accommodated itself to the legitimate needs of these people and protected all authentic human values in their sub-religions. However, this theory also removed all characteristics which were contrary to the authentic tradition of YHWH's blessing. In view of the seductive alternatives provided by the social environment, the harvest festivals in particular had become confessions of faith. Their centralization secured the integrity of the YHWH cult and was thus principally religiously motivated.

However, the deuteronomic reform did not revitalize the traditional form of divine worship simply in order to adapt itself to or resist the fertility cults or other alien cults belonging to other religions. A comparison with predeuteronomic worship of YHWH reveals a creative remaking of the sacred institutions and practices of old Israel. This had its origin in Deuteronomy's "theology of the people,"[15] which plays a decisive part in the book. As a consequence of this systematic approach, Deuteronomy rendered present what was really to be celebrated by de-sacralizing, de-ritualizing, rationalizing and humanizing the YHWH cult.[16]

The most important characteristics of the deuteronomic liturgical reform are clearly reflected in the "festival calendar" of Deuteronomy 16. In what follows, the individual deuteronomic "pilgrimage feasts" will be sketched from the standpoint of their historical development, and the theology of their revision into a "festival cycle" will be briefly outlined.

Pesaḥ-Maṣṣôt as a Commemorative Passion Celebration (Deut 16:1-8)

Strictly speaking, the deuteronomic Passover is not a *ḥag*, not a "feast,"[17] but a celebration with a prescribed ritual. In the predeuteronomic era, the Passover[18] probably constituted an apotropic blood rite (*šḥṭ pesaḥ*, Exod 12:21) belonging to the cultivated land, which was carried out in the circle of the clan (cf. also Deut 16:5). It was probably brought into connection with the exodus (Exod 12:21-23) in order to make Israel aware of the threat to its existence. Destruction threatens—the Assyrian empire presents an alternative between life and death. And through this empire, YHWH himself became dangerous to his people. However, those who listened to YHWH's Torah and followed it could escape destruction. In accordance with its demythologizing and rationalizing tendencies, the deuteronomic reform reinterprets the Passover as an immolation (*zbḥ pesaḥ*, Deut 16:2, 5, 6). Immolation was the only private sacrifice in preexilic times. Unlike the old Passover, it did not include any blood rite. Like the Passover, however, it belonged to the family sphere and was offered by the family. It culminated in a sacrificial meal. This emphasized its communal character and could also be combined with the eating of the unleavened bread.[19] Not only sheep and goats (as in Exod 12:21), but also cattle (e.g., Exod 20:24; Num 22:40) were immolated. On account of the cult centralization, however, it was no longer permitted to slaughter (verses 2, 6), cook and eat (verse 7) an animal "sacrificed to YHWH" at any place (even though it be considered divinely ordained, verse 5), but only in the place chosen by YHWH himself as a dwelling for his name. The deuteronomic Passover order is not—as is elsewhere customary in connection with sacrifices—addressed to "you and your house" (cf. 12:7). Moreover, in contrast to the ordinances regarding the participants at the Feast of Weeks and the Feast of Booths (16:9-12, 13-15), the "you" addressed is not only the free man and his wife. It means—at any rate in the present redactional context of the second discourse of Moses (5:1)—the whole of Israel (cf. 27:6-7).

If one wishes to bring the whole people together for a celebration, a common date is necessary. Thus *ḥōdeš hā'ābîb* is prescribed as the date for Passover (verse 1). This expression could be translated either "new moon"[20] or "month." The cultic symbolism which is intended here makes it unlikely, however, that "month" is the right interpretation—quite apart from the practical purpose already mentioned. As with the other liturgical regulations of Deuteronomy, Passover was to reproduce, as far as possible, in its rites, what is proper to it: the deliverance of the people from Egypt. Passover was to render present this deliverance through the celebration. Since the exodus took place "by night" (verse 1), the Passover victim must be slaughtered "in the evening, at sunset, at the hour at which you came out of Egypt" (verse 6), and none of the sacrificial meat may be kept until the next morning (verse 4).

Finally, Passover was probably fixed for the "new moon" (that is, the beginning) of the month Abib, because in older times another feast, which through the deuteronomic reform was fused with Passover (the Feast of Unleavened Bread), was probably observed at the same time. In connection with the eating of the unleavened bread, verse 3 (for the first time in the Old Testament) accentuates the "day you left the land of Egypt" (a day beginning with sunset).[21] In this way, the traditional triad of annual feasts (34:18, 22; cf. 23:14-17) could be retained without any change of calendar, in spite of the deuteronomic innovations. At the same time, the inauguration of the Passover celebration in the Temple of Jerusalem was made easier by the fact that the Feast of Unleavened Bread had already been observed there under King Hezekiah. Contrary to a widespread notion, the "origin and nature" of the Feast of Unleavened Bread was "not an agricultural feast which had been accommodated to yahwistic faith. It was a feast *for* farmers, developed as the answer of the YHWH faith to sedentary life."[22] Not only does the entire biblical tradition contradict the notion of an agrarian-Canaanite origin of the Feast of Unleavened Bread, but also, it would have been impossible to establish a feast connected with the first cutting of the (barley) harvest for the month of Abib. A seven day festival might even, in some cases, have endangered the harvesting of the produce and hence have remained a theological construction alienated from agrarian reality.[23] Unleavened cakes constitute the daily bread of any situation in which it is impossible to use prepared (that is, leavened) dough for baking. Such cakes are eaten by Bedouins and by farmers when they spend a long time on the road. Therefore, unleavened bread was *also* the bread of the hurried escape from Egypt and the desert wanderings. This is the symbolic reference used at the Feast of Unleavened Bread.

In spring, before the sheaves were brought in and therefore while the success of one's labor still hung in the balance, the unleavened bread reminded the worshipers of YHWH, who had now become farmers, of their historical beginnings, to which they owed the possession of the land with its rich produce: the departure from the land of Egypt in the month of Abib. The seven day period which, from time immemorial was essential to the Feast of Unleavened Bread and which coincided with the Israelite week, turned the commonplace custom of eating unleavened bread into a cultic rite.

With the deuteronomic liturgical reform, the Feast of Unleavened Bread was assimilated into Passover and was no longer designated as a *ḥag*, a feast (contrary to Exod 34:18; 23:15 and Deut 16:16). It is not necessary for the purposes of this study to settle the much-debated issue of the priority of Unleavened Bread or Passover strata in Deut 16:1-8.[24] It is enough to establish that, according to the final redaction, the symbolism of unleavened bread constitutes the literary and theological center of the entire celebration:[25]

> For seven days you shall eat unleavened cakes, the bread of affliction. In urgent haste you came out of Egypt, and thus as long as you live you shall commemorate the day of your coming out of Egypt.

The central position of the exodus motif in the composition of verses 1-7 corresponds perfectly with the function of this topic as the common denominator which made the cultic interweaving of the Passover and the Feast of Unleavened Bread possible. The etiological explanation of the unleavened cakes as the "food of affliction" (*leḥem ʿōnî*) is found only in this passage in the whole Old Testament. This passage also constitutes the first instance in the Old Testament of explaining the eating of unleavened bread with the haste (*ḥippazôn*)[26] with which the escape took place, and also the first evidence that the stipulation was intended to recall the day (*yôm*) of the departure from Egypt[27]—"as long as you live you shall commemorate the day of your coming out of Egypt." Both as regards content and as regards form they are an innovation proper to the deuteronomic celebration. If, however, it was only later that the Passover-Unleavend Bread regulations were expanded through the text quoted (verse 3a*β**b)—and many consider this to be the case[28]—the text only served to make explicit what the ordinance concerning the eating of unleavened bread (verse 3a*β**, 4a) already contained as liturgical kerygma.

The merging of the Passover and the Feast of Unleavened Bread enriches the celebration theologically and ritually through the reciprocal reinterpretation of the two customs. Thus the exodus is no longer seen simply as the "departure" (*yṣʾ* qal) of Israel as it had previously been, particularly in regard to the Feast of Unleavened Bread (verse 3, cf. verse 6);[29] rather, it is theologically understood as "being brought out (*yṣʾ* hi.) by YHWH," and thereby as his saving action (verse 1). The sacrificial meal of the paschal victim, now combined with the eating of unleavened bread, is a more powerful symbolic representation of the exodus than was the former practice.

What Israel had once experienced as YHWH's action and now reenacted liturgically gave rise to the remembrance (*zkr*) of the exodus event in daily life (*kol yᵉmê ḥayyêkā*, verse 3). To be more precise, this means that the memory of the distress of the departure by night is made present through the cult drama;[30] however, it does not remain limited to the commemorative passion celebration.

> The eating of unleavened bread made it clear to the participants in the cult that the fundamental exodus event also concerned him, that he also participated in the salvation experienced during the departure from Egypt. He was meant to conclude that he had to maintain a

> continuous reference to this event throughout his life. Reminded by the eating of unleavened bread of the fundamental saving act of his God, the Israelite is thereby exhorted to allow this deed to fashion his life.[31]

The exodus event, especially as interpreted by Deuteronomy, possesses various features. In the context of observing the commandments, attention is always drawn to that aspect which best corresponds to the given exhortation. But which features of the past are intended to be understood as pertinent through the cultic experience and rational remembrance of the Passover-Unleavened Bread ritual? Certainly not, as is so often maintained,[32] the liberation from slavery; but simply Israel's departure from Egypt. With this departure, the way had begun which found its destination in secure settlements (verse 5). For this reason, unleavened bread is eaten for seven days beginning with the Passover night (verse 3). To begin with, the bread, since it is shared by all, creates a unity and a living community of the whole people.

In the deuteronomic context, however, the unleavened cakes are defined as the "food of affliction," that is, as a symbol of the hasty departure (verse 3). They are not the "bread of misery," which would be "a technical term for the bondage in Egypt,"[33] thus "linking the memory of the oppression with the liberation."[34] Finally, the consumption of unleavened bread as the epitome of being under way, of not being settled, allows the return of the celebrants to become the extension of that journey which began on the night of the exodus.[35] Throughout the entire territory of Israel, nothing leavened is to be found during the week of unleavened bread (verse 4). Thus the reality of the celebration can take hold of the entire people and the whole land and is not restricted to the central sanctuary. Indeed, the change in cultic consciousness spreads so much into daily life that without the symbolism of the wandering, one's own "town" (verse 5) is transformed into "tents" (verse 7), to which one returns.

Israel celebrates the exodus as the origin of its history. "Aliens" (*gērîm*) would not fit in with the cultic representation. And so, despite the social and charitable orientation of deuteronomic legislation, they are not mentioned as participants in the Passover.[36] Neither is there any separate reference to the Levites, as there is in all other deuteronomic cult ordinances. For this celebration does not fall under priestly competence. It is the whole people who celebrates the deuteronomic Passover-Feast of Unleavened Bread.

However, this commemorative passion celebration is not merely intended to "create the holy people."[37] It constitutes an interpretation of Israel's way, from being brought out of Egypt (verse 1) to receiving the gift of town settlements (verse 5) as YHWH's action. For this reason, the Passover is celebrated "for YHWH your God" (verse 1) and the Passover sacrifice is offered "for YHWH, your God" (verse 2). On the seventh day of the week of Unleavened Bread, a "special day of celebration[38] for YHWH your God" is observed; on that day, no work may be done (verse 8).[39]

The liturgy of the deuteronomic Passover-Feast of Unleavened Bread thus constitutes a commemorative passion celebration. As such, it is liturgy in the fullest sense of the word: a cult celebrated for the people and a cult celebrated by the people. This double function cannot, however, be attributed to the two original rites, especially not on the editorial level. Certainly the Passover-Feast of Unleavened Bread is above all oriented towards worship, whereas the community aspect is dominant in the eating of unleavened bread. However, the Passover also includes a community-creating sacrificial meal, and the week of Unleavened Bread is observed with a special day of rest in honor of YHWH. In the deuteronomic liturgy of the Passover and Feast of Unleavened Bread, the people first of all render present its prototype, its departure and its wanderings and thereby reenacts an event in its history which, as a memorial of YHWH's deeds, continues to shape individual lives. Secondly, the communal celebration, the sacrifice and the rest proper to this liturgy are intended to honor YHWH.

The Feast of Weeks and the Feast of Booths as Feasts of Joy

The Feast of Weeks and the Feast of Booths can be distinguished from the Passover-Feast of Unleavened Bread celebration by means of their origin and their basic liturgical structure. True, they are also characterized by the deuteronomic "theology of the people" and are intended to be understood as the self-representation of the whole of Israel. Yet the cult reform of Deuteronomy mainly intended these two harvest festivals as answers to indigenous fertility rites, which had a seductive influence on an agrarian culture.

The Canaanite religion was a "popular religion with all its typical characteristics."[40] It attempted, often in primitive ways, to establish an intimacy between humankind and nature, to draw humans into the continuing process of creation and to balance their dependence on the deity by being elevating to the status of a collaborator with the deity.[41]

Among other things, the participant's joy at a festival and sacrificial meal was intended to bring about the joy of the deity through magical congeniality.[42] Through the cult centralization, Deuteronomy corrected popular notions regarding YHWH's presence and availability in holy places. But, beyond that, Deuteronomy was not satisfied to let one remain simply *one* element in the cultic scheme of an annual ritual. Deuteronomy made "rejoicing" its basic liturgical attitude. One does not, of course, rejoice for God's benefit or in order to obtain his favor; one rejoices in what he and he alone has granted. It is the joy of thanksgiving which Deuteronomy demands whenever a sacrifice or gift-offering from the herds or the fields is presented in the central sanctuary of Jerusalem, or when the people gathers there for the Feast of Weeks or the Feast of Booths. Joy, of course, cannot be forced, nor can it be prescribed by means of certain rites of jubilation or other concrete expressions of joy which could be obediently executed.

If, nevertheless, Deuteronomy speaks of joy only in the form of a command, this is because it intends to make it a duty for everyone to strive for the—by no means self-evident—"joy before YHWH." This is a joy which, in the final analysis has its basis and its limits in YHWH's blessing. In the Hebrew text, *śāmaḥ* (qal) is always used for this joy. It is perhaps characteristic that Deuteronomy uses only this verb to express human rejoicing and that it is found exclusively in the cultic stipulations of the Old Testament legislation (chapters 12-26).[43] "The specific place for joy is the 'divine service' of Israel . . . This is reflected upon in a systematic manner for the first time in Deuteronomy. 'Rejoicing' constitutes the key word in a festival theory."[44] This theory includes sacrifices, tributes and feasts in the strict sense of the word. Their dissimilarities are to a great extent leveled out. The kerygma of this, the oldest biblical festival theory, is formulated most clearly in the second part of the deuteronomic festival calendar, in the stipulations for the Feast of Weeks and the Feast of Booths. It is to this part that I propose to limit my study.

Even the names of the two harvest festivals and the dates at which they are celebrated reveal a new liturgico-theological accentuation in comparison with the older festival calendar. The "harvest festival" (*ḥag haqqāṣir*) is called the "Feast of Weeks" (*ḥag šābu'ōt*, Deut 16:10, cf. Exod 34:22).[45] This name comes from the process of reckoning: "Seven weeks shall be counted: start counting the seven weeks from the time when the sickle is first put to the standing corn" (Deut 16:9). This seven week period does not bring the end of the wheat harvest, which the Feast of Weeks observes, into connection with the Feast of Unleavened Bread as the beginning of the barley harvest.[46] For in the month of Abib, in which the non-agrarian Feast of Unleavened Bread is observed, the barley in Palestine is not yet ripe.[47] On the other hand, the seven day formula does establish a formal relationship with the seven days of unleavened bread (verses 4 and 8) and with the seven days during which the Feast of Booths is observed in the temple (verse 13). The choice of dates for the Feast of Weeks reflects an attempt to gather, as far as possible, the whole people in the central sanctuary of Jerusalem for a common feast. Nevertheless, in order that the festival joy may be an authentic personal experience, no absolute date is set: everyone should be able to give thanks for their own grain when it has in fact already been harvested.

So, in spite of the seven weeks limitation, the festival date varies from year to year according to the harvest, which is dependent on natural conditions. Moreover, due to local differences, it also remains flexible for the individual families. Hence the invitation to the Feast of Weeks is not addressed to the "you" of all Israel, as is the case for the Passover-Feast of Unleavened Bread celebration; rather, the festival community of the Feast of Weeks has its primary basis in the family.

The case is somewhat similar for the second harvest festival. The "Feast of the Ingathering" (*ḥag hā'āsip*) at the end of the year, when the fruit of one's labor is gathered in from the fields, as this feast is called in the earlier cultic calendar (Exod 23:16; cf. 34:22), is named the "Feast of Booths" (*ḥag hassukkôt*, Deut 16:13) for the first time in Deuteronomy. The term is not explained further. It probably reminded people of the old custom of living in huts in the vineyards during the time of gathering and pressing the grapes (cf. Judg 21:19-21). During the Feast of Booths, people dwelt for seven days—probably in a similar fashion—in and around the central sanctuary (Deut 16:15). However, the new name for the feast also implied that other than purely agrarian conditions were taken into account.

The way the date for this feast was determined makes it clearer: The Feast of Booths was to be observed "after you have brought in the produce from your threshing floor and wine press" (verse 13). This means after everything has been harvested. Yet the feast should be observed by all Israelites, including those who possess no fields. The formulation includes everyone in the festival community. When Deuteronomy does not mention the end of the agrarian year in autumn (cf. Exod 34:22; 23:16), it once more relegates the peasant elements of the feast into the background. The renaming of the feast and the date of its observation both aim at a participation of the whole people,[48] although the impossibility of predicting when the harvest would be over meant that no definite date could be fixed.

Contrary to the Passover-Feast of Unleavened Bread celebration, the Feast of Weeks and the Feast of Booths are both called *ḥag*. Since one was obliged to journey to the sanctuary of Jerusalem for all three liturgies, the specific *ḥag* aspect cannot, within the deuteronomic context, lie primarily in its pilgrimage character.[49] The elements of the deuteronomic *ḥag* (16:10, 13, 14, 16; 31:10) can thus be discovered only in the context of and in distinction to the Passover-Feast of Unleavened Bread, or at least in distinction to the Passover (cf. 16:16).

It is striking that neither the Feast of Weeks nor the Feast of Booths is observed according to a prescribed ritual. True, one is to present a freewill offering during the Feast of Weeks. Yet it is not presented explicitly "for YHWH," and its contents and size are left to the judgment of the giver (verse 10). For the Feast of Booths, no sacrifice at all is required (contrary to 16:16-17).[50] This is because the Feast of Weeks expresses gratitude "only" for YHWH's harvest blessing (verse 10), whereas the Feast of Booths expresses gratitude for the blessing which has been experienced in the produce of the land *and* in the success of one's own work (verse 15). In a similar way there are theological and anthropological shades of differences between the two feasts in the verbal formulations about feast and joy. Indeed, it is characteristic of both feasts that, beginning with Deuteronomy, they are observed explicitly "for YHWH" (cf. Exod 34:22; and, in spite of 23:14, verse 16). Yet the Feast of Weeks is called a "feast for YHWH" (Deut 16:10), whereas the Feast of Booths is called "your feast" (verse 14),[51] although it is "observed for YHWH" (*ḥāgag l^eYHWH*, verse 15). It is *the* feast and it is intended above all for men and women and their joy. It is only in regard to the Feast of Booths that—in addition to the usual exhortations to rejoice (verse 14)—we find the emphatic declaration at the end: "You shall do nothing but rejoice" (verse 15).[52]

Even though the deuteronomic festival liturgy remains more or less undetermined ritually, it is nevertheless enclosed in the corset of a local and temporal cult centralization. According to the calendar of the Covenant Book (Exod 23:14-17), people only made a pilgrimage to one of the local sanctuaries, and—especially in regard to the Harvest Festival and the Feast of Ingathering—there was no fixed date. Deuteronomy, however, created the "pilgrimage feasts" by means of its unity of time and place.[53] In spite of the "election" of the Temple of Jerusalem, this unification cannot be attributed either to the sacredness of this particular locality or to an absolute centralization. Rather, it arises as a consequence of Israel's relationship to YHWH, their God. This relationship constitutes the heart of deuteronomic theology. For the community-forming framework of one and the same sanctuary and—more or less—one and the same time, did not merely guarantee "cult purification through cult unification." More importantly, it gathered the individual families and social classes together into a united people. And this was to find its expression in the feast.

Therefore the deuteronomic festival order, which otherwise limits ritual ordinances to a minimum, makes a list of all the participants in its liturgy. To be invited are, first of all, "you" (that is, the free man as well as his wife), "your son and daughter (their family), "your male and female slaves" (that is, also the domestic staff). Even by itself, this detailed list of what is otherwise simply called "your house" is socially explosive. That it was by no means self-evident to break through class barriers and include the slaves is demonstrated by the reason given, the origins of Israel's existence: "Remember that you, too, were once slaves in Egypt" (verse 12).[54] At first sight, it appears that the "fathers," "brothers" and "neighbors" are missing. But in deuteronomic linguistic usage, "fathers" denotes the patriarchs, "brother" usually means a member of one's own people and one is related to one's neighbors through friendship rather than through blood relationship. Nevertheless, the festival community is to be widened over and beyond the extended family to include all ranks of society. Thus the "Levites who live in your towns" are included and finally the typically deuteronomic triad of social cases: "the alien, the orphan and the widow who live among you" (verses 11 and 14). This regulation decidedly expands the circle of participants compared with the older festival calendar. Reform of worship and reform of the community are very closely related in Deuteronomy. Of course, it was not always possible for each family with all its members simply to leave house and farm and set out for Jerusalem. It would be even more difficult to always bring all the needy people and provide them with sumptuous food for seven days. Deuteronomy is not concerned with the "legality" of these rubrics in the sense of casuistic regulations; it is concerned with determining the theological aim of Israel's liturgy.[55] Its parenesis may neither be depreciated into some kind of "devotion" nor exaggerated into a rigid legal obligation.[56] The legislation of the Priestly Code—with all its rigorous demands concerning a unified and precisely dated liturgy of the whole people in the central sanctuary—should prevent us from seeing the deuteronomic festival order as simply ideological and utopian.[57] The deuteronomic festival community is supported primarily by the extended family and by the individual. It structures itself, as it were, from the bottom up instead of being fashioned in descending order from the top down. Thereby Israel appears as a supradimensional family and as such it is the people of God.

This unity of the whole people which is actualized in the Feast of Weeks and the Feast of Booths is not represented explicitly by the participants eating together, as is the case for the Passover-Feast of Unleavened Bread and, for that matter, with all animal sacrifices (12:7, 18; 14:23, 26; 15:20; 27:7).[58] It is inconceivable that there should have been a seven day fast during the Feast of Booths, *the* feast of joy. When, if not after the harvest, would people have eaten and drunk in a circle of rejoicing friends and let all those in need participate in their abundance? Precisely because the usual festival practice makes the proclamation of such a meal seem natural, the fact that there is no such proclamation must be taken as a sign that this custom has been reevaluated. In remaining so consistently silent about any cultic meal during the harvest festivals, Deuteronomy is setting a theological accent which cannot be overlooked. Since the Feast of Weeks and the Feast of Booths have their liturgical center in YHWH's blessing, that is, in the fertility he has granted (16:10, 15), Deuteronomy, by not mentioning any meal, intends to put up a barrier against the festival meals of the Canaanite fertility religions. The banquet which is sure to have taken place during the harvest festivals at the central sanctuary is not thereby forbidden. It is simply stripped of its syncretistic-sacral character. This type of indirect polemic, combined with Israel's unchanging practice, can also be seen as regards "drinking." Deuteronomy includes wine among the blessings of the cultivated land (e.g., 28:39) and even encourages the consumption of alcoholic beverages at the cultic meal of the prescribed tithe (14:26). Once again, however, it is the theological symbolism of a liturgical activity which is decisive. The appeasement of human appetites ought to enter into the cultic joy, but must not be interpreted in accordance with the religion of Baal. In the Canaanite cults drinking wine together was part of the ritual. The intoxication made people experience themselves as one with God and with nature. Compared to this, Israel's harvest festivals retained a matter-of-fact distance between YHWH and his people. The purpose of this radical de-mystification, however, was the most intimate communion in "rejoicing before YHWH, your God" (verse 11).

In no other book in the Old Testament is the formula "before YHWH, your God" employed earlier or more often connected with the sacrificial meal (12:7, 18; 14:23, 26) or with cultic joy (12:12, 18; 16:11; 27:7) than in Deuteronomy. That it is omitted at the Feast of Booths must be because of the markedly "human" character of the joy at this feast (verse 15b).[59] Yet the Feast of Booths is "observed for YHWH" (verse 15a). So the following holds true: "That which takes place 'before YHWH' in the cult is also carried out 'for YHWH.'"[60] The phrase "before YHWH" means neither the area of the sanctuary nor a specific cultic action. It is rather "the expression of an inner religious attitude."[61] This attitude gives the desacralization and deritualization in Deuteronomy their proper sense. Sacredness is dissociated from objects, rituals and persons in their concrete existence or representative function; the rites are no longer invested with an absolute character—in order that a personal relationship between YHWH and his people may be free to develop fully.

It is characteristic that "within the deuteronomic cult legislation, the liturgy is never defined as 'service for YHWH.' The key word of the liturgy is not worship, but rejoicing before YHWH."[62] This is also shown by the fundamental command presupposed in 28:47-48a whose transgression was to be decisive for Israel's future disaster:

> Because you did not serve YHWH your God with joy and with a glad heart for all your blessing, you shall serve your enemies whom YHWH will send against you in hunger and thirst, in nakedness and extreme want.

In the deuteronomic/deuteronomistic literature, "to serve YHWH" does not merely mean the correct (or incorrect) cult, but a total adhesion to YHWH, which encompasses Israel's whole existence. "Joy" (*śimḥâ*) refers to the pivot point of the deuteronomic festival theory. "Kindheartedness" aims at solidarity with the "brother" in need. Joy and social charitable behavior arising from the consciousness of gratitude constitute, according to Deuteronomy, the brief formula for "serving God." Neither can they be separated from each other nor can they be measured against each other.[63] "Feast is where love rejoices" (John Chrysostom).[64]

What, then, is it that makes the Feast of Weeks and the Feast of Booths into feasts? It is the joy before YHWH which gives thanks for the natural blessings granted by him—not by Baal— and allows all those who are socially dependent or in need to participate in this blessing. In such a unity, unhindered by class barriers (although by no means classless), the whole of Israel presents itself with all its families as the people of YHWH, living in the blessed presence of its God.

Consequently, the Feast of Weeks and the Feast of Booths are not meant to be something provisional nor do they in themselves refer to a final eschatological fulfillment. According to Deuteronomy, they do not celebrate any historical deeds of God nor is a "sacrifice for YHWH" offered and communally consumed.[65] Especially because of the freedom from their concrete observance, they can hardly, according to modern linguistic usage, be said to display the character of a "celebration," but rather that of a "feast."[66] "A celebration usually has historical . . . roots. A feast, on the other hand, can, even without any external occasion, be an expression of joy."[67] "As ritual, divine worship is a celebration. Only a relatively closed group is able, after many years of practice, to follow inwardly its long evolved ceremonies and symbolism. As a feast, however, it is closer to creative play . . . strangers can also participate. For a feast, only the framework is planned in advance; what happens within it is left to the participants."[68]

The Passover-Feast of Unleavened Bread, the Feast of Weeks and the Feast of Booths

Types of Deuteronomic Popular Liturgy and Their Later History in the Holiness Code

According to the deuteronomic calendar, the Passover-Feast of Unleavened Bread as a commemorative passion celebration and the Feast of Weeks and the Feast of Booths as feasts of joy constitute two basic forms of liturgy. As cultic responses, they correspond to the two ways in which YHWH acts on Israel; his saving action in history (verse 1) and his blessing in nature (verses 10 and 15). Whereas the Passover-Feast of Unleavened Bread commemorates the common origin in YHWH's deed in the past, shining forth into the future, the Feast of Weeks and the Feast of Booths make it possible to experience the present as YHWH's gift.[69] Yet it is always the people which presents itself in the cult,[70] either as living through the hurried departure from foreign soil or in the joy over the blessings of their own land. It is the people which liturgically fulfills itself in the seven days of consuming the "bread of affliction" before securing the harvest or in the seven days of complete happiness before YHWH in the sanctuary after it has been brought in.

Before concluding, I wish to touch on the fact that the structures of the Passover-Feast of Unleavened Bread celebration on one hand and of the Feast of Weeks and the Feast of Booths on the other, which are so clearly distinguished from each other in Deuteronomy, were assimilated into each other in the later revision of the Holiness Code (Leviticus 23). A transformation of the character of "feast" into that of "celebration" in the sense already described can be observed. "The characteristic of this process is an ever increasing radicalism in the return to old traditions, which had been too quickly and too radically discarded through the deuteronomic reform movement."[71] Deuteronomy remains the basis. But the priestly officials of the Jerusalem Temple, who stand behind the legislation of the Holiness Code, attempt to reconcile the deuteronomic principles with the old traditions, softening solutions which seemed all too bold, clarifying, modifying or adding to the ritual regulations. Thus, for example, the Passover remains for the main part a national celebration, but as in predeuteronomic times it is distinguished from the autonomous Feast of Unleavened Bread, which immediately precedes it as a separate cultic act. Once again, the unleavened bread is eaten only during the feast bearing this name. This feast lasts one full week, on the first and seventh day of which a festival assembly is to be held and no work may be performed. On each of the seven days, an official sacrifice is to be offered. The dates for the Feast of Weeks and the Feast of Booths are precisely established, various sacrifices are made obligatory and detailed ceremonies are prescribed. This, however, was not enough to give the Feast of Weeks a historical origin. But the Feast of Booths was reinterpreted: it was no longer seen as a purely agrarian feast, but as a commemoration of God's guidance of Israel and of the life in huts in the desert. In consequence of this liturgical symbolism, only members of the people of Israel can participate in the feast.

Here we must conclude our outline of one chapter in the history of the Israelite cult. We have shown that, even according to the oldest theory in Deuteronomy, the "divine service"[72] of Israel cannot be limited either to a celebration of God's historical deeds through sacrifice or to the creation of the holy people. However, it is always a "liturgy of the people." According to the Second Vatican Council's Constitution on the Liturgy, every Christian liturgical celebration is also an act of the Body of Christ, the Church (SC 7) with the whole people acting as celebrant (SC 14).[73] At the same time, this document made the celebration of the Easter mystery as the work of our redemption into the fundamental motif of the liturgical renewal initiated by the Council.[74] The New Testament warrants this emphasis. Nevertheless, the divine service of the early church, where it replaces the Old Testament Passover, is fashioned by another fundamental structure[75] which finds its first biblical systematization in the book of Deuteronomy. As the preceding analysis has shown, it is clearly distinct from the commemorative passion celebration of the Passover. The central characteristic of this feast is the joy before YHWH. "All individual reforms of the divine service which do not take into account festival theory and practice are inevitably in danger of remaining too shortsighted and too superficial."[76] The liturgical renewal of the Second Vatican Council must be continued and the biblical feast with its joy should receive greater recognition and become part of the liturgy of the New Testament People of God.[77]

4
Some Remarks on the Deuteronomistic Conception of Freedom and Peace

German title: "Zur deuteronomistischen Konzeption von Freiheit und Frieden"
(see bibliography)

To speak of freedom and peace today is as topical as it is difficult. In this lecture, the "long march" to this subject takes the way of a system of predication. In the entire Old Testament, this system is found only in the Deuteronomistic History (DtrH) and in the Chronistic History. The Chronistic History, however, is dependent on the Deuteronomistic History, and thus I propose to limit my study to DtrH.

The key words of the system are *nwḥ* (hi. I) "grant, give rest" and *m^e^nûḥâ*, "(place of) rest." The subject of *nwḥ* (hi. I) is always YHWH. The indirect object is either Israel or its king. YHWH grants *m^e^nûḥâ*.

My remarks on this subject are also intended as a contribution to the recent discussion concerning the various strata of DtrH—a discussion which was started by F.M. Cross[1] and R. Smend.[2] My own analysis is related to those studies which no longer follow M. Noth in regarding Deuteronomy 5-30 as a single text block which the Deuteronomist(s) found in its finished form. Rather, as N. Lohfink has recently discussed,[3] it is possible to discover traces of several deuteronomistic (Dtr) editing processes in these chapters. By way of methodological caution, I shall at first speak only of a system of predication. That is, I shall not presuppose any stratification for the individual passages.

The importance of the theme "rest" has been acknowledged by Old testament scholarship since G. von Rad wrote his pioneering article "Es ist noch eine Ruhe vorhanden dem Volke Gottes"[4] ("There is still rest for the people of God") in 1933. Ever since, the subject has been discussed by various writers in concept-, motif- and traditio-historical studies and in one redaction-critical study.[5] However, none of these studies has succeeded in explaining how the predicational system works. Hence there seems to be good reason to conduct a fresh analysis.

Deut 12:9-10 constitutes the point of departure. These verses are found among the statutes concerning the centralization of the cult, at the beginning of the code. They outline the historical presuppositions for the enforcement of the sacrificial ordinances, which cannot yet be in force at the time of the promulgation of the Mosaic law:

> for till now you have not reached the place of rest, the patrimony which the LORD your God is giving you. You shall cross the Jordan and settle in the land which the LORD your God allots you as patrimony; he will grant you peace from your enemies on every side and you will live in security (Deut 12:9-10).

Then (verses 11-12 continue) Israel is to sacrifice in the chosen places and to rejoice before God. Verse 9 mentions "(the place of) rest" (*hamm^{e}nûḥâ*) and "(the) patrimony," (*hannaḥ^{a}lâ*) as constitutive parts of Israel's existence. These two gifts of God cannot be identified with each other. In this context, *bw' 'el hamm^{e}nûḥâ*, "arrive at (the place of) rest, come to rest" refers to the procession to the Temple of Jerusalem. In 12:4-28 (that is, in the statutes concerning the only legitimate sanctuary), *bw'* qal always refers to *'el hammāqôm*, "this place, the place" (verses 5 and 26), whereas *bw'* hi. through the combination with *šāmmâ* refers back to it (verses 6 and 11, cf. verse 5). The only other instance of "the rest which YHWH gives" is to be found in 1 Kgs 8:56 in the context of Solomon's consecration of the temple. This confirms the interpretation of *m^{e}nûḥâ* as referring to the central sanctuary in Jerusalem. Admittedly there is also a philologically as well as theologically important difference between *ntn* with the abstract substantive *m^{e}nûḥâ* as its object and the related verb *nwḥ* in hi.[6] God, the giver, and the *m^{e}nûḥâ* are closely related to each other, whereas Israel as recipient remains relatively passive. But if YHWH procures rest for his people, the people in a way "participates" in *nwḥ* hi. and becomes the subordinate subject of the action. This second expression is only found in Deut 12:10.

This verse constitutes the historical introduction to the law concerning sacrifices which follows it. The five verbal clauses are all in the form *w=qatal-x*. This syntactic form primarily denotes a continuous progress. Thus we arrive at a linear historical process: the crossing of the Jordan, the first settlement, the "coming to rest" and, as a consequence of this, living in security in the land. This sequence of events is not, however, the only way in which one can understand the *w=qatal-x* clauses. When future states of affairs are recapitulated, *w=qatal-x* can also occur. The repetition of *yšb* even suggests a kind of parallelism between verses 10a and 10b, with the second part of the sentence repeating and intensifying the first (*yšb beṭaḥ*). This gives us the following: "You will cross the Jordan and settle in the land; indeed, the Lord will procure rest for you and you will settle in security." In that case, the action denoted by *nwḥ* does not succeed, but precedes the settlement. It is possible to decide between these syntactical alternatives only after an analysis of the other instances of *nwḥ* hi. However, as will become clear, the ambiguity might well be intentional.

Deut 12:9-10 has a programmatic function. This is proved by the following three texts: 25:19 by its terminology refers back to these two verses; Josh 21:43-45 and 1 Kgs 8:56 bring out the connection with 12:10 and 12:9 respectively through their own retrospective references. Only in the Amalekite law, the "political testament" of Moses at the end of the deuteronomic "civil law" is *nwḥ* hi. combined with *naḥ^{a}lâ* or *nḥl* hi. (Deut 25:19 and 12:9-10). The motif of "rest" thus functions as a frame for the deuteronomic law code, for its cultic and social order.

In Josh 21:43-45, the conquest and the allotment of the promised land are completed by a historical summary and a report of fulfillment. In verses 43-44a, *nwḥ* hi. constitutes the last of four *wayyiqtol* clauses. This means that the conquest and the settlement have taken place before Israel is granted rest. And thus YHWH's oath to the "fathers," that is, to the Moses generation, has been fulfilled. Certainly God's oath in Deut 1:8 and 39 refers explicitly only to giving the Israelites the land. However, according to Josh 21:43-44, only the rest which YHWH grants makes the gift of the land complete. Hence this text, through a statement which is unique in the Old Testament, interprets the peace granted by YHWH as the fulfillment of his oath to the fathers. In addition, what Deut 12:10 proclaimed is now also completed.

Josh 21:43-44a suggests the retrospective reference through the combination of *yšb* and *nwḥ* hi. The only other instance of this combination is Deut 12:10. However, only *missābîb* follows. Deut 12:10 allows us to expect a second prepositional phrase, *mikkol 'ōy^{e}bîm*. And this phrase is not, in fact, missing. Josh 21:44b even adds it in two sentences: None of the enemies was able to resist; the Lord gave all enemies into Israel's hands. These two statements in the form *(w=)x-qatal* interrupt the preceding progressive sequence and depict the background of the conquest and the granting of rest. The words *ntn YHWH* which constitute a frame for verses 43-44, interpret the entire history of Israel as a gift of grace brought about by the action of God. The *m^{e}nûḥâ* granted by God is one of these gifts of grace. Finally, verse 45 also refers back to the outline of the future given in Deut 12:10. Full of pathos, verse 45 proclaims that "the whole of the good word" which YHWH has spoken to Israel has now been fulfilled.

This report of fulfillment is also found in 1 Kgs 8:56. However, the term used is not *nwḥ* hi., but the noun *m^{e}nûḥâ*. Whereas Deut 12:9 speaks of *m^{e}nûḥâ* in the context of the law concerning sacrifices as a condition which still has to be fulfilled before the laws on sacrifice can be observed, Solomon at the end of the temple consecration liturgy in 1 Kgs 8:56 praises the *m^{e}nûḥâ* which has finally been granted by YHWH. With the *m^{e}nûḥâ*, the real culmen in the history of the promises given to Israel has been reached. Hence it is through a doxology that we learn that YHWH has granted Israel rest.

There are two retrospective references. The first one, in verse 56a, mentions neither the addressee nor the mediator of the promise. If an assurance given through Moses were intended, this would merely be an (inexact) anticipation of the second reference. It therefore seems probable that the word of YHWH in verse 56a refers to the prophecy of Nathan, that is, to 2 Sam 7:13a. In order that what Nathan had proclaimed should come to pass, God in 1 Kgs 5:18-19 granted Solomon peace from all his enemies. According to 2 Sam 7:1 and 11, the same was true even of David. Later, I shall return briefly to these passages. In any case, this explains why the first retrospective reference in 1 Kgs 8:56a does not mention any name: David was the immediate recipient of the promise, yet the promise was made to Solomon. This implies that *m^{e}nûḥâ* refers to the temple of Solomon. Verse 56a then relates the reference to Nathan's prophecy concerning the sanctuary in Jerusalem to the Mosaic origins. The passage intended is Deut 12:9, the only passage where Moses uses the term *m^enûḥâ*. What Moses implicitly promises as a gift, 1 Kgs 8:56 explicitly proclaims as the fulfillment of a word of YHWH mediated through Moses. In a similar way, Josh 21:45 reinterpreted the prediction made by Moses in Deut 12:10. Thus both fulfillment texts present a theological outline of the history of Israel. In addition, in 1 Kgs 8:56, the *m^enûḥâ* for which YHWH is praised appears as a medium of the blessing which, according to verse 55, Solomon pronounces over the whole assembly of Israel. This makes possible both the granting of the petitions in verses 57-58 and the parenesis in verse 61. The function of the temple as a "(place of) rest" is not put into more explicit terms. But it is through the temple that YHWH will be with Israel and with the king of Israel and turn the hearts of the Israelites to himself. Then they will be able to observe "his commandments, his statutes and ordinances," that is, the covenantal obligations of Deuteronomy (cf. 1 Kgs 8:58b with Deut 26:17).

The *nwḥ* hi. / *m^enûḥâ* system divides the history of Israel into periods in Josh 21:43-45 and 1 Kgs 8:56. The rest which YHWH procures or grants functions as a boundary for the period of the conquest under Joshua and for the Davidic-Solomonic period when the temple was built. The "entire good word, none of which has lost its validity" resumes all historical events between the promise and the fulfillment into the unity of a history of salvation.

With the *m^enûḥâ*, Israel has been given its central sanctuary. According to Deuteronomy 12, the demand for a centralization of the cult now comes into force. And now 1-2 Kings are able to develop their cultic main theme. After the consecration of the temple, however, the Deuteronomic History no longer speaks of *nwḥ* hi. or *m^enûḥâ*. All future history can and should consist in a life of fidelity and obedience to YHWH because of this state of bliss. Later, 1 Chr 22:9 will, in connection with *m^enûḥâ* and *nwḥ* hi. characterize this state as *šālôm*, here "peace" in a wide sense.

Besides the strict system of relations which I have just described, there are certainly other texts in the Deuteronomistic History which are related to Deut 12:9-10. When God procures rest for the kings of Israel, this is because of the *m^enûḥâ* in verse 9. If the verb *nwḥ* hi. is not used, the passages usually link up with the prepositional phrases *mikkol 'ōy^ebîm* and/or *missābîb* or with the words *yšb beṭaḥ*, which in verse 10 follow on the granting of rest. The history of Israel thus contains a sequence of deliberate references to Deut 12:9-10 as the programmatic text for a theology of rest. There is, however, no connection with the notion of "resting" denoted by *šqṭ*. It is only in the Chronistic History that this notion is related to *nwḥ* hi. Under Joshua, YHWH granted Israel peace from all enemies surrounding it. This action is never repeated; apparently it has never been totally canceled. When God again grants rest, it is not the people, but the kings, David and Solomon, who receive this gift. True, even after the settlement, Israel can be in danger from its enemies. However, as Joshua explains in his "valedictory speech" at the end of the period before the judges, this rest depends entirely on Israel's relation to God (Joshua 23). And during the period of the judges, Israel does repeatedly apostatize from YHWH. As a result, its former successes against the enemies turn into defeat. The "main article" of the period of the judges, Judg 2:14, directs at Israel words which were spoken against the enemies in Josh 21:44. Only the judges appointed by YHWH can defend Israel against its enemies (cf. Judg 2:18). Samuel, at the culmen of the historical retrospect in his "valedictory speech" in 1 Sam 12:11 states that men empowered by God, especially Jerubbaal/Gideon (see also Judg 8:34) saved the Israelites from the power of the enemies surrounding them (*miyyad 'ōyᵉbîm missābîb*), so that they may dwell in safety (*yšb beṭaḥ*)." Neither of the two historical summaries, one at the beginning (Judges 2) and one at the end (1 Samuel 12) of the period of the Judges uses the verb *nwḥ* hi. Only Neh 9:28 expresses the temporally limited liberation of Israel from the threat constituted by its enemies with the help of this verb.

In the Deuteronomistic History, on the other hand, it does not occur again until 2 Sam 7:1, that is, until the time when David is moving into his palace and planning to build a temple. It is precisely through this rest "from all surrounding enemies" and the king's peace that, according to verse 11, David's era differs from the period of the judges. However, both instances of *nwḥ* hi. are related to the promise of a "dwelling for YHWH's name" in verse 13a and thus also to the *mᵉnûḥâ* of 1 Kgs 8:56. 1 Kgs 5:17-19 finally makes clear that Solomon wants to fulfill Nathan's prophecy, now that YHWH has granted him peace on all sides. Verse 18, however, uses terminology for the enemies different from that we have found in all other passages up to now. It is no longer a question of enemies of the nation but of the king's external and internal opponents. Now Israel is able not only to dwell in safety, as during the period of the judges (1 Sam 12:11), but also to enjoy a life in prosperity. According to 1 Kgs 5:4b-5, Solomon "enjoyed peace (*šālôm*) on all sides (*mikkol ... missābîb*); Judah and Israel dwelt in safety (*yšb lābeṭaḥ*); everybody sat under his own vine or fig-tree." A peaceful reign and a period of national prosperity are crowned by the construction of the temple. True, nowhere is the construction of the temple syntactically the result of *nwḥ* hi. Yet, when David and Solomon are concerned—not when Israel is concerned—the verb ultimately refers to the *m^enûḥâ* of 1 Kgs 8:56, in which Deut 12:9 is fulfilled.

Deut 3:20, Josh 1:13, 15; and 22:4 form a second text system with (only) *nwḥ* hi. These four passages are parts of speeches in which Moses or Joshua turns the two and a half tribes settled in East Jordan. In these passages, the verb *nwḥ* hi. always precedes the conquest (*yrš* qal) of the land which YHWH gives (*ntn*). Deut 3:20 and Josh 1:15 make this order clear. 22:4 constitutes an abbreviated form. The retrospective references to the other texts nevertheless allow us to conclude that the idea is the same. According to these three passages, YHWH first grants the West Jordanian tribes rest and then gives them the land of which they take possession. The half verse 1:13b, which concerns the East Jordanians, is structured in a more complicated way. It contains two clauses. The first one uses the participle of *nwḥ* hi. In the context of deuteronomistic linguistic usage, this implies a reference to the immediate future. The second clause speaks of YHWH's gift of the land in *w=qatal-x* form. This is best interpreted as referring to the future, with progress compared with the preceding action. But that means that, according to the word of Moses quoted in Josh 1:13b, YHWH will also grant the East Jordanians rest and then give them the land. For Deut 3:20 (see verse 18) and Josh 1:15, this event, related in 1:13b, is already in the past.[7] Therefore, these verses can compare the future of the West Jordanians with the past of the East Jordanians: YHWH will act towards the West Jordanian brothers as he has already acted towards the East Jordanian tribes.

What is meant by "granting rest" when *nwḥ* hi. precedes *yrš* qal and *ntn hā'āreṣ*? It must mean either "putting an end to the migrations" or "eliminating the threat constituted by the enemies." In the second case, we would have a reference to the kings who were vanquished both in East and West Jordan before Israel took possession of the land. This is recounted in Deuteronomy 2-3 and in

Joshua 2-12. In any case, there is an objective difference between this and the use of *nwḥ* hi. in Deut 12:10 and Josh 21:44. In those verses, the wars of conquest are long since past, Israel has taken possession of the land (*yrš* qal) and settled (*yšb*) in it. A fundamental security against the assault of external enemies is denoted by *nwḥ* hi., of which the book of Judges frequently speaks.

Differences in the word field also show that *nwḥ* hi. does not have the same meaning in both passages. Whereas in Deut 12:10, Josh 21:44 etc., YHWH gives rest "from the enemies on all sides," there is no such specification in Deut 3:20 or in Josh 1:13, 15 or 22:4. Where there is no reference to external enemies, *nwḥ* hi. is perhaps best interpreted as referring to the end of the migrations.

But how can the two different text systems be combined? The question becomes urgent if, with Lohfink, one assumes a Deuteronomistic History of the Conquest (DtrC), which stretches from Deuteronomy 1 to Joshua 22 and within which *nwḥ* hi. is used in a twofold way. The following answers to the question appear acceptable to me. Which answer one chooses depends on whether one assign the systems to one single stratum or to different strata.

If one assigns both "rest" systems to one and the same stratum, *nwḥ* has, in different contexts, been used for two different, although similar, states of affairs: once for the victory over external enemies before the settlement in the land or, in a more neutral way, for the end of the migrations (Deut 3:20; Josh 1:13, 15; 22:4); and once for protection against the surrounding nations after the settlement in the land (Deut 12:10; 25:19; Josh 21:44). The different forms—*nwḥ* with and without additions—and the corresponding contexts make clear what is intended. Because of the *m^{e}nûḥâ* statements in Deut 12:9 and 1 Kgs 8:56, however, this stratum cannot be assumed to reach only to Joshua 22.[8]

Another solution seems more probable to me, namely that the different uses of *nwḥ* hi. belong to different strata. In that case, Lohfink's DtrC would, without further explanation, have used *nwḥ* hi. for something preceding Israel's settlement in the land. A later redactional stratum, however, has inserted those passages in which *nwḥ* hi. is given additional determinations, and used the term for something that happened after the settlement. In Josh 21:43-45, the two strata have become interwoven. Verses 43 and 44b very probably belong to the DtrC, whereas a later redaction added verses 44a and 45, thus integrating the whole passage into the main system of *nwḥ* hi. / *m^enûḥâ*. This theory would explain why the two prepositional phrases, *mikkol-'ōy^ebîm* and *missābîb* are not found together in verse 44, as in Deut 12:10 and 25:19, but instead only *missābîb* is latched on to *nwḥ* hi. in verse 44a. The expression *mikkol-'ōy^ebîm* was used in another sense in the already existing verse 44b.

Perhaps it may now be possible to fit the ambivalence in Deut 12:10, which we noted at the beginning, into the sequence of events. The syntactic formation may have deliberately retained the possibility of a dual interpretation because the two systems had become united. There would be "granting rest" as a sequence of actions following the settlement, as in Josh 21:44, but also "granting rest" as a recapitulation of the preceding events and hence as a presupposition for Israel's settlement in the land, as in Deut 3:20 etc. Then *nwḥ* hi. could be recognized as referring to the elimination of the enemies in the programmatic text Deut 12:10, and would thus be anchored in this text.

If the two text sequences are assigned to different strata, the notion of a DtrC ending with Joshua 22 is acceptable. The "rest" system beginning with the key passage Deut 12:9-10 would then belong to a redaction of the Deuteronomistic History including at least 1 Kings 8. This may be the oldest draft of the whole work. Since everything in this work constitutes a preparation for the cult problems in 1-2 Kings, which culminate in Josiah's cult reform, the redaction may well have originated at this time. As Cross suggests, we would then have a first edition which would be preexilic. However, if, for other reasons, we assume with Smend that there was no Deuteronomistic History in existence until the exile or even later, there is nothing in the text system we have discovered to exclude this. In either case, however, the older stratum of the DtrC would have been integrated into the younger, expanded work.

If one decides to assign both text systems to a single stratum, this stratum has conceived a unified historical scheme, in which Israel is "granted rest/peace" before and after the conquest and finally receives this rest/peace as a gift. In that case, no key text has been created in this redaction. Deut 12:9-10 functions as a key text only if one assumes a later redaction which presents its message at once and in a central position.

Further reflection would now be necessary in order to assign the occurrences of *nwḥ* hi. in 2 Sam 7:1, 11 and 1 Kgs 5:18, which refer to

The Use of *nwḥ* (hiphil I) and *menûḥâ*

DtrH	*menûḥâ*	*nwḥ* hi. I syntactic formation	indirect object	*mikkol 'ōyebîm*	*missābîb*
Deut 3:20		X	West Jordanians		
12:9	X		Israel		
12:10		w=qatal-x	Israel	X	X
25:19		X	Israel	X	X
Josh 1:13		participle	East Jordanians		
1:15		X	West Jordanians		
21:44		wayyiqtol-x	Israel	v. 44b	v. 44a
22:4		w=x-qatal	West Jordanians		
23:1		X	Israel	X	X
Judg 2:14				*miyyad 'ōyebîm*	X
8:34				*miyyad kol 'ōyebîm*	X
1 Sam 12:11				*miyyad 'ōyebîm*	X
2 Sam 7:1		w=x-qatal	David	X	X
7:11		w=qatal-x	David	X	
1 Kgs 5:5					
1 Kgs 5:18		w=x-qatal	Solomon	(cf. v. 18b)	X
1 Kgs 8:56		X	Israel		

in the Deuteronomistic History

yšb (*beṭaḥ*)	*yrš* qal	*ntn* *hā'āreṣ*	report of fulfillment	retrospective reference
	after *nwḥ*	after *yrš*		
before/after *nwḥ (+ beṭaḥ)*				
		after *nwḥ*		no reference
	after *nwḥ*	after *yrš*		
before	*nwḥ*	v. 43	v. 45	to Deut 2:10 to Deut 3:20 etc.
			v. 14	X
yšb *beṭaḥ* v. 1a				
yšb lābeṭaḥ				
			X	v. 19 to 2 Sam 7:13b to 2 Sam 7:13b Deut 12:9

the *m^e^nûḥâ* of 1 Kgs 8:56 to a particular stratum of the text. In my opinion, they belong to that stratum whose program is outlined by Deut 12:9-10. The redactional relation of Josh 23:1, certainly a late deuteronomistic text, to the other "rest" passages ought to be determined. Finally, the references in Judg 2:14; 8:34, 1 Sam 12:11, 1 Kgs 5:5, which were probably written at different times, must be localized redactio-historically. In the present study, I cannot do more than mention this question. As regards the answer and the further substantiation of my theses, I refer to an extensive study which I hope to publish shortly. In this study, I have made a detailed exegetical analysis of all the "rest" texts and evaluated them from a theological point of view.

On the level of the final redaction, the history of Israel from Horeb to the construction of the temple on Zion is, through the system of *nwḥ* hi. / *m^e^nûḥâ*, characterized as a history of liberation through God and peace granted by God until, finally, the people is permitted to enjoy cultic communion with its God in the central sanctuary. According to the deuteronomistic conception of rest / peace, there are four stages before the goal of YHWH's history with Israel is reached.

1) "Granting rest" to Israel before the conquest, with *nwḥ* hi. meaning the end of the migrations or the elimination of the threat constituted by enemies living in the land (Deut 3:20; Josh 1:13, 15; 22:4).

2) "Granting rest" to Israel after the settlement in the land; *nwḥ* hi. guarantees a final security against external enemies (Deut 12:10; 25:19; Josh 21:44; further 23:1 and the references without the verb in Judg 2:14; 8:34; 1 Sam 12:11 as well as 1 Kgs 5:5.

3) "Granting rest/peace" to David through the submission of his, the king's, enemies (2 Sam 7:1, 11) and "granting rest/peace" to Solomon by eliminating his external and internal opponents (1 Kgs 5:18); *nwḥ* hi. is here the presupposition for:

4) the gift of "rest," of *m^e^nûḥâ* as the Temple of Jerusalem (Deut 12:9; 1 Kgs 8:56). With this gift, the cultic centralization of Deuteronomy comes into force.

5
Deuteronomy and the Birth of Monotheism

German title: "Das Deuteronomium und die Geburt des Monotheismus" (see bibliography)

Deuteronomy is considered to constitute a program for a "constructive restoration," which originated in "the search for a true knowledge of YHWH, intended to create a new social order in Israel."[1] The reform(s) it reflected as well as initiated was (were) carried by the pathos of a return to the origins of Israel as the people of YHWH. Its theology, however, was ecclesiology and was, from the beginning, interwoven with a Torah (2 Kgs 22:8), a social order, and a way of life. In 621 BCE, King Josiah, by a covenant, made the Torah in its contemporary literary form the constitution of his kingdom. Here the revelation of YHWH and the social renewal condition each other reciprocally. Even when it is "only" a matter of liturgical reform[2] or of theoretical reflections about God,[3] the two are interrelated.

In fact, Josiah's reform was principally concerned with the cult.[4] There were two principal aims: worship of YHWH alone and centralization of the cult, in other words, "cultic purity" and "cultic unity." Because of the demand to worship YHWH alone as the God of Israel, the alien cults disappeared. The centralization of the cult to the Temple of Jerusalem meant the elimination of all other YHWH sanctuaries. Historically speaking, the two activities probably ran parallel from a certain point in time: YHWH sanctuaries were demolished exactly as though they had been shrines of other gods, since the cult had become syncretistic. From the theological point of view, the alien cults and the cult of YHWH in the high places both constituted violations of a single commandment, the first commandment of the Decalogue. And finally, they were both forbidden in one and the same text, Deuteronomy 12.

The stipulation of a single sanctuary is unique to Deuteronomy. It is found only in the corpus of laws (12-18*; 26*) and in 31:9-13.[5] The exclusive claim of YHWH, on the other hand, is not restricted to Deuteronomy; and the obligation to eliminate alien cults also had deep roots in Israel's past (cf. Exod 34:13; 23:24).[6] But it is only in Deuteronomy that the two are found in the interpretational and formal context of a covenant theology.[7]

The demand to honor YHWH alone is found mainly within a parenetic framework (4-11; 29-30), but also in individual statutes (e.g., 12:2-3; cf. 12:29-31; 13; 17:2-7) and in the chapter of sanctions (28). In other words, it is found in all parts of the "covenant formula," as well as in an introduction to the Song of Moses (31:16-23), which constitutes a poetic summary of Israel's history of apostasy, punishment and grace.[8]

What is demanded in this context is monolatric practice.[9] Israel must realize that it is committed to YHWH as its only God. This does not imply any denial of the existence of other gods. On the contrary, YHWH is distinguished from all other gods. This is not monotheism, but one of the possibilities included in polytheism. In spite of that, Deuteronomy soon abandoned the typically polytheistic conception of the gods, in which each god is an element in a divine constellation. The monotheistic wording, however, was only developed under pressure of the Babylonian exile. Here YHWH is confessed and honored as the one God. The existence of other gods is denied. The explicit negation is emphasized as long as a monotheistic linguistic usage has to assert itself against a still existing polytheistic usage.

In the present essay, I wish to systematize the theoretical statements about YHWH found in Deuteronomy,[10] as well as to analyze them in their chronological sequence. I shall outline how the monotheistic language matured within the polytheistic reference system, in the actual case the *'ēl* predicates for YHWH. Furthermore, I shall describe the monotheistic breakthrough in Deuteronomy and enumerate the differences between this form of monotheism and the monotheism of Deutero-Isaiah. Finally, I shall demonstrate that the Song of Moses has not had any influence on the doctrine of God in Deuteronomy. In my opinion, this makes it probable that the monotheism of the Old Testament had its origin in Deuteronomy.

YHWH as *(hā)'ēl*—the Unique God

In his article "Gott im Buch Deuteronomium," which constitutes the basis for my contribution, Norbert Lohfink has made one thing clear: what is new in the doctrine of God in Deuteronomy is manifestly the interpretation of the relationship between YHWH and Israel as an all-encompassing "covenant."[11] It was conceived in analogy with ancient Near Eastern vassal treaties. Indeed, it even appears that there are Neo-Assyrian instances of a covenant with a god.[12] The type of treaty which comes into question for Deuteronomy[13] mentions the suzerain principally in a "historical prologue." Such a prologue was intended to substantiate the legal claim the overlord had on his vassal. When the preexilic Deuteronomy spoke of YHWH, this was therefore restricted almost entirely to YHWH actions within the history of Israel and, of course, to his claims on his people as his covenantal partner. This constitutes a considerable narrowing in comparison with the numerous assertions about YHWH which had been made in Israel for centuries. In the preexilic Deuteronomy, we find theoretical statements about YHWH only in 6:4 and in connection with the *'ēl* predicates.[14] Yet the *'ēl* epithets are attributed to YHWH even during the exile. From the syntactical point of view, we are dealing with nominal clauses—and what is more, with pure nominal clauses, not participial clauses, which in the last analysis are verbal. I shall now proceed to an analysis of the individual texts.

Perhaps the 621 edition of Deuteronomy began with 6:4-5 as its basic dogma and basic norm. Together with the Israel he is addressing, the speaker confesses the one God of all Israel ("YHWH, our God"). Beginning with this assumption, he announces to Israel "Hear, Israel! YHWH, our God, is the one and only." The Hebrew *YHWH 'ᵉlōhênû YHWH 'eḥād* by itself permits several interpretations. The one I have just given can be inferred from the linguistic usage of Deuteronomy. According to this usage, *'ᵉlōhênû* must be understood as an apposition to YHWH.[15] And *'eḥād* with neither article nor preposition signifies "one" in the sense of "one and only."[16]

However, the reader of the final redaction of the book of Deuteronomy does not see 6:4 until he or she has read chapter 4, in which YHWH is spoken of as the only God. Hence he or she can only understand 6:4 in a monotheistic sense. Mark 12:32, for instance, is proof of this. But how was this uniqueness meant to be understood without previous redactional information, that is, at a time when 6:4 was not yet preceded by chapter 4?

At that time, 6:4 could, no doubt, also be understood as meaning "one YHWH" in opposition to a multiplicity of deities called YHWH.[17] Such a "mono-yahwistic" interpretation[18] presupposes that YHWH had, in the various sanctuaries, assimilated various local deities and had thus disintegrated into several YHWH figures. In order to combat this, Deut 6:4 stresses his unity. The historical hypothesis of such a poly-yahwism is not sufficiently substantiated by Deuteronomy itself. However, today there no longer seems to be any source which would exclude such a hypothesis.[19]

The texts from Kuntillet ‘Ajrud, which came into being between 776 and 750 BCE speak of a "YHWH of Samaria" and a "YHWH of Teman" (*yhwh šmrn* and *yhwh tmn*).[20] Thereby they place YHWH and a town or territory in a "positively definitional relationship to each other."[21] That the reference was to a temple in which YHWH was worshiped is not very likely for Samaria and unlikely for Teman. Thus it would be precipitate to conclude from the existing material "that such definitions of YHWH as YHWH of Samaria or YHWH of Teman either constitute a stage on the way to a poly-yahwistic disintegration of YHWH or that they presuppose such a disintegration as having already taken place."[22] In any case, Deuteronomy never bases the centralization of the cult on the nature of the "one YHWH"[23] but on his will, which is at work in the historical election of Israel (cf. *bḥr* in the "centralization formula").[24] As far as the wording went, it was certainly possible to interpret Deut 6:4 mono-yawhistically on first hearing it, although there were other possible ways of understanding it. But nothing in the continuation of the text made this interpretation necessary. Indeed, the immediate context pointed in another direction.

Verses 6:4 and 6:5 together make up a brief formula, which also occurs elsewhere, and which was therefore well known to the contemporary hearers.[25]

a) an exhortation to listen
b) the address "Israel"
c) a statement
d) a demand

In the concrete case of 6:5, the demand consists in the commandment to love YHWH. Through this commandment, addressed to Israel, the YHWH predicate is given an "ecclesiological"[26] interpretation: YHWH is the one and only (*'eḥād*). Israel is to love him and be united with him with all (*kōl*) its strength.[27] The text is not speaking of the one God of monotheism.[28] Israel is commanded to love solely "the one and only," that is, YHWH, "our God." This interpretation remains valid for 6:4-5 even though the two verses may have been proclaimed as independent brief formulas of the YHWH religion[29] before being inserted in this text.

In Deuteronomy, the theological emphasis is laid more on the commandment to love God than on the statements about God. The commandment is repeated more frequently than in any comparable Old Testament text. The YHWH predicates found in connection with the love commandment, on the other hand, are always different.[30] The doctrine of God is intended to induce a behavior by the people which can be deemed worthy of YHWH. This was probably the case from the beginning of Deuteronomy. Within the deuteronomic covenant theology, the demand to love God is only one of several versions of the "chief commandment," to honor YHWH alone and have no other gods. Given this connotation, the commandment to love YHWH finally determines the YHWH predicate of 6:4—YHWH is neither one in the sense of undivided in himself nor the only god there is; he is the only god among all the gods whom Israel—and not merely the individual Israelites—is to love as its own God. In other words, YHWH is the one and only as Israel's God; he is unique only as the God loved by Israel. Thus Deut 6:4-5 implies a theoretical polytheism. This can also be concluded from the connection of this text with the first commandment of the Decalogue. For the rest, this implicit polytheism is far more strongly present in Deuteronomy than in earlier texts of the Old Testament. For in Deuteronomy, Israel and YHWH are pointedly, even polemically distinguished from other nations and their gods.[31]

In the present redaction of Deuteronomy, the passage 6:4-5 repeats the love motif of 5:10 and thus the beginning of the Decalogue, which is then given a midrash-like interpretation in 6:12-15.[32] Deut 5:9 and 6:15, however, characterize YHWH as *'ēl qannā'*, as a "jealous God." In predeuteronomic times, this predicate occurred for the first time in Exod 34:14[33]: "You shall not prostrate yourselves before any other god. For YHWH (the) jealous (one) (*qannā'*) (is) his name, a jealous God (*'ēl qannā'*) is he." The divine name is "explained" through another name, which expresses the nature of God. Strictly speaking, this is the case only for *qannā'*; *'ēl* does not characterize only YHWH. Israel is expressly forbidden to give cultic worship to any other god, *'ēl 'aḥēr.* Contrary to Exod 34:14, Deuteronomy—with the exception of the Song of Moses (Deuteronomy 32)—reserves the epithet *'ēl* for YHWH alone.[34] This linguistic usage does, however, attain its limit in statements about YHWH as the incomparable *'ēl* (3:24 and 33:26). In spite of YHWH's uniqueness, what one might call his *'ēl*-ness here constitutes the basis for a comparison with other gods. In Deuteronomy, every god other than YHWH is *'ᵉlōhîm*. The expression *'ᵉlōhîm 'ᵃḥērîm* is substituted for *'ēl 'aḥēr.* As soon as the existence of other gods has been negated, that is, as soon as the writers have begun to think monotheistically, they avoid even this term.

Taking over from Exod 34:14, Deuteronomy has, however, further developed the predicate *'ēl qannā'* for YHWH. It uses the formula three times, thus making it the most frequent *'ēl* epithet: 5:9; 6:15 and 4:24.

It is characteristic of Deuteronomy that, first of all, only *'ēl qannā'* among all the different *'ēl* epithets is associated with YHWH's exclusive claim on Israel's worship. YHWH has the right to forbid Israel to have other gods. Although no explicit reason is given for this in Exod 34:14, Deuteronomy does, in this connection, always mention the founding event in Israel's history: YHWH has brought Israel out of Egypt, the house of slavery (5:6; 6:12), the smelting furnace, that it may become the people of his inheritance, his inalienable possession (4:20). For Israel, this experience of God cannot be exchanged for any other; it is the basis for Israel's exclusive relationship with YHWH whereas in Exod 34:14, *'ēl qannā'* still refers to YHWH without the apposition "your God." This apposition is never absent in Deuteronomy.[35] This is the second characteristic.

The third one is that the designation *'ēl qannā'* is reserved for YHWH's relation to his own people. It is as *'ēl gādôl wᵉnôrā'*, as a "great and terrifying" God, that he confronts the peoples living in the promised land, who are Israel's enemies (7:21). As *hā'ēl haggādôl haggibbōr wᵉhannôrā'*, as "the great God, the hero and the terrible (God)" (10:18), he even intervenes in favor of marginal groups in society, those with no legal rights, the orphans and the widows, and the destitute aliens.

Fourthly, as in Exod 34:14, in Deuteronomy *'ēl qannā'* is always found in a substantiation clause introduced by *kî* and constitutes an explanation for the interdiction of other gods and of images which is given in the Decalogue. This function suits the supposed original setting of this confessional formula in the cult, the renunciation of other gods and the exhortation to demolish their images.[36] In spite of the claim to exclusive loyalty, *'ēl qannā'* in the first instance seems to have included both aspects of "jealousy": YHWH's strong affection for Israel, as well as his anger with Israel for worshiping other gods. Yet this trait becomes more and more of a threat, not, however, a threat against the other gods, but against Israel, of whom YHWH is jealous. This is unique in the history of religion.

Thus *'ēl qannā'* also differs from other *'ēl* predicates, which only express YHWH's benevolence, especially in favor of his people. Possibly *'ēl qannā'* has a slightly negative accent even in 5:9-10. After all, in this text the "jealous God" is characterized first by his judicial activity and only afterwards by his grace.

> You shall not prostrate yourself before other gods or serve them. For I, YHWH, your God, am a jealous God (*'ēl qannā'*). On those who are my enemies, I punish the children for the guilt of the fathers unto the third and fourth generations; on those who love me and keep my commandments, I show mercy to thousands" (5:9-10).[37]

It may be that, when the later radical reinterpretation of these Decalogue sentences about guilt and punishment took place (7:9-10), people felt that the title *'ēl qannā'* had a mainly negative connotation and this is why it was changed into *hā'ēl hanne'ᵉmān*, "the faithful God." Conversely, in 6:15, "the old motivation formula for the first commandment"[38] is intensified. The nominal clause is extended through a definition of circumstance: "For YHWH, your God, is a jealous God in your midst." As is shown by 7:21, *bᵉqirbêkā* ("in your midst") can refer to the aid provided by YHWH's presence, even if combined with an *'ēl* predicate. In the context of 6:15, however, this term expresses an opposition to "the other gods, the gods of the nations surrounding you" (verse 14). From a stylistic point of view, we here find what can be observed elsewhere regarding the *'ēl* predicates, namely that they are always chosen to harmonize perfectly with their context. And let it be said in advance: except for *'ēl qannā'*, they are frequently adapted to their context, or even specially created. In 6:15, however, *'ēl qannā'* is further explicated by allusions and "curses" taken from the treaty formula. There are references to YHWH's anger being roused and to the annihilation of Israel in the cultivated land.

As the people then, in fact, had to live in exile, they realized that their political ruin was not simply a result of the passion of a jealous God, as 6:15 still proclaims, but that it came from the very nature of YHWH, who is a consuming fire, and as such *'ēl qannā'*. In 4:24, a text from the exilic era,[39] *'ēl qannā'* is added as an apposition to the predicate *'ēš 'ōkᵉlâ*, and the two expressions are understood as identical: "For YHWH, your God, is a consuming fire, a jealous God." This theoretical statement certainly has the somber colors of those days, but in fact it can be concluded even from the Horeb theophany. At Horeb, YHWH let Israel see "his (!) great fire." At Horeb, Israel heard YHWH's words coming "out of the fire" (verse 36, cf. verse 12). In the flames which burned high on the mountain, reaching the heavens (verse 11), YHWH revealed his most profound nature and his will. Therefore, according to chapter 4, the consuming fire, YHWH as *'ēl qannā'* is not merely the reason why the first and second commandments should be kept, but also constitutes the origin of the Horeb covenant, that is, of the whole Decalogue (verses 13 and 23). If Israel had broken this covenant, was not her fall a strictly logical consequence of the nature of its God as *'ēl qannā'*? It is the same theology which explains that YHWH must send his apostate people into exile, not simply in anger but as a result of his innermost nature, and which founds every hope precisely on the nature of this same God. Although YHWH, the God who is "jealous almost to the point of murdering his beloved,"[40] has reached his utmost as *'ēl qannā'*, yet he does not completely exterminate Israel, since he is, at the same time, an *'ēl rāḥûm*, "a merciful God" (verse 31). YHWH can transcend the claim to exclusive worship which is part of his very nature, but, in the final analysis, only because he is the *only* God (*hā'ᵉlōhîm*). This is the reason given by verses 32-40 and introduced by *kî*. As soon as language about God becomes monotheistic, the formula about the jealous God loses its meaning. And in fact, neither the *'ēl qannā'* nor YHWH's *qin'â* in relation to Israel occur in later texts.[41]

In 3:24, YHWH's uniqueness is explained in a way quite different from that of the predicate *'ēl qannā'*. This verse is usually attributed to the (or a) deuteronomistic editor of the exilic period.[42] Probably, however, the verse belonged to a stratum which was intended to legitimize the expansion under King Josiah and the enforcement of the deuteronomic law. In that case, the verse is from the end of King Josiah's reign.[43] Hence I prefer to discuss this text here.

Verse 3:24 is—with the exception of Deuteronomy 32 and 33—the only text in Deuteronomy in which *'ēl* is found without an attribute. Furthermore, it is only here that the epithet is found outside any parenesis, in a historical retrospect. However, it is part of a prayer.[44] Verse 24, especially the second half, constitutes a kind of hymnic preamble.[45] The preamble is intended to render credible the hope for divine aid in answer to the petitions which follow. In the Masoretic Text, 3:24 reads: "Lord YHWH, you have begun to show your servant your greatness and your strong hand, which are such that (it is valid to ask:) What god (*'ēl*) is there in heaven or on earth who can do such works and mighty deeds as you?" The content and formulation of this statement belong entirely to the tradition of ancient Near Eastern polytheism, insofar as this polytheism included the phenomenon called henotheism as a genuine option.[46] In the hymnic setting, the person praying experiences the presence of one particular god as so overwhelming and incomparable that this god becomes the highest god, even the only god for that person. The certitude of the moment is expressed in the form of a rhetorical question. This question exudes conviction and is intended to convince others. Yet the same person can, in a different cultic situation, praise another god in exactly the same way. Even in 3:24, the rhetorical question does not constitute a denial of the existence of gods other than YHWH. The answer already contained in the question is simply that no god[47] could do what YHWH has done. His incomparability is here intended to be understood as something which others cannot attain.[48] Thus the verse affirms that YHWH is unique, not that he is the only god.[49] YHWH's greatness and might, like the *'ēl* predications elsewhere, do not transcend experience. The use of *gōdel* and *yad ḥ^{a}zākâ* in Deuteronomy makes clear[50] that YHWH's incomparability and uniqueness as *'ēl* become manifest in his historical deeds in favor of Israel, tangibly and above all in his mighty act in leading Israel out of Egypt.[51]

Deut 10:17 speaks of YHWH's uniqueness in a different and intensified way. True, as in 3:24, the *'ēl* predication here remains embedded in hymnic expressions—one might almost say in an "inflation of superlatives and designations of totality" (10:14, 17).[52] There is a certain hymnic participial style[53] (verse 18). And finally,

YHWH is even called the "praise" of Israel (verse 21). However, he is no longer simply singled out among the gods (3:24); he is given the place of El, creator god and king of the gods in the Canaanite pantheon. Even 10:14 characterizes YHWH through a nominal clause, that is, through a theoretical statement as lord of the entire cosmos and—this is suggested by a comparison with Ps 136:2-3—also as creator of the world.[54] "Behold, to YHWH your God belong the heavens and the heaven of heavens, the earth, with everything that is in it." According to verses 17-18, he is the highest god and the overlord of all earthly rulers. Deuteronomy never calls YHWH "king" (*melek*), but does make use of the "ancient Near Eastern royal ideology: the king as warrior hero, as just judge and as helper of widows and orphans."[55] The text reads: "For YHWH your God is the God above all gods, and the lord of lords, *the* great God, the hero and the terrible [God] (*hā'ēl haggādôl haggibbōr w^{e}hannôrā'*), who is no respecter of persons and accepts no bribes. He secures justice to widows and orphans and loves the aliens, whom he gives food and clothing." To begin with, god is compared with god and lord is compared with lord. In the Hebrew, the relation is expressed by the genitive case. In this context, the subsequent predicate *hā'ēl haggādôl* could be translated "the great El," with El as a proper name.[56] Such a translation would be explanatory and can be defended from the grammatical point of view.[57] This is probably the first time that this divine title is used in the Old Testament. Later it is only found in prayers.[58] It is then further explained by two expressions which we have already found linked with *'ēl*. The term *haggibbōr*, "the hero," goes back to the "probably pre-yahwistic epithet[59] *'ēl gibbôr*;[60] and *hannôrā'*, "the terrible one" is part of an *'ēl* predication even in 7:21. Incidentally, this is the only *'ēl* predication in Deuteronomy which differentiates YHWH from the gods.[61] However, in deuteronomic linguistic usage, *gādôl* and *nôrā'* are stereotypes for what is mighty and numinous.[62] When, in 10:17, this word pair is split up, the intention is to define YHWH through the old title, which probably belonged originally to the Canaanite king of the gods: YHWH is seen as El, the divine warrior and hero[63] (cf. 33:26-29).

The triad of YHWH predicates—something unique in the Old Testament—then has its stylistic echo in 10:18, where YHWH's three royal functions are listed and where we find the typically deuteronomic triad of social cases. As the El of Israel, YHWH accepts the responsibility for these cases. The definite article makes it clear that YHWH is the god *par excellence*. This does not, however, suffice to make him the only god.[64] Indeed, the use of the superlatives "god of gods" and "lord of lords" and the fact that YHWH takes over the role of El presuppose that there are several gods. Although he is creator and king of the world, no active or polemical relation to the gods or the nations is attributed to YHWH in this passage. He is, above all, Israel's God (verses 17 and 21). In fact, the cosmic horizon only serves as the background against which the particular history of Israel is narrated.[65] Within this history, YHWH as *hā'ēl haggādôl haggibbōr w^{e}hannôrā'* (verse 17) performs *'et hagg^{e}dōlōt w^e'et hannôrā'ōt*, that is, "great and terrifying deeds" (verse 21) in favor of Israel.

That YHWH is spoken of as *'ēl* in this historical context is decisive for the further development of the doctrine of God in Deuteronomy. True, YHWH's great deeds do not suffice to make his uniqueness known. Rather, YHWH's universal dominion is the prerequisite for his exclusive love of the patriarchs and for his election of Israel among all nations (verse 15).[66] And in fact, this dominion constitutes the foundation for the love and the election: originally, *kî*, "for" in verse 17 directly followed verse 15.[67] It becomes clear that, the more YHWH claims, not only to be the only god for Israel, but also to be unique and to be above all other gods, the more theological does the description of his relation to his people become. For with YHWH's relation to the fathers, his love (*'hb, ḥšq*) and his election (*bḥr*) of Israel, three new motifs are brought into the *'ēl* theology of Deuteronomy, three motifs which, from now on, will always be found in connection with this theology.[68] It is probably significant that the love theme is nowhere associated with *'ēl qannā'*, with the jealous YHWH. There is, then, a growing theological awareness that Israel's identity is dependent on the uniqueness of its God and that YHWH's union with his people is in no way self-evident. Deut 10:12 - 11:17 certainly gives no evidence of the distress of the Babylonian exile. And yet this text, the core of which is almost certainly older, was probably not incorporated into Deuteronomy before the exilic period. In the context of this book, this passage then made it possible to speak of YHWH in a manner suited to the times.[69]

According to the deuteronomic view of treaties, the catastrophe of the exile proved that the curses with which Israel had been threatened had now become reality. Israel had broken the covenant of Horeb and thus destroyed its relationship with YHWH. The first thing to be explained was "how what had happened could happen, if YHWH was, and remained, Israel's God."[70] Later on, however, the theological "key question" was: Which is the way out of this situation of guilt?[71] The logic of a treaty formula offered no possibility to start afresh once Israel had rendered itself guilty. The only hope lay in the divine covenant partner. Hence not only are there no accusations regarding the past; but beyond that, YHWH alone is made responsible for Israel's future. Deuteronomic texts of late exilic origin attempt to come to terms with the crisis through a kind of double strategy. After Israel has been found guilty, these texts are intended to assure its survival through a radical theology. Tradition conscious, this theology remains committed to the notion of a covenant, a notion which up to now has proved useful giving a systematic account of Israel's relationship with God. This is shown for instance by the fact that pericopes written or edited at that time were structured strictly on the pattern of the "covenant formula" (4:9-31; 29-30). Even the term *b^e^rît*, covenant, has been retained. The covenant relationship itself, however, is now so conceived that YHWH's fidelity extends further than Israel's apostasy, not only by a single act of grace, but basically. There no longer has to be any correspondence between YHWH's fidelity and Israel's behavior, since the measure for YHWH's fidelity is no longer found in human behavior. The measure is YHWH himself—his fidelity to himself. The strict parallelism between punishment and reward is now unilaterally changed to favor a sinful Israel. YHWH's grace exceeds his retribution and his grace is for all generations.

The covenant with the fathers replaces the Horeb covenant. And the covenant with the fathers consisted in an assurance of grace, binding YHWH alone. In the second place, the cause of Israel's downfall is eliminated at its very roots. The cause lies in Israel's turning to other gods. According to prevailing linguistic usage, this is expressed by saying that Israel has broken the first commandment of its covenant with God. Obviously, parenesis had not been enough to protect Israel from this temptation. Hence there was need for a theoretical explanation of what the other gods were and why Israel was not to trust in them, but only in YHWH—indeed, why Israel could only put its trust in YHWH. The evidence is furnished by Israel's experience of God, its history with YHWH. And it is here that we find the breakthrough to monotheism. It is not only juridically clear, but also rational and logical. Late texts in Deuteronomy, such as 8:1-18; 9:1-8[72] say nothing about any confrontation with the gods. The gods are no longer YHWH's rivals; his rival is the human self-confidence of Israel. In 30:1-10, not even the covenant with the fathers is mentioned as the reason for the grace granted to Israel. YHWH, the only God, is "reason" enough.

Within Deuteronomy 7, the theological *relecture* is incorporated in the framework of an older text.[73] Verses 9-10 recall the central text of the Horeb covenant, the first commandment of the Decalogue, but rework the YHWH predicates of 5:9b-10, which give the reason for the first commandment. The new interpretation reads: "YHWH, your God, is the God (*hā'ᵉlōhîm*), the faithful God/El (*hā'ēl hanne'ᵉmān*); with those who love him and keep his commandments, he keeps covenant (*habbᵉrît*) and faith for a thousand generations, but those who defy him and show their hatred for him he repays with destruction: he will not be slow to requite any who so hate him" (7:9-10). A comparison between 5:9-10 and 7:9-10 shows that grace now takes precedence over justice. To begin with, the old divine title *'ēl qannā'* is replaced by *hā'ēl hanne'ᵉmān*. Instead of a jealous God, we have a faithful God. For the author of this passage, the threat of retribution takes second place.

But there is more to it than that. The parity between divine punishment and divine fidelity also disappears. According to 5:9-10, YHWH punished all generations living together in an extended family for the sins of the fathers. He also promised a family his blessing, even though it have a thousand members. God's grace was as great as his retribution. According to 7:9-10, on the other hand, YHWH's fidelity extends unto a thousand, that is, unto all possible generations, and not only to a number of people within a family. God's retribution, on the other hand, which comes into effect immediately, only affects the individual sinners, and no longer several generations within a family. If Israel, while still being punished and afterwards, begins to love YHWH once more and to observe the commandments of the Decalogue, then YHWH's fidelity, and with it his whole blessing, are revived.[74]

In the third place, the fidelity of YHWH's grace is defined through a concept which is missing in 5:9-10: *bᵉrît*, "covenant." This concept no longer denotes, as it did in the context of Horeb, the duties the treaty laid on Israel,[75] but quite evidently the oath which, according to 7:8, YHWH had sworn to the patriarchs. Verse 12 recapitulates the two expressions *nišba' la'ᵃbōtêkem* and *habbᵉrît wᵉhaḥesed.*[76] The following verse 13 makes it clear that the promises to the fathers will be surpassed. In verses 12-13, the contents of the covenant and YHWH's fidelity to the covenant are explained as what is contained in the promise of YHWH's blessing.[77] For the rest, it seems possible that the author of this critical commentary on the Decalogue gave his own doctrine of individual retribution a basis in the Decalogue by adding the participles at the end of 5:9b and 10b. The addition would be intended to correct the notion of the collective guilt of several generations (24:16), since the participles serve to relate the hatred and the love of the jealous God to one generation at a time.[78] The most important novelty remains the notion of a covenant with the fathers (7:9). Before this passage, Deuteronomy only knew of an oath YHWH swore to the fathers. Through the specially created expression *hā'ēl hanne'ᵉmān*, which is found nowhere else in the Old Testament, the notion of such a covenant became part of the doctrine of God in this book. But does this mean that YHWH became other?[79]

Until now, the *'ēl* predications were used to justify the first commandment (the causal *kî* always precedes *'ēl qannā'* statements: 5:9; 6:15; 4:24 and 10:17, in the final redaction of the pericope after verse 16), or to explain YHWH's deeds in the history of Israel (10:17, originally directly after verses 14-15), or else they are used to specify YHWH's stature as incomparable (3:24). In 7:9-10, on the other hand, the conception of the faithful God follows from YHWH's earlier history with the patriarchs and with Israel. In addition, a typically deuteronomic wording is used, the "schema of the presentation of evidence." In its freer triple form, present in 7:8-11, a historical retrospect gives rise to a basic and doctrinal conclusion. This conclusion then has consequences for Israel's conduct, in the actual case regarding the observance of the laws. Verse 8[80] cites the following historical acts: YHWH brought Israel out of Egypt, the house of slavery, with a strong hand, and redeemed it out of pure love and because of an oath he had sworn to the fathers. Verses 9-10 then bring the theoretical conclusion to be drawn from these facts, introducing the solemn assertion of YHWH's nature by the formula "you shall know that" (*wᵉyāda'tā kî*). Then follows the text quoted above. The formula here functions as an assertion of the ultimate goal of salvation history: "The ultimate intention of God's action becomes clear through this assertion. God does not act for his own sake, but for the sake of human beings. The intention is to bring them to know YHWH ... which also means to confess him."[81] In spite of the imperative components of the formula of knowledge in this version, it retains its ultimate function.[82] According to verse 11, which concludes the schema, this knowledge is expressed by practical observance of the deuteronomic law. YHWH, Israel's God, is rightly called *hā'ēl hanne'ᵉmān* because of the historical evidence for his love and constancy. But above that, he is "*the* God" (*hā'ᵉlōhîm)*. Other gods are not mentioned; neither is their existence explicitly denied.[83] We are on the threshold of monotheism.[84]

The YHWH predications in 7:9-10 have their prototypes in the hymnic confessional formula of Exod 34:6-7,[85] which prepares the way for the forgiveness in verse 9. Thus in Exod 34:6 YHWH is addressed as *'ēl rāḥûm wᵉḥannûn*, as a "compassionate and merciful God." The latest *'ēl* title in Deuteronomy (in 4:31) links up with this.[86] As previously mentioned, this predicate was intended as a contrast to *'ēl qannā'* in verse 24. Nevertheless, the polarity in God depicted in 4:23-31 appears to have a factual basis in Exodus 34. After all, the words about a "jealous God" have their origin there, taken from Exod 34:14, which belongs to the "cultic Decalogue." In Deuteronomy 4, however, the sequence of YHWH predications is the reverse of Exodus 34. First, we have *'ēl qannā'* and his "law," then *'ēl rāḥûm* and his "good news" of the forgiveness of sinners. In order to heighten the tension within YHWH between the jealous God and the compassionate God by stylistic means, Deut 4:31 omits the second of the adjectives *rāḥûm wᵉḥannûn*. With one possible exception, these predicates are used only of YHWH in the entire OT. Thus Deut 4:31 creates a new *'ēl* epithet, one which is certainly dependent on tradition, but differently worded and unique in the OT. This epithet is *'ēl rāḥûm*, the "compassionate God." The epithets *'ēl qannā'* and *'ēl rāḥûm* are incorporated in YHWH's historical actions towards Israel. This corresponds well with the old way of speaking about God, characteristic of Deuteronomy. In the last analysis, the predicates explain the way YHWH acts towards Israel (*kî* in verses 24 and 31). In the past, the Israelites suffered through the curses of a jealous God (verses 25-28). Now the same YHWH, as a compassionate God, makes future bliss possible. Or, to be exact, he makes possible the prerequisite for such bliss, Israel's conversion to YHWH as its God and a renewed obedience (verses 29-30).

The tension within God himself, revealed through the dramatic antitheses of verses 23-31,[87] is reminiscent of the struggle within YHWH which Hos 11:8-9 describes by the term "remorse"—because YHWH is "*'ēl* and not a man" (Hos 11:9).[88] In a similar way, Deut 4:31 characterizes YHWH as a "compassionate *'ēl*" in his relationship to Israel. He will not bring about Israel's ruin (verse 25, *šḥt* hi.). He will not forget his covenant with the fathers (verse 23, *škḥ b^{e}rît*). A comparison with the not much older, also exilic verse 1 Kgs 8:50,[89] which only asks that the conquerors be merciful towards the exiles, illustrates the determinedly *theological* intent of the deuteronomic passage.

Deut 7:9 is mainly interested in the validity of the covenant with the fathers. This covenant remains valid only if Israel loves YHWH and observes the commandments of the Decalogue (verse 12). Deut 4:31, on the other hand, considers matters from a far more radical point of view: it asserts the enduring existence of the covenant with the fathers and sees it as founded on grace. Furthermore, in contrast to 7:9, 4:31 views everything that happens from YHWH's perspective and presents it as an inference from his nature. Whereas, according to 7:8 the covenant with the fathers and the exodus led to knowledge of the "faithful God," in 4:31 everything has its origin in the "compassionate God," who does not abandon his people even in exile[90] nor forget the covenant with the fathers. It is also the "compassionate God," not primarily the covenant with the fathers, who enables Israel to rediscover YHWH and return to him (verses 29-30). In the end, those who are certain of his mercy no longer need even the reassurance of the covenant with the fathers (30:3).[91]

Neither in 4:24 nor in 4:31 do the *'ēl* predicates take the definite article. Obviously they intend—unlike 10:17 and 7:9—to avoid associating YHWH with the Canaanite El, now that YHWH is conceived monotheistically and not merely described as incomparable. The *'ēl* theology continues to evolve within the framework of the treaty formula. For Deuteronomy 4, this only constitutes the penultimate step towards recognizing that YHWH is the only God.

YHWH as *hā'^{e}lōhîm*—The Only God

Deut 4:1-40 forms an independent synthesis of deuteronomic theology on the subject of YHWH's divinity and Israel's relationship with God through the Torah. The text—a literary unity—was created for its present context and inserted between the older chapters 1-3 and 5.[92] Hence the reader is meant to read all that follows in Deuteronomy through the—as will become clear, monotheistic—viewpoint of chapter 4. The text probably has its origin in the advanced, but not in the late exilic period. This may be inferred on one hand from the historicized curse sanctions (verses 25-28), which precede the future blessing (verses 29-31), and on the other from the expression of hope for the future, which is still focussed entirely on the essential relationship with God. Elsewhere it is merely suggested (cf., for instance, 30:1-10).[93]

The doctrine of God in 4:1-40 may be gathered first of all from the precise theological terminology of this chapter.[94] YHWH, *'ᵉlōhîm*, and *'ēl* are used in accordance with stringent definitions. The juxtaposition of YHWH and *'ᵉlōhîm* reflects YHWH's relationship with Israel; however, when YHWH's divinity is being discussed, *'ᵉlōhîm* is not found in apposition to YHWH. In what follows, I propose to discuss first the way the terms are used, then the debate concerning YHWH and the gods, which is carried out with the aid of the term *'ᵉlōhîm*.

The divine name YHWH without "my, your, our God" is used when YHWH acts in the manner of an absolute ruler and keeps his distance from that which is unlike him. He is ruler and lord as the judge who punishes Israel (verse 3) and Moses (verse 21), in the violent liberation of Israel from the smelting furnace of Egypt (verse 20), and also as legislator in the Horeb theophany (verses 10, 12, and 15) and as the only powerful god in world history (verses 35 and 39). *'ᵉlōhîm* occurs as an appellative only when the term refers to the gods (verse 28) or is used in a comparison between YHWH and the gods (verses 7, 33 and 34)—unless, of course, tradition should dictate otherwise (verse 32). This will be further discussed below. However, there is no instance of YHWH alone being called *'ᵉlōhîm*, "God"; instead, he is *hā'ᵉlōhîm*, "the God" (verses 35 and 39). The phrase YHWH *'ᵉlōhêkā/kem*, "YHWH, your God," on the other hand, in spite of being a formula, to a greater or lesser degree emphasizes the close relationship YHWH as its "personal" God has with his people. The changes in number in the enclitic pronoun referring to Israel have stylistic functions. By saying YHWH *'ᵉlōhāy*, "YHWH, my God" (verse 5), Moses contrasts himself as a legislator whose authority comes from God with Israel as recipient of the law. This makes Moses comparable to YHWH in the promulgation of the Decalogue.

It is only in relation to the gods of other nations that the mediator integrates himself with his people by using the "national we" in his speech: *ʾelōhênû*, "our God" (verse 7).[95] And finally, from the very beginning of the text, the phrase *YHWH ʾelōhê ʾabōtêkem*, "YHWH, the God of your fathers" (verse 1), announces the image of God which the author is going to develop in his text—the compassionate god of the covenant with the fathers (verse 31), an image appropriate for his time. This is the God who, out of love for the patriarchs, made the entire history of their descendants into a history of salvation (verses 37-38). The *ʾēl* predicates are only found in those passages in which—albeit within the Mosaic fiction—the guilt of the recent past is revealed to the authentic addressees and hope for the future is expressed.

For 4:1-40, as well as for the preceding strata of Deuteronomy, *ʾelōhîm*, unlike YHWH or *ʾēl*, is not (yet) a divine name and thus is not reserved for YHWH. It is a designation for the numinous/divine in general.[96] This implies that a monotheistic God must claim this title for himself alone. In monotheistic language, *ʾelōhîm* may neither be given the restricted meaning of "God for a certain people" nor may it be used in classifying other entities. This means that if YHWH were only "my, your, our God" or if there were "other gods" beside him, he would not be the only God. The rules for the theological use of language in Deuteronomy 4 are adapted to this. In the very commentary on the first/second commandment of the Decalogue, nothing is said about *ʾelōhîm ʾaḥērîm*, "other gods" (verses 16-19). When Deuteronomy 4 speaks of the gods of the other nations, the term *ʾelōhîm* is either used in the course of a "de-divinizing" polemic (verse 28) or entirely avoided and replaced by a list of demythologized stars or a prohibition of "graven images" (verses 19, 16-18, 23, 25). In addition, even the preceding text denies, with a determination which can hardly be surpassed, that YHWH has any form or that it is possible to make an image of him (verses 12 and 15). I have already spoken of *ʾelōhîm* as a prerequisite for the creation (verse 32) and *ʾelōhîm* in assertions of incomparability (verses 7, 33, 34). It is characteristic, however, that *ʾelōhîm* is only used for "some divinity," that is, always in the singular,[97] which means that the term is ready to be used exclusively for YHWH, indeed is already aimed at this use. In spite of the prevailing, still unmistakably polytheistic framework, the language of the entire pericope is already consistently monotheistic.[98] This monotheism, however, does not take the form of an independent doctrine of the only God, but is presented with pastoral regard for an Israel that has been dispersed among the nations. This monotheism expresses Israel's identity and incomparability.[99] This forms the background for a continuing "twilight of the gods."

As early as in verse 7, Israel, which has YHWH as its *'ᵉlōhîm qᵉrōbîm*, a "god close at hand," is compared to other nations and their gods. By paraphrasing the verse, we get: Which great nation has a god[100] so close at hand as YHWH—not some god, but the highest god—our god—the personal god of every member of the people as well as of the whole people—every time when we call on him—directly. Verse 8 then explains that God's presence and aid are found in tangible form in the just laws of the social order and in the observance of this Torah, that God is always present in the Torah.[101] Israel is unique because of its God. On the other hand, it is never clearly explained what the gods are like, what their relation to YHWH is, how close they are to the nations, or to what extent they are able to help them. Hence their difference from YHWH is never defined.

It is necessary to give a theoretical explanation of the historical circumstances in which other nations honor gods other than YHWH, sometimes the stars, sometimes "images." The explanation follows in verses 19 and 28. As I have already remarked, verse 19 deliberately avoids the qualification *'ᵉlōhîm 'ᵃḥērîm*, "other gods." The sun, the moon and the stars—the entire "heavenly host"—are reduced to purely "secular" status. In addition, YHWH himself is said to have given them to the other nations as objects of worship (cf. 29:25). This (only apparently) liberal acceptance[102] of a kind of "natural religion" serves to bridge the gulf between YHWH's universal power and uniqueness on one hand and the plain fact that other nations do not worship him on the other.[103]

YHWH's world dominion does not remain in the realm of speculation; it constitutes the background for his unique relationship with Israel, the people of his heritage (verse 20). Should Israel, in spite of that, make an image (verse 25), it is not even necessary to point out that it cannot be of *'ᵉlōhîm*. The situation is, however, different when we come to the imposing cult of the nations before their images. According to the principle of the *talio*, Israel in the exile is punished by having to worship these gods. True, verse 28 calls them *'ᵉlōhîm*, but in the same breath derides them as made by human hands and lifeless.

Finally, verses 33 and 34 expose the inability of these gods to make an impact on world history. As far as form and content go, these verses are reminiscent of verses 7 and 8, which speak of Israel's exceptional position among the nations. The irregularity which they question is clearly envisaged from the viewpoint of YHWH's deeds in the already canonical salvation history of Israel. The word *'ᵉlōhîm* refers to the two types of gods already mentioned, the stars and the "images." Neither stars nor products of human hands are capable of surmounting their own nature and letting *qôl 'ᵉlōhîm*, "the voice of God," be heard and then saving men from its deadly power. Neither can these gods appear in order to save one nation from the power of another. Only Israel has such a god, and so only Israel is able to bear witness to its god because of its unique experience. And this is how the explication of *'ᵉlōhîm* culminates: in the assertion that YHWH alone is *hā'ᵉlōhîm*, "the God." We shall presently see how this comes about. At all events, it does not simply mean that the dogmatic question concerning the relation between YHWH and *'ᵉlōhîm* has been solved in a manner which is not surpassed anywhere in Deuteronomy. Because (*kî*, verse 32!) YHWH is *the* God, he can change the course of history in favor of his people, in spite of the iron laws of world history. At least, it is the implicit hope of his people that he will do so once more.

Deuteronomy 4 did not introduce monotheism only by means of the terms predicated of God. It also developed and, in a unique way, intensified the formal language used by older texts in order to express YHWH's incomparability. Rhetorical questions are repeated[104] and answered; the incomparability they speak of is not simply one which, in fact, has never been matched (3:24; cf. 10:14, 17). It is something quite exceptional.[105] The line of argument (7:8-11) is run through twice, or rather, the first and second steps are. The pleading in 4:32-40 continues to use prevalent language about YHWH and the same may be said of the *'ēl* predicates in verses 24 and 31. But the assertions in 4:32-40, with their almost hymnic rhetoric, surpass all former traditions.[106] In verse 32—correctly introduced by "search" (*š'l*) instead of the traditional "remember" (*zkr*)—the field of "religio-historical comparison"[107] is extended to the outermost limits of time and space: "Search into days gone by, long before your time, beginning at the day when God created man on earth, search from one end of heaven to the other,[108] and ask if any deed as mighty as this has been seen or heard."

In the course of performing this (double) universal historical research,[109] Deuteronomy poses not only the usual rhetorical question but a double question. This question concerns the efficacy of the divine word and divine activity in history. In both cases, we are concerned with a rescue of a type not normally to be expected. What is required of an *'elōhîm* aiming at demonstrating his divinity and his equality with YHWH is, therefore, that he change those laws of history which have obtained always and everywhere. According to verses 33 and 34, this concretely means: "Did any people ever hear the voice of God speaking out of the fire, as you heard it, and remain alive? Or did ever a god attempt to come and take a nation for himself away from another nation, with a challenge and with signs, portents and wars, with a strong hand and an outstretched arm, and with great deeds of terror, as YHWH your God did for you in Egypt in the sight of you all?"

Although rhetorical questions do not really need an explicit answer, since the answers are already contained in the questions (cf. 3:24), the answer is given. It is suggested in the comparative clauses of verses 33 and 34, it is put in a nutshell in verse 35, and finally verses 36-38 develop it fully. The events we have spoken of are found only in the traditions of Israel, indeed the history of Israel, attested as being brought about by YHWH, even surpasses the conditions given.

There is only one image of God which fits the framework of verses 33 and 34. As the second step of the argument, verse 35a draws the theoretical conclusion: "To you it has been shown, that you might know that YHWH is God" (*'attâ hor'ētā lada'at kî YHWH hû' hā'elōhîm*). Although God is invisible (verses 12 and 15), Israel's knowledge of God[110] is the result of "seeing the events with their own eyes." As a witness, Israel is able to transmit this experience to later generations (verse 9). Not only have the events been caused by God (verse 34), but also, the very experience of seeing such things is a gift of grace (*r'h* ho. verse 35; cf. 29:3). The facts by themselves are not, then, sufficient to give knowledge of God.[111] The purpose of every divine action is to give Israel an understanding of its own history, actually experienced or transmitted by earlier generations, and to enable the Israelites to recognize this history as the revelation of YHWH, and of YHWH as the only God.[112]

Verse 35a gives the conclusion drawn by Israel in a deuteronomistic formula: YHWH *hû' hā'elōhîm*, "YHWH is the

God"–thus 1 Kgs 18:39;[113] 2 Sam 7:28 and Deut 7:9 (cf. 10:17).[114] Taken by itself, this confession would still mean no more than that YHWH is the only God who fulfills all the conditions investigated.[115] Hence verse 35b expressly excludes the possibility of comparing YHWH with other gods by using the superlative and asserts: *'ên 'ôd mill^{e}baddô*, "no one but he is (God)." Assertions of incomparability and uniqueness can also be made in the negative form. But then the second half of the verse ought to continue *'ên kāmōhû*, "no one is like him" (cf. 33:26). The formulation chosen for verse 35b has developed through comparisons and demarcations within a polytheistic reference system. In addition, the verse is in the negative form. Later, the same phrase is used in its positive form, in 2 Kgs 19:15 (= Isa 37:16; cf. 2 Kgs 19:19), in the prayer of King Hezekiah: "You (YHWH) alone are God" (*'attâ hû' hā'^{e}lōhîm l^{e}badd^{e}kā*). Yet Deut 4:35b does not merely "open the door to monotheism"[116] or "attain the immediate proximity of a theoretical assertion of monotheism."[117] Monotheism was actually born in Deuteronomy.

Verses 36-38 establish from the experiences of Israel that YHWH is the only God in heaven as on earth, that is, in all spheres of reality. In verse 37, we find YHWH's love and election of Israel. The context of the assertions of incomparability in chapters 7 and 10 makes it clear that Israel's history has its roots in YHWH's love and election. For the rest, YHWH's traditional deeds are listed: first the Horeb theophany, in which Israel is constituted as a *qāhāl*, an assembly of believers, a "church" (cf. 4:10); then the exodus from Egypt, and finally, the gift of the promised land. But precisely this gift remains open–not least because of the Mosaic fiction–even for the immediate future. Apart from that, no new facts or future experiences are mentioned. Evidently, all that is necessary for recognizing YHWH as the only God is a knowledge of the history of Israel during the "pre-" or "non-"state period. Thus Israel's history does not merely belong to the past, it is not something that is over and done with, but is a source of knowledge in the present and hence serves to introduce the future. Verse 39, differing clearly from the formula of knowledge in verse 35, therefore exhorts: "This day, then, know (*w^{e}yāda'tā*) and take to heart that YHWH is God in heaven above and on earth below; there is no other." The world–from the stars in the sky to the "images" on earth–is de-divinized and seen as belonging to YHWH, its only God.

If it were only a question of YHWH's incomparability, it would have been sufficient to say, in analogy with 1 Kgs 8:23: "No one is god as he (YHWH, Israel's God) is, whether in heaven above or on earth below." In Deut 4:39, however, the wording is unmistakably monotheistic. With this knowledge, the text is primarily addressed to an Israel suffering under the "curse sanctions." This Israel can trust YHWH, its judge, to become its redeemer, since he is the only God who can act and hence the only God there is. For the monotheism of Deuteronomy is not an end in itself. According to verse 40 (the third step in the argumentation), which concludes the whole pericope, monotheism is a prerequisite for Israel's being able to live in conformity with its social order—which in its turn entails a long and happy life in the promised land.[118]

Our analysis has shown that the texts of Deuteronomy, chronologically arranged, exhibit a continuous development of the doctrine of God. They range from "YHWH is one" (6:4), belonging to the still polytheistic reference system of the late monarchic period to the monotheistic assertions of the Babylonian exile: "YHWH is God, there is no other god" (4:35). Yet the assertions of incomparability and uniqueness belonging to the different literary strata are always theologized in a typically deuteronomic manner. Even where the Canaanite conceptions of El are used to elucidate the image of YHWH, this image remains entirely dependent on Israel's experiences and traditions. As long as the language remains monolatric (which means polytheistic), Deuteronomy develops its theoretical doctrine of YHWH with the aid of *'ēl* predicates.

1. As a "jealous God" (*'ēl qannā'*, 5:9; 6:15; 4:24), YHWH claims the right to an exclusive relationship with Israel. Here Deuteronomy takes up an older *'ēl* predicate, which characterizes Israel's relation to God and which in the course of time receives more and more threatening features. During the exile, it becomes identified with YHWH as a "consuming fire."

2. In a prayer, YHWH is praised as "a god" (*'ēl*, 3:24) whose deeds can be matched by no god in heaven or on earth (*'ēl* without attributes or article in a hymnic context)—an expression of YHWH's incomparability in the sense of what has not been matched. The form is that of a rhetorical question.

3. As a "great and terrible god" (*'ēl gādôl w^{e}nôrā'*, 7:21), YHWH wages war on Israel's enemies (*'ēl* predication with the typically

deuteronomic way of expressing the numinous through a juxtaposition of attributes without the article). The context is parenetic.

4. As the highest god and lord (10:14), YHWH takes over the role of the creator god and king of the gods, El. As "the great god, the hero and the terrible (one)" (*hā'ēl hāggādôl haggibbōr wᵉhannôrā'*, 10:17), he protects and aids. He makes possible the history of the fathers and of Israel (*'ēl* predication with attributes and with the definite article). A new linguistic creation using older elements, the incomparability is hymnically expressed through superlatives; this constitutes the basis for a parenesis. YHWH's cosmic sovereignty constitutes the prerequisite for his history with the patriarchs and with Israel.

5. During the catastrophe of the exile, YHWH is recognized as "*the* God" (*hā'ᵉlōhîm*) and "the faithful God" (*hā'ēl hanne'ᵉmān*, 7:9), who adheres to his covenant of grace with the fathers. This recognition no longer serves to found the first commandment of the broken Horeb covenant. Instead, the logic of faith discloses this understanding of God as the purpose of YHWH's actions in favor of the patriarchs and of Israel (*'ēl* predication in the singular, with an attribute and with the definite article), adapted to the covenant with the fathers, a consequence of YHWH's history with the patriarchs and with Israel: a theoretical inference within a schema of argumentation.

6. Finally, the covenant with the fathers has its source in YHWH himself as a "compassionate God" (*'ēl rāḥûm*, 4:31). The experience of the exile is precisely what makes it possible to understand the opposition between the jealous God and the compassionate God as an opposition between two polar characteristics within YHWH (4:24 and 31, *'ēl rāḥûm* as part of an older divine title, but conceived in opposition to *'ēl qannā'*). Both predicates occur in both the curse and in the blessing sections (which are given the form of a historical fiction) of a covenant formula. They belong to a predication about God which has already become monotheistic.

7. Monotheism breaks through, since YHWH alone in world history has proved himself to be God. The extraordinary experiences in the salvation history of Israel make it clear that he alone is "the God" (*hā'ᵉlōhîm*, 4:35, 39)—double expressions for the now exceptional incomparability in the form of rhetorical questions within

the schema of argumentation and explicit denial of the existence of other gods.

Deuteronomy develops this systematic theology from the authentic traditions of Israelite faith in YHWH. Deuteronomy's monotheism has no need of any inspiration from Zarathustra's "monotheistic" religion.[119] Neither does it constitute a revolutionary innovation.[120]

Deuteronomy's Doctrine of God and Deutero-Isaiah's Monotheism

H. Vorländer has recently defended the thesis that Old Testament monotheism "can be discerned for the first time in Deut.-Is. 43:10-13."[121] Vorländer admits that "apart from Deutero-Isaiah, the deuteronomistic school particularly stresses that YHWH is the only God." However, "Deut 4:35 uses the characteristically Deutero-Isaianic phrase 'no one' else (*'ên 'ôd*) and is thus clearly dependent on Deutero-Isaiah."[122] Does this affirmation assess justly the relation between the monotheism of Deuteronomy and the monotheism expounded in Deutero-Isaiah? Since we already have W. Wildberger's study of Deutero-Isaiah's monotheism,[123] the following comparison can be restricted to linguistic phenomena. There are two questions. The first one is: How did Deutero-Isaiah use the divine appellation *'ēl*? The second one is: Do Deut 4:35 and 39 take up expressions used by Deutero-Isaiah?

In Deutero-Isaiah, *'ēl* is usually an appellative, but "with a very clearly defined meaning: a god who really exists."[124] Since this is true of YHWH, Deutero-Isaiah uses *'ēl* mainly[125] in assertions of monotheism. Within the Book of Deutero-Isaiah, *'ēl* occurs for the first time in 40:18. In so far as one may speak chronologically, this text is probably from the early period of the prophet's public activity. Yet the issue is already YHWH's claim to be the only God and no longer whether it is possible to make any image at all of the deity: "What likeness will you find for God (*'ēl*) or what form to resemble his?"[126] Here, *'ēl* replaces the name YHWH and is used by itself. "YHWH as *'ēl*, that is, as the god who alone is truly God, cannot be compared to any other (god)."[127] Hence 42:5 can create the appositional relation "YHWH the God" (YHWH *hā'ēl*), which is unique in the Old Testament.

In 43:12, YHWH then (continuing verse 10) says of himself: "I am God" (*'anî 'ēl*). In this context, that means: There is no God but YHWH. Verses 45:14, 22 and 46:9 then elucidate this self-predication by "no one else" (*'ên 'ôd*).

In Deutero-Isaiah, *'ēl* is always without attributes, except for 45:15 and 21. Furthermore, the *'ēl* epithet cannot be explained either as the "use of an old liturgical formula" or as a sign of Deutero-Isaiah's "general inclination towards archaic language."[128]

Finally, *'ēl* can denote gods other than YHWH; in the actual case, a pagan idol 44:10, 15, 17(bis); 45:20; 46:6. However, these passages are probably secondary insertions in Deutero-Isaiah.[129]

The linguistic usage of Deuteronomy differs almost completely from the way in which Deutero-Isaiah uses the term *'ēl*. In Deuteronomy, *'ēl* is certainly reserved entirely for YHWH. However, the term is never found in monotheistic assertions. When Deuteronomy 4 speaks of YHWH as the only God, it uses *hā'elōhîm*, not *'ēl*.

Nowhere in Deuteronomy does *'ēl* replace the name YHWH. Except for the formulation of incomparability in 3:24, *'ēl* is not, syntactically speaking, either the predicate of a clause whose subject is "YHWH your God" (YHWH *'elōhêkā*, 4:31; 5:9; 6:15; 7:21) or an apposition to the predicate in such a clause (4:24; 7:9; 10:17).

In no case does Deuteronomy explicitly deny the existence of other gods while using an *'ēl* predicate. The phrase *'ên 'ôd* is associated with *hā'elōhîm* (4:35, 39).

It is only in Deut 3:24 that *'ēl* remains without an attribute, presumably in order that the range of comparison be as wide as possible. To some extent, the *'ēl* predicates of Deuteronomy repeat ancient and liturgical formulas, for instance *'ēl qannā'* and *'ēl rāḥûm*.

In Deuteronomy, no god except YHWH is ever called *'ēl*.

That is, the theology of Deutero-Isaiah starts where the doctrine of God in Deuteronomy 4 left off. To begin with, in Deutero-Isaiah, *'ēl* is no longer part of a monolatric language, but belongs to a monotheistic one. In the second place, in Deutero-Isaiah, *'ēl* has partly become a proper name instead of being a generic designation or part of a YHWH predicate.

It is almost certain that the exiles exchanged opinions among themselves, especially on central theological problems. Probably there was a similar exchange of ideas between the exiles and those who had remained in the land. We need not attempt to decide here to what extent linguistic similarities in the exilic literature should be seen as indicating literary dependence and to what extent they simply show the linguistic usage of the times.[130] We may, however, pose the question: Can Deutero-Isaiah's monotheism be shown to have had an influence on Deut 4:35 (39)?

Deut 4:35a expresses YHWH's uniqueness as God: YHWH *hû' hā'ᵉlōhîm*, "YHWH is the God" (cf. verse 39). The same statement is found in other deuteronomistic texts: Deut 7:9; 10:17; 1 Kgs 8:60; 18:39 (cf. verse 37); 2 Kgs 19:15 (cf. verse 19). In Deutero-Isaiah, it occurs only in Isa 45:18a. Probably, however, *hā'ᵉlōhîm* must in this instance be understood as, from the syntactic point of view, constituting an apposition to *hû'*, in which case the correct translation would be "he, (the) God."[131] If one assumes that there is a(n inserted) sentence "he is (the) God," what is missing in this passage is a reference to his being the only God, the phrase *'ên 'ôd*, "there is no other."

In Deut 4:35b, this phrase follows immediately. It is true that in Isa 45:18, this assertion occurs in the second half of the verse. It is, however, combined with a formula of self-predication unknown to Deuteronomy 4. Isa 45:18b reads: "I am YHWH, there is no other." This text will be discussed below. It would seem that the formulation used in Deut 4:35a is from the deuteronomistic tradition, not from Deutero-Isaiah.

In Deut 4:35b, the phrase *'ên 'ôd millᵉbaddô*, "there is no (god) but he" makes it quite certain that YHWH is the only God. Now Solomon's petition in 1 Kgs 8:60 also makes use of the phrase *'ên 'ôd* in order to deny the existence of any other god, whereas in 2 Kgs 19:15 (= Isa 37:16), Hezekiah praises YHWH as the only God— *'attâ hû' hā'ᵉlōhîm lᵉbaddᵉkā*. In 2 Kgs 19:19, Hezekiah prays in a way reminiscent of 1 Kgs 8:60 that "all the kingdoms of the earth" may recognize "that only you, YHWH, are God" (*lᵉbaddᵉkā*). However, the extension of the knowledge of YHWH to the entire world and the positive wording of the assertion of uniqueness suggest a stage of development at the earliest contemporary to, or later than Deut 4:35.[132] As the wording goes, these two texts nevertheless come closest to Deut 4:35.

Deutero-Isaiah employs the phrase *'ên 'ôd*[133] seven times in order to reject the existence of any other god, six times in Isaiah 45. But the immediate context never quite corresponds to Deut 4:35. In contrast to the two deuteronomistic prayers in the book of Kings and to the parenesis of Deuteronomy 4, Deutero-Isaiah is no longer concerned with human beings who confess their monotheistic faith: it is YHWH himself who claims to be the only God.

In Isa 45:5, 6, and 18b, the assertion of uniqueness follows on the self-predication, "I am YHWH and there is no other" (*’^{a}nî YHWH w^{e}’ên ‘ôd*). Here the proper name YHWH has already taken over the meaning of the appellative "God." In Deuteronomy, the name does not yet fulfill this function. In an exact parallel to this, Isa 45:22 stresses the exclusiveness of YHWH’s divinity. "I am God and there is no other" (*’^{a}nî ’ēl w^{e}’ên ‘ôd*). YHWH and *’ēl* have become identical.

Isa 45:14 and 21 are even further removed from Deut 4:35. In Isa 45:14, YHWH promises Israel that the pagans will confess: "Surely God (*’ēl*) is among you and there is no other (*w^{e}’ên ‘ôd*), no other god (*’epes ’^{e}lōhîm*)." YHWH’s self-predication in Isa 46:9 is similar. In both passages, *’ēl* and *’^{e}lōhîm* are understood as synonyms. Such an identification between *’ēl* and *’^{e}lōhîm* is unknown to Deuteronomy.

Like Isa 45:14, 21; 46:9 (cf. also 44:6 and 45:5), Isa 45:21 denies that the designation *’^{e}lōhîm* can be attributed to anyone but YHWH: "(I am YHWH) and there is no god but me" (*w^{e}’ên ‘ôd ’^{e}lōhîm mibbal ‘āday*).

A comparison between Deut 4:35(39) and related formulations in Deutero-Isaiah leads to the following conclusion. Although the wording is similar, there are no exact parallels. It is not possible to discern any influence of Deutero-Isaiah’s monotheism on that of Deuteronomy. On the contrary, it is precisely the closest linguistic resemblances which demonstrate that the monotheism of Deutero-Isaiah is further developed than that of Deuteronomy. True, for the prophet, only YHWH is *’ēl* or *’^{e}lōhîm*. But there is no longer any need to add any predicate to the name of YHWH. YHWH simply means God and the only God there is.

We may thus conclude that the monotheism of Deuteronomy did not, as far as can be discerned, receive any "midwifely assistance" from Deutero-Isaiah. It was the deuteronomistic theology which made the monotheism of Deuteronomy part of Israel’s faith.[134]

The Song of Moses (Deuteronomy 32) and Deuteronomy's Doctrine of God

N. Lohfink has suggested that late deuteronomic texts learned the language they used about YHWH from the Song of Moses.[135] True, Deuteronomy 32:1-43 "has not yet renounced the polytheistic mental and linguistic structures. However, YHWH is no longer merely the only possible God for Israel. Even though we consider the question merely theoretically, he is God in a manner in which no other god ever could be."[136] What, then, is the position of this didactic poem – as it is rightly described by the preamble in 31:19 – in the development of the doctrine of God in Deuteronomy?

The composition of the Song of Moses gives us no help with this question. In the present state of research, it is impossible to say with any certainty whether the text of the song belongs to the late exilic or to the early postexilic period.[137] Only if this could be decided would it be possible to exclude from the beginning that the song had any decisive influence. Hence we must, in this case too, have recourse to a terminological comparison in order to decide whether the doctrine of God is dependent on the Song of Moses.

Deuteronomy 32 wishes, above all, to make it known that YHWH is "the rock": "I will make known the/a name of YHWH the rock (*haṣṣûr*). His works are perfect ... He is a faithful God (*'ēl 'ᵉmûnâ*) who commits no injustice" (verses 3-4). The YHWH predicate "rock" then becomes a key motif for the whole song. It occurs seven times(!) and in a strictly systematized manner. After its programmatic introduction in the nominal clauses of verse 4, *ṣûr* is later on in the poem identified with other YHWH epithets through the *parallelismus membrorum*. It is also made clear that other gods are not *ṣûr*. Verse 15 identifies *ṣûr* with *'ᵉlôᵃh*, "God." Verse 18 identifies *ṣûr* with *'ēl*, "God." And verse 30 identifies *ṣûr* with YHWH. On the other hand, verse 31 explains that Israel's *ṣûr* does not resemble the *ṣûr* of its enemies and verse 37 affirms that the *'ᵉlōhîm* do not protect as *ṣûr*.

Apart from *ṣûr*, *'ᵉlôᵃh* and *'ēl*, two designations for "God" are also used with a definite purpose. Both terms are reserved for YHWH. Verses 15 and 18 place these terms in parallel with *ṣûr*. Verses 17 and 21 make it clear that they are not applicable to the gods. The gods are declared to be *lō' 'ᵉlôᵃh* (verse 17) and *lō' 'ēl* (verse 21). Thus even when the formulation is negative, *'ᵉlôᵃh* and *'ēl* are declared to be reserved for YHWH. This nomenclature is only found in the singular. Therefore the singular is found even when the confrontation with several gods demands the plural.[138] Since the singulars *'elô^ah* and *'ēl* have been taken by YHWH, and *'elōhîm* is used for the gods, it is necessary to have recourse to an attributive relation when speaking of one other god. Therefore verse 12 uses the phrase *'ēl nēkār*, "an alien god." Given the language of the Song of Moses, this must be taken as the singular corresponding to *'elōhîm*, "gods." This may be inferred from a comparison of the immediate context with verse 43, where we find the same formulation as in verse 12, only with *'elōhîm*. At the same time, the phrase *'ēl nēkār* carries with it a suggestion of equality with the *'ēl* YHWH. Although *'ēl nēkār* occurs in Ps 81:10, it might well be an innovation of Deuteronomy 32.[139] This is certainly true of the YHWH predicate *'ēl 'emûnâ*, "faithful God."[140] In verse 4, this title elucidates the new metaphor for YHWH, *haṣṣûr*, "the rock"; it is not found elsewhere in the Old Testament.

With the exception of verse 3, where YHWH is called *'elōhênû*, "our God," the Song of Moses applies the term *'elōhîm* only to the gods. They are *lō' 'elô^ah* (verse 17) and do not have the power to protect of a *ṣûr* (verse 37). For Israel, therefore, there can be no *'elōhîm* besides YHWH: "See now that I am he, only I, and there are no gods beside me (*'ên 'elōhîm 'immadî*). I put to death and I make alive again. I have wounded; now I will heal" (verse 39).

This rejection of any kind of co-operation from the gods corresponds to what is said in verse 12: "YHWH alone led him (Jacob); there was no alien god at his side (*'ên 'immô 'ēl nēkār*)."

Verses 12 and 39 make it clear that YHWH's exclusive claim comprises his entire historical activity on behalf of Israel. The existence of other gods is not explicitly denied. But even on the conceptual level, there is an essential difference between these gods and YHWH. Because of its past experiences, Israel realizes that they are powerless.

However, YHWH's sovereignty also extends to other nations and their gods. This means that it reaches backwards to the beginning of time and also determines the end of time. The metahistorical frame for the history of Israel is given an entirely mythological coloring. This explains the attempts of the textual tradition to demythologize this linguistic usage which later became offensive to the YHWH faith.[141] YHWH appears as *'elyôn*, "the most high." Not only is he creator (of Israel, verse 6), but he also rises above the pantheon of the gods. In verses 8 and 43, the $b^e n\hat{e}$ $^{\prime e}l\bar{o}h\hat{i}m$, the "sons of God," surround him as a kind of heavenly court. "When the Most High ($^\prime ely\hat{o}n$) parceled out the nations (among the gods), and dispersed the children of man, he laid down the boundaries of every nation according to the number of the Sons of God ($b^e n\hat{e}$ $^{\prime e}l\bar{o}h\hat{i}m$)" (verse 8).[142] In the background, we have the old tradition of the "Most High" parceling out the world. Humankind is divided into nations according to the number of the gods. It is characteristic that in the Song of Moses this distribution of the nations among their gods (cf. 4:19) through which YHWH limits his own power in history is only suggested (or at least is not explicitly formulated). This implies a greater dependence of the gods on YHWH. In the last verse of the song, this dependence is increased to the point of becoming adoration: the $b^e n\hat{e}$ $^{\prime e}l\bar{o}h\hat{i}m$, "the sons of God" prostrate themselves before YHWH. "Rejoice with him (YHWH), you heavens, bow down before him, all you sons of God ($b^e n\hat{e}$ $^{\prime e}l\bar{o}h\hat{i}m$)" (verse 43).[143] Thus YHWH's power over the history of his people forces the gods to surrender to the only powerful God. This is expressed in a "legal doxology."

The skillful structuring of the Song of Moses, using the terms for God which we have analyzed, shows that this theology is theoretical in character and very precisely systematized.

As far as the "theological" concepts go, the Song of Moses is almost entirely different from the rest of Deuteronomy. Nowhere else in Deuteronomy do we find $\d{s}\hat{u}r$, "rock," $^\prime \bar{e}l$ $^{\prime e}m\hat{u}n\hat{a}$, "faithful God," $^\prime ely\hat{o}n$, "the Most High," $^{\prime e}l\hat{o}^a h$, "God" or $^\prime \bar{e}l$, "God" without an attribute for YHWH.[144] Nor do we find $b^e n\hat{e}$ $^{\prime e}l\bar{o}h\hat{i}m$, "the sons of God," $^\prime \bar{e}l$ $n\bar{e}k\bar{a}r$, "an alien god,"[145] or $\d{s}\hat{u}r$[146] used of the gods or $l\bar{o}^\prime$ $^{\prime e}l\hat{o}^a h$, "no(t) god," or $l\bar{o}^\prime$ $^\prime \bar{e}l$, "no(t) god," or $l\bar{o}^\prime$ $\d{s}\hat{u}r$, "no(t) rock," as what distinguishes the gods from YHWH. Hence there are no signs that the Song of Moses influenced the doctrine of God in Deuteronomy, even less that this doctrine is dependent on the Song of Moses. Deuteronomy 4 took the step to monotheism on its own.

Designations of God in the Song of Moses

(Deuteronomy 32)

Verse					
3	YHWH				’^{e}lōhênû
4				haṣṣûr - ’ēl ’^{e}mûnâ	
8	‘elyôn				
		b^{e}nê ’^{e}lōhîm			
12			’ên ’ēl nēkār ‘immô		
15				ṣûr - ’^{e}lô^{a}h	
17				lō’ ’^{e}lô^{a}h - ’^{e}lōhîm	
18				ṣûr - ’ēl	
21				lō’ ’ēl	
30				ṣûr - YHWH	
31				ṣûrām - lō’ ṣûrênû[147]	
37				ṣûr - ’ê ’^{e}lōhêmô[148]	
39			’ên ’^{e}lōhîm ‘immadî		
43		b^{e}nê ’^{e}lōhîm			

3	YHWH				our ’^{e}lōhîm
4				*the* rock - the faithful ’ēl	
8	the Most High				
		sons of God			
12			no alien ’ēl with him		
15				rock - ’^{e}lô^{a}h	
17				no(t) - ’^{e}lô^{a}h - ’^{e}lōhîm	
18				rock - ’ēl	
21				no(t) ’ēl	
30				rock - YHWH	
31				their rock - not our rock	
37				rock - where are their ’^{e}lōhîm	
39			no ’^{e}lōhîm with him		
43		sons of God			

6
Deuteronomy and Human Rights

German title: "Das Deuteronomium und die Menschenrechte" (see bibliography)

In our day, those committed to rendering our world more humane usually take the concept of human rights as their point of reference. In the intellectual history of humankind, the basis for human rights is found first of all in the doctrine of natural law and in humanist schools of thought such as the Enlightenment. However, if one compares, for instance, the articles of the Universal Declaration of Human Rights (HR) of 10 December 1948 with the stipulations of the Book of Deuteronomy, one finds surprisingly many correspondences, or at least common tendencies. I propose to enumerate briefly those human rights articles which come into question and to refer to certain deuteronomic statutes to which they are directly or indirectly related:

Art. 1: Liberty, equality, fraternity—this brief formula of human rights will serve as a fundamental model for all further analysis.

Art. 2: The prohibition of discrimination—regarding women, cf. Deut 15:12; 22:13-19; regarding an escaped slave, 23:16-17; regarding aliens and former enemies, 23:8-9.

Art. 3: The right to life and liberty—cf. Deut 5:17; 18:10; 22:8; 27:24-25 (life); Deut 15:12; 23:16-17 (liberty).

Art. 4: The prohibition of slavery and of the slave trade—new ideas penetrate the deuteronomic legislation and there are considerable changes in practice, cf. Deut 5:14; 15:12-18; 16:11, 14; 23:16-17; concerning the slave trade, cf. Deut 21:14; 24:7.

Art. 5: The prohibition of inhuman and degrading punishment—cf. Deut 25:3.

Art. 6: The entitlement to be recognized as a person before the law—cf. Deut 1:16-17; 16:18-19; concerning slaves, cf. 15:16.

Art. 7: Equality before the law – cf. Deut 1:17; 16:19; 24:17; 27:19; 29:9-14 (all free people are included in the covenant with YHWH and enjoy the benefits of his law).
Art. 8: The entitlement to an effective remedy against violations – cf. e.g. Deut 17:8-13; 19:16-21 (as a realization of 5:20).
Art. 10: The right to a public hearing by an impartial tribunal – cf. Deut 1:16-17; 16:18-20; 17:8-13; 19:16-19.
Art. 11: Conviction only after guilt has been proved and only according to a law that was in force at the time when the act was committed – cf. Deut 13:15; 17:4, 6; 19:15; 24:16.
Art. 12: Protection of the privacy of the individual – cf. Deut 15:12-18; 23:16-17; 24:10-13.
Art. 13: The right to choose one's residence freely – according to Deut 23:17, even for the escaped slave.
Art. 14: The right to asylum – cf. Deut 19:1-10; 23:16-17.
Art. 16: Freedom to marry and protection of the family – cf. Deut 21:10-13; 25:5-10 (freedom to marry); Deut 5:18; 15:12-15 (as an amendment to the older provision in Exod 21:2-4); Deut 22:22; 23:1.
Art. 17: Protection of property – cf. Deut 5:19, 21; 19:14; 22:1-3; 24:6.
Art. 18: Freedom of conscience and religious liberty – for aliens, cf. Deut 14:21. As 29:9-14 makes clear, slaves are not forced to observe the law, and thus follow the religion of their Israelite masters.
Art. 22: The right to social security – cf. Deut 14:27, 28-29; 15:1-6, 7-11, 12-18; 23:25-26; 24:10-13, 19, 20-22.
Art. 23: The right to just and equitable remuneration – cf. Deut 24:14-15.
Art. 24: The right to rest and leisure – cf. Deut 5:14.
Art. 25: The right to social protection – cf. Deut 5:16; 10:19; 15:4, 7-11; 16:11, 14; 18:1-8; 22:4.
Art. 28: The right to an equitable social order – cf. Deut 4:8.
Art. 29: Duties towards the community, which alone makes possible the free and full development of the human personality – Deut 6:20-25.

In addition, it should be stressed that the human right to happiness embodied in the Virginia Declaration of Rights (section 1) has its predecessor in Deuteronomy. For instance, in Deuteronomy a man who has recently married is exempt from military service and even from holding any public office for a year so "that he may remain at home and give happiness to the woman he has married" (Deut 24:5; cf. 20:5-7). Finally, the entire deuteronomic social order and the blessing it implies is intended to ensure that:

> you, and after you your descendants prosper and that you may live long in the land that YHWH your God gives you for all time (Deut 4:40 et passim).

The wording of the human rights charters could, then, have been influenced by Deuteronomy. In any case, the numerous correspondences regarding the contents, as well as the fact that the social philosophers of the seventeenth and eighteenth centuries to whom we owe the classic catalog of human rights had a good knowledge of the Bible, suggest this as a possibility. Perhaps it may one day become possible to show by historical methods that there is a dependence. It would hardly be fortuitous. Deuteronomy is proud of its uniquely just laws (4:8).[1] Traditio-historically, their roots go back to the period before Israel became a state. At that time, Israel constituted an acephalic segmentary society.[2] Its characteristic features were a great desire for liberty and an egalitarian pathos. Social relations were to a large extent determined by the "fraternal" solidarity which obtains within a family. YHWH, the god of this tribal society, the god to whom they ascribed their liberation from the Egyptian slave state and from the Canaanite feudal state, demanded a just society.

It was this ideal from Israel's beginnings that King Josiah of Judah had in mind as he reformed his state. This reform took place during the crisis caused by the pressure of Assyrian cultural and political supremacy in the seventh century. The plan for a just society to which Josiah pledged the whole people in 621 BCE and which his court scribes made their measure in presenting the history of Israel forms the nucleus of the "deuteronomic law." The heading describes it as a social order "which Moses proclaimed to the Israelites when they came out of Egypt" (Deut 4:45).

Is this claim borne out by the facts? In other words, to what extent does the deuteronomic law project into the legal sphere the historical experience of an exodus from inhuman conditions and the original vision of an equitable tribal society consisting of free and equal peasants in order to create a law and an ethos of liberty, equality and fraternity for life in the promised land? If the statutes of Deuteronomy show that such structures constitute a possible concept for social life, then they are essentially in agreement with the modern human rights charters.[3] True, the modern declarations derive their arguments from the nature and dignity of every human being. Nevertheless, for systematic and historical reasons,[4] the deuteronomic triad of "liberty-equality-fraternity" (or participation or solidarity) today counts as "the normative foundation of all human rights."[5]

In what follows, I shall select certain statutes in Deuteronomy in which these three fundamental rights become manifest in a tangible manner and emerge as a fundamental concern of the YHWH religion. I propose, as a general rule, to pay no attention to literary-historical differentiations, but to read Deuteronomy as a synchronic system, in the form in which it was finally accepted in the biblical canon. The narrow boundaries of our theme force us to dispense almost entirely with traditio-historical comparisons with other ancient Oriental law codes. In the section on preserving liberty, I shall explore the historical preamble to the Decalogue and a version of Israel's credo. They both pledge the people to observe the ten commandments or the deuteronomic law because YHWH has brought them out of (that is, liberated them from) Egypt, the slave state.

In the section on granting freedom, I propose to discuss those individual precepts in which the Israelites are exhorted to remember "their" slavery in Egypt and therefore grant others their freedom in a specified way. The emphasis of my interpretation of Deuteronomy lies in these two sections. The lists of the participants in sacrifices and feasts in the section titled "Raising to Equality" are intended to illustrate where in Israel the class society was overthrown and a fundamental equality was created in spite of all remaining inequalities. In "Fraternity in Practice," I shall give an outline of the ethics explicitly associated with the term "brother." Therein, I propose to relate each of the selected laws, on the basis of the formula used or of a particular terminology, to one of the three fundamental human rights categories. However, liberty, equality and fraternity condition each other mutually and remain related to each other even in the phraseology of the individual laws. In a way, these cases even serve to illustrate the hermeneutic rule of modern human rights articles: "Every individual human right, even though it be especially close to one of the three basic rights, should be interpreted with regard to all three."[6] Finally, in the last section, I want to give an idea of the special features of biblical thought on human rights.

Preserving Liberty

The Book of Deuteronomy regards its "statutes and ordinances " (12:2 - 26:16) as provisions for fulfilling the Decalogue (5:6-21) that YHWH himself proclaimed on Mount Horeb.[7] According to the prologue of the Decalogue, both the deuteronomic law corpus and the ten commandments are preceded by the exodus through which YHWH brought his people "out of Egypt, the slave state" (5:6). Israel did not understand this event as "principally emancipation, rebellion, change, migration, expectation" (Ernst Bloch), but as a saving act of God. Deuteronomy, therefore, never gives "leaving" (*yṣ'* qal) as the reason for the commandments, but speaks—strictly theologically—of "being brought out" (*yṣ'* hi.) by YHWH. (There may be one exception, 16:3.) It is not simply a matter of leaving Egypt. "To bring out" is a legal term for manumission. A slave who received his or her freedom was "brought out." This liberating act on the part of God is what gives meaning to the Decalogue and to the deuteronomic law. In Deuteronomy, human rights are not grounded in a freedom which belongs to human beings because of their nature, but on an act of God which is free, based on grace, and unique in history.

The Decalogue itself is not the sum of a universally valid human ethos, but thematizes "the elementary demands which have to be fulfilled if the freedom described in the prologue is to be preserved. To break one of the commandments in this catalog of what is necessary for freedom would harm or abolish the freedom which is presupposed. Within the framework of this theme, the Decalogue strives for and achieves completeness."[8]

Israel's exodus from Egypt does not, as has already been pointed out, legitimize only the brief official formula of the Decalogue, but also the deuteronomic social order in general. In order to make this connection clear, Deuteronomy draws up its own credo.[9] The parents are instructed how to answer their children when, one day, the children discover the difference between their society and the nations around them and ask why the Israelites do not live as other people do. The catechetic formula is to be something like this:

> We were Pharaoh's slaves in Egypt, and the LORD brought us out of Egypt with his strong hand, sending great disasters, signs and portents against the Egyptians and against Pharaoh and all his family, as we saw for ourselves. But he led us out from there to bring us into the land and

> give it to us as he had promised our forefathers. The LORD commanded us to observe all these statutes and to fear the LORD our God; it will be for our own good at all times and he will continue to preserve our lives. It will be counted to our credit if we keep all these commandments in the sight of the LORD our God as he has bidden us (Deut 6:21-25).

The exodus from Egypt is here entirely adapted to the entry into a new society. Both exodus and entry are depicted with the emancipation of a slave as a model. The person who "brought out" a slave, that is, according to the particular meaning of this expression, emancipated him or her, became the slave's new master. He could "bring him into" his house. This legal term refers to the slave becoming the property of the new master.

The emancipation of Israel from its servitude in Egypt was a legal act of this kind. Israel was freed from the rule of Pharaoh in order to come under the rule of YHWH. The sovereignty of this God abolished human sovereignty. This will emerge even more clearly later on. In any case, in Deuteronomy the formula "exodus from Egypt, the slave state" stands for a liberation brought about by YHWH. This liberation takes the form of a social order. Through this social order, YHWH establishes a society which is the opposite of the system from which Israel has escaped. YHWH then brings this new society into the promised land. And there liberty means life in plenitude in a society that has finally become just.

Our "nutshell credo" (6:21-25) gives the following explanation of the deuteronomic human rights: They are not granted to the individual in a kind of individualistic isolation but only within the new society which God himself has founded. The "we" or "us" which can be spoken by the whole community[10] constitutes the aimed at freedom. From the very beginning, this freedom has a political-theological dimension. Furthermore, justice[11] is possible only if Israel understands its social order (and the human rights contained within it) as divine right and implements this order in its social life (cf. HR 28-29).

Granting Freedom

After delivering Israel from foreign domination in Egypt, YHWH brought his people into the promised land, which became a space for freedom. In the deuteronomic Decalogue, however, he obliged his people exiled in foreign Babylon to keep the sabbath[12] free from work (cf. HR 24). During the exile, the sabbath became the one decisive sign of faith. Yet even before Israel became a state, there was a day on which work was forbidden:

> For six days you shall work but on the seventh day you shall cease work; even at plowing time and harvest, you shall cease work (Exod 34:21).

This life cycle is an original creation of the YHWH religion and implies a social revolution. Its seven day rhythm breaks with the course of the month and the year, even when—as at plowing or harvest time—the natural order as well as economic necessity make continuous work seem reasonable, even unavoidable. Israel does not owe its (agrarian) life to the mythic power of the earth but to having been freed by God from all systems of exploitation and oppression. Even in the old cultic Decalogue, the seventh day probably constituted a powerful sign of Israel's exodus freedom (cf. Exod 34:18). At any rate, the deuteronomic Decalogue grounds the periodic rest from work in the exodus event:

> Remember that you were slaves in Egypt and the LORD your God brought you out with a strong hand and an outstretched arm, and for that reason the LORD your God commanded you to keep the sabbath day (Deut 5:15).

The parenesis associates (but only in this passage in Deuteronomy)[13] the memory of Israel's bondage in Egypt with the exodus. In Deuteronomy, the formula first used—"remember that you were slaves in Egypt"—is reserved for cultic laws with social and charitable contents and for social laws which concern those living on the margins of society: male and female slaves (5:15; 15:15; 16:12), aliens, orphans and widows (24:18, 22; cf. 10:[18-]19; 23:8). The exhortation to think back to the slavery they had themselves suffered under was intended to strengthen the free Israelites in their decision to grant freedom to those who were economically dependent. We shall go on to examine all the laws concerned.

In this context, it is important to realize that even the sabbath commandment demands such a liberating practice. This commandment also refers back to the exodus from Egypt, which the prologue has made the presupposition for the whole Decalogue. However, the sabbath commandment, unlike other Decalogue commandments, does not merely preserve the freedom YHWH has granted to the Israelites. It demands that even people who do not belong to those "freed from the slavery in Egypt" (to whom the prologue, 5:6, is addressed) be granted freedom by being granted free time.

Of old, Israelite law differed from current practice elsewhere in antiquity by not sharing out leisure and work according to social status, granting leisure to the well-to-do and making the underprivileged work (Exod 23:12). In the deuteronomic sabbath commandment, this restructuring of the social system takes its place in the literary and theological center of the Decalogue. This is not the case for the parallel in Exod 20:8-11. Furthermore, the sabbath commandment in Deuteronomy differs from the version in the book of Exodus in several details[14] in order to stress and support the social and humanitarian concern for the right to rest and leisure. In both texts, the sabbath removes the class distinctions between the workers in a "family workers' pool." It is evidently because of the shattering impact of this provision that we are given a list of those who have the right to a day of rest. The list shows changes which are slight from a literary point of view but important in their effects:

> But the seventh day is a sabbath of the LORD, your God. That day you shall not do any work, neither you, your son, or your daughter, nor your male or female slaves, nor your ox, your ass or any of your cattle, nor the alien within your gates (Deut 5:14).

The prohibition concerns a "house" as a working pool. The only "you" which is directly addressed and hence made responsible for keeping the sabbath is the free man as well as the free woman.[15] Then Deuteronomy puts the members of the family, the staff and the animals used for work on the same level. This is accomplished by means of a(n) "(n)or" (really a *waw*, of course), which does not occur in the Exodus parallel, but appears here between those who are free and those who are unfree, that is, between "son and daughter" and "male and female slaves." Among the domestic animals, the ox and the ass, who work hardest, are mentioned first and explicitly. But then all farm animals are granted the freedom of the sabbath as a matter of principle. The list ends with the alien. He or she is a worker who does not belong to the house, yet when employed is in a certain way associated with the family; he or she is "your" alien. This distinguishes the alien from the other social cases, the Levite, the orphan and the widow, who are not mentioned in this list.

In contrast to the Exodus model, the deuteronomic sabbath commandment once more emphasizes:

> so that your male and female slaves may rest as you do.
> (Deut 5:14)

The words "as you do," which are not found in the old law of Exod 23:12, use the extreme case of the slave to demonstrate that the right to sabbath rest is related to equality and to participation in this basic right. As in the triad of the basic human rights principles, the three aspects cannot be separated from each other. Equality and participation, however, are consequences of the freedom which has been granted and preserved. To emancipate the socially disadvantaged and show solidarity with them is demanded by the memory of Israel's bondage and of the exodus event brought about by YHWH. Thus argues the final substantiation of the law (5:15), which has already been cited.

Anyone who has known the hardships of forced labor and then become a full member of society ought to be capable of empathy with those who are in a similar situation and ought to understand that they need rest. He or she ought to feel solidarity with them and therefore to develop a strategy for changing such alienating structures. However, Deuteronomy does not merely make a psychological appeal to the experience of the Israelites; the most important thing is the theological reference to YHWH as redeemer. If free Israelites allow the unfree members of their household to participate in their own lot, they do not merely accept these as their equals but also, by emancipating them, act in a way resembling God's. In the last analysis, the sabbath commandment goes back to YHWH as legislator. Thus it is ultimately YHWH's supremacy which grants human rights to those who have no rights and which protects these rights as being divinely instituted. Furthermore, YHWH's supremacy is an incitement to abolish the class barriers.

Since the earliest times, slavery was part of the socioeconomic structure, even of the *ius gentium* of the ancient Orient. However, we must not simply identify this form of slavery with the Graeco-Roman institution and then judge it from our modern point of view. In Israel, the term *'ebed*—the usual term for a slave—is not restricted to this status or this social sphere, but denotes any relation of a subordinate to his master. The *'ebed* relation cannot exist between two members of the same family. "Fraternity" is not compatible with slavery. And all Israelites are brothers, since YHWH has delivered them from bondage in Egypt in order that they may become his people (*'am*), that is, his family (e.g. Deut 4:20). If there are nevertheless Israelite(!) slaves, this is, in fact, only in order to help these people socially and economically by bringing them into another family when they find themselves in distress. At any rate, this is the view held by Deuteronomy.

The institution of slavery is therefore allowed to remain, but is humanized so as to take human rights into account. This emerges very clearly from the Hebrew slave law.[16] This law argues—as does the sabbath commandment—from the solidarity existing between people who have been liberated, then adds the concept of brotherhood. The first case to be discussed is that of the Israelite who, in desperate straits, gives up independent existence and sells himself or herself to a fellow countryman in order to pay his or her debts.

> When a fellow Hebrew, man or woman, sells himself to you as a slave, he shall serve you for six years and in the seventh year you shall set him free. But when you set him free, do not let him go empty-handed. Give to him lavishly from your flock, from your threshing floor and your wine press. Be generous to him because the LORD your God has blessed you. Do not take it amiss when you have to set him free, for his six years' service to you has been worth twice the wages of a hired man. Then the LORD your God will bless you in everything you do. Remember that you were slaves in Egypt and the LORD your God redeemed you; that is why I am giving you this commandment today.
>
> (Deut 15:12-15)

The characteristic features of this deuteronomic provision are not evident when compared to the version of the slave law found in the Covenant Book, the oldest collection of laws in the Old Testament (Exod 21:1-6). Deuteronomy does not take as its point of departure the needs of the buyer (as Exod 21:2 does), but the desperate situation of the person who chooses to become a slave. That person acquires legal status and dignity. The transaction is not seen as an unproblematic business deal, but as a regrettable, though unavoidable, exception. In a sense, it can be called the last safety net in the social welfare system of chapter 15, and it may only be used when there is no other way of preventing economic disaster. After all, the prospective slave is "your brother, a Hebrew man or woman." The Covenant Book merely speaks of "a Hebrew slave." The term "Hebrew" does not define him as an Israelite, but as a member of a class on the lowest step of the social ladder, which constituted a cheap labor pool. In Deuteronomy, on the other hand, "Hebrew" denotes an Israelite and a fellow citizen. When the text expressly mentions "a Hebrew woman," this is in order to guarantee the position of women as legally emancipated (cf. HR 2) and as "brothers." The work to be accomplished is limited to six years' service. Since Israelite slaves were set free again in the seventh year of their bondage, the slave law of Deuteronomy is related to the year of release.[17] According to the Covenant Book, the slave was free to "leave" in the seventh year. Deuteronomy, on the other hand, obliges the creditor to "release" his slave (cf. HR 4).

Thus Deuteronomy deliberately changes the subject of the action – in comparison to the provisions of the Covenant Book – both at the beginning and at the all-important conclusion of the contract of employment. In other words, Deuteronomy does not allow the slave to do something, but obliges his or her master to do something. This is typical of the deuteronomic laws with their bias in favor of the weak and the poor. The Covenant Book certainly excludes any payment on the part of the slave and obliges the owner to let the slave go "without compensation." However, letting a slave go may take the perverted form of sending him or her away, namely in those cases where, although discharged of the first debt, the slave is in danger of having to sell himself or herself once again. It was precisely from this risk that the Israelites had to be protected. Whereas the Covenant Book simply determines what belongs to the released slave and what belongs to the former master (Exod 21:3-4), Deuteronomy firmly enjoins the master to ensure that his slave is in a position to establish himself or herself as an independent member of society (HR 3). When the moment of release comes, the slave must be "liberally furnished" with livestock, corn and wine. The literal meaning of this expression, which is only used once more in the Old Testament, is "to put a necklace round someone's neck" (Ps 73:6). It is not, then, a matter of "dispatch casuistry" – it would in fact be quite impossible to bring away the foodstuffs mentioned in the way described! – but of honorable provision and of treating the former slave with dignity.

It is hard to find a legal justification for this kind of social rehabilitation and economic integration, but there is certainly a theological one. To begin with, it is a question of participating in blessings received from God. That is the standard used. Ultimately, however, such freedom – not simply "release" – is granted because YHWH "has redeemed the Israelites who were slaves in Egypt." To "remember" is to allow those Israelites who are now slaves to participate in this freedom, since they are "brothers." The final consequence of this would be to abolish the very institution of slavery.

If this institution is still allowed to exist, it is only as a way out for those who need it in order to survive. Indeed, Deuteronomy sees it as a possibility to give not only economic, but also all-embracing human assistance. This can be concluded from the following subsidiary case. In spite of all fidelity to principles, no authentic human relationship may be destroyed, even if it originated in slavery. The free decision of the slave must be respected (cf. HR 6) if he or she explains:

> I do not wish to be released by you

And the text goes on:

> because he loves you and your family since he fares well with you then you shall take an awl and pierce through his ear to the door and he will be your slave for life. You shall treat a female slave in the same way (Deut 15:16-17).

In contrast to the Covenant Book (Exod 21:5), the slave's wish to remain is not determined by his love for his wife and children, who would remain the property of his master after his release, but solely by the fact that he had been well treated, was content with his lot and wanted to continue living in this way. In a symbolic act, he becomes a bondsman forever by being nailed to the house in which he wishes to remain. His right to happiness takes precedence over every ordained release (cf. the Virginia Bill of Rights, section 1). In some cases, being released from slavery could mean social degradation, namely if the former slave could not establish himself or herself as an independent member of society, but had to live an insecure life as a day laborer. Deuteronomy deliberately leaves out those passages of the Covenant Book which concern the wife and children of someone who has sold himself as a slave (Exod 21:3-4). According to Deuteronomy, a slave's family also enjoys protection from being seized (cf. HR 16). Even a slave's private life and intimate sphere were to remain free: one "sells" one's working capacity, not one's person. It is not, therefore, a coincidence that the deuteronomic slave law avoids the title of master: both male and female slaves are "brothers."

We can thus establish that the law concerning debt slavery, like the sabbath commandment, contains the triad of human rights principles. It is, however, fraternity which restores those who have been redeemed by YHWH to freedom and renewed equality. Even within the institution of slavery, this notion transforms the structures of oppression into a loving and happy life together.

If, however, a master exploited and oppressed his slave, the slave could escape by flight. Deuteronomy supports the slave in this. It does not defend the claim of the slave owner, but the human rights of the slave. The law which was to be applied in such a case can only be hypothetically reconstructed. It was probably elaborated later and given a new meaning.[18] The original rule is likely to have been:

> You shall not surrender a slave who seeks protection from his master with you to that master (Deut 23:16).

Such a protection is contrary to the entire ancient Oriental legal tradition. Israel's experiences in Egypt are not here given as the reason for the statute. However, the verb *nṣl*, which is here used (in ni.) for "seek protection, save oneself," is a keyword for the redemption (*nṣl* hi.) of Israel from the power of the Egyptians.[19] By using this term, Deuteronomy could therefore suggest that the protection offered by an Israelite to a runaway slave could be compared to the redemption to which Israel owed its freedom. There are no conditions attached to this reception. The slave alone decides whether he or she is to remain a slave or not (cf. HR 12). Thus the institution of slavery is, in practice, abandoned as soon as it has ceased to fulfill its function as a form of social assistance.

This slave law later developed into a right to asylum for foreign refugees independent of their social position (cf. HR 14). The old law of 23:16 was reinterpreted by the addition of verse 17. This addition reads as follows:

> Let him (the escaped *'ebed*) stay with you anywhere he chooses in any of your settlements, wherever suits him best. You shall not force him.

In this context, *'ebed* (23:16) means anyone in a subordinate position,[20] a minister as well as a slave. "You" no longer designates the individual Israelite, but the whole people amongst whom the refugee finds shelter. The legal protection offered is unique in the entire ancient Orient. Other treaties and law codes decreed that escaped subjects had to be returned to their foreign lords. Deuteronomy does not merely refuse such a demand for extradition, but grants the refugee a higher social status. It ensures that the escaped *'ebed* becomes a protected person (*gēr*) in Israel, that is, a resident alien. This probably constitutes a radicalization of a provision in the Covenant Book which decreed:

> You shall not wrong an alien or be hard upon him, for you were yourselves aliens in Egypt (Exod 22:20).

The formula, up to now a feature of the liberation laws in Deuteronomy, belongs to the traditional background of the deuteronomic asylum law. The refugee is not interned, but may freely choose to reside where he or she likes (cf. HR 3). Incidentally, otherwise Deuteronomy claims this privilege only for God. The stateless are to be fully integrated—"in your midst"[21]—and to live where they choose.[22] It is forbidden to exploit their legally secure but socially weak position—just as it is forbidden to exploit that of the alien.

The resident alien (*gēr*) belonged to a free class. However, Israel's own past showed how precarious the position of a resident alien could become. Therefore even the Covenant Book appealed to the empathy and the Egyptian experience of the Israelites:

> You shall not oppress the alien, for you know how it feels to be an alien; you were aliens yourselves in Egypt.
>
> (Exod 23:9, cf. 22:20)

The argumentation is reminiscent of the "golden rule." This rule would have more or less the following wording: Treat aliens as you would have liked to be treated when you were aliens in Egypt.[23] The corresponding ordinance in Deuteronomy also reminds the Israelites of the common historical fate, but then moves beyond human solidarity. The solicitude for the alien is given a theological foundation. Israel is to imitate the love God shows to all strangers:

> (YHWH) loves the alien who lives among you, giving him food and clothing. You too must love the alien, for you once lived as aliens in Egypt (Deut 10:18-19).

It is no longer merely that oppression is prohibited; love is demanded (cf. HR 25). This love gives the alien what he or she needs for livelihood and thus protects him or her from economic pressure which could all too easily end in slavery. Both participation and freedom are here founded on the fundamental equality of Israelites and aliens before God. Both are in need of his love and his blessing, which he gives—unconditionally. Not even the former slave owners are to be excluded (cf. HR 2):

> The Egyptian shall not be an abomination to you, for you were aliens in his land. The third generation of children born to them may become members of the assembly of the LORD (Deut 23:8-9).

Charity does not dispense from justice. Aliens had a legally defined position. In fact, however, they—like other members of the lower classes—had difficulty in obtaining justice against those who had more social and economic power. Therefore Deuteronomy demands, concerning these people who may be in extreme need of protection:

> You shall not deprive aliens who are orphans of justice. Remember that you were slaves in Egypt and the LORD your God redeemed you from there; that is why I command you to do this (Deut 24:17-18).

Origin, social position, sex, or even religion are not to determine whether the law is to have force. Israel *must* accept equality before the law (cf. HR 7). The Israelites were themselves degraded to slaves. Redeemed, they are now under the dominion of YHWH.

Orphans (even when they are aliens) are, through their claim to justice, the equals of the widows (27:19)—indeed of all Israelites (16:19). They may not be deprived of justice (cf. HR 7). Deuteronomy stresses this particularly in the case of aliens, orphans and widows because these people were especially exposed to judicial arbitrariness. They did not belong to a family and usually did not own property, which meant that they had neither influence at the local court of justice nor sufficient means. Deuteronomy therefore unites aliens, orphans and widows in a hitherto proverbial triad of people in need of assistance and entrusts these social cases to public welfare. In order to guarantee their livelihood (cf. HR 22), Deuteronomy establishes a kind of social security. Every third year, the tithes which were formerly delivered to the Temple are to be stored in the locality so that:

> the aliens, orphans and widows in your settlements may come and eat their fill (Deut 14:29; cf. 26:12).

This welfare institution is extended by the right to gleaning which Deuteronomy grants these three groups (24:19, 20-21). In this context, Israel is once more reminded of its former existence in slavery (24:22). As long as there are the "poor," Israel is, in a certain manner, still in the same situation as it was in Egypt and during the exodus. On the margins of Israelite society, this insecure existence was repeatedly reexperienced.

For Deuteronomy, general prosperity is not a social utopia, but something which God demands. In the middle of the law concerning the remission of debts in the sabbath year, which aims at liberating the whole people from poverty, we find the following fundamental affirmation concerning the society of Israel:

> But there should be no poor among you, for the LORD will bless you in the land, which your God gives you for an inheritance and of which you take possession (Deut 15:4).

Thus the scandal of poverty can be removed in Israel (cf. HR 25). The blessing only depends on whether Israel implements its just social order (15:5—cf. HR 28-29). Since this is open to question, Deuteronomy does contain "poor laws."

Raising to Equality

In spite of all social differences which still exist in Israel, there is one occasion on which the society of status and class has already been overcome in its very foundations. This is the feast (16:9-12, 13-15).[24] Because Israel constitutes a single family—the "family" (*'am*) of YHWH—the Israelites celebrate their feasts together in one single sanctuary. When they hold a meal together and rejoice before YHWH, that is, in mystical union with their God, there can no longer be any divisions. All the needy and dependent are to participate in a harvest blessed by YHWH. The deuteronomic cult order, otherwise very restrained in the matter of cultic rubrics, goes further than the old festival calendar (Exod 34:22; 23:16) and defines the group of participants. The festival community is based on the family; that is, it is not formed from above but, so to speak, constructed from below. The following are to be invited:

> You (that means the free man as well as the free woman) shall rejoice before the LORD your God, with your sons and daughters, your male and female slaves, the Levites who live in your settlements, and the aliens, orphans and widows (those who are not in a position to form a festival community) who live among you (and who are therefore neighbors, Deut 16:11; cf. 16:14).

We have already found a similar list in the sabbath commandment of the Decalogue (5:14). Other comparable catalogs determine who is to enjoy the sacrificial meal (12:7, 12, 18), tithes (14:26-27) and first produce (15:20; 26:11). The underprivileged are not merely to be able to rest "as you do" (5:14). They are also to taste their equality. Why does the joy of the festival reach its culmen only when all are together? There can be only one reason for this: "Remember—You were yourselves slaves in Egypt" (16:12).

Fraternity in Practice

Israel has been liberated in order to live a fraternal life.[25] In Deuteronomy, the word *'aḥ*, which is usually translated "brother," does not specify the sex of a person; it includes women (15:12). The deuteronomic ideal of brotherhood has associations with the time before Israel became a state. Through the exodus from the slave state Egypt and from the oppressive systems of the Canaanite city states, Israel emerged as a tribal society. During the monarchic period, this fraternal Israel was gradually transformed into a stratified society. The deuteronomic law attempts to reform this state by emphasizing the original equality of all Israelites. In this way, it permeates the entire social system with fraternal structures. And it goes much further than the older Covenant Book, in which the term "brother" never occurs.

Deuteronomy does not abolish the king. But it teaches him "not to raise his heart above his brothers" (17:20). The disgrace of the stratified society is attacked where it had its beginnings. In addition, Deuteronomy outlines a state in which the powers are separated, instead of a hierarchic state. Through the fraternal relation, the laws regarding public offices (16:18 - 18:22) abolish every distance between "superior" and "inferior" members of society. Thus judges are to treat every litigation among their brothers (1:16). Both king (17:15) and prophet (18:15) come from the midst of their brothers. The priestly tribe of Levi is to live among the Israelites, their brothers (18:2). The Levites who live in the country have the same rights as their levitic brothers who are employed at the temple of Jerusalem, the principal sanctuary (18:7-8).

The notion of fraternity transforms the other end of the social scale as well. It comes into effect in 15:1-18 when those who, in various ways are unfree, are liberated. Later, some of the humanitarian provisions in 19-25 again make use of the term "brother." In the liturgical sphere, the language of brotherhood does not occur. In this sphere, the class distinctions have already been overcome.

The ethics of brotherhood is, as we were able to determine from the law concerning Hebrew slaves, a consequence of the liberation of Israel by YHWH (15:15). However, the YHWH family will truly become a people of brothers and sisters only when every single Israelite recognizes a needy neighbor as "brother" and treats him or her accordingly (15:2, 7—cf. 23:20; 15:12). Even a personal enemy amongst one's fellow countrymen must be able to count on unselfish help because of this fraternal solidarity. True, even the Covenant Book decrees:

> When you come upon your enemy's ox or ass straying, you shall take it back to him. When you see the ass of someone who hates you lying helpless under its load, however unwilling you may be, you must give him a hand with it.
>
> (Exod 23:4-5)

Deuteronomy takes up these ordinances, reinforcing and expanding them (22:1-3, 4) Above all, the "enemy " is now called "brother." The word "love" is not actually used. But is this fraternal solicitude not in fact the same as love of one's enemies?

The brother must be protected from false witnesses (19:18-19), from being taken as a slave (24:7) and from being degraded (25:11). When it is a question of survival, for instance when a day laborer is not paid, then the alien – "the alien within your gates" – may claim the same rights as a poor and distressed Israelite brother (24:14-15). The alien Edomites may even, as brothers – presumably as participants in the same cult – become members of the assembly of YHWH (23:8). Deuteronomy goes further than any "right" and makes Israel into a space where the same rules of behavior obtain as within a family.[26]

Human Rights and Justice in the Society of God

This fragmentary perusal of Deuteronomy was intended to clarify some features it shares with the human rights articles which I have mentioned at the beginning. Strictly speaking, I have only treated one aspect of my theme. The other aspect, which is at least as important, consists of all those "human rights" which Deuteronomy has formulated but which have no equivalent in any of the many human rights charters. I am thinking of, for instance, the right to celebrate feasts through which Israel lives and fulfills itself as a free society of sisters and brothers. This right can be compared to the right Christian communities have to participate in the Eucharist.

In conclusion, there are two issues which still must be discussed. The first is how the connection we have found between Deuteronomy and the modern human rights definitions can be explained factually. The second is the nature of the fundamental basis of the specific features of biblical human rights as transmitted by Deuteronomy.

As I remarked at the beginning, the human rights discussion was at first a product of the Enlightenment. People spoke of "fundamental rights" (for the first time in France in 1770) and of "natural rights" (1779) which belong autonomously to all human beings because of their nature and dignity. According to Deuteronomy, on the other hand, human rights are, as we have noted, theonomous and are mediated by Israel. In other words, human rights, as defined in Deuteronomy, are part of liberation or redemption, through which God gives his people a just social order and thus brings them justice (6:21-25). This apparently irreconcilable contrast can probably be resolved both in theological and in historical terms. The authentic human face, so the Bible teaches us, can be seen only where human beings are liberated from the "worldly" societies which oppress their true nature. Only through redemption by God does human nature become itself. This history of liberation and redemption does not start with all humanity but reaches all human beings through a people chosen by God for this mission—through Israel. Even in Deuteronomy, Israel is less an ethnic and political entity than a social and religious one. In this society of God, then—later continued in the Church of Jesus—an authentically human life is possible. Only here, "human rights" can be truly recognized.

In spite of the excellent knowledge of Scripture possessed by many of its leading men, the Enlightenment defined authentic human nature and human rights in opposition to "Christian" societies. The main reason for this was that these so-called Christian societies were, at least in their basic structures, in fact largely unchristian and therefore inhuman, suppressing human rights. Yet they continued to transmit the biblical and Christian ideology. This ideology, then, was known, but had to be resisted as inhuman—because of its perversion—in the name of authentic humanity. Thus autonomous human nature became, for the Enlightenment, the point of departure for what was defined as human rights. The philosophers of the Enlightenment knew these rights from the Bible, but defined them in opposition to a Christian society which claimed to follow the Bible.

When we ask for specific features of biblical thought on human rights, we should put the expression "human rights" within quotation marks. We are concerned with a merely analogical concept, and this in a dual sense. As regards the element "human beings," strictly speaking, only believers are meant. For in the end, only they come into their own. Within the people of God, they are granted the liberating justice of God. As regards the element "rights," an essential aspect of ordinary "rights" must be left out of account, and that is the recourse to force. The society of God is a non-violent society. In Deuteronomy, this is expressed by the fact that human rights are spoken of above all in parenetic form and that the exodus from Egypt is given as the reason why they are to be put into practice. Other deuteronomic laws rely on sanctions in cases of human failure or evil–that is, on force, although on legally canalized force. Only the New Testament counterpart to the deuteronomic Torah, that is, the Sermon on the Mount, which also contains all essential demands contained in the modern human rights declarations,[27] is radically non-violent. I have restricted my study to the beginning of this way, to the deuteronomic laws as the Magna Carta of "liberty-equality-fraternity"–the very basis for modern human rights. This may demand "greater justice" precisely from us Christians and may thus lead to human rights being realized in a true sense.

7

The Development of the Doctrine of Justification in the Redactional Strata of the Book of Deuteronomy

A Contribution to the Clarification of the Necessary Conditions for Pauline Theology

German title: "Die Entstehung der Rechtfertigungslehre in den Bearbeitungsschichten des Buches Deuteronomium" (see bibliography)

W. Zimmerli probably expressed a wide-spread view of the difference between the Old and the New Testaments when he wrote:

> The dialectic between law and gospel is not yet openly present in the Old Testament, since in the Old Testament, the name of Christ has not yet been openly spoken . . . In the Old Testament the gift of God and the justice of God remain interwoven. The phenomenon of the law as Paul understood it has not yet become apparent, and could not have. This is possible only in the presence of Christ, in whom divine justice—"the "righteousness of God"—is revealed as the perfect event of grace.[1]

I propose to test this thesis within a limited but central textual domain of the Old Testament, the Book of Deuteronomy.

Some time ago, in my article "Gesetz als Evangelium: Rechtfertigung und Begnadigung nach der deuteronomischen Tora" ("Law and Gospel: Justification and Grace According to the Deuteronomistic Torah"),[2] I tried to show that the deuteronomistic Torah is structured according to a concept of grace. I based my study primarily on the concepts *ṣ^edāqâ* and *šwb*. In 6:25 and 24:13, *ṣ^edāqâ* denotes righteousness as "justifying grace" which becomes effective in the observance of the deuteronomic law. In 9:4-6, on the other hand, we are dealing with Israel's "own righteousness," to which the people wanted to appeal before God. This righteousness, however, is denied both for theological reasons and because of the entire history of Israel. When in 4:30 and 30:1-10, the term *šwb* is used to denote the conversion of Israel, this conversion is understood as a fruit of divine grace which precedes any observance of the law.

Quite independently of my reflections on the subject, M. Köckert in his essay "Das nahe Wort: Zum entscheidenden Wandel des Gesetzesverständnisses im Alten Testament" ("The Word That Is Near: Concerning the Decisive Change in the Old Testament Conception of the Law")[3] has studied the same topic. His methods are, however, mainly traditio- and redactio-historical, and he also takes into account the deuteronomistic literature outside Deuteronomy. In spite of exegetical divergences regarding details, Köckert's conclusions generally agree with my own evaluation of the law. In his literary-historical analysis, Köckert is greatly indebted to the school of R. Smend. Hence he assumes that the deuteronomistic interpretations are not to be dated earlier than the period of the exile. To begin with, they give rise to "nomistic hopes": it is possible to fulfill the law. Taking possession of the promised land is dependent on observance of the laws, and Israel is able to control its future fate. This conception, however, entails the danger of emphasizing one's own achievement. Hence the sequel criticizes the conditional connection between the law and the land. But it is only in late deuteronomistic texts that the non-fulfillment of the law is counteracted by the promise that YHWH, preceding all human action, will render Israel capable of obedience.

Recently, O. Hofius has, in the second volume of the *Jahrbuch für Biblische Theologie*, which has as its theme "the one God of both Testaments", made a broad outline of the Old Testament prehistory of the Pauline doctrine of justification.[4] His investigation is based on Hosea, Jeremiah, Deutero-Isaiah and the Yahwist. He also mentions a number of psalms as further subjects of study. In this context, Hofius also refers to my essay, mentioned above, without, however, commenting on it.[5] Perhaps what Köckert and I have written on the subject is too astonishing. It therefore seems important to attempt to explain things yet more cogently.

This contribution takes into account both Köckert's article and my own earlier article and, in a sense, carries on where they left off.[6] Whereas my former essay was mainly systematic, this one is historically oriented. Unlike Köckert's, my essay is, to a large extent, based on the redactio-critical view held by N. Lohfink.[7] Lohfink accepts the theory of the school of F. M. Cross and assumes that there was a preexilic redaction of the Deuteronomistic History. However, it is also possible that there were several partial editions and that they were not collected in a single work until the period of the exile. In addition, Lohfink assumes that there were several redactions of the exilic edition. Here he also accepts elements of Smend's theory. In what follows, I wish to show that the dialectic between law and gospel was developed as early as in the passage from one of these redactional strata to another during Deuteronomy's discussion of the "law."

According to 2 Kings 23, the version of Deuteronomy to which King Josiah through an oath pledged himself and the whole people appears to have been a treaty. It is explicitly described as a treaty document (*sēper habb^{e}rît*). It contains precepts, more precisely, the basic demand of adherence to YHWH (*hlk 'aḥ^{a}rê* YHWH)—which means being faithful to him alone—and the observance of his "commandments, statutes and laws" (*miṣwōt 'ēdôt* and *ḥuqqîm*), that is, the form the full allegiance to YHWH is actually to take (2 Kgs 23:3). Finally, this treaty document must also have contained threats and "curses" (2 Kgs 22:16). As regards its structure, it was probably modeled on Hittite and Assyrian vassal treaties. On the other hand, there was probably no "historical introduction." At least I can find no clear instance of such a "history" in any of those texts in Deuteronomy which I now assume probably belonged to Josiah's treaty document. Therefore, I shall leave aside all theological reflections related to the systematization of the YHWH faith through the category of a treaty with God and particularly its historical prologue. I shall start immediately with a version of the text which, although it still has its origins in the times of King Josiah, yet contains an excellent theological interpretation of his "covenantal document."

It is a stratum of the text which—with, for instance, the school of F.M. Cross—must be defined as deuteronomistic. Lohfink calls this preexilic redaction the "Deuteronomistic Narrative of the Conquest."[8] In his view, this narrative corresponds to the essential parts of Deuteronomy 1 to Joshua 22. In fact, I think it may have extended even further.[9] In the present context, however, this issue is of no importance. This Deuteronomistic Conquest Narrative was intended, on the one hand, to provide a historical justification for the territorial claims of King Josiah, and on the other, to locate the deuteronomic law in the very beginning of Israel's history by inserting it here. The treaty document of 622 probably had the form of a YHWH speech. Now the deuteronomic law was presented as the speech Moses made before he died and Israel crossed the Jordan in order to take possession of the promised land. In Deuteronomy 1-3, the proclamation of the law, now announced in a preamble, precedes Moses' retrospective view of the events between Horeb and the time at which he makes his speech. In a second speech by Moses, the Mosaic law is presented as the social order for Israel's new existence in the promised land and in this way as a yardstick for its history.

The narratives of the proclamation of the law at Horeb (Deuteronomy 5*) and of the rupture and the renewal of the covenant at Horeb (Deuteronomy 9-10*) had probably already been inserted. The authentic narrative of the author only begins in Deuteronomy 31 and recounts the military occupation and the distribution of the land west of Jordan under Joshua. We are concerned with the two interrelated themes, the law and the land. It is important that the land of which Israel takes possession (e.g., the "link and frame" verses, Deut 1:8 and Josh 21:43) is self-evidently seen as the place where the law is to be observed and the blessing to be experienced (e.g., Deut 5:31, 33).

As a textual example of the conception of law in this preexilic Deuteronomistic Conquest Narrative, I have chosen the so-called "catechismal credo," Deut 6:20-25. It is directly related to 6:17, a verse which I would consider to belong to the covenantal document of King Josiah (cf. 2 Kgs 23:3G/ 2 Chr 34:31). This verse reads:

> You must diligently keep the commandments (*miṣwōt*) of the LORD your God as well as the precepts (*'ēdōt*) and statutes (*ḥuqqîm*) which he gave you.

In 6:20, the children ask questions about the commitment to these precepts, statutes and laws. The "family catechism" first answers with a "redemption narrative." YHWH's bringing Israel out of Egypt is interpreted according to the legal model of the manumission of a slave. Whoever "brought out" a slave, that is, freed the slave, according to the special legal meaning of the term, became his or her new owner and could "bring him into" his house, in other words, make him or her his slave. Against the domain of the old bondage, the land of Egypt, the credo posits a new domain, the land promised to the patriarchs. It does not, however, affirm what one might expect, namely that Israel has become a slave in the land of YHWH. The result of the exodus from Egypt, that Israel was brought into the land of Canaan, is mentioned only in a subsidiary clause.

On the contrary, Deut 6:24-25 give as the ultimate goal (in an explanatory translation):

> YHWH commanded us to observe all these statutes (*kol haḥuqqîm hā'ēlleh*) as an expression of our fear of YHWH our God, that it may be for our own good at all times, in order to preserve our lives as (they are) today. (Only then) will we be justified (before God) (*ûṣ^{e}dāqâ tiḥyeh lānû*), if we keep this whole commandment (*kol hammiṣwâ hazzō't*) before YHWH our God as he has commanded us.

The entire salvation history thus ends in the people's commitment to the law. Within the legal logic of the credo, observing the statutes constitutes an expression of the total submission of the "slave" Israel to its new lord, YHWH, the "fear of YHWH." That YHWH has commanded Israel to keep the statutes (the chief commandment and the individual commandments) also constitutes part of his redemptive act. From the New Testament point of view, this means that it is proclaimed as "gospel." It is only as a consequence of this that the observance of the laws means blessing and life for Israel, in other words, earthly happiness as it is described in the blessings of Deuteronomy. Finally it is of importance that the text is structured in such a way that "well-being" and "preserving one's life" together with "being justified" (*ṣ^{e}dāqâ tiḥyeh*) are projected on to one and the same level and identified as instances of divine grace. What "well-being" and "life" describe as an anthropological state is given a legal and theological interpretation through the expression "to be justified (before God)": Israel will remain in a state of well-being and lead a full life in the land—"as things are today" (6:23)—only if it also behaves according to the state described as "being justified," that is, if it keeps all the commandments, as YHWH has ordered.

The next redaction which is relevant for the present discussion is from the period of the exile. In order to explain the problems present in this text, I must first give a brief outline of the situation it presupposes.[10] Those who lived in exile soon discovered that there were several statutes which could not be observed in this new existence, particularly those connected with the land and with the Temple of Jerusalem. Therefore the obligatory character of the "statutes and ordinances" (*haḥuqqîm wᵉhammišpāṭîm* 12:2 - 26:16*) is defined in a preamble (12:1) according to a realm and a time of validity. They are to be kept in the land of which the Israelites are to take possession, as already prescribed by 5:31 within the Deuteronomistic Conquest Narrative. However, 12:1 specifies "These are the statutes and laws that you shall be careful to observe in the land"—that is, only in the land and only from the time of the settlement until the time they left. This accommodation to reality was a relief for exiles with sensitive consciences, who regarded the law introduced by Joshua as obligatory. The legal differentiation in 12:1 does not, however, imply any laxity. The law remains in force as the will of YHWH which has been communicated once and for all. The differentiation simply takes into account the possibilities of putting it into practice at the present moment. In spite of the freedom granted in the present situation of exile, it is made clear that the law is to be fulfilled again in the future in the land of Israel. For the rest, the ordinances preceding 12:1, which are mainly comments on the first commandment of the Decalogue, and the Decalogue itself (*miṣwōṭay*, 5:29), are not affected by this limitation. They are, of course, to be kept always and everywhere, even in Babylon (5:29, 31; 6:1-2).

However, the longer the major part of Israel lived in exile and established themselves there, the stronger became the reverse interest, that is, putting as much as possible of the deuteronomic social order into practice in the diaspora. The calming of consciences was not to be allowed to turn into indifference towards the entire law. The restriction in 12:1 no longer corresponded to the situation in which the exiles found themselves. This constitutes the psychological and pragmatic context for the strong reaction of the so-called Deuteronomistic Nomist. In order to counteract a general relaxation of moral standards, he emphasized that it is only if Israel begins to observe its law again that it can hope to recover the land. This redactional stratum can be followed until the Book of Judges. I shall, however, restrict myself to the instances in Deuteronomy. Lohfink[11] includes 6:17-19 (now corrected to 6:18-19); 8:1; 11:8, 22-25 (and possibly 16:20). These texts are deliberately used to reinterpret their older contexts. I shall choose 11:22-25 and 6:18-19 as examples.

The "Nomist" has reinterpreted 12:1 by adding 11:22-25 just before this preamble to the individual precepts. These verses demand—in the code of the Mosaic fiction—that the exiles "observe carefully the whole of this commandment (*kol hammiṣwâ hazzō't*)" and that they "love YHWH" (verse 25). For it is only on condition that the Israelites observe the laws, that YHWH will destroy the nations so that Israel may take possession of a land stretching as far as the river Euphrates. Since the text preceding 12:1 stresses that the entire law must be observed outside the land, 12:1 in fact only affirms that it is always to be observed in the land as well.

Deut 6:18-19 has been inserted in a place which is crucial from the point of view of pastoral theology. It is preceded by 6:17, a verse which in all probability was part of Josiah's treaty document. Its exhortation to observe the commandments of YHWH was, even in the preexilic Deuteronomistic Conquest Narrative, the point of departure for a fundamental reflection on the obligation and the meaning of observing the laws. It was developed in the catechismal credo of 6:20-25, which has already been mentioned and which originally followed immediately on 6:17. The exilic Deuteronomistic Nomist reinterprets both texts—6:17 and 6:20-25—by inserting verses 18-19. Deut 6:17 reads "You must diligently keep the commandments (*miṣwōt*) of YHWH your God as well as the precepts (*'ēdōt*) and statutes (*ḥuqqîm*) which he gave you." Now the two nomistic verses (18-19) add:

> You must do what is right and good (*hayyāšār wᵉhaṭṭôb*) in YHWH's eyes so that (*lᵉma'an*) all may go well with you and you may enter and occupy the rich land which YHWH your God promised by oath to your forefathers; then you shall drive out all your enemies before you, as YHWH promised.

The old verse 17 speaks of YHWH's *miṣwōt*, *'ēdōt* and *ḥuqqîm*. These concepts are elucidated by the nomistic verse 18 as "what is right and good" *hayyāšār wᵉhaṭṭôb* in YHWH's eyes. This expression explicitly qualifies the law as "salutary" (*ṭôb*), cf. 12:28. At the same time, the law is detached from the possession of the land and made comprehensible in its fundamental, divinely ordained function in the present situation. The impossibility of keeping certain commandments, for instance of making a pilgrimage to the central sanctuary, does not constitute a dispensation from what YHWH—not Moses—considers right and good. If Israel fulfills this, all will be well (*yîṭab*) with it, even here and now, outside the land. Furthermore, by doing what is just and right, Israel will enter the "good land" (*hā'āreṣ haṭṭôbâ*) and take possession of it. The laws, then, should be observed immediately, even outside the promised land; indeed, observing them constitutes a prerequisite for the conquest. This constitutes an introduction to the topic "observance of the laws and possession of the land," a topic which is also treated in the "catechismal credo" of 6:20-25.

Verses 6:20-25 speak only briefly of being brought into the land and of the gift of "the land that YHWH promised our fathers by oath" (verse 23). Everything is aimed at founding Israel's observance of the laws given by YHWH – not by Moses – on the promise of the land and at showing the salutary effects it will have there (verse 24). The preceding nomistic verses 18b* and 19 refer to this through their terminology (*ṭôb*, the land promised to the fathers). But in a way, they retroject this statement into the time before the promised land. And this becomes important for those living in exile. The Nomist stresses that the possession of the land is a consequence of Israel's behavior. This thesis must not, however, be dissociated from the salvation history which follows in verses 20-23. And the thesis is formulated without any rigidity. The land which is to be "merited" – taken possession of – constitutes the fulfillment of an entirely unmerited promise, an assurance of pure grace, which YHWH gave the fathers by an oath, before Israel existed. And even after Israel has taken possession of the land, it remains a gift. If Israel or YHWH – the infinitive *l^ahadōp* in verse 19 could have either as its subject – drives out the enemies, this is in any case because of a totally unmerited promise which YHWH made to Israel. Hence it is not, even for the Nomist, a question of a demand which could be fulfilled without God, but of a demand which can be successfully fulfilled only if God makes this possible beforehand and accompanies the fulfillment. Thus it is not an external observance of the laws which is praised, but an obedience which YHWH himself has commanded which is rewarded.

In the later exilic period, the Nomist was contradicted from a strictly theological point of view. There was the risk that his parenesis would reduce the dialectic between "grace" and "merit," between divine activity and human achievement in a one-sided way. Lohfink calls the theologian who, as early as in Deuteronomy wrote to counteract this view the "Deuteronomistic Reviser." The final version of Deuteronomy 7 was probably written by him, as were Deuteronomy 8 and 9:1-8, 22-24.[12] The nomistic thesis of 8:1 – Israel is to keep "the entire commandment" (*kol hammiṣwâ*) so that (*l^ema'an*) it can enter "the land that YHWH promised the fathers by an oath" and take possession of it – is, in the subsequent text of Deuteronomy 8 combined with a warning: although it be through its fidelity to the law in the land that Israel has achieved prosperity, it may never ascribe what it has achieved to its own efforts. It was YHWH alone who gave Israel the strength to procure these riches (8:17-18). Beginning with 9:1, it is made clear as a basic fact that there can be no causal connection between taking possession of the land – for the Israelites in exile, this means returning to the land – and any preceding achievement of their own or righteousness of their own (cf. Rom 10:3). There is no such *ṣ^edāqâ*, as is shown by the entire history of Israel, a history of defiance and unbelief (Deut 9:7, 23, 24) from the beginning.

I should like to explore the theologically decisive text 9:1-6 yet more in detail. It alludes to the nomistic passage we have just discussed, 6:18-19 (9:4 *hdp*, "drive away," cf. 6:19; 9:5 *yōšer*, "righteousness" cf. 6:18 *hayyāšār*, "what is right"; 9:6 *hā'āreṣ haṭṭôbâ*, "the good land," cf. 6:18). Above all, the Deuteronomistic Nomist's "key root," *yrš* in qal ("take possession of") and hi. ("destroy") constitutes the crucial motif of 9:1-6. The verb *yrš* occurs seven times, with the qal and hi. stems succeeding each other regularly.

In the background of 9:1-6, we have the conquest of West Jordan. To the ancient Oriental mind, a war was a law suit. The legal decision was made through victory or defeat: the one who was in the right won, the one who was in the wrong lost. Israel could, therefore, conclude from its future successes in war that it was in the right. Now verses 1-3 make it abundantly clear that the conquest of the land west of Jordan is a war waged by YHWH. Israel is aware of this and must therefore regard its history as a kind of ordeal. Hence it sees itself as "justified," *hiṣdāqâ*, not only before the nations but also before YHWH. The criticism in verses 4-6 contradicts this view. These verses first relate the presumption of Israel, who affirms a right to possess the land, then place this affirmation of self-righteousness under divine judgment.

The text reads (in an explanatory translation):

> (v. 4a) When YHWH your God drives them [the peoples of Canaan] out before you, do not think: 'I am in the right, therefore [*b^{e}ṣidqātî*, because of my righteousness] YHWH has brought me into this land so that I may take possession of it. [Whether the quotation of what Israel says stops here or only after verse 4b, as well as whether verse 4b may not be secondary from a literary-critical point of view is controversial. I understand verse 4b as a continuation of Israel's thoughts.]
>
> (v. 4b) These peoples are wicked, therefore [*b^{e}riš'at*] YHWH has destroyed them before you,
>
> (v. 5a) [for] it is not because of your righteousness [*b^{e}ṣidqāt^{e}kā*] or your upright heart that you are able to enter the land and take possession of it.
>
> (v. 5b) Because these peoples are wicked [*b^{e}riš'at*], YHWH your God is destroying them before you, as well as in order to fulfill the promise YHWH gave your fathers Abraham, Isaac and Jacob with an oath.
>
> (v. 6) Know, then, that it is not because of your righteousness [*b^{e}ṣidqāt^{e}kā*] that YHWH your God gives you this good land to occupy. For indeed you are a stubborn people.

Verse 4 regards the war against the Canaanites as a lawsuit. Israel admits that it is YHWH who drives out the peoples of Canaan and allows Israel to enter the land. However, Israel sees the reason for this in its own "righteousness" (v. 4a) and in the "wickedness" of the peoples (v. 4b). The Mosaic speaker develops an antithesis both in verse 5a and in verse 5b. He interprets the entry into the land in conformity with the temple entrance liturgy. The key words *ṣ^{e}dāqâ* and *riš'â* refer to this institution. Nowhere else in the Old Testament are these two polar concepts so closely related to each other as in Ezekiel 18 and 33:10-20 (except for Prov 11:5; 13:6). The background for these Ezekiel texts is constituted by the temple entrance liturgy, with *ṣ^{e}dāqâ* and *riš'â* as technical terms. Thus Deut 9:5 either refers directly to the gate liturgy which had disappeared with the temple of Jerusalem or alludes to it indirectly, through Ezekiel 18 or 33.

Let us assume that the first alternative is the right one. The wording of 9:5 is directly dependent on the temple entrance liturgy. In that case, this verse affirms: If Israel—this constitutes the first argument—in 9:4a wants to appeal to its *ṣ^{e}dāqâ*, this must, according to verse 5a, be a *ṣ^{e}dāqâ* in the sense of an "upright heart" (*yōšer lēbāb*), which YHWH judges in a kind of gate liturgy before allowing Israel to enter the land. *yōšer lēbāb* also suggests a cultic background (cf. for instance Psalms 7 and 11). Verses 6-8 make it clear that Israel does not have an "upright heart." However—this constitutes the second argument—when Israel in verse 4b points out the wickedness of the peoples already living in the land, the accusation is true. Yet YHWH also destroys them—verse 5b affirms that this must be added— because of his promise to the patriarchs, which he now fulfills. In the final analysis, we are concerned with a decision about Israel, not about the Canaanites. This is made clear by verse 6. This verse no longer speaks of the wickedness of the other peoples, but only of Israel, which is a "stubborn people" and has no legal claim to the land. This does away with the difference between the "righteousness" which Israel claims to possess, its *ṣ^{e}dāqâ*, and the "wickedness" of the peoples as far as Israel's relation to God is concerned. History shows that they are all "under the power of sin" (cf. for instance Rom 3:9). That Israel can, nevertheless, take possession of the land is due entirely to YHWH's promise to the fathers (verse 5).

A brief comment on the second alternative: that *ṣ^{e}dāqâ* and *riš'â* in Deut 9:4-6 refer not only to the temple entrance liturgy but also to Ezekiel 18 (and 33:10-20). In plain language, this would mean what, for instance, Ezek 18:5-9 (independently of any connection with the land of Palestine or with the sanctuary of Jerusalem) defines as the ethical and social norm for life in a foreign country. A norm on which *ṣ^{e}dāqâ* and *riš'â*, life and death depend, does not, according to Deut 9:1-6 imply any right to take possession of the land, that is, to return to the native land.

The strong theological emphasis of the Deuteronomistic Reviser, who, in 9:4-6 prevented the nomistic misconception that Israel had a claim because of its righteousness, could, however, lead to another misinterpretation: that every effort made by the people who had to live in exile was senseless. Hence within Deut 4:1-40,[13] verses 29-31 (and then above all 30:1-10 late in the exilic period) specify what is the result of YHWH's grace and what is Israel's achievement. This takes the form of an explicit reference to the crisis, made in the hope of surmounting it. These two texts are connected mainly by the verb *šwb*. Nowhere else in Deuteronomy is this verb given its religious meaning. The importance of the "conversion theology" of these two pericopes is shown by their position. These pericopes are found in the first and the last of the parenetic texts of Deuteronomy and constitute a kind of frame for the kernel of the book, the second speech of Moses (chapters 5-28). I shall limit my investigation to 30:1-10.

Within chapters 29-30, which appear to have been edited roughly in conformity with the structure of a Hittite vassal treaty formula, 30:1-10 forms the blessings section. Written during the exile, this section has been historicized. The verses have been given an elaborate concentric structure. Yet the theme—the return to the land and the observance of the commandments—is developed in intermittent stages. The key word is *šwb*. It occurs more frequently in quick succession than anywhere else in the Old Testament, seven times, with different shades of meaning. The consequence of breaking the covenant, the exile, is the reason for a self-examination by the exiles:

> When all these things have befallen you, the blessing and the curse of which I have offered you the choice, if you and your children take them to heart (*šwb 'el lēbāb*) there among all the peoples among whom YHWH your God has scattered you (Deut 30:1).

What gives Israel cause to examine itself is "all these things/words" (*kol hadd*ᵉ*bārîm*). This refers to the blessings and curses of the deuteronomic treaty document. When the "words" have come true and Israel has experienced YHWH's action, what verses 2 and 3 explicate becomes possible:

> And if you turn back to (*šwb ʿad*) YHWH your God and hear his voice in all that I command you today (*w*ᵉ*šāmaʿtā b*ᵉ*qōlô k*ᵉ*kōl 'ᵃšer 'ānōkî m*ᵉ*ṣaww*ᵉ*kā hayyôm*), you and your children, with all your heart and all your soul, then YHWH your God will restore (*šwb*) your fortunes. He will have compassion on you, turn (*šwb*) to you and gather you again from all the peoples among whom he has scattered you. . .

Unlike the nomistic texts, the return to YHWH here precedes any observance of the commandments, which in any case can only be partially fulfilled outside Palestine. This passage deliberately avoids the terminology of the commandments. In contrast to the preamble of 12:1, obedience in this situation is not suspended, but is limited to hearing YHWH's voice in all that Moses commands. In contrast to the Deuteronomistic Reviser, the restoration of Israel's fortunes is here explained as a consequence of YHWH's gift, of his compassion, but is no longer founded in the covenant with the patriarchs.

According to verses 4-5, YHWH himself will then gather together those who had been scattered to the ends of the earth and bring them back into the land of their fathers, the forefathers of the exilic generation.

With verses 6-8 we have reached the literary and theological center of the concentric structure. I quote verses 6 and 8:

> YHWH your God will circumcise your hearts and the hearts of your descendants so that you will love him with all your heart and all your soul that you may live... You will turn back (*šwb*) and listen to the voice of YHWH and keep all his commandments (*miṣwōt*) which I give you this day.

To love YHWH with all one's heart and all one's soul was, presumably, the first commandment Israel had to fulfill according to Josiah's treaty document (6:5, cf. the Nomist's command to love YHWH in 11:22). Here this is promised as a gift and a blessing. The circumcision of the heart, demanded by 10:16 is now performed by YHWH himself. It is only through this circumcision that Israel will become able to love its God. Verse 8 explains this love of God made possible by YHWH himself as conversion and obedience. Since Israel is already living in the land, obedience is not, as in verse 2, understood merely as "hearing the voice of YHWH," but also as keeping YHWH's commandments as they were promulgated by Moses. The circumcision of the hearts by God precedes the conversion of Israel and is what enables Israel to observe the main commandment and the individual commandments. For the rest, the circumcision of the hearts is not described as something YHWH does once for the generation of the exiles; it is promised to all future generations. For them, too, this grace is necessary if they are to receive the blessing through obedience. According to verse 9, the blessing of all labor and of the fruit of the body, the cattle and the earth will, in its abundance, surpass anything that has gone before. This abundance shows, as does the obedience after the change of heart, that it is not a question of restoring what has been, but of a surpassing new beginning, where YHWH again turns to (*šwb*) Israel and rejoices in doing good (*ṭôb*) for the returning exiles, as he once did for their forefathers.

The concluding verse, verse 10, alludes to verses 2 and 8 and intensifies their message. It describes—as a ground for the blessing in the land—what the full conversion of Israel implies:

> You will listen to the voice of YHWH your God and observe his commandments (*miṣwōt*) and statutes (*ḥuqqōt*), as they are written in this book of the Torah (*sēper hattôrâ*); for you will turn back to (*šwb 'el*) YHWH your God with all your heart and all your soul.

Thus Israel, whose heart was circumcised by YHWH (cf. Rom 2:28-29) is able to follow the deuteronomic social order, not only because the change of heart brought about by YHWH disposes Israel to act in this way, but also because, according to verses 30:11-14, the law is "very near to you, upon your lips and in your heart, so that you can keep it" (verse 14). Here the deuteronomic Torah, according to the explicit witness of Rom 10:6-10, which rightly quotes this passage, expresses "the righteousness that comes by faith" (Rom 10:6). The truly internalized deuteronomic law is "a word of faith" (Rom 10:8), that is, "gospel" (Rom 10:16).

The dialectic between law and gospel determines the attitude to the revealed will of God, even in the Old Testament. It is even likely that Paul's theology and way of expressing himself are deliberate reminiscences of Deuteronomy. What is new in the New Testament is that it introduces the event of Christ as the concrete form which God's saving action takes and (in comparison with Deuteronomy) includes the nations in the justification and in the people of God.

8
The Rejection of the Goddess Asherah in Israel

Was the Rejection as Late as Deuteronomistic and Did It Further the Oppression of Women in Israel?

German title: "Die Ablehnung der Göttin Aschera in Israel" (see bibliography)

Did the Old Testament, in rejecting the goddess Asherah, simultaneously remove women from participation in public worship, perhaps even without providing any compensation for the loss of their former role?[1] This supposition seems reasonable, especially if the Asherah cult did not simply associate female elements with the conception of YHWH, but also offered women a possibility of participating actively in the cult.[2] Such a social change in favor of one sex would indeed cast doubt on the humanism claimed for the YHWH faith. Therefore, the research into the history of the goddess Asherah does not merely concern a chapter in the history of the YHWH-only worship; it also concerns the roles of men and women within the Old Testament world view. More exactly, it concerns those roles within a quite particular construction of the society "Israel," the one which is to be found in the legislation of Deuteronomy. For here there is a second problem. The biblical polemic against the wooden cult object and the goddess[3] it represents is nowadays almost generally considered an innovation of Deuteronomy. Saul M. Olyan, author of the most recent Asherah monograph,[4] may be considered a typical representative of the opinion common today. In his view, the deuteronomistic school did not reject a pagan element alien to the YHWH cult. The worship of the goddess and her cult symbol was regarded as traditionally legitimate by the state cults in Israel and Judah, by popular religion and by strictly conservative believers in YHWH. During the period of the monarchy, it enjoyed great popularity. It was not until the deuteronomistic innovator that the worship of the asherah, because of a conscious association with the cult of Baal, was branded as apostasy—wrongly so, since Canaanite religion at this time did not associate Baal and Asherah with each other.[5] Formerly, it was possible to be against Baal without opposing the asherah. The religio-historical problem this gives rise to may, according to Olyan, be formulated as follows: "It is extremely difficult to explain why one group of anti-Baal Yahwists (Dtr) would oppose the asherah while other anti-Baal circles seem not to have opposed it, and possibly even approved of it.[6] His solution is that the deuteronomists gave a logical extension to YHWH's exclusive claim.[7] In other words, it is an intellectual operation. To begin with, there was rivalry only between YHWH and Baal, two male deities. Asherah belonged peacefully to YHWH. Then she became tendentiously related to Baal. It was logical, therefore, that she should become, so to speak, part of the opposition.

The assumption that, up to the time of Deuteronomy, Asherah had a self-evident place in Israel's religion is based mainly on extrabiblical sources. Biblical remarks on the subject are, unless they may be considered deuteronomistic or later on the basis of literary or redactio-critical considerations, made to fit into this picture.

Regarding this complex of questions, obviously treated on several levels simultaneously, I should like to make some remarks in the following order:

1. What does non-biblical material really allow us to infer regarding worship of the goddess Asherah in predeuteronomistic or early deuteronomistic times? What should be presented here is the picture of Asherah worship in Israel suggested by the religio-historically relevant material from the Iron II period.

2. Is it really true that the rejection of Asherah cannot be documented in biblical sources earlier than Deuteronomy or the deuteronomists? Here particular attention should be paid to Hosea and to the reports in the book of Kings.

3. Did Deuteronomy, in connection with its undoubted condemnation of any kind of Asherah cult also relegate women to a more marginal position in society? It can be shown that Deuteronomy contains a tendency which runs in exactly the opposite direction.

Archaeology and Inscriptions
A Religious Revolution in the Eighth Century?

John S. Holladay, Jr., in his article "Religion in Israel and Judah Under the Monarchy: An Explicitly Archaeological Approach,"[8] treats statistically all archaeological data concerning cultic architecture and "religious artifacts" found at "non-conformist" cult sites or in dwelling houses, and evaluates them for religious practice. The picture is obviously dependent on the epochs from which there are strata and on the available reports from excavations, most of which concern important cities. Nevertheless, Holladay's study provides us with two results which are important for our own questions.

In the first place, the location, size and style of a "sanctuary," as well as the accumulation of religious "equipment," offer archaeological criteria for distinguishing clearly the official national temples and religious services from other cult sites and cults which, although non-conformist, yet were tolerated.[9]

Particular interest should be paid to the numerous and varied female figurines which in addition to horse-and-rider figurines, zoomorphic figurines, vessels for food, model furniture and lamps and other items were discovered both in Israelite and in Judean private houses.[10]

The same kinds of female figurines have been found in Philistine and Phoenician sanctuaries, as well as at non-conformist cult sites in Israel and Judah. This allows us to infer that the objects fulfilled a religious function. In residential parts of the towns, they are—as is shown by the best documented excavations in Beer-sheba, Tell beit Mirsim, Tell en-Nasbeh and Hazor—found regularly, although their distribution is unequal. The statistically dominant figurines are the so-called "pillar figurines."[11] These female statuettes were evidently the central religious objects of the individual households. In none of the houses of Tell Beit Mirsim or Beer-sheba, for instance, has more than one copy of this statuette been found.[12] The pillar figurines were obviously "household icons," but could also be dedicated to a sanctuary with a particular petitionary prayer as votives or be buried with the dead.[13] Scholars are not agreed as to which goddess they represent. Often they are interpreted as figurines of Asherah, who may have assumed attributes of Anath and Astarte.[14] The presence of these female figurines has led to the conclusion that YHWH's claim to exclusive worship was not too well respected in Israel and that the figurines belonged to the "sediment" of pious popularity.[15] Holladay has interpreted the finds according to their presence in the individual strata.[16] It turns out that these domestic cults were not practiced with the same intensity in every epoch. In Hazor, for instance—of which we have the best stratigraphy for the Iron II period—the number of religious objects in Stratum V (after 750 BCE) is, on the average 500 per cent higher than in the preceding Strata XI-VI or in the following Strata IV-III. In Lachish, the cult of the *dea nutrix* appears to have been practiced only in the last period of the site, that is, from about 720 to 587 BCE, or from about 610 to 587 BCE (depending on whether one dates Lachish III to 701 BCE or to 597 BCE). Much the same is true of Jerusalem Cave 1 and of Samaria E 207.[17] In any case, the enormous increase in pillar-based figurines, characteristic of the Iron IIC period in the second half of the eighth and in the seventh century appears to reflect a leap forward in the popularity of the worship of the goddess, probably Asherah.

An inscription in Khirbet el-Qôm, as well as the material from Kuntillet 'Ajrud explicitly mention Asherah. If the word **'šrh* were here used only as a noun meaning "woman, consort"—for which there is, however, no evidence in Hebrew—it would remain an open question who this goddess was.[18] But even in that case, the choice of the word **'šrh* would point to the name of the goddess being Asherah.

The burial inscription in Khirbet el-Qôm, 14 km. south of Hebron, that is, in the heart of Judah, is dated to about 750[19] or 700[20] BCE. In other words, it belongs to a period in which the pillar figurines suddenly increase. The text was written by a man called Uriyahu, described as "rich," hence cannot be regarded as a relict of "popular religion," to be found only in the lower classes. Both the transcription and the translation of the inscription are disputed.[21] However, there are strong arguments for the supposition that YHWH blesses Uriyahu and saves him from his enemies[22] with the aid of his A/asherah, that is, at the very least with the aid of the sacred pole of the goddess associated with the altar of YHWH. Although (the) A/asherah is subordinate to YHWH, there is a suggestion of independence which cannot be shown to have been attributed to cultic objects such as altars and *maṣṣēbôt*[23].

There is no need to reduce the asherah to an aspect of YHWH's power to bless, made visible in the wooden pole.[24] It is equally possible that we have to deal with Asherah as an independent goddess, related or subordinated to YHWH. One may, for instance, interpret *lyhwh* and *l'šrth* as a kind of stereotypic hendiadys.[25] Indeed, in the eighth century, the formula "May you be blessed by YHWH and his Asherah" was in all probability a popular blessing.[26]

This blessing is found on two pithoi liberally ornamented with drawings and inscriptions discovered at Kuntillet 'Ajrud, 50 km. south of Kadesh-Barnea.[27] In all probability, this site was not a desert shrine or a religious center, but a caravanserai or a way station.[28] According to the most recent interpretation, those passages of the most important pithos inscriptions which are of interest to us read as follows: "... I bless you by YHWH of Samaria and by his asherah" (Pithos A)[29] and "... I bless you by YHWH of Teman and by his asherah. May he bless you and keep you..." (Pithos B).[30] The blessing formula *brk l-* with the preposition can only refer to a divine persona or agency.[31] To judge by the paleographic evidence, the two texts were probably written between 776 and 750 BCE.[32] This means that they are close in time to the finds we have been discussing. Whether or not the two figurines which resemble Bes[33] represent YHWH and the goddess Asherah is disputed.[34] It is certain that the accompanying lyre player, whose sex is uncertain, cannot be identified with Asherah.[35] It is also possible that the goddess is depicted in symbolic form, in the tree of life flanked by two ibexes on the opposite side of Pithos A.[36] The fact that this motif is found above a lion constitutes an argument for this identification.[37] In addition to this, there are many other fragmentarily preserved petitions and blessings on stone vessels, walls and doorposts where, besides YHWH, El, Baal and Asherah are invoked.[38] Taken all in all, the inscriptions and religious representations seem to bear witness to a multicultural origin.[39] Thus we will have to say that Kuntillet 'Ajrud gives us no information about "the specific area of corporate religious activity in Israel or Judah during the united monarchy."[40]

Recently, a further witness to the presence of Asherah has been brought to light in the Philistine territory at the boundary of Judah.[41] Fifteen inscriptions, fragments of inscriptions, and single characters were discovered in Tell Miqne, the old Philistine town of Ekron. They were found on large pithoi from a seventh-century building in the "elite zone" of the town. This building evidently served cultic purposes, for in the same room as the pithoi were found small horned altars and disinterred calices. It cannot be determined with certainty whether the inscriptions are in Old Hebrew, in Phoenician or in Philistine. Among the six completely extant words, we find *l'šrt*, "to Asherah" and *qdš*, "holy" on one vessel.[42] Further (according only to American information) "for the shrine" and "oil"[43] on other vessels. According to the leader of the excavations, Seymour Gitin, the engraved pithoi may have contained oil for a rite honoring the goddess Asherah.[44]

The combination of a sacred tree with Asherah on the two pithoi from Kuntillet 'Ajrud has been thoroughly investigated by Silvia Schroer in her article "Die Zweiggöttin in Palästina/Israel. Von der Mittelbronze II-B-Zeit bis zu Jesus Sirach" ("The Twig Goddess in Palestine/Israel. From the Middle Bronze IIB period to Jesus Sirach").[45] She shows that the tree or twig or pubic triangle are iconographically interchangeable with a type of goddess which she calls "twig goddess." In Palestine, the pictorial tradition reaches back to the Middle Bronze Age (1750 BCE). The life promoting and renewing twig-goddess was later identified with the wooden asherah. In the Israel of the Iron Age, she is found—apart from a clay stand from Taanach (tenth century BCE)[46] and the pithoi from Kuntillet 'Ajrud—on a group of scaraboid seals.[47] They are mainly from large towns. A stylized tree is flanked by two worshipers, usually with one arm or both arms raised in order to invoke a blessing. This motif is found all over Palestine in the twelfth century and can be followed until the eighth century.[48] It is striking that in the Iron Age, female deities are no longer portrayed anthropomorphically,[49] or symbolized by a pubis, as they were in the Middle and Late Bronze Ages. The originally primarily female connotation of the stylized tree arises only from the designation of sacred trees as asherahs. In the Iron II period, the motif of a single worshiper standing or sitting before a tree becomes very rare.[50]

The extrabiblical onomastic material from the monarchic period, whose theophoric elements from the ninth century onwards have been analyzed by Jeffrey H. Tigay,[51] contrasts with the architectonic and iconographic finds. According to Tigay's study, 557 of the 592 theophoric names known from the inscriptions are yahwistic.[52] That makes 94.1 percent. Only 35 (5.9 percent) probably refer to other gods. These are mainly from the border districts of the country. Five of the six baalic names are from the territory of Samaria and from the ninth century.[53] For the rest, Baal is the only one among the gods who is also mentioned in the Old Testament. There are no goddesses to be found here.[54] The onomastic evidence does not, however, always mirror exactly the actual religious worship of a time and place; even less does it mirror popular piety.[55]

This means that, during the monarchy, there existed in Israel and Judah, beside the official non-pictorial YHWH cultus, a non-conformist cultus, represented both in the sanctuaries outside the towns and in the residential parts of the towns. There were "images," especially portrayals of the goddess, probably of Asherah.[56] To judge by the archaeological evidence, this cultus was, to begin with, only a thin rivulet, but grew enormously in importance during the crisis-shaken second half of the eighth century. This is why there existed a polemic against Baal in the times of Hosea, but only sporadic rejection of the goddess Asherah. This silence should not be taken as an indication that she was accepted as legitimately worshiped together with YHWH. The cult of the goddess did not spread until the last decades of the Southern Kingdom. At that time, it became an unsolved problem for the YHWH faith and began to influence the minds of large groups. Yet we have established that personal names with theophoric elements were still almost entirely yahwistic. A possible explanation of this fact is that it was too risky to show by one's choice of personal names that one belonged to a non-conformist cultus. Obviously, there was a social barrier. After all, in the choice of location and style for non-conformist sanctuaries, one did not exceed certain limits.

The non-conformist cultus existed but could not be admitted into the public sphere of identification by the choice of names, which had long been yahwistic. This sphere remained reserved for YHWH. Regarded from this point of view, the taboo on non-conformist theophoric names is, in its way, an indication of mono-yahwism. But this does not exclude that much went on behind the scenes which was tolerated, although it was contrary to the official YHWH cultus and was felt not to be quite legitimate.

The Bible
A Struggle Against Goddesses even before Deuteronomy

It was not until the deuteronomic-deuteronomistic literature, that is, until the seventh and sixth centuries, that there was widespread rejection of (the) A/asherah.[57] Probably the only older mentions of "asherahs" are those in the precept to demolish alien cult objects in Exod 34:13, in the narrative of the destruction of the Baal altar and the asherah beside it in Ophrah in Judg *6:25-32,[58] and in the interdiction of cultic poles and stone pillars in Deut 16:21-22.[59] Hosea's speech in 4:18 against "the (goddess) whose shields are ignominy" is predeuteronomic. Hos 14:9 appears to engage in a polemic against female deities, with the aid of word play and of the comparison of YHWH with a luxuriant green tree carrying fruits. To these reactions of the prophet towards the end of the Northern Kingdom, we may add a number of reports in the book of Kings concerning Asherah (the asherah) in Jerusalem during the last decades of the Southern Kingdom.

Hos 4:18 and 14:9.[60] The traditional exegesis of the book of Hosea sees Baal or the baals as the rival(s) of YHWH for his beloved "Israel." Scholars commonly think that the single name "Baal" may refer to various deities which were worshiped in the land, all with different names, sanctuaries and cults; primarily, of course, to fertility deities. One cannot exclude the thought that goddesses too may have been meant.[61] However, because Israel is seen as female, Hosea includes them all under a common masculine name, "Baal." According to many writers, the name "Baal" may even have referred to YHWH himself insofar as his image and worship had more and more come to resemble those of Baal. Hence the name "Baal" was used to distinguish this image of YHWH from the "true" YHWH. This is normally affirmed for the entire book of Hosea. In fact, however, it appears to be true mainly of chapter 2 (2:10, 15, (18), 19).[62] Outside that very special part of the book, Hosea 1-3, to which all these instances belong, the word "Baal" only occurs three times (9:10; 11:2; 13:1). However, these verses probably do not refer to a divine rival of YHWH's in the days of Hosea, but to a divinity connected with the historical sins of Israel.[63] If, then, Baal is not present in the whole book, and if Hosea 1-3 has a different literary history from the textual units which follow,[64] the figure of Baal cannot be automatically introduced every time Hosea attacks the orgiastic cult in the high places. Thus there can be a renewed discussion regarding the cult against which the prophet's polemic is directed. There are texts which tend to make one think of a fertility goddess, even though Hosea does not used the name *ʾašērâ*.[65]

In an article as yet unpublished, Norbert Lohfink[66] demonstrates that Hos 4:4-19 specifically accuses Israel of serving a goddess. The symbolic gender roles are not distributed in the same way as in chapters 1-3. The man Israel-Ephraim has, according to 4:16-17, gotten himself into a disastrous situation without issue, which makes it impossible for YHWH to shepherd him: "Ephraim has been joined to an idol—abandon him!" (4:17).[67] However, the idol which exercises an almost magical fascination for Israel is a goddess. The following scene from the sacrificial cult with its liberal wine drinking and its sacral sexual intercourse illustrates the kind of union in which the men indulged.

> When their wine drinking is finished,
> they take their fill of fornication.
> With intense desire, they love
> *the* (goddess) *whose shields are ignominy* (Hos 4:18).[68]

Hosea does not deign to give the goddess any name,[69] but denigrates her by identifying her only through her emblems. The context shows that she is a goddess of love. Whether her name was Asherah, Anath or Astarte must remain an open question.[70]

The full description of cultic practice and of the catastrophic effects of these sexual practices on women can be found in 4:11-14. The exterior frame is constituted by orgiastic sacrificial meals where alcohol and divination lead the people astray and give them a "promiscuous spirit" (*rûaḥ zᵉnûnîm*, 4:12bα). The men (!) "act promiscuously, are unfaithful to their God" (*wayyiznû mittaḥaṯ ʾᵉlōhêhem*),[71] and sacrifice and burn incense (4:12bβ-13a).

The key statement occurs in 4:13b, 14aα. The real victims of the cult of the goddess are said to be the women, above all the "daughters" and "daughters-in-law," obliged to submit to sacral intercourse.[72] In the last analysis, the priests are responsible for this sexual abuse of women in the name of the goddess. During the sacrificial feasts, the priests themselves have recourse both to "secular" prostitutes (*ʿim hazzônôt*) and temple prostitutes (*ʿim haqqᵉdēšôt*, 4:14aβb). Through their example, they ruin the people, who are lacking in understanding (4:14b). Because the priests have "rejected knowledge" and "forgotten the Torah" (4:6), the fundamental institution of human affection (*ḥesed*, cf. 4:1), marriage, has been destroyed.[73] Hosea, at any rate, considers that the cult of the goddess attributes a humiliating role to women and exploits them, not that they find human fulfillment in this cult.[74]

It is possible that Hos 10:5-8 also speaks of a goddess. Francis F. Andersen and David Noel Freedman in their commentary play with this possibility without, however, making up their minds about it.[75]

Hence I only mention the notion without exploring it further.[76]

At the end of the book of Hosea, the "love dialogue"[77] which YHWH maintains with Israel makes it obvious that there is no need for a goddess of love and fertility. In 14:9, YHWH says:

A Ephraim—what have I[78] (in common) with the idol?[79]

B I myself answer (*'ānîtî*) and watch over him (*wa'ešûrennû*)

B′ I am like a luxuriant[80] juniper[81]

A′ I bear fruit for you (*peryekā*).

Even from a stylistic point of view, the prepositional phrases (*lî* and *mimmenû*) referring to YHWH accentuate the two exterior members (A - A′), and the emphasized "I" (*'anî*) of the middle members (B - B′)[82] accentuate YHWH's exclusive claim on Israel. In this passage, too, the rival of YHWH is probably not Baal but a goddess, who in 4:17 is apostrophized together with the "idol" (*'aṣabbîm*).[83] This also appears probable from the formulation *'ānîtî wa'ašûrrenû* with its phonetic allusions to Anath and Asherah.[84] That both the imagination and practice of Israel associated YHWH with these figures is testified to by the question "What have I in common with the idol?" YHWH alone fulfills the functions which Israel ascribes to the goddess of love and fertility.[85] For like a luxuriant juniper he surpasses the tree or the wooden pole of the goddess (14:9).[86] It is only through him that "Ephraim" obtains his "fruit" (cf. 9:16).[87]

The Reports in the book of Kings. In some passages in the book of Kings, too, Asherah appears to be an independent goddess. Klaus Koch[88] has pointed out that it is only in connection with the capitals Samaria (1 Kgs 16:33; 2 Kgs 13:6) and Jerusalem (1 Kgs 15:13; 2 Kgs 18:4; 21:7 [differently in verse 3]; 23:4, 6-7) that (the) A/asherah (*hā'ašērâ*) is mentioned—at least if we exclude Judges 6:25-30 and the text-critically uncertain reference in 1 Kgs 18:19. The Jerusalem texts, to which Koch limits his analysis, show that the asherah played "a major part in the idolatrous practices at the temple." The asherah "was considered the great temptation for the court as well as for the people. It is true that 2 Kgs 21:3 and 23:4 give her a Baal as a companion, but his role remains vague. In contrast to his female partner, he remains in the background." In contrast to Asherah in 1 Kgs 15:13 and 2 Kgs 21:7, "he is honored neither by a *mipleṣet* nor by a *pesel*."[89] To the extent that the reports in the book of Kings allow us to draw retrojective historical conclusions regarding the role of Asherah in the ninth and eighth centuries, they fit well into the overall archaeological picture, once we have discounted the deuteronomistic qualifications.

Every now and then, especially in the major temples, there was an Asherah cult. But it is on the whole unlikely that this cult actually left its mark on popular religious life.[90] Yet even in predeuteronomic times, there was a struggle against the Asherah. At the beginning of the ninth century, for instance, King Asah according to a report which was probably historical[91] in 1 Kgs 15:13, had the image that his grandmother Maacah had had made cut down and burnt. However, in the eighth century, there was a revitalization of the cult. Therefore, Hezekiah (2 Kgs 18:4) had the sacred pole of Asherah removed from the Jerusalem temple. After a restoration under Manasseh (2 Kgs 21:3, 7), Josiah in the seventh century did the same thing (2 Kgs 23:6). This happened in the context of an extensive cult reform for which there is also archaeological evidence.[92]

To sum up: It is perfectly possible to gain an idea of the part played by Asherah in the predeuteronomic/predeuteronomistic religion of Israel. This part varies in importance according to the period. It is only in the eighth century that the cult of Asherah is revitalized and again becomes wide-spread. The asherahs of the official national sanctuaries correspond to the pillar figurines which are increasingly worshiped at non-conformist sanctuaries and in many private households. As soon as a particular threshold has been crossed, the sociologico-archaeological classification of the cult sites and the difference between the dominant religion and personal piety prove irrelevant for prophetic criticism. The cult of the goddess cannot be tolerated by the authentic YHWH faith. It makes no difference whether it takes place in the "high places" or in private houses or in national sanctuaries such as the temples of Samaria and Jerusalem.[93] There is immediate resistance in the name of YHWH. This is obvious from Hosea, but the same thing happened in Judah. The deuteronomists are not the originators. Rather, one might say that historical distance enables them to move to the level of reflection.

Deuteronomy
Denigration of Asherah, Promotion of Women.

What Hosea attacked as an acute danger for the authentic YHWH faith and its social ethos, Deuteronomy attempted to control through a theologico-pastoral strategy, systematically and with the aid of legislation. Against the background of the texts quoted above, this means that Deuteronomy resisted the conceptions of love and fertility present in popular piety, but integrated what was authentic in these experiences in the YHWH faith. It prohibited magical rites as well as all forms of cultic sexual exploitation of women or men,[94] but took over some genuinely human values and made them part of the harvest festivals.[95] At the same time, Deuteronomy made sure, by introducing a new conception of instruction, that all Israelites would assimilate its liturgical and social programs, irrespective of the priests.[96] Of course, the religio-historical relations I have spoken of must be worked out more in detail. In what follows, I shall restrict myself to the third question posed at the beginning: How did the extermination of the goddess influence the image of YHWH and, above all, the status of women in the cultus and in society?

From the Goddess to Fertility as YHWH's Blessing. Hosea criticized a cult in which Israel was "joined to" (Hos 4:17) the "idol" (*'ᵃṣabbîm*) of a goddess and expected to receive its "fruits" from this idol (cf. Hos 14:9). A cultic image representing a goddess is no longer compatible with the exclusive claim of YHWH. Therefore Hosea parodies and disqualifies the idol in various ways (cf. Hos 10:5-6). Perhaps there is an echo of his polemic against the *pᵉsilîm*[97] (Hos 11:2) in the singular formulations "obscene idol of Asherah" (*mipleṣet lā'ᵃšērâ*, 1 Kgs 15:13) and the "image of Asherah" (*pesel hā'ᵃšērâ*, 2 Kgs 21:7). But whereas these designations still show Asherah's claim to divine status, Deuteronomy in the context of its cultic purification (7:5; 12:3; 16:21)[98] only mentions a cultic pole, lacking in any numinous dimension. Such an asherah is not conceivable within the YHWH religion (cf. Hos 14:9); it merely belongs to the requisites "the nations" needed in order to "worship their gods" (Deut 12:2) or which they used to persuade Israel to worship other gods (Deut 7:4). The asherah of Deuteronomy does not manifest any particular relation to vegetation rites. This is true even of the expression (occurring only in Deuteronomy) "to plant an asherah" (*nt' 'ᵃšērâ*, Deut 16:21). This expression should be interpreted in analogy with the Akkadian expression "to erect a stele."[99] For the rest, the asherah is not even explicitly criticized, it is simply forbidden, along with other "foreign" cultic objects (Deut 7:5 and 12:3, probably in connection with Exod 34:13). The list of individual objects in the "high places" became more and more detailed as time went on. Whereas Hosea only mentioned altars and stone pillars (10:1, 2; cf. 3:4) and Exod 34:13 added the cultic poles, Deut 7:5 and 12:3, in commanding the annihilation of all such objects, added a fourth object, the "cultic image(s)" (*pᵉsilîm*). These are distinguished from the *maṣṣēbôt* and *'ᵃšērôt* already mentioned and serve to rob them of their last glimmer of divinity.[100] The verbs associated with the cultic objects manage to reduce these to destructible matter. An "asherah" is simply "wood" (*'ēṣ*) that Israel must not "plant" (*nṭ'*, Deut 16:21); "asherahs" are to be "cut down" (*gd'* pi., Deut 7:5) or "burnt in fire" (*śrp bā'ēš*, Deut 12:3).

Deuteronomy managed to demythologize Astarte in an even more radical manner. She is present—in a "desemanticized," yet etymologically transparent manner—when in Deut 7:13, 28:4, YHWH blesses (or in 28:18, 51 curses) "the offspring of your herds[101] and the lambing[102] of your flocks" (*šᵉgar 'alāpêkā wᵉ'ašṭᵉrōt ṣō'nêkā*). Used here in parallel, *šeger* and **'ašteret* occur in Ugarit as the names of Canaanite goddesses, and also in an inscription from Tell Deir 'Alla, dating from the end of the ninth or the beginning of the eighth century.[103] Behind *'ašṭᵉrôt ṣō'n*, we discover Astarte as "ruler of the animals," or rather, as "nurturer of goats,"[104] symbolized by a (female) sheep or honored by sacrifices of (female) sheep.[105] Deuteronomy[106] dedivinized the names **'ašteret* and *šeger*, which formerly referred to fertility deities, by using these terms to designate what was formerly the bounty of these deities.[107]

Indeed, fertility and increase follow from the blessing which only YHWH can give. This is creative and innovative use of language. In fact, the demythologization took place earlier. As Othmar Keel concludes from the glyptic, "the reduction of female deities to the bounty they distributed (suckling animals, trees) which took place, in iconography at least, in the Iron II period, made it easier to transfer the power to bless to one (male) deity."[108]

That Deuteronomy scorns the goddess or mentions her only under the guise of fertility, is, however, merely the negative side of its extensive theology of blessing. This can be shown even for those passages which order the destruction of the asherah. In the context of its radical dissociation from all alien cults (7:4-5, 25-26), chapter 7 promises that the fertility of human beings, of the land, and of the herds will exceed that of the nations. This has its origin in the unique love between YHWH and Israel, which is indissolubly bound up with the cultic and social orders of Deuteronomy (7:12-14). Therefore the sacrifices, which according to chapter 12, are to be offered in the one legitimate sanctuary, in clear opposition to Canaanite cultic practice (12:2-3, 29-31; cf. 16:21-22), do not function as a ritual for securing future fertility, but express the common rejoicing of men and women "before YHWH," because YHWH has blessed them (12:4-28).

Both Men and Women Had the Right to Bring Sacrifices to YHWH.[109] Deuteronomy differs from ancient Near Eastern legislation, as well as from biblical legislation elsewhere, in that it is not simply male-centered, but regards men and women as brothers and sisters.[110] This is true, at any rate, of the final version of the book. This final version is to be understood as a systematic overall design for Israel as a society. The fraternal view is seen mainly in the attitude towards the classic fringe groups—the orphans, the widows the resident aliens and the strangers. These groups are "demarginalized" and saved from destitution.[111] The same leading principle brings about a change in the position of women. In 15:12, the word "brother" (*'aḥ*) explicitly refers to women as well as to men. Deuteronomy has a strong inclination towards the emancipation of women.[112] Hence we have reason to expect the deuteronomic social reform to offer women new opportunities in the liturgical realm as well. In the actual case, this would mean that women, too, could bring sacrifices. Such a permission may, however, be expressed only with extreme caution. There has been little discussion of this possibility among exegetes. In what follows, I shall assume a unity of intent in the deuteronomic legislation on liturgical renewal. In general, I shall make use of a synchronic reading of the final redaction.

Before considering the main question, we should make it clear that the offering of sacrifices in Deuteronomy is not the task of the priests, but of every Israelite. Deut 18:3 explicitly states that "members of the people," and not the priests, offer sacrifices. The priests receive a due from the people (*me'et hā'am*), from those who offer sacrifices (*me'et zōbḥê hazzebaḥ*). There is a fixed tariff. But the priests are not paid for offering sacrifices. This is equally true of their "Levite brethren" when these come to Jerusalem and begin to exercise priestly functions in the temple (18:6-8). These functions are related to the Torah, kept in the central sanctuary with the Ark. Sacrifice and cult are not mentioned as priestly tasks. As for the Levites living in other towns, deuteronomic cultic legislation desires their participation in various liturgical acts, but never explicitly mentions sacrifices in this connection.[113]

Women are never excluded from "those among the people" mentioned in 18:3 as offering sacrifices and distinguished from the priests. On the contrary, according to 29:10, they are among those entering into the covenant at Moab, a covenant through which YHWH makes Israel his own people (29:9-14). Deut 31:12 explicitly mentions them in the context of the Feast of Booths. Every seventh year, all Israel is to recall the content of the Torah by reciting it in a festival ritual. This constitutes a renewal of the Horeb situation, the origin of this social order (31:10-13). In spite of that, we cannot, of course, infer from 18:3 alone that women had the right to offer sacrifices.

What was specific about the deuteronomic liturgical reform was that the entire cult was concentrated to the Jerusalem Temple as the only legitimate YHWH sanctuary. The reasons for this liturgical reform need not be presented here.[114]

In any case, this reform also changed the status of the sacrifices. The deuteronomic understanding of sacrifices must not be harmonized with texts from the Priestly Writings. Deuteronomy distinguishes between "profane slaughtering" in order to eat the flesh, a slaughtering which is permitted always and everywhere (12:15, 21), and slaughtering for sacrificial purposes, which is restricted to the central sanctuary (12:27). Even vegetable offerings had to be brought there (12:6). The new order also corresponded to the deuteronomic "theology of the people of YHWH." What had formerly been a private form of piety now became part of the symbolic realization of the society of Israel in the cult.[115] Did women have to pay the price for this centralization, since, with the abolition of the local sanctuaries, they lost the shrines at which they had been accustomed to seek "guidance, release and consolation"?[116]

In our context, the lists of participants and the sequence of the sacrificial acts in the cultic order of Deuteronomy[117] are of interest. Since the sacrifices and offerings are made mainly in gratitude for the blessing YHWH has bestowed on a family (12:7; 14:24; 16:10, 17; 26:11), all family members participate. To them, we can normally add the local Levites, for whose social integration Deuteronomy provides with the aid of sacrifices and feasts. This "public interest" of Israelite society constitutes a reason for not classifying even the sacrifices of these family feasts at the central sanctuary as "private sacrifices."

The shortest list of participants reads "you and your family" (14:26; 15:20; cf. 26:11) or "you and your families" (12:7). This formula existed before Deuteronomy and was used later as well.[118] But the formula could have an explosive impact on society. This becomes obvious only when the cultic legislation interprets it and lists the members of the family—or, to be precise, of the "household" (*bayit*)—in detail and expands it in various ways, depending on the context. According to 12:18, the following persons are invited to participate in the sacrifice: "you, your son and your daughter, your male and female slaves, as well as the Levites living in your settlements." The same is the case for the Feast of Weeks and the Feast of Booths (16:11 and 16:14) and the sabbath (5:14). The same list can be found with the participants in the plural (12:12).

The list aims at completeness. Of the people normally found in an Israelite extended family, the "fathers" and "brothers" are missing. So are the "neighbors." But they all have families of their own and are thus directly addressed by the "you" of the ordinances. It is all the more remarkable that "your wife" is not mentioned. This can mean one of two things: either the free woman and housewife was included in the "you" or the family mother had to stay at home alone, take care of the house and do all the work, while the whole family, including the slaves, went off on a pilgrimage, enjoyed the sacrificial meal and rejoiced in Jerusalem. The second alternative is highly improbable.[119] Such an interpretation would run contrary not only to the older pilgrimage tradition (1 Samuel 1), but also to the equal esteem for men and women shown elsewhere in Deuteronomy.

Nevertheless, it seems quite as improbable that a family should simply leave their house and farm empty and set off for Jerusalem with all their servants. Must we, then, conclude that the ordinance was the "impracticable theory of an ideologist"? The other liturgical regulations show that Deuteronomy was not interested in rubrical casuistry, but in theological goals. It was probably presupposed as self-evident that a few people had to stay at home—but there is nothing to suggest that this was the particular task of the housewife and mother. If the entire family was invited to the sacrifice and the feast, it is, given the world-view of Deuteronomy, just as likely that a woman set off for Jerusalem at the head of her family—for instance if her husband was busy looking after the farm or was doing war service or was, perhaps, a prisoner of war. Evidently, the "you" (*'attâ, 'attem*) of the list addresses women as well as men.[120] Other observations support this view.

The literary technique through which Deuteronomy imperceptibly allows women to approach the altar is, however, clearly different from the way in which it formulates central items of its program, such as the centralization of the cult. There may be various reasons for this. In any case, Deuteronomy does not explicitly state that women are also allowed to offer sacrifices. Deuteronomy leaves, so to speak, the door partially open for future legal development. The intention is, nevertheless, obvious. Those who read carefully notice it.

From the formal structure of the list of participants, one would expect the housewife to be explicitly, not implicitly mentioned. If the "you" in the list addresses men alone, why is there no "and your wife" added to "your sons and daughters," "your male and female slaves"? It is obvious that the difference in the formulation in Deuteronomy is deliberate. The "you" addressed does not in fact yet belong to an authentic list; and now the moment has come to elucidate a certain vagueness in the explanations up to now. Deuteronomy wishes to define the same right to offer sacrifices for men and women, while excluding the still dependent sons and daughters, as well as the farm hands and maids from this right. Syntactically speaking, the authentic list forms a parenthesis, inserted only where the ritual concerns all participants, that is, together with "eat" (*'kl*) and/or "rejoice" (*śmḥ*). If the family mother were mentioned here, the other finite verbs would refer only to the free man. As things are, however, all masculine singular forms in the statutes concerning sacrifices and festivals refer, text-pragmatically speaking, to women as well as to men.[121] Since the "you" refers to women as well and since the free woman is not mentioned in the authentic list, women are not counted simply as part of the household. They are as competent as men to perform any act connected with the sacrifices.

To affirm that a woman could perform cultic sacrifices is not, of course, the same as to affirm that she had to do the whole work alone. No doubt several people assisted in the slaughtering of an animal. This was certainly the case in the temple as well, where the entire household, including farm hands, participated in the sacrifice. The decisive point is not who did the actual slaughtering, but whether a woman could formally be the one to perform the sacrifice, for instance by pouring the blood on the altar (12:27) or by setting the basket with the first fruits before the altar (26:10; cf. 26:4).

It was probably not until Deuteronomy that women were granted the right to offer sacrifices. It all happens in an almost hidden fashion and with great caution. This may also be inferred from the differences between the addressees of the regulations for the Feast of Weeks and the Feast of Booths in 16:9-12, 13-15 and in 16:16-17. One can argue about whether the old text of 16:16-17 is reinterpreted by the preceding unit or whether 16:9-12, 13-15 was relativized and restricted by the addition of 16:16-17 as a redactional summary of the festival calendar.[122] In that case, the reinterpretation would have meant a reintroduction of the original practice.[123]

On the basis of the source material in our possession, it cannot be determined whether Israelite women in deuteronomic times performed important functions in non-yahwistic cults,[124] or even what proportion of them participated in these cults at all.[125] Neither do we know to what extent the deuteronomic outline of a social order, including the equality and active participation of women in the cult, became reality or remained a utopian program. In any case, this outline, which is based on faith in YHWH, sees equality in the liturgical domain as a possibility in the legal order of Israel.[126]

In comparison with the book of Hosea, which combats the erotic female deities, but includes some of their features in its image of YHWH through the daring metaphor of 14:9, Deuteronomy distances itself much further from such deities. It rejects Asherah and her cultic symbol, and, in a very subtle way, reduces Astarte to her fertility function and attributes the granting of fertility to YHWH. Whereas Hosea only pities women as the victims of male transgressions in the legal and cultic domains, Deuteronomy to a high degree attempts to give them equal social and cultic rights with men. And there is more to it than that: All Israel is to experience true humaneness in the joy of the feast before YHWH and in the blessing of his social order.

9
Deuteronomy and the Commemorative Culture of Israel

Redactio-Historical Observations on the Use of למד

German title: "Das Deuteronomium und die Gedächtniskultur Israels" (see bibliography)

Jan Assmann in his book *Das kulturelle Gedächnis* calls Deuteronomy the "basic text of a form of collective mnemonics, which constituted something entirely new in the contemporary world and, together with a new form of religion simultaneously founded a new type of cultural memory and identity."[1] This new technique needed neither king nor temple nor a territory as natural focussing points for the collective memory.[2] It becomes possible "to remember in the land ties which originated outside the land and belong to the extraterritorial history of Israel: Egypt – Sinai – the desert – Moab." Hence it is also possible "to remember Israel outside Israel and that means . . . not forgetting Jerusalem in the Babylonian exile."[3] For the identity which through the mnemonics of Deuteronomy develops into a "new, interiorized and spiritualized form" is based only on the Torah as a "portable motherland" (Heinrich Heine).[4] "Whoever lives according to these laws never for a moment forgets who he is and where he belongs. This form of life is so difficult that it can only be realized if the laws are ceaselessly memorized and kept in mind."[5]

In his case studies of the interrelations between writing, memory and political identity in the higher civilizations of antiquity, Assmann rightly chose Deuteronomy as a "paradigm of cultural mnemonics"[6] for Israel, although he offered no inner-biblical reasons for this. For under King Josiah, who in 621 BCE pledged Judah to observe Deuteronomy as "state law," "for the first time in the history of Israel, the process of learning became a technocratic way of promoting faith in YHWH."[7] Afterwards, both in Jerusalem and later in the Babylonian exile, people strove to actualize the new conception of an authentic society of YHWH in the future YHWH state. No other document in the Old Testament used למד, the most important verb for "teaching" and "learning" as often as Deuteronomy.[8] The only instances of this root in the Pentateuch are found in Deuteronomy. Of course, the didactic culture of Deuteronomy is not restricted to the use of למד. Yet the instances of this lexeme must be differentiated from the literary-historical point of view as well as subjected to sociological analysis.[9] Assmann analyzes Deuteronomy as we possess it, in its final redaction. He neither discusses its terminology nor takes into account any change in the educational institutions of Israel during the deuteronomic-deuteronomistic period. Yet the experiences and needs of the inhabitants of Judah in the last period of the monarchy were fundamentally different from those of the exiles in Babylon. Probably this cannot be expected in this kind of extensive and all-encompassing comparison between the civilizations of Egypt, Israel and Greece that Assmann makes. In the following contribution, I shall take up his challenge from the point of view of biblical scholarship.

I propose to take as my point of departure Norbert Lohfink's recent survey of the "people of God in the Bible as a teaching and learning community."[10] In this survey, Lohfink reads Deuteronomy with its notion of instruction synchronically, as a unity. My own study, however, is diachronic. I wish to observe the mnemonics of Deuteronomy on the basis of the instances of למד in their immediate contexts and draw redactio-historical conclusions.[11] Many of my theses must remain hypothetical, given the present state of the literary-critical discussion and the lack of unanimity regarding methods and results. Nevertheless, I wish to risk the attempt. It is intended as a small sign of my gratitude towards my teacher Norbert Lohfink, S.J., who at the Pontifical Biblical Institute in Rome introduced me to the world of Deuteronomy and taught me to love it, and who even today remains my guide in the deuteronomic world.

For the purposes of this study, I shall distinguish between the following strata:

- I predeuteronomistic: 6:6-9 (probably without the promulgation in verse 6)
- II deuteronomistic, preexilic: 5:31 and 6:1, somewhat later 5:1; 11:18-21 (which, however, might be exilic); 31:9-13

III deuteronomistic, exilic: 14:23 (which however, might be wholly or partly older); 17:19; 18:9; 20:18; 31:19, 22
IV deuteronomistic, late exilic: 4:1, 5, 10, 14

A Predeuteronomistic Text (6:6*-9)

Perhaps even the first outline of the deuteronomic law should be understood as a "textbook" interpretation of the divine will.[12] This might be concluded from the probably oldest extant heading in 4:45*,[13] if the translation of עדת[14] which has recently been proposed and which is based on convincing reasons is correct. This translation is: "These are the doctrines (or "this is the doctrine") [העדת] that Moses gave the Israelites as they departed from Egypt."[15] Later, the juridical character of this document was changed by the addition of blessings and curses; however, the book of law evidently remained known as a textbook. For when it was discovered in the temple in 621 BCE, it was identified as ספר התורה (2 Kgs 22:8). Following the changes in linguistic usage, this might be interpreted as "textbook" or "manual." This "manual of the law of YHWH" was made valid by King Josiah through a ritual oath. This is why the narrative also calls it ספר הברית (2 Kgs 23:2). The Josianic Deuteronomy probably began with 6:4-5, that is with the confession of YHWH as the only God of Israel and the command to love him.[16]

Today, this is followed by a parenesis about teaching and learning, probably the oldest parenesis in Deuteronomy (6:6-9). The aim is not to instruct an elite: all Israel is addressed (the "you" is the same "you" as in 6:4), all generations and both sexes. The places where the text is to be perpetually recited (דבר בם),[17] as well as its all-penetrating presence, renders it impossible to exclude the daughters from learning it (and hence the women from "repeating" it).[18] The text is recited when "sitting" and when "walking," that is, in every position; "indoors," that is, in the private sphere; and "out of doors," that is, in the public sphere – in other words, everywhere; "when lying down" and "when rising," that is, always (verse 7). The words themselves are written "on your heart" (verse 6) and are also "bound to" the body as ornaments and as a confession (verse 8). They are available to the individual (verse 8); they are also found inscribed for the family and the community on the wall near the doorposts of the houses and on the gates of the town (verse 9). Thus they are perpetually heard, felt, seen. One moves, so to speak, in them with all senses as one moves in a landscape.[19]

These stipulations are of the greatest importance for the commemorative culture. If a memory is not to be lost, it must be "transposed from the biographical to the cultural memory." This happens through collective mnemonics."[20] In 6:6-9, Assmann discovers half of altogether eight forms of culturally shaped memory in Deuteronomy:

1. Making and becoming aware of, taking to one's heart—writing on one's heart (verse 6).
2. Education—transmitting a memory to the following generations through communication, circulation—speaking of it everywhere and always (verse 7).
3. Making visible—a sign on the brow [bodily mark] (verse 8).
4. Boundary symbols—inscriptions on the doorposts [the boundaries of one's property] (verse9).[21]

The text constitutes a literary-critical unity. The only probable secondary insertion is the relative clause in verse 6, which refers to the Mosaic promulgation of הדברים האלה.[22] With the exception of this promulgation clause, the whole pericope may be assumed to have belonged to the Josianic treaty document. Probably it had not yet been explained as a law mediated through Moses.[23] This does not exclude the possibility that Moses may already have been mentioned, for instance in the heading in 4:45.[24] Nevertheless, it was probably only as the Josianic edition was reshaped and became Moses' valedictory speech—and this only happened in the deuteronomistic redaction—that the notion of Moses pledging the people to observe these commandments was introduced into Deuteronomy. The earliest date for this is the last years of King Josiah.[25] Lohfink has called the framework stretching from Deuteronomy 1 to Joshua 22 the "Deuteronomistic Conquest Narrative."[26] Within this framework, the flashback from Deuteronomy 5 to the theophanic proclamation of the Decalogue (verses 2-22) and the commissioning of Moses as mediator of the law (verses 23-31) and the following parenesis, reaching up to 6:1(2a), with its "global theory of the essence of deuteronomic legislation,"[27] in the concrete instance of the relation between the Decalogue and other laws, was inserted before 6:4-9.[28]

That 6:6*-9 is predeuteronomistic is suggested first of all by the different terms used for "teach," "instruct" in 6:7(שנן pi.) and 5:31, and

6:1 (למד pi.). Semantically speaking, the two verbs are equivalent. In both cases, we are dealing with a typically pedagogical transmission of texts, although in this text the transmission is the task of the parents.[29] This is made clear above all by the later parallel to 6:7 which we find in 11:19.[30] There, למד pi. replaces שׁנן pi. The intention was evidently to substitute the more common למד for שׁנן, used for the recital of texts only in 6:7. The legal term דברים constitutes a second indication that 6:6-9 is older than 5:31 and 6:1. If 6:6 were contemporary with or later than 5:31 and 6:1, the author would probably have chosen one of the terms used for law in these verses and indicated clearly the content of the doctrine with the aid of this concept. Originally, דברים probably referred to דבר pi., the verb for promulgating the law in the old heading of 4:45.[31] Now it does not appear to refer to anything in particular.[32] However, this argument presupposes that the expression in 6:6 (and possibly also in 1:18) only designates the parenesis and the individual commandments. However, since 6:6-9 also aims at universal education, it is possible that הדברים האלה in 6:6 originally referred to the entire text of the Josianic covenant document, including the blessings and curses. In the third place, 6:6-9 obviously does not yet know the association of law and land which is typical of 5:31 and 6:1. This is found only in the later variant, in 11:18-21. However, it is typical of the "Deuteronomistic Conquest Narrative" to combine the themes of law and land.[33]

Verses 6:6-9, the germ cell of the deuteronomic didactic systematics, are found in an appropriate place – after 6:4-5, the basic covenantal dogma and norm, and before 6:17 with its exhortation to observe the law. Within the text, the didactic parenesis appears on one hand as a first realization of the commandment to love, and on the other hand as a preparation for the observance of the law. Deut 6:10-16 already constitutes a commentary on the first commandment of the Decalogue.[34] Hence it can hardly have been introduced into Deuteronomy at an earlier date than that of chapter 5. The sequence מצות יהוה אלהיכם ועדתיו[35] וחקיו mentioned in 6:17 probably forms the self-designation of the Book of the Torah found in the temple.[36] At least this is suggested by a comparison with 2 Kgs 23:3.[37] Its laws are – and this is also suggested by 6:17 – still given by YHWH and not by Moses. Perhaps 6:18abα still belonged to it.[38] Together with verses 18bβγ-19, these verses "nomistically" demand that what is "right and good" be done as a prerequisite for entering the promised land. The passage before us is exilic.[39] The "catechismal instruction" in 6:20-25, which originally followed on 6:17 (and 18abα)[40] is somewhat later than 6:6-9. It does not employ the verb למד, but factually, it belongs to the domain of education and at the very beginning of the parenesis it explains the significance of the commandments.[41] The two pedagogical arrangements complement each other. According to 6:6-9, the text is continuously recited and thus committed to memory. According to 6:20-25, however, it is discussed with reference to the actual situation; that is, it is learned in a rational manner.

The "meditation" on the new deuteronomic social order went much further than any mnemonics and was intended to create a new consciousness.[42] With the centralization of the cult in the Temple of Jerusalem, it constituted the second institutional structure with the aid of which King Josiah intended to preserve the identity of Israel as the people of YHWH. As the "festival theory" helped to effect the cult reform,[43] so the theology of teaching and learning served to socialize the entire people in the observance of the deuteronomic law. We see that 6:6-9 is only one member of a system of assertions constructed with the aid of the key term למד and intended to found the social change. Probably it was created under Josiah; in any case, it is preexilic. In structurally decisive places—reading the text in its present order, synchronically—it discusses what is learned and why (5:1), who teaches (5:31; 6:1), how Israel is to handle the deuteronomic law (6:6-9; 11:18-21) and what attitude is learned (31:12-13). This does not mean that a particular aspect is not also mentioned elsewhere in connection with למד. But it does not in that case constitute the authentic reference for למד. In these passages, "to teach," למד pi., always has to do with a recital: the recital of the parents (דבר ב pi. 6:7; 11:19), the speech of Moses (דבר qal 5:1), reading the Torah to the people (קרא נגד 31:11). What is repeated and learned by heart (למד qal 5:1) in listening (שמע 5:1; 31:12, 13) is intended to lead to action (עשׂה 5:31; 6:1 and שמר לעשׂת 5:1; 31:12) and/or the fear of YHWH (ירא 31:12 and 31:13).

Preexilic Deuteronomistic Texts
(5:31; 6:1; 5:1; 11:18-21; 31:9-13)

The old heading (4:45) without further explanation introduced Moses as Israel's legislator בצאתם ממצרים; that is, in the early period or at Horeb. Moses' power to promulgate laws did not receive a theological explanation until chapter 5 with its inserted Horeb narrative. At Horeb, Israel asked YHWH to give them Moses as a mediator. According to 5:31, YHWH therefore wants to impart (דבר pi.) כל-המצוה החקים[44] והמשׁטים which he is to "teach" Israel. In 6:1, Moses begins to carry out this mission. This takes place within the framework of a kind of address, that is, in a programmatic way. The content remains כל-המצוה החקים והמשׁטים, for Moses is only a faithful mediator.

In 6:2a, the mediating authority of Moses (מצוה) is explicitly added to the authority of YHWH in 6:1 (צוה); this may be a later addition.[45] When the law is given, YHWH does not "teach" (למד pi.),[46] nor does Moses learn (למד qal)—a common linguistic usage in Deuteronomy. The parents who teach in 6:6 stand within a chain of transmission whose archetypical prototypes are the teacher Moses, and the initiator, YHWH himself.

Deut 6:6-9 exhorts the Israelites to assimilate the ever-present text. Then 5:31 and 6:1, together with the mediating teaching authority of Moses, also establish the practical purpose of his teaching: keeping the law (עשׂה). However, it is not a question of a parenesis on keeping the commandments—as in 5:1—but a strict juridical regulation of the domain of validity of the law (the land they are to possess). Nevertheless, 6:2a first mentions the fear of YHWH, expressed in the observance of the law, before determining the duration of the validity of the law ("all your life") and the persons concerned (all the generations of the extended family, not merely those Israelites who were directly addressed). Independently of whether 6:2a is a literary-critically original or a secondary continuation of 6:1, factually and syntactically, it is only in 31:12, 13 that the fear of YHWH is thematized as the authentic purpose of learning the law.

Whereas 5:31 and 6:1 are concerned with Moses' teaching authority, 5:1 stresses above all that the whole of Israel is to learn and observe the law. This again takes place at a structural intersection and is also embedded in the framework of the parenesis (5:1; 11:32) and the individual laws (12:1; 26:16). The author of 5:31 and 6:1 seems to be the earliest possible author of this system, as is evident from the history of the key term חקים ומשׁטים, but there is no reason why it should not be later still.[47]

Moses summons a formal assembly of the people. He begins his speech in 5:1a with a didactic opening formula,[48] שמע ישראל את, which is followed by the laws. This is not so much of a key motif in the following Sinai narrative of Deuteronomy 5.[49] It is rather that 5:1a and the double expression שמר לעשת at the end of verse 1b anticipate certain phrases in 5:27a and 6:3a.[50] There, too, they have special positions at the beginning of verses belonging to the frame of a transitional structure between chapter 5 and verse 6:4. They are related to each other by palindromic key word connections.[51] If the intention of the formulation in 5:1 has been correctly interpreted and 6:3 was added later as a counterpart to 5:27,[52] 5:1 must be later than 5:31 and 6:1. There is a further observation which supports this: if 5:1 is a secondary insertion before the proclamation of the Decalogue, then the narrative of 5:2, 5b* (לאמר) once began in the same way as the introductory speech 1:6a. Deut 5:2 was a reminder of the passage which once constituted the beginning of the entire structure of the Deuteronomistic Conquest Narrative, including the flashback in chapter 5.[53] This parallel is all the more important as 1:6-8 and 5:6-21 contain the only words of God addressed to all Israel reported by Moses in his speeches in the entire book of Deuteronomy. Deut 5:1 stands out as a characterization of the speech.

The promulgation of the law was formulated with the aid of the extremely rare,[54] solemn phrase דבר באזנים (qal). In this way, the relation between the speaker (דבר pi.), YHWH, and Moses, who is commissioned to teach (למד pi., 5:31), continues in 5:1 as Moses speaks (דבר pi.) and Israel learns (למד qal). The actuality of the Mosaic discourse is emphasized by היום, which is found nowhere else in Deuteronomy in a context of teaching and learning.[55]

שמע and למד qal, the verbs describing the process of assimilation, are found together only in 31:12-13. And it is only in 31:12 that למד also refers to the double phrase שמר לעשת for observing the commandments of the Torah (cf. also 17:19). What 5:1 only formulated as the political aim of the Mosaic promulgation of the law, 31:12 now subordinates to the theologico-mystical prerequisite of all the laws, the fear of YHWH.

Deut 11:18-21 is a variant of 6:6-9. The text is obviously meant to recall the old admonition to actualize the law which we find in an analogous position in the composition. Whereas 6:6-9 is situated at the beginning of a parenesis on the commandments, 11:18-21 might either constitute the end of this parenesis by a kind of inclusional correspondence or prepare for learning the following individual commandments. Through the allusion to 6:7—the one verbal agreement, albeit with a change in number—and through its way of elucidating the central motif of teaching, the passage shows itself to be secondary and to belong to a different stratum.[56]

In order to make its intention clearer, 11:18-21 repeats the statements of its prototype in a new order, and even partially reformulates them. The text is palindromically structured.[57] The center is teaching the children (למד pi.). The ever-present recital becomes a single process (לדבר ב, "while ..."). It is now entirely devoted to transmitting a knowledge of the text to the next generation. It is emphasized that the parents themselves must learn the text by heart (instead of היה על לבב, as in 6:6, we have in 11:18a the verb שׂים)[58] and be able to speak of it (the addition of נפשׁ may here refer to the throat as the seat of language).[59] The Mosaic laws appear as living speeches, as דברי, which is quite unique in Deuteronomy. For this reason, the promulgatory statement is unnecessary. The "frame" verses, 18a and 21 refer to each other and offer the most all-encompassing affirmation: "Lay these words on your heart, then you will possess the land forever."[60]

Besides the concentration on teaching the children, the promise for the future in 11:21 is new in relation to the prototype. The combination of the exhortation to "learn and teach" with the promise of a long life in the promised land makes 11:18-21 into a parenetic scheme.[61] The fundamental notion of this form is transformed in a unique way: the "blessing" usually given for observing the law here already applies to learning and teaching the Mosaic law.

Even the phraseology of the reference to the blessing in verse 21 is, apart from YHWH's oath to the fathers, completely undeuteronomic. The way in which the formulation refers to the context—the oath to the fathers in 11:9a and the words "heaven" and "earth" in 10:14 and 11:11—is rather vague.[62] However, if 11:21 is adapted to the cosmic perspective of 10:12 - 11:17, then 11:18-21 probably was not written until the time of the exile.[63] The relationship between the law of the king (17:14-20) and 11:21 must be similarly determined. There are good reasons to regard the law of the king as exilic.[64] Verses 17:18-20 allude to 6:6-9 and 31:9-13.[65] Like 11:21, 17:20b contains an assurance of blessing for the daily recitation of the Torah by the king as well as the key words ימים and בנים. Nevertheless, 11:18-21 cannot be dated with any certainty.

The pericope 31:9-13 constitutes a literary unity.[66] It belongs to a deuteronomistic but probably Josianic stratum.[67] The verses narrate how Moses wrote down the Torah and gave it to the levitic priests, who carried the Ark, and to the elders of Israel (verse 9). They are responsible not merely for the preservation of the Torah, but also for its living transmission. Therefore, both groups are given the task of solemnly reciting the Torah at the Feast of Booths, before all Israel (verses 10-11), every year of remission,[68] when all debts are remitted and the original equality is restored (cf. chapter 15).

The audience is not listed according to social class, as are those invited to the Feast of Booths (16:14), but according to age, sex and affiliation to Israel (31:12). The individual families are assimilated into the unity of the people. The order to recite the Torah probably always had its place towards the end of the Book of the Torah, which through King Josiah's covenant became a treaty document. The Hittite vassal treaties which provided the structural model for King Josiah's document also normally ended with the obligation to recite the treaty formula regularly in the presence of all those concerned. The recitation includes the treaty stipulations, the historical preamble, and the sanctions. Its purpose is "knowledge" and "preservation" of the treaty text.[69]

Deut 31:10-13, unlike the didactic parenesis, is not addressed to all Israel (6:6-9) but to the leaders of the people. The command in verse 11b is expanded as a solemn ritual of teaching and learning"[70] in verses 12-13. The priests and elders are to assemble "the men, the women, the children, the old people and the aliens" for the feast (קהל hi. verse 12). The archetypical place for this assembly is Horeb (קהלכם 5:22), where YHWH spoke to the Israelites and entered into a covenant with them and where they "feared" him (ירא 5:29). This "day of assembly" (18:16) is described at the beginning of the Torah, in chapter 5. Therefore this original situation can be reestablished when the Torah is recited. When the Torah is recited in this context, it is the assembly of Israel in the land of Moab that is to be re-actualized. This was where, for the first time, Moses read the whole of the Torah – including the Horeb theophany – and made the covenant. For the narrative of Deuteronomy (that is, the sequence of events as it is described in the book) knows of only one solemn assembly and one covenant: the assembly and the covenant of the plains of Moab,[71] and this in spite of the fact that 29:1 speaks of a second assembly being called (קרא אל as in 5:1). קרא באזנים in 31:11 may therefore allude to the solemn proclamation דבר באזנים in 5:1.

Above all, 31:12b takes up all the verbs in the proclamation of the Torah to Israel in 5:1 (שׁמר לעשׂת, למד qal, שׁמע). Deut 31:12b inserts the phrase ירא את יהוה אלהיכם into the sequence of verbs. When Israel performs this "public ritual of learning,"[72] it again finds itself on the threshold of the promised land, receives its social order and is "reborn in the collective consciousness as the society of YHWH."[73]

"To fear YHWH" is the theological didactic goal of the periodic recital of the Torah; this is implicit in the Horeb theophany (5:29, cf. 6:2a) and becomes explicit at Moab. Through different syntactic constructions, with למד and ירא in 31:12 and 13, it is formulated in different ways for adults and for children.[74] In verse 12bα, the two verbs are paratactically construed: learning is stressed in its own right. In this context, למד qal means above all that the Torah "be repeated," that is, that it be spoken and then repeated, as was the custom in schools at that time. It does not mean that the text was to be learned on this occasion.[75] For anyone who, as 6:7 demands, continually repeats (cf. שׁנן pi.) the דברים must already know the text by heart.[76]

The common recitation of the Torah occasions the "fearful, numinous experience of the God of Israel who reveals himself and his will for the particular structure of the world."[77] Since the Horeb theophany, Deuteronomy has defined this experience as the "fear of YHWH" (ירא את-יהוה). It distinguishes between the daily recitation of the law within the family and the public cultic recitation by the whole of Israel. Only when this occurs does it become possible to attain the practical goal, to live as the text demands:

ושׁמרו לעשׂת את-כל-דברי התורה הזאת (31:12bβ).

"Mysticism mediates between the text and reality ... As every detail is assimilated into the unity of the encounter with God, it becomes possible to return to the manifold new social reality concretely outlined by 'this Torah'".[78] The children do not yet know the ritual (לא ידעת without an object). They hear, for the first time, the "great waves of sound as the Levitic priests and the elders recite the Torah and it is repeated in chorus by the thousands assembled"[79] and in this way they "learn" to "fear YHWH." This is why verse 13 unites למד qal syntactically with the infinitive construction ליראה את-יהוה אלהיכם. This is the fundamental attitude which the children must learn, even before they learn the laws by heart. They are not even required to observe the laws. The pedagogical custom and the experience of God made by the entire Israelite society are presupposed and belong to the feast. The children learn to "believe" through "hearing."

למד qal in the sense of "repeating" the text of the Torah when it is recited and thus "being confronted with YHWH in trembling and fascination" and the "cultic singularity"[80] of this way of learning imply something new which 31:12-13 introduces into the system of למד statements. The collective learning process which frames the entire proclamation (from 5:1 to 31:12-13) till we reach the recitation of the written document is now the alpha and the omega of the deuteronomic Torah.

Deuteronomistic Texts from the Exile
(14:23; 17:19; 18:9; 20:18; 31:19, 22)

The four instances taken from the deuteronomic code (12:1 - 26:16) form a system of their own. They "show two typical phrases in the commentary on the laws"[81] which may belong to a single redaction. The two texts from the preamble to the Song of Moses (31:16-22) correspond to each other as task and achievement. In the individual laws, למד qal/pi. refers to attitudes and reactions; in the song, למד pi. refers to the text written by Moses.

Deut 17:19 in the law on the king (17:14-20) and 18:9 in the law on the prophets (18:9-22) belong to the outline of the constitution (Deut 16:18 - 18:22). This outline forms a systematic legal unity.[82] Both passages are exilic.[83] The sacrificial stipulations concerning tithes and firstlings (14:23) in the final redaction of the book become part of a large palindromic structure encompassing the seven "sacrificial" texts of the deuteronomic code and is related to 18:3-4, about the priests' due.[84] Deut 14:23 could indeed be preexilic and would in that case have become part of the system only through the deuteronomistic redaction. It seems probable, however, that at least the final sentence in 14:23b is exilic, since the programmatically formulated sequence of "fear of YHWH and (as a consequence of this attitude) observance of the laws" (31:12) is reversed in 14:23. Deut 20:18 was—probably in analogy to 18:9b—inserted into the law on war (20:10-18) only during the exile.[85]

In any case, the four texts, according to their sequence in the book, correspond to each other in pairs. Learning the fear of YHWH

(למען תלמד/ילמד ליראה יהוה אלהיך/אלהיו) in mentioned in both 14:23 and 17:19. Deut 18:9 prohibits learning the abominable things[86] done by the inhabitants of the land (לא-תלמד לעשות כתועבת הגוים). In 20:18, לא-ילמדו אתכם לעשות ככל תועבתם precludes allowing them to teach such things. In 14:23 and 17:19, למד qal comes from a concrete practice which, although in a different way, belongs to the liturgy of the Feast of Booths: the law is learned yearly when the tithes of the harvest and the firstlings are consumed (14:23),[87] as well as through the king's daily reading of the Torah (17:19) directed towards the public recitation in the temple (31:12). In 18:9 and 20:18, למד qal has to do with forbidden customs: the magic and the oracles of the inhabitants of the land (18:10b-11) and the Canaanite cultic practice (20:18; 18:10a). In all four cases, we are clearly concerned with an actualization of the first commandment—the fear of YHWH (14:23; 17:19) or the danger of apostatizing from YHWH to other gods (18:12-13; 20:18). Deut 14:23 and 17:19 go further than 31:12 and affirm that the mystical depths of the fear of YHWH can also be experienced in the joy of the yearly festival and in the "meditation" on the Torah in everyday life.

According to 31:19, 22, Moses receives the mission to teach the בני ישׂראל yet another song (32:1-43), which they are to recite regularly (לא תשכח מפי ודעו 31:21).[88] This song anticipates Israel's apostasy to "abominable practices" (תועבת 32:16) and YHWH's consequent anger, but also his compassion for his people. Assmann calls this "poetry as a codification of remembered history"[89] in the shape of culturally formed memory. The introduction (31:16-22),[90] however, does not take into account the hopeful salvation assurances, but only the gloomy accusations in the first part of the song (32:1-25). The song constitutes YHWH's prophetic "witness" (עד) against the Israelites (31:21); that is, it functions as a theodicy. Such a commentary on the Song of Moses makes us conclude that the introduction dates from the (early) exile. למד pi. here serves the attempt "to come to terms with an undesirable marginal possibility in the history of the society of YHWH . . . before it becomes a reality."[91] From the perspective of the times of Moses, the instances of למד after the proclamation of the law anticipate something in the far future, the Babylonian exile. The following instances from Deuteronomy 4 at the beginning of the Mosaic proclamation of the law recall the Horeb theophany where, for the first time, Israel learned. In both textual domains, the danger of forgetting is pointed out.[92] Learning and teaching, as we encounter them in these texts, form the last and most all-encompassing framework for the proclamation of the law by Moses.

A Deuteronomistic Stratum from the Late Exile (4:1, 5, 10, 14)

In the late period of the Babylonian exile,[93] 4:1-40 was added in front of the text of the Torah of Moses (4:44) as an interpretation of it (see 4:8). In this passage, the Torah supplants the king, the state and the temple. When the nations come to know (שׁמע) this law code, they will praise Israel as a wise and understanding people. The unique closeness to God and the incomparable social justice which Israel experiences through its observance of the Torah determine its identity as a "great nation" (verses 6-8).[94] Assmann's characterization of the deuteronomic commemorative culture, which I quoted at the beginning of this article, fits the view of chapter 4 particularly well.

The background of the pericope, which constitutes a literary unity,[95] may be the discussion concerning the validity of the deuteronomic law, which was obviously a matter of discussion among the exiles.[96] For the period of the *gôlâ*, it was enough to transmit the knowledge of the law. The "text" (הדברים) becomes canonized as a "complete course of doctrine with binding force"[97] ("you shall not add to . . . nor take from it" 4:2). According to Assmann,[98] this binding force constitutes the most decisive form of collective mnemonics.

למד is used four times in pi. (4:1, 5, 10, 14) and once in qal (4:10). This fairly high number of instances and their positions in the structure of verses 1-14[99] make the verb a key word in the parenesis on the commandments. Does the preference for this promulgatory verb mirror a dangerous break in the tradition, a break which has to be counteracted? In any case, the accents in 4:1, 5, 14 are new in relation to 5:1 and 5:31. It is above all the החקים והמשׁפטים which are learned (למד pi.).[100] Nowhere else is Moses depicted as "teacher" to such an extent.[101] Whereas in 4:1a, Moses promulgates the laws and teaches them, Israel only has to "listen."[102] Then it will live and YHWH will give it the land to possess (4:1b). In 4:1, the statement formulated with למד is an element in a parenetic scheme, as it is only in 11:18-21. Whereas, according to 11:18-21, the future depends on teaching; according to 4:1, it is hearing the laws that decides the future. This hearing is, however, merely a matter of acknowledgement, which, however, includes the readiness to obey (לעשׂות). It is only "within the land" that the laws have to be kept. Deut 4:5 thus clarifies the validity of the law as it was defined in 12:1, but also thematizes Moses as a teacher—in accordance with the purpose of chapter 4. At Horeb, YHWH authorized him as such. Therefore verse 5 in a subsidiary clause refers to the commissioning to teach in verse 14. Factually, 4:14 goes back to 5:31, where YHWH transmits to Moses כל-המצוה החקים והמשׁפטים. Yet the accents are different from 5:31, since 4:14 takes over the formulation of 6:1 almost word for word. Because of the narrative evidence, it is no longer stated that the laws were transmitted by YHWH. The abbreviated formulation of 6:1 in place of the explicit formulation of 5:31, which one might have expected, is "a distinct new statement, because it is, so to speak, a zero statement."[103] God has only "ordered Moses to teach the people 'statutes and laws" (*ḥuqqîm ûmišpaṭîm*—without an article) . . . The emphasis is on the reality of the Mosaic law."[104]

After speaking of Moab and of hearing the laws taught by Moses, 4:10 narratively recalls Horeb, where YHWH told Moses to assemble the people (קהל hi., in Deuteronomy also in 31:12, 28) in order to make them listen (שׁמע hi. 4:10a) to his words (דברי). The goal of this verbal revelation is emphasized stylistically by the inclusion of the final clause[105] through למד qal and pi. (verse 10b). Israel is to "learn" directly from God (למד qal).[106] What the people assimilate in this way is not, however, the Decalogue—YHWH will give it in writing later on (verse 13)—but the habit of lifelong fear of YHWH (ליראה אתי verse 10b). They are also to teach (למד pi.) their children. Nothing similar is said about Moses anywhere. למד pi. here means transmitting what one has learned oneself. This happens when Israel "makes the younger generations know" (ידע hi. verse 9) the דברים, the events/words of the Horeb theophany, and thus recounts its own experience. The details of the transmission remain open. For the situation in the land, this is a matter of individual stipulations. One thing only is certain: As the laws must continue to be taught in Israel in order that Israel may live, so the living tradition of the personal experience of faith must not be broken.

Conclusion

The redactio-historical evolution of the deuteronomic-deuteronomistic theology of "teaching and learning" in the changing society of Israel can be summarized as follows: 6:6*-9 at the beginning of the Josianic treaty document intends to socialize the whole people in the deuteronomic social order by means of the ubiquitous recitation of the law of Moses. It is no longer learned at school, but in the family. In 5:31 and 6:1, the early deuteronomistic Horeb narrative, which was early on inserted in front of the oldest parenesis on learning, authorized Moses to teach as the archetypical teacher commissioned by YHWH. Deut 5:1, the introduction which was added later, stresses the deuteronomic law as a didactic program and as a principle for action. Finally, teaching the children is made the central concern by 11:18-21, a variant of 6:6-9, which may be as late as the late exile. This passage comes at the end of the parenetic part and promises a long life in the land if the children are taught the law. According to the Mosaic promulgation of the law in 31:10-13, the priests are obliged to read the Torah at a public ceremony on the Feast of Booths during the year of remission. When hearing and repeating this social order in the cult, the second place for learning the law, Israel experiences the fear of YHWH as it did in Moab and can renew its social life. The exilic instances of the deuteronomic code in 14:23 and 17:19 also refer to the fear of YHWH, which Israel or the king is now to learn through offering sacrifices or meditating on the Torah. Deut 18:9 and 20:18 prohibit learning forbidden mantic practices such as the Canaanite cultic practices. Finally, the four individual laws are concerned with fulfilling the first commandment. After the promulgation of the law, YHWH commissions Moses (31:19, 22) to teach the Israelites a song in case the catastrophe of the exile should occur. Chapter 4, in the late exile, emphasizes hearing and teaching the laws (verses 1, 5 and 14) in order that Israel may survive. Above all, they have to transmit the fear of YHWH which they themselves learned at the time of the Horeb theophany. This means transmitting their own experience to coming generations (verse 10). Deuteronomy, then, is first and foremost concerned with teaching and learning a faith related to the community.

NOTES

(Refer to bibliography for complete citations.)

Chapter 1. Wisdom, Divine Presence and Law

1. Eissfeldt, *Jahve*, pp. 10-11.

2. See for instance H.J. Kraus, *Gesetzesverständnis*.

3. This constitutes Eissfeldt's (*Jahve*, p. 11) final description of the relation to God in the New Testament.

4. The translation has been kept as close as possible to the Hebrew original. Words which are necessary for understanding the translated text but which are not found in the Masoretic Text are in brackets. Concerning the division into speech lines, see Braulik, *Rhetorik*.

5. The SAM and the LXX offer – probably they are adapting to the fact that all through verses 5-8, Israel is addressed in the plural – *r*[e]*'u* and ἴδετε. This interjection-like imperative is, however, always used in the singular in Deuteronomy; cf. e.g., 11:26; 30:15.

6. Regarding the rendering of *limmadtî* in the present in order to indicate coincidence, cf. the recent study by Gross, *Verbform*, p. 37. Cf. further, for instance, the German *Einheitsübersetzung* of the Bible.

7. Missing in the LXX.

8. It is, however, possible that *kēn*, here as in Amos 5:14 and in Ps 61:9 conveys the meaning "then."

9. The LXX adds πάντων; cf. 2:25; further 4:9, 27.

10. Concerning the translation of *raq*, cf. Jongeling, p. 104: "rien d'autre," "sans doute."

11. Cf. the LXX θεὸς ἐγγίζων. See further note 98 below.

12. I have presented the literary-critical analysis of this text in Braulik, "Literarkritik und archäologische Stratigraphie." The theory that verses 5-8 constitute a literary-critical unity has recently been defended by Mittmann, *Deuteronomium 1,1 - 6,3*, pp. 117-118.

13. Cf. Lohfink, *Höre Israel*, p. 91. However, in a recent study (Kaiser, "Exegese," p. 42), Otto Kaiser assumes that Deut 4:1-8 should be dated "at least as late as the period of the reconsolidation of Judaism as a religious community" because of the "combination of legal, cultic and sapiential terminology" and the "religious evaluation of Israel's position among the nations, which is found only in verses 6-8."

14. See, for instance, Noth, *Überlieferungsgeschichtliche Studien*, p. 14. This view will receive further confirmation from the reinterpretation of central deuteronomic conceptions (see below).

15. For a substantiation of the following introductory remarks, see Braulik, *Rhetorik*, passim.

16. See Lohfink, "Darstellungskunst," pp. 124-125. Further Halbe, *Privilegrecht*, pp. 100-103. Halbe (pp. 102-103) refers to the extensive use and many-sided application of this scheme, which does not constitute a genre and for which no particular legal field can be determined.

17. According to Halbe, *Privilegrecht*, pp. 102-103, this scheme makes possible "a linguistic expression of the real confrontation between the partners so that—remaining with this confrontation and without for a moment losing sight of one's partner—the behavior which one side demands from or allows the other is immediately understood as obligatory or allowed. The basis for this can be found in the state of affairs which the affirmative clause not merely denotes but creates as a legal reality. A correspondence is expressed in such a way that the speaker's declaration lays the foundation for a corresponding behavior on the part of the other side. In this declaration, the person addressed discerns the necessity and the freedom of his own actions."

18. Regarding the stylistic arrangement of verses 5-8, for instance, through successive divisions, parallelisms and so on, see Braulik, *Rhetorik*.

19. Regarding this term, see Gross, *Bileam*, p. 181 note 25.

20. Broide, p. 65, expresses a different opinion, as he combines the first two members and thus finds a triple rhythm which he has also discovered elsewhere and which he considers characteristic of the deuteronomic style.

21. The formula is used for the presentation of laws in Deut 11:32. In connection with this, but related to the blessings and curses, the same formula is used in 11:26 and 30:15. It is found in 1:8, 21; 2:24, 31 as a "formula of release" without any relation to any legal theme.

22. For instance, Landsberger, p. 220, has shown that Old Babylonian had no term expressing what we mean by "law" and that expressions like "observe the laws," "the laws are in force," "condemned according to paragraph so-an-so of the law" are unknown. According to F.R. Kraus, p. 286, the characteristic limitation of the "laws" of the Code of Hammurapi to conflictual situations constitutes the essential difference between Old Babylonian and modern law. This is suggested by the Old Babylonian laws being defined as legal decisions, as particular cases which had been decided. "There appears to have been no place for legislation as we understand it in the Old Mesopotamian social and legal orders" (p. 296). The designation of ancient Near Eastern legal collections as "laws"

or "codes" is misleading. However, since the term is an established one, I shall continue to use it.

23. See note 164 below.

24. See e.g., Eilers, p. 4.

25. Schmökel, p. 67.

26. F.R. Kraus, p. 291. Renger (pp. 286-287) points out that the Code of Hammurapi contains no reference to any proclamation or coming-into-effect of its legal decisions which would give them legal force. However, about a century later, learned scribes, because of the colophon *ṣimdat Hammurapi*, interpreted these legal decisions as a summary of a royal decree. This view is decisive for our textual comparison.

27. See in more detail p. 34 above.

28. It corresponds to *š^{e}ma'* *('el)* in verse 1.

29. This structural analysis is not accepted by Broide (p. 66). He constructs a triple rhythm: *r^{e}'ēh* (1), verse 5a (2), verse 5b (3).

30. 14:23; 17:19; 18:9; 20:18.

31. 4:1, 5, 10 (bis), 14; 5:1, 31; 6:1; 11:19; 31:12-13.

32. 31:19, 22. See Becker, *Gottesfurcht*, p. 104.

33. Cf. for instance the description of the "parenetic process" in Lohfink, *Hauptgebot*, pp. 261-285.

34. 6:7, for instance, exhorts the Israelites to repeat (*šnn* pi.) the deuteronomic obligations to their sons, whereas the later parallel in 11:19 speaks of "teaching" (*lmd* pi.). [See note 100 on p. 270 in the present volume for my current opinion on this.]

35. Like the LXX, commentators and grammars generally interpret *'^{a}šer* in this passage as final (cf. Joüon, para. 168-169). This would mean that we are dealing with acquisition of an attitude of true worship of YHWH. Becker, on the other hand (*Gottesfurcht*, pp. 104-105) correctly interprets *'^{a}šer* as a relative particle. Certainly *d^{e}bārîm* in the same passage should not be equated with the Mosaic law (see further below). Derousseaux (pp. 214-215) explicitly rejects Becker's interpretation, according to which *l^{e}yir'â 'ōtî* is a final or a consecutive clause. There is, however a counter argument against the arguments cited: *yr'* in this passage may not be interpreted according to Exod 20:20 as "to fear" in the sense of "to experience the terrifying presence of God," but must be understood strictly in its context, where it occurs together with "my words." Furthermore, the change in number in the use of *lmd* (plural in verses 1, 5, 14 and singular in verse 10) should not be interpreted as an indication of literary-critical stratification or of different denotations.

36. For a definition of the deuteronomic/deuteronomistic concept of "fearing God" as "worshiping God," see Becker, *Gottesfurcht*, p. 85.

37. See verse 13 as fulfillment of the prediction in verse 10; further Braulik, "Ausdrücke," pp. 45-46.

38. See Lohfink, *Hauptgebot*, p. 59.

39. The use of *škḥ* in late deuteronomic texts corresponds to this. While in the parenesis (6:12; 8:11, 14, 19) and in the Song of Moses (32:18), *škḥ* is used as a verb indicating the relation to God, in the deuteronomistic passages 4:9, 23, it refers to *d^{e}bārîm* and *b^{e}rît* (cf 2 Kgs 17:38), in 31:21 to the Song of Moses. Finally, it occurs in the prayer formula of 26:13, taking *miṣwōt* as an object.

40. Braulik, "Ausdrücke," pp. 61-62.

41. See Eissfeldt, *Mein Gott*, p. 37.

42. Macholz, p. 100.

43. This change in the text, which was necessary if one wished to remain faithful to the spirit of the older law in the face of a changing world does not, therefore, constitute a contradiction of the command in verse 2 neither to add nor to take away anything.

44. See Lohfink, "Sicherung," pp. 153-154.

45. See the episode recounted in verses 3-4 concerning the apostasy of the Israelites to Baal of Peor and the punishment of the apostates; further the description of the return to YHWH in verses 29-30 (in Deuteronomy, *šmʿ b^{e}qôl* does not refer to the observance of the laws—see Lohfink, *Hauptgebot*, p. 65).

46. Localizing the observance of the laws in the promised land is no contradiction of verse 1, where, through the subordinate final clause, the conquest and the possession of the land are made dependent on the observance of the commandments. The conquest of the land, which is about to take place, cannot be either a regard for keeping the laws or the purpose of the present teaching of the laws (see Mittmann, *Deuteronomium 1,1 - 6,3*, p. 115). The final clause in verse 1b refers back to *šmʿ* and cannot be excised by literary-critical methods by being said to be "far away and hidden by the relative clause" (against Mittmann, *Deuteronomium 1,1 - 6,3*, p. 115)—cf. the structure of verse 5b. The New English Bible renders the passage as follows: "Now, Israel, listen to the statutes and laws which I am teaching you, and obey them; then you will live and go in and occupy the land which the LORD the God of your fathers is giving you" (NEB, OUP/CUP edition, 1970, p. 199). Although "listen" does not, in this verse, mean "obey," it does not simply denote taking notice of what is being said. This is a type of listening "which includes the readiness to observe the laws. In the last analysis, this means deciding *for* the divine author of the law—here and now" (Mittmann, *Deuteronomium 1,1 - 6,3*, p. 126). The opposition between verses 1 and 5 follows from the literary fiction of Deuteronomy (Diepold, p. 94 note 2.

Diepold here argues against Macholz's assumption of different strata—see Macholz, pp. 101-102). The different formulations in verses 1 and 5 are caused by the two different levels of argumentation, the promulgation of the law immediately before entering the land and the authentic address to the exiles. Finally, there also seems to be a difference in the meaning of the word "life." "Understood only from the literary situation of Moses addressing the second-generation exodus Israelites, 'life' is a promise for the nation which involves closely their land, while at the same time, 'life' in the land is conditional and rests on obedience to the law. Understood, on the other hand, as an address for people who had lost the promise and the land through disobedience, Moses' sermon in 4:1-40 offers hope to that nation in the insistence that the law of Yahweh delivered on Horeb means life for them in their exile situation." (Jacobs, p. 156).

47. Lohfink, *Höre Israel*, p. 99.

48. Cf. Janssen, p. 74.

49. Lohfink, *Hauptgebot*, pp. 68ff, esp. p. 69; *ûš^{e}martem* does not, then, oblige the Israelites to learn the law as a prerequisite to acting in accordance with it (against D. Hoffmann, *Deuteronomium*, p. 52).

50. Cf. Lohfink, *Höre Israel*, p. 100.

51. This is not simply "public evidence of your wisdom in the eyes of the world" (in opposition to S. R. Driver, *Deuteronomy*). The correct interpretation is found as early as in Bertholet, p. 65.

52. Contrary to what is maintained by, for instance, Whybray (pp. 87-88), who considers it the evident intention of verse 6 "to characterize the Deuteronomic Code as the highest *ḥokmâ* whose possession is infinitely superior to any *ḥokmâ* which other peoples may claim to possess." Our text must not be claimed as the biblical starting point for a nomistic tendency in the sapiential tradition. Only a misinterpretation could lead to the kind of development which Hempel (p. 103) characterizes as follows: "Such a heightened self-assurance through belief in election becomes dangerous in the religious sphere when the thought that one possesses (sic) the true law leads to a 'resting on the law' and thus to the notion that one has a claim on God."

53. In opposition to S. R. Driver, *Deuteronomy*, p. 54.

54. Against, for instance, Weinfeld (*Deuteronomic School*, p. 256). Concerning the linking of wisdom and law in later texts, see Zenger, pp. 43-56; and Marböck. According to Würthwein (p. 53), "the appropriation of the law through the sapiential tradition and its becoming imbued with spirit was crucial for the evolution of Jewish 'monism.'" Because the wisdom which was originally formulated in experiential statements was identified with the law, "the images of man and God transmitted by the

sapiential tradition give a new meaning to the law. Action is transferred from God to human beings, who themselves determine their temporal and eternal salvation. In the Old Testament, this notion can only be faintly discerned; it becomes decisive for late Judaism and its understanding of the law. It is fatal to ascribe this interpretation of the law to the Old Testament" ("Sinn des Gesetzes," p. 54).

55. See Reventlow, and Zimmerli, "Wahrheitserweis."

56. It is not, however, stated that the nations will hear "that YHWH has committed His laws to His people" (in opposition to Thompson, p. 103.

57. Braulik, "Ausdrücke," p. 52.

58. This often occurs in connection with Malfroy, pp. 45-65; see, for instance, Johannes, p. 192; further Weinfeld, *Deuteronomic School*, pp. 244-319, concerning Deut 4:6, esp. pp. 255-256. However, Weinfeld does not merely attempt to discover similarities in phraseology between Deuteronomy and sapiential literature (*Deuteronomic School*, pp. 362-363). As Whybray remarks (p. 121 note 191), several of these affinities simply "belonged to the common speech of Israel." But Weinfeld also attempts to discover a common sapiential structure.

59. Murphy (p. 104) states: "Wisdom language does not constitute wisdom. The literary method of 'anthological compositions' . . . cannot be considered sufficient in itself to justify the classification of a given text as wisdom. Nor is it sufficient to make one of the 'topoi' . . . determinative." See further, Crenshaw, pp. 129-142, esp. pp. 132-133.

60. See Boston, pp. 169-202. Verse 16:19b is probably a sapiential sentence. Concerning 1:13, 15, see below.

61. This is in spite of what Whybray affirms (pp. 142-143, 150). Characteristically, the Deuteronomic History, with the exception of the succession narrative, which was taken over from other sources, never mentions the wisdom of a ruler (*Intellectual Tradition*, pp. 109-110). Nevertheless, we need not assume that the text was not written by the Deuteronomic Historian, but by "another writer who *did* see the Deuteronomic Code as *ḥokmâ* and wrote an introduction to stress this point of view" (as Whybray thinks, p. 111). Moore (p. 127) speaks of the adoption of an early monarchic wisdom tradition "with the addition of a bit of anti-wisdom," since a sharp distinction is made between the wisdom of Israel and that of other nations.

62. For an account of the use of these terms in the Old Testament, see Whybray *Intellectual Tradition*.

63. Whybray, p. 145. On the other hand, according to Wildberger (*Jesaja*, vol. 1, p. 449), "*ḥokmâ* means rather the wisdom necessary for coping with everyday problems, whereas *bînâ* refers mainly to the intellect,

to the intellectual faculties necessary for sizing up a situation, drawing the correct conclusions from it and making the right decisions."

64. Wildberger, *Jesaja*, vol. 1, p. 448. Concerning the judiciary office of the king, see *Jesaja*, vol. 1, pp. 450ff.

65. See O. Kaiser, *Jesaja 13-39*, p. 218.

66. According to Proksch, pp. 377-378, it is possible that Isa 29:13-14 refers to a superficial understanding of Deuteronomy. However, in spite of the verbal affinities, there is not enough foundation for this assumption.

67. In poetic texts, the dual expression is always broken up and its members are distributed over the hemistichoi of the verse. The order *ḥākām - nābôn* is much more frequent than the reverse one.

68. Thus e.g., Noth, *Könige*, pp. 44-45; and Görg, p. 29.

69. See Johannes, pp. 42-56.

70. Görg, p. 47, assumes (on the basis of a comparison between verse 12 and Solomon's prayer in verse 9 for a "hearing heart (*lēb šōmēa'*) . . . in order to distinguish (*lᵉhābîn*) good from evil") that Solomon is granted insight, a quality of a wise heart.

71. In opposition to Egyptian models for the pericope about the revelatory dream in Gibeon (3:4-15), Solomon does not participate in the godhead. His uniqueness on the human level is explained as YHWH's gracious elevation of him. Compared to the absolute uniqueness of YHWH, this is only a relative uniqueness. See Görg, pp. 100-104.

72. Noth, *Könige*, p. 53.

73. See, for instance, von Rad, "Josephsgeschichte," pp. 273ff.

74. See, for instance, Ruppert, pp. 78-81.

75. For what follows, see Ruppert, pp. 81-82.

76. Noth, "Bewährung," p. 108.

77. Ruppert, p. 81.

78. Regarding the relation of Deut 1:9-18 to 1 Kgs 3:4-15, see Weinfeld, *Deuteronomic School*, p. 246. The deuteronomic passages speak of *'ᵃnāšîm ḥᵃkāmîm ûnᵉbōnîm wîdu'îm*, that is, through the triple enumeration they differ from 4:6; 1 Kgs 3:12 and Gen 41:33, 39. The entire tendency is also different. Hence we need not take them into account when interpreting our text.

79. See, for instance, D. Baltzer, pp. 141-149. Regarding the collectivizing transfer of the royal idea to the entire people, a transfer which took place in the context of a theocratic current both within the book of Isaiah and elsewhere, see Becker, *Messiaserwartungen*, pp. 63-73.

80. See, for instance, Perlitt, *Bundestheologie*, pp. 167-181.

81. See Weinfeld, *Deuteronomic School*, p. 37 note 4; Görg, p. 213.

82. Regarding the *ḥ^{a}kāmîm* in Jer 8:8-9, see McKane, pp. 102-112. According to this study, the designation is not dependent on Deut 4:6 (against Lindblom, p. 195), nor are verses 6-8 corrected by Jer 8:8-9 (against Altmann, p. 23).

83. See 4:37 (*bḥr*) and 19-20; further Altmann, pp. 15-18.

84. E.g., the exhortation to "wisdom" addressed to everyone in Proverbs 8:1-21, which in verses 14-16 appears as a virtue for rulers and judges; further the ideal image of the wise and judicious (*ḥākām, nābôn*) person in 1:5; 16:21; 17:28; 18:15; Qoh. 9:11.

85. Regarding these passages, see Fohrer, "Weisheit," pp. 258-259.

86. Cf. 1 Kgs 3:28; Isa 11:2; further Deut 1:13, 15.

87. Gen 41:39; Isa 29:14.

88. See 1 Kgs 9:1-9 at the end of the positive part of the Solomon narrative and the relation of this second theophany to the revelatory dream at the beginning of Solomon's reign described in 3:4-15; further 1 Kings 11. The exhortations in the "model for the king" (Deut 17:16-17), which form part of the law on the king (17:14-20) are probably also the result of the negative experiences of the YHWH faith during the reign of Solomon.

89. See Mosis, TWAT 1:953-955; English translation TDOT 2:414ff.

90. Jer 6:22; 50:41.

91. See Wolff, "Kerygma," p. 356.

92. Hulst, "'am/gôy," pp. 312-313.

93. The designation of Israel as a *gôy gādôl* is, according to this view, to be explained as a reference to the terminology of promise (cf. Hulst, "'am/gôy," p. 313). Otherwise Israel's unrivaled special status among the nations, based on its election, could have been expressed by the term *'am*, the customary one in chapter 4. Note the synonymous use of *gôy* and *'am* in verses 27, 33-34 (against Perlitt, *Bundestheologie*, p. 174). Perlitt, affirms that, during the exile, the *'am* became a *gôy*, although the substance of the deuteronomic theology of the people of God as well as the context of the election were retained.

94. Cf. Mosis, TWAT 1:954ff; English translation TDOT 2:414-415.

95. Regarding their elements, see Johannes, pp. 81-89.

96. See Labuschagne, *Incomparability*, pp. 16-28.

97. There exists a second type, differing in meaning as well as in syntactic structure, in which the explanatory additions come only after the comparison introduced by *kî* and should always be understood as being in the real mood. (See, for instance, 2 Sam 7:23, where for this reason the *gôy 'eḥād* of the MT should be maintained.)

98. Since YHWH is not compared to other gods, but Israel (which has YHWH as its God) is compared to other nations, Labuschagne, *Incomparability*, pp. 16-19 (following B. Gemser), defends the translation "God" for *'elōhîm* in verse 7. The same translation is given by Ringgren, TWAT 1:303; English translation TDOT 1:282.

99. According to verse 38, the election of Israel is shown in the possession of the land. Cf. what was said above concerning the promises to the patriarchs.

100. Cf. Johannes, p. 195.

101. For what follows, cf. Metzger, pp. 139-158; Weinfeld, *Deuteronomic School*, pp. 191-209.

102. De Vaux. I have been unable to obtain S. McBride, *Name Theology*.

103. Nelson, *Redactional Duality*, offers an overall view of the literary-critical analysis of 1 Kings 8*.

104. Metzger, p. 151.

105. For a more detailed explanation, see Braulik, "Spuren."

106. Deut 4:11-12 and 36 probably also serve to correct a temple theology which distinguishes between YHWH dwelling in heaven and his name being present on earth. To begin with, a contrast is made between heaven and earth. According to verse 11, the mountain where the revelation took place was "ablaze with fire to the very skies." According to verse 36, YHWH let the Israelites hear his voice from heaven and see his fire on earth. Then, however, the two spheres merge. Israel heard the words of YHWH out of the fire. A comparison with the parallel text of 5:24 reveals a further shift in emphasis. In connection with the Horeb theophany, 5:24 speaks of seeing the "glory (*kābôd*) of YHWH." When Deuteronomy 4 avoids this expression, typical of the temple theology, it is not least because YHWH's verbal revelation, that is, the proclamation of the Decalogue (verse 13) is given pride of place. This was already pointed out by Lohfink, *Höre Israel*, p. 117. Weinfeld, *Deuteronomic School*, pp. 206ff has a slightly different view.

107. Regarding the expression YHWH *'elōhênû* in Deuteronomy, see Lohfink, "Gott im Deuteronomium," p. 109 note 33. Regarding the use of the "national we" by the great mediator figures of the Old Testament, see Scharbert, *Heilsmittler*, p. 312 et passim.

108. The expression *'elōhîm qerōbîm* is not found elsewhere in the Old Testament. The use of this expression and of some other turns of phrase clearly demonstrates the linguistic and theological independence of our text, in spite of all affinities to other texts. Regarding YHWH and *'elōhîm qārôb*, see Viganò, pp. 193-196.

109. The scene of the Horeb theophany shows how completely and deliberately Deuteronomy avoids ascribing any cultic prerogative to Moses. According to verse 11, the entire people assembles as though for the cult, approaches (*qrb*) the scene of the revelation, and stands (*'md*) at the foot of Horeb. In contrast to 5:26-27, their access is not restricted in any way, nor is Moses said to have approached more closely to god, in spite of his special mission (verse 14; see also p. 34 above). When, in verse 7, Moses unites himself with Israel in calling on God, one may even suppose that not merely the people, but also the legislator—that is, the authority acting in the name of Moses (cf. 18:15-18)—is being pledged to observe the law as a medium of the divine presence and of YHWH's answer to all those who call on him (see below). Cf. also the status of Solomon in 1 Kgs 8:59.

110. On the other hand, Solomon in 1 Kgs 8:59 expects the assistance of YHWH, not only for his people, but also for himself. Moses in Deut 4:7 unites himself with his people and participates in their supplication.

111. Here, *mišpāṭ* is employed in a different sense than in verse 58 (cf. also verses 45 and 49). Admittedly, it is characteristic that the insertion occurs in a context where observance of the commandments (verses 58 and 61) is appealed for or demanded. Thus YHWH's help in the exile (concretely speaking, his bringing Israel back to the promised land) could be understood as a prerequisite for observing the law.

112. If, as verse 60 states, this is to lead the nations to a knowledge of YHWH as the only God (cf. Deut 4:35, 39), this can be expected only on the condition that the gods of the nations do not grant any prayers; that is, that they are at any rate too distant as well as too lacking in authority (Johannes, pp. 194-195).

113. In a similar way, verses 12 and 36 reject a "theology of the presence of YHWH in the temple" in favor of a "theology of the divine word." YHWH is present, not through his invisible figure or his name, but above all through his helping word. See further note 106 above. However, our survey shows that 4:7 never referred to YHWH's presence in the Ark and that the interpolation "as often as we call on him" was not a way of spiritualizing his presence after the capture of the Ark (against Dus, pp. 198-199. Neither does our text understand the proximity of God as a historical proximity (against M. Schmidt, *Prophet und Tempel*, pp. 69-74. Finally, the immediate context indicates no reason for interpreting YHWH's presence as "steadfast covenant love" or "covenant relation" (against Labuschagne, *Incomparability*, p. 104).

114. Von Rad, *Old Testament Theology*, 1:95. German original *Theologie*, p. 108.

115. How unconditional YHWH's behavior towards Israel is and how greatly he respects the free decisions of his people is illustrated by verses 26-30. First, they provide a gloomy contrast to the elevating prospect for the future depicted in verses 6-8 (cf. Mittmann, *Deuteronomium 1,1 - 6,3*, pp. 126-127). If Israel devotes itself to idols, it will not remain long in its own land as other peoples do; instead, it will lead a miserable existence, dispersed among them. Far from the place where YHWH was formerly adored, the exiles will worship idols as a punishment—idols made by human hands from dead matter like wood and stone, incapable of giving the most elementary sign of life. Through their mediation, the remnant of Israel hopes to experience the divine presence. However, even in a foreign country, YHWH is not far from his people. If Israel seeks and finds him there, that is only because YHWH's word has already reached Israel and granted it the grace of conversion and of listening to his voice (cf. Lohfink, *Höre Israel*, pp. 112-113). In Isa 55:6, we find a terminological association of verses 7 and 29: *diršû YHWH b*^{e}*himmāṣ*^{e}*'ô q*^{e}*rā'uhû bihyôtô qārôb*. However, the notion that YHWH is near when Israel calls to him has a different meaning in this text and is changed into an exhortation to penance: the presence of YHWH as an offer of salvation will not remain forever. A swift conversion is necessary.

116. Isa 55:6; Ps 34:18-19 (cf. verse 17); 69:4, 19; 119:145-152; 145:18; Lam 3:57. Although these texts are from the exilic and postexilic periods, they bear witness to a widespread notion which even the author of Deuteronomy 4 must have been acquainted with. See further Amirtam, pp. 37-38.

117. 1 Kgs 8:52 and Isa 55:6 speak of the supplications of the people.

118. Here, as in 4:7, we find a wordplay on *qrb* and *qr'*. In Deuteronomy, this occurs again in 20:10 and 31:14.

119. Except for 4:7, Deuteronomy does not speak of the nearness of God. In 30:14, the notion of "being near" is not applied to God but to the entire law promulgated by Moses. Ps 119:145-152 draws the conclusion from Deut 4:7-8. See Deissler, *Psalm 119*. As far as the word field is concerned, Isa 58:2b—a later text than the passage we are concerned with—deserves attention. In this text, YHWH approves his people's desire for an immediate oral transmission of his will: *yiš'ālûnî mišp*^{e}*ṭê-ṣedeq qirbat '*^{e}*lōhîm yeḥpāṣûn*. Note the related promise in verse 8 (*qr'*). Finally, Isa 66:1-2 appears to be a radicalized formulation of, amongst other things, the words in Deut 4:7, implying that the presence of YHWH in the temple is not necessary. YHWH does not turn towards his people at a particular sanctuary, but through his word. (For a detailed analysis of this exilic or early postexilic text, which is mainly deuteronomistic in origin, see Sehmsdorf, esp. pp. 530-542 and 557-561.)

120. Weinfeld, *Deuteronomic School*, p. 256 even says: "the Deuteronomist regarded Solomon's juridical perspicacity, not his knowledge, as the major component of his unparalleled wisdom (1 Kgs 3:12) . . . The scribes of the seventh century . . . began conceiving it in a juridical sense and in terms of his ability to discern between social good and evil."

121. Stamm, pp. 318-319. Note the relation to the category of calling (upon).

122. Stamm, p. 319.

123. Stamm, p. 189 ("konkreter Dank"), cf. p. 319. Note the relation to hearing (or listening) which belongs to the same category as calling.

124. Stamm, p. 167 ("Gebetsnamen"), cf. p. 319. See also the names formed with *šemû* pp. 166-167.

125. Stamm, p. 193 ("Danknamen").

126. Stamm, p. 314 ("Sklavennamen").

127. Von Soden, *Handwörterbuch*, 2:915.

128. Prümm, "Griechen," p. 320.

129. Cf. Prümm, *Handbuch*, p. 36.

130. Regarding the somewhat different relations between personal piety and official cult in Egypt, see Morenz, pp. 108-116.

131. See Vorländer, *Vorstellungen*.

132. Vorländer, *Vorstellungen*, p. 69.

133. Jacobsen, pp. 228-229.

134. When Israel's relation to God (verse 7) is included in the praise of the observance of the law and of the law itself (verses 6 and 8), this is not a digression. (Against Steuernagel, p. 65.)

135. Johannes, p. 279 note 14 (to p. 192).

136. The German *Einheitsübersetzung*, p. 282. Bertholet (p. 16) gives a similar translation: "*ṣaddîqim*—ihrem Zweck innerlich entsprechend" (corresponding inherently to their purpose).

137. Thus von Rad, *Theologie*, p. 209, with reference to 4:8.

138. Von Rad, *Theologie*, p. 387.

139. Cf. Gesenius and Buhl, pp. 673-674. Cf. Ps 19:10; 119.

140. Regarding this view of what behavior *ṣdq* is, see, for instance, Koch, "ṣdq," TWAT 2:515-516.

141. See Kramer and Falkenstein; and Finkelstein.

142. Castellino, pp. 106-132.

143. Falkenstein and San Nicolò; Haase, pp. 17-20.

144. Falkenstein and von Soden, pp. 123-126, 126-130.

145. Kapp.

146. Falkenstein and von Soden, pp. 120-123.

147. See Driver and Miles, *Babylonian Laws*, 1:40-41.

148. Cf. von Soden, "Religion und Sittlichkeit," pp. 149-150.

149. Von Soden, "Religion und Sittlichkeit," p. 151.

150. Böhl, *Babylonische Fürstenspiegel.*

151. xxiv b 1-2. See Driver and Miles, *Babylonian Laws*, vol 2. See also Weinfeld, *Deuteronomic School*, pp. 150-151.

152. Landsberger, p. 223. Since the laws of Hammurapi are in fact legal decisions, it is obvious why Hammurapi failed to bestow upon himself the title of "legislator" (F.R. Kraus, p. 287).

153. Cf. Landsberger, p. 224.

154. Schmökel, p. 67. According to F.R. Kraus, p. 287, *mišarum* generally means "justice" and occasionally "both the typical professional ethics of a judge and the ideal of judging in the Babylon conception."

155. I a 32; V a 21; XXIV b 2, 77, 87; XXV b 7, 64, 96; XXVI b 13, 17.

156. Cf. the prologue (I a 32-39): "to cause justice to prevail in the land, / to destroy the wicked and the evil, / that the strong may not oppress the weak, / to rise like the sun over the blackheaded people, / and to light up the land.

The epilogue (XXIV b 59-62, 74-78) reads: "in order that the strong may not oppress the weak, / that justice might be dealt the orphan (and) the widow ... I wrote my precious words on my stela, / and in the presence of the statue of me, the king of justice, / I set it up" (translations according to ANET, pp. 164, 178).

"The law that is found in the Code of Hammurapi is based on cases in which the king had pronounced judgment—cases in which he and his officials were associated, as is shown by the king's letters; cases which concerned his interest and that of the state; cases where he could demonstrate his sense of justice in a special way; cases in which he could intervene in favor of the weak, the widows and the orphans, against the strong, who were often his own officials. When it says on the stela that the oppressed man is to understand his case from reading the stela and to have his mind set at rest (see below), this refers less to a legal than to a moral aspect—an assurance to the 'oppressed man who has a cause,' and an obligation for Hammurapi's successor on the throne. This obligation is based on Hammurapi's exemplary acts from which the stela on which the just decisions of the king are written down takes its name "the king of justice" (Renger, p. 234).

157. Schmökel, p. 69.

158. XXIV b 77; XXV b 7, 96; XXVI b 13. See also Driver and Miles, *Babylonian Laws*, 1:37-38.

159. Schmökel, p. 94. Regarding the last statement, see note 156 above.

160. XXV b 3-38; translation from *ANET* p. 178.

161. "Even the composition of the relief on the stela expresses, as has been persuasively argued, Hammurapi's extreme self-confidence. The respectful distance normally obtaining between the king and the god has become smaller. Hammurapi stands before Shamash in a respectful, but not devout, attitude. It is not Marduk who grants the king his triumph, but Hammurapi who secures the triumph of Marduk. Shamash and Marduk even appear as the tutelary gods of the ruler. Subordinate gods act as advocates and helpers for simple mortals" (Schmökel, p. 93). See further the predications of the prologue and XXIV b (40-)53-54 (*lamasia* without the divine determinative DINGIR).

162. Yet Hammurapi, in spite of various semi-divine titles, refused the traditional divinization of the king. (Schmökel, pp. 81-82). Later generations, however, may have received a different impression of Hammurapi from the Code.

163. See the passages mentioned in notes 155 and 158 above, further I a 32-34; IV a 53; V a 20-21; XXIV b 62, 70-72; XXV 38, 68; XXVI 6, 27.

164. III a 17; IV a 7; XXIV b 26, 57; XXV b 103 - XXVI b 1. According to F.R. Kraus, p. 289, the Code of Hammurapi bears the stamp of wisdom ideology. It is a "work belonging to Old Babylonian wisdom literature." In their phraseology and in their characterization of the judge and legislator Hammurapi as a wise man, the authors depicted themselves. Weinfeld, *Deuteronomic School*, p. 151 note 1, sees this as a parallel to the identification of wisdom and law in the (deuteronomic) literary compositions written by the scribes—wise men at the court of Jerusalem. If the Code of Hammurapi constitutes an account of the exercise of royal wisdom (*emqum*) addressed to the god and not to the people, then, having regard to the present state of scholarship, it seems advisable "not to consider the laws of Hammurapi as merely an academic collection of decisions, but as part of the means whereby the Babylonians sought to preserve law and order as a living and continuing tradition. It will still remain to decide how far Hammurapi's royal judgments (*dinat šarrim*), as recounted by him, include measures intended as actual reforms" (Wiseman, p. 166).

165. XXIV b 79-83.

166. XXV b 99 - XXVI b 1 (see the text quoted below).

167. XXV b 95 - XXVI b 1 (translation from *ANET* p. 178).

168. For what follows, see Schmökel, pp. 74-76, 95-96.

169. Perhaps there is a relation between the canon formula used in 4:2 and the demand that the law be inviolable. This demand is found for the first time in connection with formal legislation in the Code of Hammurapi. (See Mühl, pp. 90-91, 122-123.)

170. A comparison between certain individual statutes in the Code of Hammurapi and in the Old Testament laws can be found, for instance, in Boecker, pp. 69-115.

171. According to van der Ploeg, p. 81, "the law of Deuteronomy is an improvement, it is more human, it tries to find a place in society for the slave, enabling him to begin his life anew. The Code of Hammurapi asks that a debt-slave should be set free after three years (§ 117), but this is not necessarily a milder regulation; it all depended on the work a slave had to do, the treatment he had to undergo and also on the easiness to become a debt-slave."

172. See Fensham.

173. Menes, p. 85.

174. Rücker, p. 110.

175. Oettli, p. 88.

176. Von Rad, *Gottesvolk*, p. 63.

177. Regarding the last-mentioned aspect, Mühl, pp. 87-88 remarks: "The Israelite law is—in contrast to Hammurapi's law—closely bound up with religion. Indeed, even in the ramifications of civil law, it is dependent on religious reasons."

178. See Braulik, "Ausdrücke," p. 65.

179. See Braulik, "Ausdrücke," pp. 61-62.

180. The law is not identified with wisdom (see above). Furthermore, the way in which the term *tôrâ* is used is characteristic. In Proverbs and in the Psalms, *tôrâ* never takes the article but is always indefinite or in the construct state or takes an enclitic personal pronoun. In Deuteronomy, on the other hand, *tôrâ* is found only with the definite article (the only exception is Deut 33:4, 10, the Benediction of Moses). If *tôrâ* really "was favored by the Deuteronomic editors because of their didactic purpose" (Lindars, p. 135), then Deuteronomy has at any rate changed the "chokmatic" use of *tôrâ* in a decisive manner. In spite of "didactic overtones," *tôrâ* must not, however, be understood as "the book of the divine instruction" (contrary to what Lindars affirms on p. 131). For in Deuteronomy, *tôrâ* is never directly related to YHWH (Braulik, "Ausdrücke," p. 65 note 6). Much the same can be said of von Rad's interpretation of the concept (*Theologie*, p. 235). According to von Rad, *tôrâ* in Deuteronomy means "the whole of YHWH's healing activity in favor of Israel."

181. J.M. Schmidt, "Vergegenwärtigung," p. 198.

182. Much the same is true of the deuteronomistic passage Jer 31:31-34. This vision of the future was written during a period of transition during which, because of the Babylonian exile, no substitute had been found for the former institutions. People lived without these

institutions and therefore thought they would be able to get on without them in the future, too. Because of these sociological facts, the text does not mention any institutions. neither does it explicitly reject them.

183. Wildberger, "Neuinterpretation," p. 323. See also the differences and resemblances between the ways in which this problem is mastered in Deutero-Isaiah and in Deuteronomy. Chapter 4 bears considerable resemblance to Deutero-Isaiah.

184. Thomas Aquinas (Thomas de Aquino), *De re spirituali. Opuscula Theologica*, vol. 2. Turin: 1954, p. 277.

Chapter 2. The Joy of the Feast

1. Ratzinger, p. 488.

2. Ratzinger, p. 499. Something similar had been written earlier by the Protestant theologian Volp (pp. 57-58), "If there is a topic which unites the arts with faith, if there is a constant among the manifold types of Christian liturgy and if, in the future, there is to be one characteristic of the Christian assembly, then this is festivity and the feast . . . Many experts are reluctant to describe the divine service as a feast . . . European irrationalism has shown itself as too dangerous in forcing through uncontrolled claims to power. The churches are seen as merely of social importance and a vague 'public' is to be kept satisfied with modern celebrations which are both oversized and often of a petit bourgeois type. Biblical sobriety and even the dimension of prayer were quickly washed away by general emotionalism. But precisely because there is a danger that a wave of hasty ideas about what a feast means may only make the situation worse, it is necessary to ask oneself how to speak of 'feast' in a way that is theologically meaningful today."

3. Martin, *Fest*.

4. De sancta pentecoste. Hom. 1. Migne, Patrologia Graeca 50 col. 455.

5. Ratzinger, p. 490.

6. Pieper, p. 43.

7. Pieper, p. 54.

8. Köhler, p. 139. On this subject, see e.g., Ammermann. Toit, p. 9 offers a table showing how exceptionally rich in words signifying various aspects of the concept of "you" Old Testament Hebrew was.

9. König, p. 80. Concerning this topic, see also Rahner, esp. pp. 166-167.

10. König, pp. 83-84.

11. See Lohfink, "Bundesformel." The "covenant formula" occurs in Deuteronomy in its twofold form in 26:17-19 and 29:12. Elsewhere, only the second part of the formula – Israel as the people of YHWH – is found: 4:20; 7:6; 14:2; 27:9; 28:9. This is typical of the deuteronomic "theology of the people of God."

12. Cogan (pp. 88-96) regards the evolution in Judah in the eighth and seventh centuries as "acculturation and assimilation": "In a word, the diminutive Judahite state was buffeted on all sides by the cultural patterns dominant in the Assyrian empire. Although Assyria made no formal demands for cultural uniformity among its subjects, one of the by-products of political and economic subjugation was a tendency toward cultural homogeneity. Involved as it was in imperial affairs, Judah was faced with the problem of assimilation of foreign norms, on a national scale, for the first time in its history . . . A feeling of disillusionment in YHWH's ability to change the fortunes of his people was abroad . . . Owing to this political decline, Judahites succumbed to the lure of new gods" (*Imperialism and Religion*, p. 95).

13. Perhaps Hezekiah rebelled against the Assyrians not once, but twice. In that case, he would have been forced to submit in 701 BCE and have rebelled for the second time in 688 BCE. During the second Assyrian invasion, Jerusalem would have been miraculously preserved from capture and occupation by the Assyrian army. See Nicholson, pp. 380-389.

14. See for instance McKay, *Religion*, pp. 20-27; Dietrich, pp. 95-103.

15. See H. Barth, pp. 245-260.

16. McKay, *Religion*, p. 60 and elsewhere; Cogan, p. 112 et passim.

17. See Weinfeld, "Molech."

18. See, for instance, Kornfeld.

19. Lohfink, "Pluralismus," pp. 24-43, esp. pp. 37-41.

20. In the struggle "of Deuteronomy against Canaanite religion, we discern a reaction of fundamental importance. Indeed, its importance can hardly be overestimated, for the functional and universal figure of Baal was much closer to natural man than was YHWH. This powerful rival had every advantage. As regards the worldview, he had the simplest, most obvious logic on his side and he had a wide scale of points of attraction down to every lure connected with sexual orgies. It is particularly instructive to see how Deuteronomy combats this type of religion" (von Rad, *Gottesvolk*, p. 37).

21. Cf. Herrmann.

22. Cf. Craig, vol. 1, tables 22-23 II 10-26. See also Lohfink, "Gott im Deuteronomium," p. 115 note 52.

23. For what follows, cf. Rose, pp. 77-100.

24. According to the literary-critical stratification assumed by Rose (pp. 65-78), apart from single phrases, only 14b and 18b are secondary.

25. Cf. Rose, pp. 87-77. King Hezekiah also appears to have been the first to centralize the cult. Today one can no longer deny that the information in 2 Kgs 18:4a, 22 is historical (thus among others H. Barth, p. 254 note 78). The temple of YHWH in Tell Arad constitutes an archaeological illustration. After the destruction of Stratum VIII, which belongs to the times of Hezekiah, the sanctuary was rebuilt in Stratum VII, but without an altar for burnt offerings. After a second destruction during the reign of King Josiah, the temple was not rebuilt in Stratum VI. On the contrary, a wall was deliberately built diagonally across the temple area. Thus one can distinguish between the abolition of sacrifices outside Jerusalem under Hezekiah and the destruction of the rural shrines under Josiah (Aharoni, p. 27). Probably Hezekiah also let the whole people celebrate the Feast of Unleavened Bread in Jerusalem (see Haag, "Mazzenfest"). Within Deuteronomy, the oldest occurrences of the centralization formula should therefore probably be dated to the reign of King Hezekiah (cf. Rose, p. 97).

26. Von Rad, *Theologie*, pp. 197-198.

27. 12:14, 18, 26; 14:25; 15:20; 16:7, 15, 16; 17:8, 10; 18:6; 31:11. Some of these passages also belong to later strata.

28. See S. McBride, *Name Theology*.

29. 12:11; 14:23; 16:2, 6, 11; 26:2.

30. 12:5, 21; 14:24.

31. Thus Rose, pp. 83-84; against de Vaux.

32. See among others Fohrer, "Kanaanäische Religion," and Gese. (Regarding the cult and a general characteristic, see esp. pp. 173-181.)

33. Fohrer, "Kanaanäische Religion," p. 7.

34. Gese, p. 181.

35. See Seitz, pp. 261-262.

36. Seitz, pp. 289-290.

37. Seitz, p. 290.

38. Thus in 4:28; 28:36, 64.

39. Cf. Floss, pp. 530-535.

40. Floss, pp. 181-235, 551-557 et passim.

41. Floss, p. 535.

42. See Baumgartner, p. 282.

43. In the Greek translation of Codex Vaticanus, the expression "in thirst and nakedness" is missing. This expression occurs nowhere else in Deuteronomy. The rhetoric of the passage is diminished (see Seitz, p. 290), but the terminological correspondences are more noticeable.

44. It is only in this passage that Deuteronomy speaks of "need" (*ḥāsar*, 15:8) and also of hardness of heart (verse 7)—in the argumentation—and of wickedness of heart—grudging (verse 10). Concerning this text, see Schwantes, pp. 66-75.

45. Schwantes, p. 69.

46. According to the statistics of Humbert, in the old historical works Judg 16:23, 2 Sam 6:12; perhaps also 1 Sam 6:13; 11:15; 1 Kgs 1:40, 45; 2 Kgs 11:20; Deut 33:18; in the preexilic prophets, Hos 9:1; Isa 9:2(ter); 22:13; 30:29. The psalms frequently use the root *śmḥ* (Humbert, pp. 195, 196-197), but these instances cannot be dated with any certainty.

47. E.g., von Rad, *Deuteronomium*, p. 148.

48. Reindl, pp. 26-27.

49. Hos 9:1; Isa 9:2(ter); 22:13; 30:29. Humbert, p. 194.

50. Especially Humbert, pp. 195-204, et passim.

51. I have translated this text-critically difficult passage in accordance with Wolff, *Hosea*, p. 192.

52. Mansfeld (pp. 50-53) even supposes that Israel's cultic joy could have been occasioned by the cry "Aleyn Baal is risen!"

53. Rudolph, *Hosea*, p. 175.

54. Against Wolff, *Hosea*, p. 197. Before Wolff, both Humbert (p. 198) and Harvey (pp. 116-127) drew the same conclusions.

55. This is also suggested by the grammatical form of the vetitive, since it is characteristic of the vetitive to be dependent on persons or situations.

56. Wolff, *Hosea*, p. 197.

57. Westermann, "*gîl*—jauchzen," col. 418.

58. Crüsemann, *Studien zur Formgeschichte*. Cf. C. Barth, TWAT 1:1016.

59. See O. Kaiser, *Jesaja 13-39*, pp. 111-117; Wildberger, *Jesaja*, vol. 2, pp. 804-830.

60. O. Kaiser, *Jesaja 13-39*, p. 115.

61. Wildberger, *Jesaja*, vol. 2, p. 827.

62. Concerning the textual criticism and the translation, the genre and the temporal relevance of Isa 8:23b - 9:6, see H. Barth, pp. 141, 177.

63. On the other hand, Wildberger (*Jesaja*, vol. 2, p. 374) affirms that "*śimḥâ* is a quite generally used word for joy"—in verse 2b the joy of the harvest period is given as an example. On the other hand, "*gîl* is more particular" and "(with its derivatives) constitutes a cultic term"; it refers "particularly to joy before God (cf. *l^epānêkā* in verse 2b)." However, precisely this verse employs *gîl* for the quite uncultic sharing out of the

plunder and associates *l^e^pānêkā* with *śāmaḥ*. Other connotations from an alien context should not be introduced here.

64. Against Humbert (pp. 199-200). It is true that verse 5 refers to the birth and enthronement of Josiah (H. Barth, pp. 166-170). However, the passage (8:23b - 9:6), reminiscent of a thanksgiving hymn, mentions several instances of YHWH's favor. There is an immediate factual relation, but not a temporal one (H. Barth, p. 168). The phrase *śām^e^ḥû l^e^pānêkā* in verse 2 cannot, therefore, be definitely connected with the royal ritual.

65. Cf. Reindl, p. 29.

66. Like 8:23b - 9:6, 30:27-33 is not an authentic Isaianic passage, but belongs to the "Assyrian redaction" of proto-Isaiah, dated to the reign of King Josiah (H. Barth, pp. 92-103).

67. Wildberger (*Jesaja*, p. 1207), among others, translates 30:29 as follows, "You will sing a song as in the night in which one consecrates oneself." Concerning the translation see H. Barth, p. 94.

68. Cf. also the later texts Exod 12:42; 34:25; Lev 23:5.

69. Contrary to what H. Barth, among others, affirms (p. 103).

70. Cf. Jeremias, *Theophanie*, pp. 57-58; de Moor, *New Year*, 1:5-6 and note 15; O. Kaiser, *Jesaja 13-39*, p. 245.

71. H. Barth, pp. 99-100.

72. Ruprecht, 2:829-830.

73. Ruprecht, 2:830.

74. This is affirmed by Ruprecht, 2:830.

75. Deut 12:7 (in the plural), 12 (in the plural), 18; 14:26; 16:11, 14; 26:11. Further, 27:7 uses the verb *śāmaḥ*. The change in number in the address in this case probably results from the different strata. Yet even those exhortations which are in the singular are always addressed to several people. The adjective *śāmē^a^ḥ* is found in 16:15, the noun *śimḥâ* only in 28:47.

76. Apart from the instances mentioned in the preceding note, the verb *śāmaḥ* occurs once more in Deuteronomy, in 24:5, not however, in qal as elsewhere, but in piel. There is no parallel elsewhere in the Old Testament to what is stipulated here, namely that a newly married man be exempt from military service and other duties in order to "gladden the heart of the woman he has married." That YHWH "rejoices" is expressed by the verb *śwś*, found only in two late exilic passages, 28:63, (bis) and 30:9(bis). (See von Rad, *Deuteronomium*, pp. 126, 131.) For the rest, in Deuteronomy YHWH's joy—like Israel's—is closely connected with the divine blessing—or with the refusal of this blessing.

77. Kasper, p. 24.

78. From the frequency and fairly early occurrence of *śmḥ* in religious contexts in Deuteronomy, Humbert (pp. 195, 200-201, 208-209) concludes that it was only Deuteronomy which adapted this term from the cultic language and used it in its polemics against the licentious baalistic religion.

79. This has to do with the solemn occasions connected with *śmḥ*, for instance, the sacrifices (12:4-7, 8-12, 13-19; 27:1-8), including the tithes (14:22-27) and the offering of the first fruits (26:1-11), as well as those liturgical events explicitly defined as feast (16:9-12, 13-15). On the redactional level at least, these pericopes form a textual system. In what follows, literary criticism will therefore be largely left out of account. The texts cited have—as I shall demonstrate—much in common in the use of formulas and in the structure of the individual elements. This will be explored mainly from a theological perspective. Yet the order varies (cf., for instance, Seitz, pp. 198-199). From this, however, only hints of the course of events during the feast can be gleaned. In any case, one cannot discern any particular ritual, which seems to be quite in accordance with the general intention of Deuteronomy. The deuteronomic festival theory, which is examined herein, has not been recognized even monographs as extensive as Hulst, *Karakter van den cultus*, or Otto and Schramm, *Fest und Freude*.

80. Concerning the "humanism" of Deuteronomy, see Weinfeld *Deuteronomic School*, pp. 282-297. The problems connected with this concept had been noted earlier by von Rad, *Gottesvolk*, pp. 50-51.

81. Cf. Kasper's definition of Christian joy (p. 29).

82. Cf. Humbert, p. 214.

83. E.g., Humbert, pp. 208-209 et passim. Mansfeld (p. 145) also rejects the notion that *gîl* was always understood as pagan and scandalous or that it referred to a characteristic feature of the Canaanite cultic dance.

84. Harvey, p. 120. In the Ugaritic Baal cycle, the root *śmḥ* is even used fairly frequently, whereas the root *gîl* is used only twice (both times in connection with *śmḥ*, Mansfeld, p. 51 note 5). The root *gîl* appears in the Old Testament mainly in parallel with *śmḥ*.

85. C. Barth, TWAT 1:1018.

86. C. Barth, TWAT 1:1016; Barth does not, however, intend to explain the fact that *gîl* is not found in the deuteronomic tradition.

87. Isa 9:2; Deut 12:12, 18; 16:11; 27:7; Lev 23:40; Ps 68:4. Cf. also Deut 12:7 and 14:26, where *śmḥ* is closely connected with the sacrificial meal before YHWH (*'kl lipnê YHWH*) and 26:10-11, where it is connected with prostrating oneself before YHWH (*hšṭḥh lipnê YHWH*).

88. The only exception is the priestly verse Lev 23:40. See Mansfeld, *Ruf*, for other exhortations to joy which are different from the syntactic point of view and which are only found in poetic texts—unless they are of a non-religious character.

89. For a discussion of the quotation, see Splett, "Mensch und Freude," p. 99 (with a reference to Seneca, *Ad Lucil.* III 2).

90. The revised text of the new German *Einheitsübersetzung* no longer renders this Hebrew word as "cheerful," but translates it "rejoice," a term which cannot be misunderstood. Although *śmḥ* means much more than a casual and spontaneous feeling, one cannot conclude that "c'était alors un véritable rite, commandé par la circonstance ou prévu par le rituel, un rite s'imposant à tout avec la force d'un usage sacré." (Contrary to what Humbert affirms, p. 198.)

91. It is a question of much more than Haag affirms ("Fröhlich sein," p. 39) about "commanding people to be joyful . . . experience teaches that a change in exterior behavior can bring about a fundamental change for people suffering from an anxiety psychosis or some other form of mental disorder. The principle is: Change your behavior, and what ought to be there, the inner root, will grow (A. Görres). The indefatigable appeals to joy in the Old Testament correspond to a psychological law." However, Haag is right in stressing that "only joyful people are loving people. The task of being joyful is the task of changing the world, ultimately the task of realizing the kingdom of God."

92. Against Ratzinger (p. 490), for whom the "authorization" to rejoice is "valid only if it holds out against death."

93. See Seitz, p. 275.

94. For *mišlaḥ*, see 28:8 (and, in the curse section, verse 20). For *ma‘*^{a}*śeh* see 28:12.

95. Von Rad, *Gottesvolk*, pp. 49-50.

96. Von Rad, *Gottesvolk*, p. 50.

97. Westermann, *Segen*, p. 49.

98. Concerning the consequences of this conception of God, see, for instance, G. Ebeling, pp. 233-234. This approach to the first commandment does not necessarily contradict an orientation of worship in accordance with the third (or fourth) commandment, the sabbath commandment, of which it has been maintained that it is limited to the cult. The deuteronomic Decalogue makes the sabbath commandment the primary commandment and makes it—from a theological as well as a literary point of view—the heart of the Ten Commandments.

99. The authentic content of the faith of Israel, which made it possible to proclaim the Feast of Weeks and the Feast of Booths as feasts for YHWH must be evaluated with more discrimination than is usually the

case. This is also true of Sauer, p. 140. The difference between the religion of Israel and those of the neighboring peoples cannot, in the cultic domain, be described as the difference between a "historical religion" and a "natural religion." In Deuteronomy at any rate, the old harvest festivals were not historicized. 16:12b gives the reason for the preceding humanitarian stipulations. Literary criticism usually ascribes this verse to a later editor (see, for instance, Nebeling, p. 108). The festal joy of Israel does not, according to Deuteronomy, express the redemption Israel has experienced in its history (contrary to what Hulst affirms, *Karakter van den cultus*, p. 88).

100. Halbe, "Passa-Massot," pp. 234-356. For a discussion of the difference in the basic liturgical structure of the Passover-Feast of Unleavened Bread as well as the Feast of Weeks and the Feast of Booths, see chapter 3 in the present volume.

101. Cf. Köhler, p. 139, although admittedly Köhler does not prove this and regards it as something common to the whole Old Testament. Regarding this notion of joy, see also Karl Barth's reflection in *Lehre von der Schöpfung*, pp. 428-429.

102. Schulte, p. 42.

103. Splett, "Mensch und Freud," pp. 100-101. On p. 101 note 27, he also refers to the first entry in Haecker. "Distrust every joy which is not at the same time gratitude."

104. Pieper, pp. 45-54.

105. Splett, "Was bedeutet," p. 8.

106. See Gaster.

107. See among others Hvidberg.

108. Weinfeld, *Deuteronomic School*, p. 213; Galling, pp. 126-127.

109. Concerning the translation and the interpretation, see Cazelles.

110. Probably one should not think of the god Mot ("death"), but of Baal; this is maintained by Worden.

111. This is also admitted by von Rad (*Deuteronomium*, p. 115), although he assumes that an old purification ritual was taken over and given a secular context. He does call this a "rather diffuse compromise." In this context, the pericope about the clean and unclean animals (14:3-21a) and the exhortation concerning leprosy (24:8-9) should also be mentioned. "The accent on the concern for being ritually correct in this form is alien to the authentic deuteronomic view" (von Rad, *Gottesvolk*, p. 76).

112. Von Rad, *Gottesvolk*, p. 72.

113. Harvey, pp. 121-126. The myths of Ras Shamra (Ugarit) show, however, that in speaking of the Canaanite conceptions of cult and sacrifice, one must distinguish between popular piety and the beginnings of theological reflection. The religious certitude that Baal would, in the end, achieve a victory over his enemies could lead to a simplistic understanding of his salvific actions. The myth combats these primitive notions. Therefore it explains a longer absence of rain with the highhandedness and sovereignty of Baal. "Human pleading for rain, as well as sacrifices and rites performed in this context create a further prerequisite for Baal's power becoming present, but they cannot force Baal to intervene in the course of nature" (Kinet, "Theologische Reflexion," p. 242).

114. See Harvey, pp. 122-125. As an example from the Neo-Assyrian epoch, I shall cite a hymn written by Aššurnaṣirpal II to the goddess Ishtar (German translation by E. Ebeling, p. 61).

> May the queen of heaven rejoice,
> may Assur rejoice in Ehersaggula.
> May Anu, the king of heaven, rejoice,
> may all the heavenly gods rejoice.
> May Ea rejoice in the depths of the ocean,
> may the gods of the depths be radiant.
> May the — the goddesses of the land rejoice.
> May all those who sacrifice dance,
> may their hearts rejoice and sing.

115. See Braulik, *Sage, was du glaubst*.

116. Pieper, pp. 57-58.

117. In general, it is true of Deuteronomy that "L'auteur du code deutéronomique vient répondre à l'aspiration de son peuple, et il a compris la crise des temps. Il ne se contente plus de fixer les institutions, les rites et les lois et d'ordonner en formules lapidaires, il donne des explications, il expose des motifs rationnels, et, quel que soit son respect pour l'antique coutûme, il n'hésite par à l'interpréter et à la transformer conformément aux exigences de son idéal réformiste. En fait, c'est une autre conception de la loi et de l'institution sociale qu'il apporte; et, au point de départ de cette conception, il y a la rationalisation de l'idée même d'alliance" (Causse, *Groupe ethnique*, p. 126).

118. Von Rad, *Gottesvolk*, p. 39.

119. This date for the priestly stratum of the Pentateuch must be maintained against Weinfeld, *Deuteronomic School*. Otherwise, however, what follows is partly based on Weinfeld's observations concerning the various cult stipulations (Weinfeld, *Deuteronomic School*, pp. 210-224).

120. Weinfeld (*Deuteronomic School*, pp. 211-212) even states: "The constant emphasis on the obligation to share the sacrificial repast with indigent persons creates the impression that the principal purpose of the offering is to provide nutriment for the destitute elements of Israelite society."

121. The phrase "to fulfill a promise" (*šillam neder*) is, characteristically, found only in Deut 23:22.

122. 15:21 and 17:1 do not constitute exceptions to this rule, since they forbid the sacrifice of imperfect victims. However, according to 27:6, which is part of a chapter that was later inserted into Deuteronomy, sacrifices are to be offered to YHWH on Gerizim. It is particularly striking that the Passover victim is to be slaughtered "for YHWH" (16:2).

123. For what follows, see Steuernagel, p. 96.

124. The only procedure of expiation which is extensively explained in Deuteronomy is not a sacrificial ceremony and has only symbolic value. This is the removal of the blood guilt brought on the community by murder committed by an unknown person (21:1-9). The whole process shows, as clearly as possible, that it is not the rite as such which expiates for the crime. On the contrary, after confession and prayer, YHWH absolves the sin himself, without recourse to any intermediary. Thus the manner in which this old custom is introduced into the deuteronomic code makes the deuteronomic attitude to sacrifices clear (see Weinfeld, *Deuteronomic School*, pp. 210-211).

125. Rose (p. 89 note 2) rightly points out that this established concept must not be understood as "creating a space detached from YHWH; on the contrary, the old cult stipulations are still valid for 'profane slaughtering (verses 23-24).'" "Profane" here means simply "outside the sacred domain."

126. This roughly chiastic structure of the statements in verses 13-19, with the individual elements being repeated in the inverse order in the second part, differs from the chiastic structure which is announced by particular phrases or introductory particles. The structure proposed by Rose (p. 67 note 3) does not quite do justice to verses 13-19, since it does not take verse 18b into account. For the rest, the text analyzed herein is always the present, redactional version of Deuteronomy.

127. Rendtorff, *Geschichte des Opfers*, p. 39.

128. Only the pericope 27:1-8, which is undeuteronomic both as to theme and as to wording, demands that burnt offerings and sacrifices be offered "to YHWH."

129. Von Rad, *Deuteronomium*, pp. 65-66.

130. Von Rad, *Deuteronomium*, p. 73.

131. Von Rad, *Gottesvolk*, p. 38.

132. Weinfeld, *Deuteronomic School*, p. 215.

133. Regarding the possible reasons for these rules, see Weinfeld, *Deuteronomic School*, p. 216.

134. At a later period, 16:16-17 establishes this for all three pilgrimage feasts, that is, for the Feast of Unleavened Bread, the Feast of Weeks and the Feast of Booths: "No one shall come into the presence of YHWH empty-handed. Each of you shall bring such gifts as he can in proportion to the blessing which YHWH your God has given you."

135. For the Feast of Booths, cf., for instance, Lev 23:39-41; Num 29:12; Zech 14:16, 18, 19. Deut 16:10, 13 employs the expression "to organize a feast" (*'śh ḥag*).

136. This occurs even in connection with the Holiness Code (Lev 23:40). The Priestly Code uses *śāmaḥ* only in this passage, *śimḥâ* in Num 10:10, *śāmē^{a}ḥ* nowhere.

137. Deut 31:10-13 also provides for reading "the whole of this Torah," (that is, Deuteronomy) at the Feast of Booths every seventh year (that is, every year of remission).

138. Von Rad, *Gottesvolk*, p. 44.

139. Von Rad, *Gottesvolk*, p. 65.

140. Cf. Martin, p. 75.

141. Von Rad, *Gottesvolk*, p. 40.

142. Auerbach, p. 16.

143. Von Rad, *Gottesvolk*, pp. 42-43.

144. The deuteronomic centralization laws are to be understood as a "reinterpretation of an ancient cult order," a reinterpretation which had become necessary "partly because of the unsatisfactory state of affairs, partly because of new knowledge of YHWH and his relationship with Israel. And this last element, the new theological conception of Israel's relationship with YHWH, constitutes the decisive point" (von Rad, *Deuteronomium*, p. 65).

145. Splett, "Was bedeutet," p. 7.

146. Cf. K. Barth, pp. 432-433.

147. Rombold, p. 12.

148. Seitz, p. 191 note 288.

149. See Bächli, pp. 119-128.

150. For what follows, see Weinfeld, *Deuteronomic School*, pp. 291-292.

151. See the old custom of a family pilgrimage to the sanctuary in 1 Samuel 1. Cf. further Deut 29:10, 17 and 31:12.

152. Lohfink, "Freizeit," p. 191.

153. Albertz, p. 174. Although chapter 28 puts the alternatives blessing or curse before the entire people, verses 3-6 of this chapter take up a blessing which is unambiguously addressed to the individual family. Verses 7:12-15 also show how decisively the promises to bless Israel remain related to the blessings experienced in the life of an individual family (pp. 174-175).

154. Emerton, "Priests and Levites."

155. See Lohfink, "Gewaltenteilung," p. 68.

156. In Deuteronomy as well, the original conception is displaced in favor of an "exaggerated emphasis on the cultic element ... In one stratum of the additions, particular importance is given to the Levitical priests. The earlier version puts no particular stress on this class. Indeed, far from being important, the Levites were in need of help and Deuteronomy wanted to give them equal status. This emphasis on the priestly functions of the Levites (18:1; 19:17; 20:2ff; 21:5; 27:9; 31:9ff) breaks up the harmonic deuteronomic system with its characteristic notion of the people" (von Rad, *Gottesvolk*, p. 76).

157. In Deuteronomy, it is only found twice more, in 14:26 and 15:20. In 15:19-23, the central statement is the prohibition against sacrificing a defective first-born animal to YHWH. The first-born animals of both herd and flock are to be eaten by the family every year. The pericope says nothing either about the Levites or about joy. In 14:26, however, the joy is closely related to the joint meal. Only in verse 27 is the obligation to take care of the Levites stressed (see below). Probably the different dates of the texts explain these differences. On the redactional level, however, it is possible to consider that the two passages complete each other and are therefore compatible.

158. "When it is nevertheless affirmed that the tithes and the other sacrifices are to be consumed at a meal, the parts that belong to the deity and to the priest are ignored and the text only mentions the person who brings the sacrifice and his protégés as those who are to profit from the sacrificial gift. Hence one cannot, in spite of the fact that it is always stated that the offerings should be used for a meal, conclude that the entire offerings were so used" (Eissfeldt, *Erstlinge*, pp. 49-50).

159. Fensham, pp. 129-130.

160. Apart from 14:29, cf. also 10:18-19; 16:11, 14; 24:17, 19, 20, 21; 26:12, 13; 27:19 and see Rose, p. 128 note 5.

161. Eissfeldt, *Erstlinge*, pp. 53-54.

162. Regarding the function of the priests at the offering of the first fruits, see verses 26:3-4, which were later inserted into the text. For a literary-critical evaluation, see Seitz, p. 245.

163. The priestly Holiness Code, on the other hand, concludes (in Lev 23:42-43) from the history of Israel that aliens are not to be allowed at the Feast of Booths. Living in booths, a custom which is here, for the first time given a historical explanation, was intended to remind Israel of its origin as a nation in the times of Moses, when YHWH led his people out of Egypt and had to let them temporarily live in such booths during the desert march, before they entered the promised land (Elliger, *Leviticus*, p. 323.

164. Concerning the connection between Israel's life in Egypt and Israel's own attitude towards aliens, see 16:12 regarding the cult (cf. note 99 above). For the social domain, see 10:19; 24:18, 22.

165. Von Rad, *Gottesvolk*, p. 54. See also Bächli, pp. 127-128, regarding the alien in Deuteronomy.

166. See pp. 44-45 in the present volume.

167. Fohrer, "Kanaanäische Religion," p. 7.

168. Regarding the tendency of Deuteronomy to concentrate increasingly on the family as responsible for the traditions of the YHWH religion, see Albertz, pp. 177-178.

169. "Deuteronomy explicitly stresses the continued and inner unity of the people it addresses . . . The strikingly frequent use of *kōl yiśrāʾēl* (all Israel), the way of including, without any distinction, the many ranks and classes of the people in a big family of *ʾāḥîm* (brothers), living in one *naḥ^{a}lâ* (inherited land)—all this, no doubt, expresses the desire for a united undivided Israel . . . The author is thinking of an ideal Israel . . . This endeavor corresponds to the summing up and unification of the cult which we have already discussed" (von Rad, *Gottesvolk*, p. 58).

170. What is usually rendered "people of God" should, according to the Old Testament, be rendered "the family of YHWH"—see Lohfink, "Gottesvolk," pp. 113-117.

171. Wolff, *Anthropologie*, pp. 273-274.

172. Golomb, p. 55.

173. Wolff, *Anthropologie*, p. 273. Regarding the concrete terms of the idea of fraternity in Deuteronomy, see Causse, "L'idéal politique."

174. Cf. Schultz, pp. 65-66.

175. Von Rad, *Gottesvolk*, p. 63.

176. Splett, "Was bedeutet," p. 14.

177. Splett, "Was bedeutet," p. 14.

178. Von Rad (*Gottesvolk*, p. 40) uses an expression which is at any rate easily misunderstood when he writes "Is there anything Deuteronomy cares more about than to express joy over YHWH's blessing and allow the poor to share in this joy?"

179. 15:20 (see note 191 below), but not 16:7, also uses this expression in the context of the Passover. 12:27 regulates the sacrificial rite and therefore mentions neither "eating before YHWH" nor joy. The three passages are not part of the textual system of the deuteronomic festival theory. The only exception is constituted by the originally non-deuteronomic verse 27:7.

180. Smend, "Essen und Trinken," p. 457.

181. Ibid.

182. Splett, "Was bedeutet," p. 14.

183. Thomassin, p. 40; quoted in Pieper, p. 60.

184. Verse 11 speaks of "all your choice gifts" after Israel has received the land. Because of the combination with the tithes, "heave offering" (12:6, 11, 17) has often been taken to be what "is lifted up with the hand" from the first fruits, since this offering would otherwise be missing from the enumeration, which is intended to be complete. However, the expression does not fit in this context. It seems more likely that we are dealing with the priests' share of the tithes or with a kind of "cult tax" for the sanctuary. The term cannot, however, be defined with any certainty (see Eissfeldt, *Erstlinge*, pp. 56-59).

185. This is reflected in the criticisms of Hosea; see May, pp. 93-94.

186. Eissfeldt (*Erstlinge*, p. 53 note 2) already thought it important for a correct understanding of Deuteronomy to stress "its conservative traits as well as its progressive tendency, the endeavor to centralize the cult. These conservative traits appear in the piety towards old customs and usages." See also *Erstlinge*, pp. 51-52.

187. Stolz, *Strukturen und Figuren*, pp. 227-228. Cf. further de Moor, *New Year*, 1:6, 10-11, 14.

188. Von Rad, *Gottesvolk*, p. 41.

189. G. Ebeling, p. 240.

190. This term is from Seitz, p. 193.

191. Apart from the festival theory texts, the phrase is also used in 15:20 (see note 179 above). Outside Deuteronomy, it is found in Exod 18:12 (belonging to the priestly tradition); Ezek 44:3; 1 Chr 29:22.

192. See p. 38-39 in the present volume concerning Isa 9:2, which is from the deuteronomic period but in which *lipnê YHWH* cannot be given the same meaning as in the deuteronomic cult legislation. The phrase is also found in Lev 23:40 (priestly).

193. Outside the pericopal system of the deuteronomic festival theory, "eating" and "rejoicing" before YHWH occur only in Deut 15:20 and 18:6-7. In 15:20, however, "before YHWH" is almost a statement of place (Seitz, p. 189 note 279). "To stand before YHWH" in 18:7, however,

means "to serve." Therefore a "there" is necessary in order to make the reference to the chosen site clear.

194. In the context of the Passover, too, the cult formula is missing; however, the sacrifice is slaughtered "for YHWH" (16:2).

195. Reindl, p. 28. According to Nötscher (p. 104) "'to eat before YHWH' means 'to hold a meal with sacrificial meat' or 'to be YHWH's guest.' The locational meaning is not entirely suppressed, but the spiritual relation to YHWH is crucial. Every sacrificial feast is a feast for YHWH . . . insofar as it is a feast in YHWH's honor."

196. This is demanded only when the first fruits are brought in (26:10, *hištaḥ^{a}weh*).

197. Cf. Splett, "Mensch und Freud," p. 94.

198. Reindl, p. 29. As his statistics show (p. 33), Deuteronomy uses *lipnê YHWH* as a cultic technical term with a partly local meaning eight times and as an expression for a religious attitude or act twelve times. (This second meaning is dependent on the first.) In the priestly tradition, the formula occurs ninety-eight times as a cultic concept and only twice in order to express a religious attitude.

199. "One characteristic feature of Deuteronomy is the theological effort to highlight the *fascinosum* aspect (in Rudolf Otto's sense) of the God of revelation and thus of revealed religion. It was not without reason that this was, in some sense, the favorite book of Jesus. 'What does not sparkle is not attractive' constitutes an important principle not merely for the orientation of the divine message of the Bible, but also for worship itself. If the form religious worship takes does not make it clear that God loves human beings (Titus 3:4), the diminished importance given to worship cannot be blamed on 'the decrease in faith among the faithful' alone. Nietzsch's famous criticism of the lack of joy among Christians, a lack which means that they do not give the impression of being 'saved,' is still valid. Above all, those who are responsible for the form worship takes in the new covenant ought to feel concerned and dismayed at this—especially when they consider how Deuteronomy characterized the temple liturgy: 'to rejoice before YHWH'" (Deissler, "Priestertum," p. 34 note 65).

200. See Braulik, "Menuchah," p. 76.

201. Cf. Mühlen, *Entsakralisierung*.

202. Schulte, p. 44. The quotation from Gregory is to be found in *Moralia* 8, 18 Migne, Patrologia Latine 75 col. 821 C. From the point of view of biblical theology, human beings encounter their creator in his

blessings. Deuteronomy exhorts them to render thanks for these blessings through cultic festive joy. According to Deuteronomy, God's love for Israel finds its expression in the election of the people, in their redemption from Egypt, as well as in the gift of the promised land with its blessings (e.g., 7:6-16). The people's love for God, which constitutes a response to this love, is, according to Deuteronomy, the principal commandment of the covenant and describes Israel's exclusive relation to YHWH as its God (6:4-5).

203. See Humbert, pp. 201-204.

204. Humbert, p. 211; C. Barth, TWAT 1:1015-1016.

205. See the various articles about "peace" by Beyreuther.

206. A detailed survey of the terms used for "joy" in the NT is offered by Backherms, pp. 27-43.

207. Beyreuther, p. 382.

208. Beyreuther, p. 33.

209. Beyreuther, p. 381.

210. Of the sixteen occurrences of the word group **εὐφραίνειν** / **εὐφροσύνη** in the New Testament, ten are found in the Lucan writings. Of the sixteen occurrences of the word group **ἀγαλλιᾶσθαι** / **ἀγαλλίασις**, seven are found in the Acts or the Gospel of Luke.

211. Cf. Acts 3:22-26 with Deut 18:15-19 and see Martini.

212. Gulin, 1:122.

213. For an interpretation of the joyous meal of the first Christians, see, for instance, Toit, pp. 103-139.

214. Weiser, pp. 17-19.

215. Reicke, p. 25.

216. Reicke, p. 31.

217. "This *koinōnia* is the effect of the working of the Spirit in the community. It is based on faith, finds its expression in cult and its concrete realisation in the sharing of material goods. Under these different aspects it differs from and surpasses the *koinōnia* concept in Hellenism and in the Qumran community" (Panikulam, p. 129).

218. Here the Christian Easter is realized. See Braulik, "Pascha." See further Braulik, "Eucharistie." Suggestions on how to realize this today are offered by, for instance, Reifenberg, pp. 52-60.

219. Reicke, p. 203.

Chapter 3. Commemoration of Passion and Feast of Joy

1. Neunheuser, "Vom Sinn der Feier," p. 20. Neunheuser refers to paragraphs 2, 7 and 18 of "Sacrosanctum Concilium" (SC).

2. Neunheuser, "Vom Sinn der Feier," p. 18.

3. Haag, "Kult," p. 662.

4. As regards the genre, the common denotation "calendar" is admittedly incorrect. See Morgan, pp. 155-159.

5. Von Rad, *Theologie*, p. 227.

6. Regarding similarities and differences between the two cult centralizations, see for instance Haran, pp. 132-146. The historicity of the two cult centralizations is denied by H.D. Hoffmann, *Reform*, pp. 155, 269. However, if the texts are analyzed more extensively than they are in this work, and the archaeological material—for instance that of Arad—is taken into account, Hoffmann's thesis cannot be sustained.

7. The cult centralization with Jerusalem as the center was, according to, for instance, Maag (pp. 92-93), made possible by the belief that the Temple of Jerusalem had been chosen by God. Historically and theologically, this election was made evident by the fact that only the sanctuary in Jerusalem had been preserved when the Assyrian king, Sennacherib made his punishing expedition in 701 BCE. The political aspect of the reform has been particularly stressed by Weinfeld, "Cult Centralization." The cult centralization also had political features, although it seems probable that the Assyrians had never forced Judah to follow their own cult. Concerning this, see Cogan, p. 95. Cf. also the religio-political function of the feast which, according to 1 Kgs 12:32-33, Jeroboam centered in Bethel for the Northern Kingdom in order to have a counterpart to the Feast of Booths in the Southern Kingdom.

8. Concerning what follows, see Lohfink, "Pluralismus."

9. See Haag, "Mazzenfest."

10. Lohfink, "Beobachtungen," pp. 239-290.

11. Only Haran, pp. 342-343 assumes a predeuteronomic paschal sacrifice in the temple.

12. Concerning this characterization of the intention of Deuteronomy, see Herrmann, pp. 169-170.

13. Nicolsky, p. 185.

14. Nicolsky, pp. 186-187.

15. See von Rad, *Gottesvolk*.

16. See chapter 2 in the present volume.

17. Even Nicolsky stresses this (pp. 172-174). In Exod 34:25b, the *pesaḥ* theme is secondary. It was inserted later because of the deuteronomistic *pesaḥ-maṣṣôt*. If the Passover had been a pilgrimage feast (*ḥag*) from the beginning, it would have had its place in the context of the three pilgrimage feasts. The strong position of the concept *ḥag* in the traditio-historical parallel in 23:18 argues against eliminating this term from 34:25.

18. See Schreiner.

19. According to Elliger (*Leviticus*, p. 99), leavened bread seems to have been the rule for *zebaḥ*, the meal sacrifice; unleavened bread the exception. In any case, Exod 34:25 and 23:18 do not allow us to conclude that there was a predeuteronomic relation between the Feast of Unleavened Bread and the Passover—contrary to Haran's view (pp. 327-342). See, for instance, Halbe, *Privilegrecht*, pp. 195-198. There is no predeuteronomic evidence for a custom of eating unleavened bread at Passover even before the Passover became related to the Feast of Unleavened Bread. The same is true of Josh 5:10-12. See also Otto and Schramm, p. 162 note 1.

20. With similar arguments, Wijngaard has pleaded for this in *Deuteronomium*, p. 168. Concerning the dating of predeuteronomic Feast of Unleavened Bread to the new moon, see Otto, p. 182 and note 5. Auerbach's theses that whenever the word *ḥōdeš* is used in preexilic texts, it means "new moon" is, however, false; see Cholewiński, p. 183 note 22. Kutsch, p. 19, considers it probable that the Passover was celebrated on 14/15 Nisan, that is, in the night of the full moon, not only during the exile but previously as well. Against the preexilic date, see Otto, pp. 183-184; against identifying the 14/15 of Nisan with the night of the full moon, see McKay, "Date of Passover." Kutsch, however, also objects to the notion that there was a whole month within which the paschal slaughtering could take place. For "at least as regards life in a cultivated land (that is, sedentary life), one must assume that a feast like the Passover, even if it was celebrated at home within the family and not in the central sanctuary, was celebrated at the same date everywhere" ("Erwägungen," p. 19). Even more must this be the case for the Passover that was centralized in Jerusalem. Thus it would seem that *ḥōdeš* does mean "new moon" in this context.

21. See W. Gross, "Herausführungsformel," pp. 439-440. Hos 2:17 is the only non-deuteronomic and older instance of this formula. But whereas Deut 16:3 uses *yṣ'*, Hos 2:17 uses *'lh*.

22. Halbe, "Erwägungen," p. 345. Cf. Wambacq, pp. 31-54.

23. See Halbe, "Erwägungen," passim.

24. See the most recent publications which discusses the older literature: Cholewiński, pp. 179-180; Halbe, "Passa-Massot"; Halbe, "Erwägungen"; Otto, pp. 178-182. Apart from literary-critical considerations, the centralization of the Feast of Unleavened Bread as early as Hezekiah and the wording of the oldest cult centralization text in Deuteronomy under the same king are both arguments for the interpolation of a *pesaḥ* stratum into a preexisting *maṣṣôt* text.

25. This remains true even though the correspondences in the concentric structure must be determined somewhat differently from what Halbe, "Passa-Massot," p. 153 proposes.

26. The expression is, apart from Deut 16:3, found only in the priestly verse Exod 12:11 and in the exilic Isa 52:12.

27. The formula (together with *yṣ'*) is, apart from Deut 16:3, found only in the deuteronomistic texts Jer 7:22; 11:4; 34:13 and in the late postexilic Mic 7:15.

28. See, for instance, Halbe, "Passa-Massot," pp. 167-168. However, verse 3a*β**b cannot be shown to belong to the priestly tradition.

29. See Exod 34:18; 23:15. Hence Deut 16:1b must be considered to belong entirely to the "pascha stratum" (contrary to Halbe, "Passa-Massot," pp. 155-156 and note 46).

30. Schottroff (p. 126) underestimates this aspect when he states, "A memorial is not the experience of a cultic act but the result of this act."

31. Schottroff, p. 126.

32. See Gross, *Bileam*, pp. 425-427, who opposes the thesis that "the formula of bringing out, together with *yṣ'* hi., from the beginning interpreted the exodus as a liberation from servitude and oppression."

33. Against Füglister, *Heilsbedeutung*, p. 108.

34. Füglister, *Heilsbedeutung*, p. 109. It was only later that the eating of unleavened bread acquired this and other memorial functions. See *Heilsbedeutung*, pp. 107-114 and Zeilinger.

35. The holiday (see note 38 below) and the rest from work which are prescribed in verse 8 do not, in the editorial deuteronomic context, necessarily demand that one be present in the central sanctuary, especially as nothing is said about where the unleavened bread should be eaten. According to Caloz, p. 57, "holiday" (*'ᵃṣeret*) in Deut 16:8 replaces the feast (*ḥag*) in the central sanctuary in the older parallel Exod 13:6.

36. However, when the first produce is brought to the temple and the short historical credo is recited in order to remind the Israelites of their life as aliens in Egypt (Deut 26:5), the "aliens" are to participate in the joy of this cultic act (verse 11). Compare 16:14 with Lev 23:42-43.

37. Cf. p. 67 and note 3 above.

38. Concerning this meaning of *ᵃṣeret*, see Cholewiński, p. 188 note 36 and p. 191 note 42.

39. To judge by Exod 13:6 (see also note 35), the particular festival character of the seventh day seems to have been an old feature of the Feast of Unleavened Bread; cf. Cholewiński, p. 185. Concerning the different interpretations of Deut 16:8, refer to the short survey in *Heiligkeitsgesetz*, p. 186 note 32. In any case, verse 8 could later be understood in accordance with the priestly legislation or be reinterpreted.

40. Cf. Fohrer, "Kanaanäische Religion," p. 7.

41. See Gese, pp. 173-181.

42. See Harvey, pp. 122-125.

43. 27:7 does not constitute a genuine exception, since this cultic ordinance is to be observed only once, immediately after crossing the Jordan, whereas the corpus of laws contains generally valid ordinances. Only *śāmaḥ* pi., "make happy" is used in 24:5 outside any liturgical contest. Concerning 28:47, where the noun "joy," *śimḥâ* is found, see p. 83 above.

44. See page 52 in the present volume. The term "feast of joy," which might appear tautological, is meant to show that the concept of joy is explicitly thematized in the feasts of Deuteronomy.

45. This change of name remains characteristic of the deuteronomic calendar, even though Exod 34:22 be older than 23:16 and thus the feast was called Feast of Weeks from the beginning (according to Laaf, pp. 177-178). For this proper name was replaced by the designation "harvest festival" even before Deuteronomy (Exod 23:16). Whether this was, as Laaf assumes (p. 178), an early attempt to force the Canaanite features into the background is, however, open to question.

46. Against, for instance, H.J. Kraus, *Gottesdienst*, p. 73.

47. See Halbe, "Erwägungen," pp. 326-327.

48. Since Hölscher, pp. 186-187, defines the addressees and dates of both the Passover-Feast of Unleavened Bread and the Feast of Weeks and the Feast of Booths wrongly, he can discern "no image of reality" in the deuteronomic feast regulations (p. 186). But the legislator has not "mechanically transported to Jerusalem institutions which were suitable only for the local cults in the high places" (p. 185). The deuteronomic feast regulations do not constitute an "impracticable theory" (p. 186). See also p. 81 in the present volume. Cf. further, the programmatic character of ancient oriental legislation, e.g., the Code of Hammurapi.

49. Against, for instance, Cholewiński, p. 196.

50. These decrees regard the three yearly pilgrimages to the central sanctuary primarily as an act of confession. Bringing gifts is an integral part of this confession as worship of YHWH, who gives his blessing. Cf.

Horst, p. 97. It is above all the responsibility of the heads of the families to proclaim this confession of YHWH.

51. Concerning the celebration of the Feast of Booths *l^ekā* (verse 13), see Cholewiński, p. 202 note 73.

52. In this sense, I wish to correct or qualify certain statements in chapter 2 of the present volume.

53. Cf. Auerbach, p. 16.

54. This exhortation does not refer only to humanitarian decisions (cf. 15:15; 24:18, 22). It should not be understood as a historicization of the Feast of Weeks through the redemption experienced by Israel in the exodus event – contrary to what Laaf says, (pp. 175, 181).

55. See p. 57 in the present volume. In this context, the differences in the lists of the individual members of the festival community are important. They reflect the aim of each cultic stipulation in a liturgical and symbolic way (see pp. 52-57 in the present volume), further the eloquent silence concerning a cultic meal at the Feast of Weeks and the Feast of Booths (see pp. 81-82 in the present volume).

56. Contrary to what Horst affirms (p. 125).

57. Contrary to what Hölscher (p. 185) affirms. See Cholewiński, pp. 214-215.

58. This is true in spite of the exhortation to offer a freewill gift at the Feast of Weeks (verse 10), or, according to another version (verse 16), not to come empty-handed to "see the face of YHWH" at any of the three pilgrimage feasts.

59. That the formula "to rejoice before YHWH" characterizes the Feast of Booths because of Lev 23:40, must be excluded, especially as this verse is concerned with a stipulation in the Holiness Code which presupposes the deuteronomic festival calendar (against Merendino, p. 135).

60. Reindl, p. 28.

61. Reindl, p. 29.

62. See p. 61-62 in the present volume.

63. Fore more detail, see pp. 34-35 in the present volume.

64. See Pieper, *Zustimmung*.

65. All this is contrary to Neunheuser's undifferentiated characterization of "all feasts of the Old Testament people of god" quoted above (p. 67). If the Old Testament liturgy is not to be seen as a mere precursor of the New Testament "fulfillment" and as totally irrelevant to the liturgical customs of the Church, the individual cultic ordinances must be understood according to the specific fundamental structures and kerygmas, historically as well as theologically. Nor may the Old Testament

cult be limited to the priestly legislation and then be rejected as "surpassed" by Christianity.

66. See Martin, pp. 74-75. However, Martin stresses (p. 75) that it is a question of "where the differences belong rather than of the mere differences as such." "The concept of *feast* seems to me to have a wider range of meaning and several connotations. A feast can contain moments of celebration." Cf. Klauser, p. 747: "Every feast contains a moment of celebration, but not every celebration is a feast, since the decisive element, the joy of the feast, is lacking in many celebrations."

67. Martin, p. 74.

68. Cox, p. 25, "A festival embraces the moment. According to Pieper, it is in no way tied to other goals, it has been removed from all 'so that' and 'in order to.' In festive excess we delight in the here and now . . . *Celebration* links us both to past and to future . . . Celebration thus helps us affirm dimensions of time we might ordinarily fear, ignore or deny."

69. Moltmann, pp. 90-91.

70. "If the essential presupposition for celebrating feasts . . . is that all are assembled for a common purpose, the actual celebration of a feast is something different; the community is given visible expression. This includes the possibility that an existing community which is not always taken sufficiently into account may become conscious of itself as a community by expressing itself in this way. Such a self-expression is not a superfluous addition to what is already certain and well-known, but adds a new element, which makes it possible to know and recognize what is already there . . . It is at the same time a confirmation and a reinforcement of the common element which is being celebrated and which constitutes a unifying factor . . . Representation is not something purely external which can be regarded as non-essential. It adds to being" (Gadamer, pp. 65-66). The same is true of the New Testament people of God: "The divine service of the first Christians constitutes a self-presentation of the congregation of Christ, the one Kyrios and Lord. This community is not primarily a community of the faithful who turn to their God, but the congregation of Christ, the congregation of God, his property (1 Cor 11:22)" (Neuenzeit, p. 15).

71. Cholewiński, p. 212. This thesis is the result of an extensive textual comparison, pp. 179-216. Only a number of characteristic features can be mentioned here.

72. This quite generally used term has no real counterpart in Deuteronomy. The wording found in 28:47, "serve YHWH," must not be understood as referring to cult or worship.

73. This knowledge that one is performing a liturgical act is what Guardini in 1964 characterized as the decisive task of liturgical education

today. I shall therefore quote his opinion, which remains relevant: "If I understand things correctly, the typical nineteenth century person was not able to perform this act, indeed did not even realize what it was. Religious behavior was simply individual and internal and became official and solemn in the liturgy. The meaning of the liturgical act was lost, for what the believer performed was not a liturgical act but a ceremonially colored private and internal act." Vatican II has made the liturgical element explicit again. Someone who was looking for its essence concluded that "the liturgical act is performed by the individual, but by the individual as a sociological entity, a 'corpus'—the congregation or the church present in the congregation. Not only spiritual interiority but the human being as a whole, mind and body, is present in this act. The exterior act is prayer, is religious—the times, places, things which belong to the process are not external ornaments but elements of the whole act and they must be present" (Guardini, pp. 9-10).

74. See, for instance, Neunheuser, "Mysterium," including the statement by the commission which he quotes on p. 26: "Above all, the liturgy celebrates the paschal mystery by proclaiming it in the light of the Old Testament, celebrating it in the eucharist and in the other sacraments as well as in the feast days of the Lord, participating in his divine presence and grace and expecting the blessed fulfillment of what she hopes for." As a kind of "preparation" for this, Casel wrote in "Art und Sinn," p. 46: "the old Christian Easter is the feast of the Church and hence constitutes the liturgical expression of Christianity."

75. See pp. 63-65 in the present volume.

76. Martin, p. 77.

77. See Braulik, "Pascha."

Chapter 4. Some Remarks on the Deuteronomistic Conception of Freedom and Peace

1. Cross, "Themes"; Nelson, *Double Redaction*.

2. Smend, *Entstehung*, pp.11-125.

3. Lohfink, "Kerygmata."

4. Von Rad, "Ruhe," pp. 101-108).

5. Frankowski, pp. 124-149, 225-240; Braulik, "Menuchah"; Hulst, "m^{e}nûḥâ," pp. 62-78; W.C. Kaiser; Schulz, pp. 11-162; Roth, pp. 5-14; Stolz, "*nū^{a}ḥ* ruhen."

6. Labuschagne, "*ntn* geben," 128-129.

7. Whereas Joshua's speech in Josh 1:13a, 14-15 is strongly reminiscent of Moses' speech in Deut 3:18-20, the word of Moses mentioned in Josh 1:13b has not been transmitted anywhere in Deuteronomy 1-3. In the narrative, it must be assumed to come before Deut 2:32.

8. If it were absolutely necessary, one could postulate a stage of the Deuteronomistic History during which it did not yet form a unity, but was created in individual parts, such as Deuteronomy, Joshua, Judges, Kings, although by the same group of writers. Then one could stop at the one DtrC and assume that Deut 12:9 contains a reference to a work of the same school concerning the monarchic period.

Chapter 5. Deuteronomy and the Birth of Monotheism

1. Herrmann, pp.155-170, p. 170.
2. See pp. 52-60 in the present volume.
3. Concerning the entire Old Testament, see Lohfink, "Gesellschaftlicher Wandel"; Lohfink, "Monotheismus."
4. See Lohfink, "Cult Reform."
5. The formula "the place which YHWH has chosen" is characteristic. It is found in 12:5, 11, 14, 18, 21, 26; 14:23, 24, 25; 15:20; 16:2, 6, 7, 11, 15, 16; 17:8; 18:6; 26:2 and outside the individual laws also in 31:11. Cf. Lohfink, "Zentralisationsformel."
6. "For Jahwism's exclusive claim certainly repudiated any peaceable co-existence of the cults right from the beginning. Jahwism without the first commandment is positively inconceivable." (von Rad, *Old Testament Theology*, 1:26. German original *Theologie*, p. 39). However, this is not yet monotheism—contrary to what Lang affirms in "Geschichte des Monotheismus," p. 55, cf. p. 57.
7. Even "before the exile," there is a "reflective theology with an exclusive claim" (against Vorländer, "Monotheismus," p. 137 note 72). Concerning this book, which provided the inspiration for the present study, see also my review in *TRev* 80 (1984):11-15.
8. In Deuteronomy, *'elōhîm* means other gods: 4:28; 5:7; 6:14 (bis); 7:4, 16, 25; 8:19; 11:16, 28; 12:2, 3, 30 (bis), 31; 13:3, 7, 8, 14; 17:3; 18:20; 20:18; 28:14, 36, 64; 29:17, 25 (bis); 30:17; 31:16, 18, 20.
9. Concerning the definitions of the concepts "henotheism," "monolatry" and "monotheism," cf. Rose, pp. 9-13. With the term "henolatry," Hartmann (pp. 78-79) introduced a further differentiation.

10. Passages from Deuteronomy 32 and 33 – two originally independent texts, later inserted into the book, but "non-deuteronomic" – as well as passages from the Deuteronomistic History will be cited only in so far as they are important for the interpretation of the rest of Deuteronomy or for collation. For Deuteronomy 32, however, see pp. 126-129 in the present volume.

11. Lohfink, "Gott im Deuteronomium," pp. 112-113.

12. Craig, vol. 1, tables 22-23 II 10-26; 23 II 27-32; 23-24 II 33-36 and III 1′-14′. Cf. Lohfink, "Gott im Deuteronomium," p. 115, note 52; further Ishida, pp. 115-116. A further text is offered by Zevit, "Phoenician Inscription."

13. These treaties are known above all from the archives of Bogazköy and Ras Shamra. Yet the same type of treaty, together with another type, was still in use during the Neo-Assyrian epoch; cf. Campbell, pp. 534-535. The text discussed in this article has been published in Deller and Parpola, pp. 464ff; Borger in TUAT I/2 p. 177; cf. further Buis.

14. Lohfink, "Gott im Deuteronomium," pp. 112-113 restricts these to *'ēl qannā'* – leaving out of account 10:12-22, a text which it is difficult to assign to any particular stratum. This title is certainly the oldest *'ēl* predication in Deuteronomy.

15. Thus, e.g. Lohfink, "Gott im Deuteronomium," pp. 108-109.

16. Deut 6:4; 17:6; 19:5; 28:7, 25; 32:30.

17. Deut 6:4 could in that case be translated "YHWH, our God, is one (and only one) YHWH" or "YHWH, our God, YHWH is one." It is not, however, possible to translate YHWH *'eḥād* as "(YHWH is our God), YHWH alone." Cf. Rose, pp. 134-135.

18. Bade (pp. 81-90) is fundamental. Since then, the same view has frequently been defended.

19. Höffken; with greater caution, Emerton, "New Light."

20. Lemaire, "Date et origine," pp. 138-139.

21. Höffken, p. 89.

22. Against Höffken, p. 89. According to Emerton, "New Light," p. 19, the phrase "Yahweh of Samaria" was probably used by someone who normally shared in the cult in that city, and it supports the theory that, though the unity of Yahweh may not have been denied, his cult took a variety of forms. It does not prove, though it perhaps favors, the view that different manifestations of Yahweh were associated with such differences in the cult . . . The phrase "Yahweh of Teman" is to be explained differently. The blessing that uses his name invokes the protection of the God who comes from the southern region (cf. Hab 3:3) for a traveler in the south.

23. Against Rose, pp. 136-140 and several others.

24. Thus also Höffken, p. 89, note 8.

25. The same structure is found in Deut 20:3-4 and 27:9-10; see Lohfink and Bergman, "'eḥād," *TWAT* 1:214; English translation *TDOT* 1:196. See also Halbe, "Gemeinschaft," p. 57.

26. Against Höffken, p. 93. Höffken holds that Deut 6:5, in spite of the union with the vocative "Israel" in verse 4, affirms "*re vera* of the one." Of course, verse 4 might be older than its present context and reflect a stage of yahwism instanced by the texts from Kuntillet ʿAjrud and best described as a *via negativa*. But this is unlikely. *YHWH 'elōhênû* in verse 4, as in 1:6 and 5:2, would appear to correspond to deuteronomic linguistic usage at the beginning of longer speeches. Cf. Lohfink, "Gott im Deuteronomium," p. 109. The "you" of verse 6:5, inextricably bound up with verse 4, must therefore be interpreted collectively.

27. Cf. Lohfink, "Gott im Deuteronomium," pp. 110-111, who, citing the Canticle of Canticles 6:8-9, shows that *'eḥād* belongs to the language of love. That Deut 6:4, 5 must be interpreted together is now also stressed by Nielsen, p. 292.

28. Thus also recently Peter.

29. Cf. Lohfink, *Hauptgebot*, p. 163. Lohfink and Bergman (*TWAT* 1:214; English translation *TDOT* 1:196) limit the formula to Deut 6:4. In that case, the meaning would be less definite.

30. Lohfink and Bergman, *TWAT* 1:213.

31. See the works by Bächli and Rössler in the bibliography.

32. Lohfink, *Hauptgebot*, p. 164. This may be true even of the phase in which Deuteronomy began with 6:4, since the commentary in 6:12-15 presupposes knowledge of the Decalogue.

33. Halbe, *Privilegrecht*, pp. 134-140.

34. This is the case only for *'ēl* in attributive phrases. Outside of the Song of Moses, this is—with the single exception of 3:24—the way Deuteronomy forms its *'ēl* predications. Concerning *'ēl* in Deuteronomy 32, see below.

35. This is also true of the parallels to Deut 5:9 in Exod 20:5, but not of the two instances of *'ēl qannô'* in Josh 24:19 and Nah 1:2.

36. Halbe, *Privilegrecht*, pp. 139-140.

37. However, see pp. 111-112 above and note 78 below.

38. Lohfink, *Hauptgebot*, p. 156.

39. Braulik, *Rhetorik*.

40. Lohfink, "Gott: Sprechen von Gott," p. 129. Concerning YHWH's love and jealousy, see also below.

41. Berg.

42. Largely in agreement with Noth, *Überlieferungsgeschichtliche Studien*, p. 37. Mittmann (*Deuteronomium 1,1 - 6,3*, p. 113) assigns Deut 3:24 to a redactional stratum which already presupposes the Priestly Narrative.

43. Lohfink, "Kerygmata," pp. 92-96.

44. Concerning what follows, cf. Rose, pp. 150-152.

45. It is characteristic that *'ēl*, "God," *ma'ᵃśeh*, "work(s)" and *gᵉbûrâ*, "mighty deeds" are nowhere found more frequently than in the psalms, where, as in Deut 3:24, they refer to YHWH.

46. The comparative material has been assembled by Labuschagne, *Incomparability*. The Old Testament material has also been evaluated by Johannes, pp. 9-24. Rose, p. 150 note 7 quotes two Mesopotamian texts which are of particular interest for the understanding of Deut 3:24.

47. According to Labuschagne, *Incomparability*, p. 79 and p. 86 note 2, it is highly probable that the phrase "god in heaven or on earth" alludes to the divine beings surrounding YHWH and to the gods honored on earth. Cf. 1 Kgs 8:23 and Ps 113:5-6.

48. Concerning this category, see Johannes, *Unvergleichlichkeits-formulierungen*.

49. Labuschagne, *Incomparability*, pp. 72-73 does not interpret Deut 3:24 monotheistically, but in principle maintains that "to Israel incomparability implied both a 'being different' and a 'being unique' and although the terms cannot grammatically be regarded as synonyms, they nevertheless had similar connotations. We can, therefore, consider the confessions of the incomparability of Yahweh as confessions of his uniqueness, or, if we chose to use Hartmann's term, we may regard them as 'monotheistic formulae'" (pp. 145-146).

50. Both expressions occur more frequently in Deuteronomy than in any other part of the Old Testament. With one significant exception, it is always a question of YHWH's "greatness" or "strong hand." The phrase *yad ḥᵃzākâ* refers exclusively to the exodus from Egypt, which only Deut 34:12 attributes to the incomparable Moses. In 9:26 and 11:2, *gōdel* is also found together with *yad ḥᵃzākâ* in this context. In 3:24, then, the linkage of both expressions must also, in spite of the preceding narrative about the victory over the two Amorite kings, be interpreted with the aid of Exodus. This interpretation is strengthened by the fact that, in Deuteronomy, YHWH's "works" (*ma'ᵃśîm*) are mentioned only in 3:24 and 11:3, and that this expression refers first to YHWH's actions in Egypt, then also to his actions during the march through the desert. Then 11:7 summarizes the whole exodus narrative and the desert journey as *kol ma'ᵃśeh YHWH gādôl*. The word *gᵉbûrâ*, "mighty deeds," is a *hapax*

legomenon in Deuteronomy. In 3:24, it probably corresponds to *yad ḥ^{a}zākâ*. In 5:24, YHWH's *gōdel* is seen together with his *kābôd* during the Horeb theophany. 32:3 requires the Israelites to give "our God," YHWH, *gōdel*, that is, to praise him.

51. The incomparability phrase in Deut 3:24 "who is . . . like" (*mî . . . k^{e}*) has a related negative form: "no one is . . . like" (*'ên . . . k^{e}*). In Deuteronomy, the only instance of this form is found in the hymnic conclusion of the old Blessing of Moses. In the Deuteronomistic History, the only instances are found in 1 Sam 2:2; 2 Sam 7:22; 1 Kgs 8:23. Deut 33:26 praises YHWH as the mighty helper of his people with the incomparability formulation "No one is like the God of Jeshurun" (*'ên k^{e}'ēl y^{e}šurûn*); we need not here discuss the problem of the masoretic vocalization *kā'ēl*. Here YHWH as *'ēl* is related to Israel by a genitive relationship. According to 33:29, Israel, too, is incomparable because of its God. (Cf. 2 Sam 7:23, following on verse 22, further Deut 4:7-8 and 4:33-34).

52. Rose, p. 125.

53. Concerning this kind of confrontation between YHWH and the gods, cf. Crüsemann, *Studien zur Formgeschichte*, pp. 81-154.

54. This does not mean that statements about YHWH's all-encompassing dominion in any way constitute a theology of creation, as Rose, pp. 125-126 stresses for Deuteronomy 10 in contrast to Psalm 136.

55. Lohfink, *Hauptgebot*, p. 222.

56. Lohfink, *Höre Israel*, p. 118.

57. "Nouns can be used especially in combination with the divine names and can then take the article or an enclitic personal pronoun" (Richter, p. 177).

58. Ps 77:14 is, according to H.J. Kraus, *Psalms 2*, p. 114, exilic or postexilic. Ps 95:3 (*Psalms 2*, p. 246) is later than the publication of Deuteronomy. The only other occurrence is in Dan 9:4.

59. Cross, *TWAT* 1:276, English translation *TDOT* 1:261.

60. Isa 9:5; 10:21.

61. Regarding the assertions of YHWH's kingship in Deut 10:17-18, it is probably significant that, according to 7:24, YHWH as a "great and terrible God" gives the kings(!) of the nations into Israel's power. Later, the *'ēl* epithet is only found in hymnic addresses to YHWH, in combination with an allusion to the beginning of the Decalogue, reminiscent of 7:9. Then it takes the article: Jer 32:18; Dan 9:4; Neh 1:5; 9:32.

62. Deut 1:19; 7:21; 8:15; 10:17, 21. The only exception—*nôrā'* without *gādôl*—is 28:58. Cf. also 2 Sam 7:23.

63. Miller, p. 56.

64. Against Labuschagne, *Incomparability*, p. 121 note 2.

65. Rose, p. 125.

66. This passage in no way provides evidence for the affirmation "that it is possible to speak of the election of Israel among all nations only if YHWH is known and affirmed as the one and only God"–against Rendtorff, "Erwählung," p. 83. Rendtorff considers this verse as a "classic instance" of the theology of election as understood in the deuteronomistic theology (p. 82 note 30).

67. Lohfink, *Hauptgebot*, p. 225.

68. The verbs *ḥšq, 'hb, and bḥr* are not found together until in Deuteronomy: 10:15; 7:7-8; 4:37 (where, however, *ḥšq* is missing). The subject is always YHWH, the objects vary. Whereas in 10:15 and 4:37, YHWH loves the fathers and chooses the seed of the father or fathers, according to 7:7-8, YHWH's affection and election concern only Israel. For the rest, the emotionally colored *ḥšq*, "take to one's heart" (21:11) is nowhere in the OT used more frequently than in Deuteronomy.

69. Lohfink, "Gott im Deuteronomium," p. 112 note 45 and p. 117.

70. Perlitt, "Anklage," p. 298.

71. Contrary to what Perlitt affirms in "Anklage." Perlitt considers that the work of the deuteronomists was written only under the pressure of the accusations leveled against God by Israel in exile. According to his interpretation, the deuteronomists eliminated the question "why?" posed by their contemporaries, and explained the failure of their ancestors with the aid of the notion of *b^{e}rît*, "covenant" and thus declared YHWH not guilty. However, they were able to do this only by accusing those who were already beaten. But this interpretation in the last analysis presents us with a perversion, not only of a theory of literary origin, but also of the principal intention of deuteronomistic theology.

72. Lohfink, "Kerygmata," pp. 99-100.

73. For what follows, cf. Lohfink, "Gott im Deuteronomium," pp. 122-123.

74. The deuteronomists did not, then, merely "find the accused God not guilty." They also took "the further step of declaring the accused human beings not guilty." It is precisely the analysis of the text which shows that "in the coordinate system of guilt and punishment . . . the sons' responsibility for the madness of the fathers" was *not* to remain "the basic law of history"–against Perlitt, "Anklage," p. 301.

75. Braulik, "Ausdrücke," pp. 43-44.

76. Concerning the stylistic technique, cf. Braulik, "Aufbrechen."

77. Lohfink, *Hauptgebot*, pp. 187. In 30:6, the first commandment even becomes the content of the promise of blessing (ibid.).

78. Thus Hossfeld, pp. 275-276.

79. Perlitt, "Anklage," p. 299 affirms that this is true of the God of Deuteronomy. Since Perlitt assigns the theology of the covenant with the fathers to an early literary stratum of Deuteronomy, he concludes: "Whereas if the deuteronomic fathers had taken him" (that is, God) "at his word and believed his promise, the deuteronomistic sons—obsessed with causality, like all sons—defended him by appealing to his retributive justice."

80. Deut 7:8 founds the election of Israel as a nation, spoken of in verses 6-7. This changes the content of 10:15. Cf. Lohfink, *Hauptgebot*, p. 226. However, Lohfink mistakenly speaks of an "election" of the fathers.

81. Zimmerli, "Erkenntnis," p. 51.

82. This is stressed by Floss, pp. 586-589.

83. The older, presupposed context in Deut 7:4-5, 16, 25-26 speaks of the gods.

84. The presence of the article in *hā'ᵉlōhîm* and *hā'ēl* does not yet imply monotheism.

85. See Scharbert, "Formgeschichte und Exegese von Ex. 34, 6f." Halbe, *Privilegrecht*, pp. 281-286, considers 34:6-7, 9 jehovistic.

86. There is another "textual bridge" formed by the "ownership" relation between YHWH and Israel. Exod 34:9 pleads with YHWH to make Israel his possession. Deut 4:20, however, defines Israel as *'am naḥᵃlâ*, the "people of his inheritance," knowing that, with the exodus from Egypt, this relation is given once and for all.

87. Cf. Braulik, *Rhetorik*, pp. 59-60.

88. Besides Isaiah, Hosea is the prophet before Deutero-Isaiah who most frequently speaks of YHWH as *'ēl*: Hos 2:1; 11:9; 12:1.

89. Braulik, "Spuren."

90. The only other instances in Deuteronomy of *rph* hi. with YHWH as subject are 31:6, 8. In those passages, *rph* is paralleled with *'zb*, "abandon." In 31:17, the verb *'zb* explains the exile.

91. Concerning the theology of grace in 4:29ff and 30:1-10, cf. Braulik, "Gesetz als Evangelium," pp. 152-160.

92. Braulik, "Literarkritik."

93. Concerning Deut 30:1-10, cf. Vanoni. In spite of the correspondences in content and form between 4:1-40 and 30:1-10 ("Geist und Buchstabe," p. 89), I am now inclined to date 30:1-10 later than chapter 4, both because 30:1-10 has a more radical conception of grace (there is no covenant with the fathers—cf. 4:31 with 30:3, where it is only said that YHWH shows compassion [*rḥm* pi.]; the first commandment is the very content of the blessing—cf. 10:16; 6:5 with 30:6) and because of its much more tangible expectations for the future.

94. Concerning what follows, cf. Braulik, *Rhetorik*, pp. 112-113 and 119-120. In what follows, I shall, however, specify and add to what *Rhetorik* shows of the systematization in 4:1-40. However, Schulz (p. 44) is, in spite of a detailed investigation of the designations of God in 4:1-28, unable to find any general rule.

95. *'elōhênû*, "our God" is a stylistically skillful way of linking up with the speech of Moses, after quoting what the nations say (Deut 4:6). Hence it is entirely necessary in this context – contrary to what Lohfink affirms in "Gott im Deuteronomium," p. 109 note 33.

96. On the other hand, in the late deuteronomistic passage 1 Kgs 8:27, *'elōhîm* has already become an appellative: YHWH is simply "God." In Deut 9:10 possibly also in 21:23 and 33:1, *'elōhîm* has a purely superlative function – Lohfink, "Gott im Deuteronomium," p. 103.

97. Concerning Deut 4:7, cf. note 100 below. In 4:32, 33, 34, the predicate is in the singular, as it is in 5:24, 26 (cf. 4:33); cf. Rose, p. 154. Lohfink, on the contrary, in "Gott im Deuteronomium," p. 103 note 10, takes into account the possibility of an indefinite use of *'elōhîm* in the sense of "some gods" in the plural.

98. Against Lohfink, "Gott im Deuteronomium," pp. 124-126.

99. Therefore, a stratum related to Deuteronomy 4 adds the uniqueness of Israel, the *gôy 'eḥād* in 2 Sam 7:23-24 to the uniqueness of YHWH in 2 Sam 7:22. Cf. Braulik, "Spuren," p. 33 note 1. However, I no longer count verse 22 as part of the Israel redaction of 2 Samuel 7.

100. Concerning rendering *'elōhîm qerōbîm* in the singular, cf. Labuschagne, *Incomparability*, p. 23.

101. See chapter 1 in the present volume.

102. Against von Rad, *Deuteronomium*, p. 36.

103. Rose, p. 155, According to Balscheit, p. 130, Deut 4:19-20 answers two questions, "in the first place the question of the relation between divine guidance and free human politics, in the second place the question of the relation between YHWH, who guides the nations, and the gods worshiped by these nations . . ." For Balscheit (p. 133), "in the entire context" – of 4:35 for instance – Deut 4:19 is "no longer merely a bridge to monotheism."

104. Cf. the similar double rhetorical question concerning Israel's incomparability in Deut 4:7-8.

105. Johannes, pp. 188-200.

106. Cf. Braulik, *Rhetorik*, pp. 61-76.

107. Cf. Lohfink, *Höre Israel*, p. 115.

108. Characteristically, when speaking of the nations and their gods, Deuteronomy only uses the phrase "from one end of the *earth* to the other end of the *earth*" (13:8), where in the dispersion of the exile, Israel is

forced to serve them (28:64). In contrast to this, YHWH will gather the dispersed Israel "from the ends of *heaven*" (30:4).

109. Wolff, "Geschichtsverständnis," p. 300 note 16.

110. Cf. Seeligmann, pp. 415, 438-440.

111. Against Botterweck, *TWAT* 3:503, English translation *TDOT* 5:448-481.

112. Concerning the relation between *r'h*, "to see" and *yd'*, "to know" what has been revealed, cf. Knierim. The roots of monotheism are to be found in this knowledge granted by grace, not in penitence and conversion to YHWH as the only God, which would have constituted the foundations of the leadership claim in the *gôlâ*—against Vorländer, "Monotheismus," pp. 88-93. Vorländer affirms: "By their complete conversion to YHWH alone, the exiles confessed their monotheistic faith" (p. 93). Such a conversion would constitute a response to YHWH's claim to exclusive worship while yet remaining in the monolatric sphere.

113. Cf. Lohfink, "Gott im Deuteronomium," pp. 106-108.

114. 1 Kgs 8:60 should not be cited in this context. This verse links up with Deuteronomy 4 and constitutes a prayer that YHWH may become known as the only God, and this among all nations.

115. Cf. Rose, p. 154, note 1.

116. Against Rose, p. 154.

117. Against Lohfink, "Gott im Deuteronomium," p. 121; cf. pp. 124ff. Later, Lohfink, as the translator of Deuteronomy in the German *Einheitsübersetzung* commented on 4:35 that, there "as in Isa 41:22-23; 43:10-13; 44:6 and 45:5, a strictly monotheistic assertion is arrived at."

118. Thus the only God, YHWH, and his unique people, Israel (4:7-8) are both indissolubly united with the Torah.

119. Against Vorländer, "Monotheismus," pp. 103-106—partly in accordance with Lessing, §§ 39-40. Also against Lang, "Yahweh-Alone Movement," pp. 47-48. Lang affirms that, through Deutero-Isaiah, the influence reaches Deuteronomy. Mayer, p. 57 also affirms that Old Testament monotheism did not originate in the religion of Zarathustra. He refers to the "long prehistory" within the Old Testament and states that "even the purified monotheistic concept of God which we find in Second Isaiah" is "so strongly bound up with inherited Old Testament conceptions that it need not, indeed cannot, be derived from Iran."

120. Against Pettazoni, p. 117: "Monotheism does not emerge from evolution, but is the result of revolution. The birth of a monotheistic religion is always associated with a religious revolution." Lang does not accept this crude revolutionary concept for the monotheism of Israel (Lang, "Jahwe-allein-Bewegung," cf. Lang, "Geschichte des Monotheismus," p. 57) . Nevertheless, he is quite willing to accept a "sequence of

revolutions" in the history of the YHWH alone movement, ending with the transformation of monolatry into monotheism. Lang here follows Keel, "Gedanken," p. 21. Keel affirms that "the model of a sequence of successive revolutions directed towards monotheism and following rapidly on one another seems inescapable to me."

121. Vorländer, "Monotheismus," p. 93.

122. Vorländer, "Monotheismus," p. 95.

123. Wildberger, "Monotheismus." However, what he says concerning *'ēl* and *'[e]lōhîm* on p. 266 is misleading.

124. Elliger, *Deuterojesaja 1*, p. 72.

125. If one does not count as Deutero-Isaianic those texts in which *'ēl*, in accordance with the pagan notions, is identified with the image of a god (see further below), the authentic Deutero-Isaiah uses *'ēl* only in monotheistic contexts.

126. Elliger, *Deuterojesaja 1*, pp. 70-72.

127. Elliger, *Deuterojesaja 1*, p. 73.

128. Against Cross, *TWAT* 1:277-278, English translation *TDOT* 1:259-260; cf. Wildberger, "Monotheismus," p. 266 note 55.

129. Elliger, *Deuterojesaja 1*, p. 72.

130. Thus Wildberger, "Monotheismus," p. 262.

131. This is affirmed by, amongst others, Wildberger, "Monotheismus," p. 256).

132. See note above 116 and pp. 119-120 in the present volume.

133. In the Old Testament, this formula is used to deny the existence of other gods. Apart from Deut 4:35, 39; 1 Kgs 8:60; Isa 45:5, 6, 14, 18, 21, 22; 46:9, it occurs only in Joel 2:27.

134. Wildberger, "Monotheismus," thinks, although without giving any reasons, that "Deutero-Isaiah, according to the parallels cited" (among which he cites Deut 4:35, 39) "is not the first witness to monotheism in the Old Testament. But there is no other book in which the assertions of monotheism are anything like as important as they are in Deutero-Isaiah."

134. Lohfink, "Gott im Deuteronomium," p. 120.

135. Ibid.

136. The following scholars among others argue that the song should be dated late: Carillo Alday, passim; Hidal, p. 20; Luyten.

137. Ibid.

138. Much the same would appear to be true of *ṣûr* in 32:37.

139. H.J. Kraus, *Psalms 2*, thinks Psalm 81 may be postexilic.

140. In parallel to the subsequent construct relationship *'ên 'āwel, 'ēl '[e]mûnâ* should probably be regarded as a genitive construction, not as a nominal clause.

141. Regarding the textual criticism, see Volkwein, *Textkritische Untersuchung*. This dissertation, which has unfortunately not been published, constitutes the basis for the following text-critical decisions concerning verses 8 and 43.

142. This is how the verse should be read and how it reads in the LXX and in 4QDtn^{g}.

143. This reading should be regarded as a preliminary stage of the LXX, partly substantiated by 4QDtn^{o}. Another possible interpretation is offered by Bogaert's reconstruction in "Trois rédactions," p. 333: "Faites rójouissance, *'elōhîm* (cieux?) avec Lui" (Rejoice with Him, *'elōhîm* [heavens?]). According to this interpretation, the gods, and no longer the sons of God, would surround YHWH and rejoice with him.

144. The incomparability formulation in Deut 3:24 constitutes the only exception.

145. Characteristically, in 31:16, in the first introduction to the Song of Moses, we find the expression *'elōhê nēkar-hā'āreṣ*. In analogy to this, Deuteronomy replaces the designation *'ēl 'aḥēr* (Exod 34:14) by *'elōhîm 'aḥērîm*.

146. The only further occurrence of *ṣûr* is in Deut 8:5 in the phrase "water from the rock"; cf. 32:13.

147. Since *ṣûr*, "rock" in verse 31 occurs in a comparison between the gods and verse 37 affirms that the gods do not function as rocks, there is, of course, no YHWH predicate as a positive counterpart, as there is in verses 12, 18 and 30. This does not mean that the constructional pattern has been broken.

148. *'elōhîm*, "gods" occurs in the first and in the last negative positions of the quintuple sequence of *ṣûr* identifications.

Chapter 6. Deuteronomy and Human Rights

1. See pp. 18-24 in the present volume.
2. See the articles by Engel, Jüngling and Lohfink in *Bibel und Kirche* 38 (1983) concerning "Israel's origins." Further Schäfer-Lichtenberger, *Stadt und Eidgenossenschaft*, pp. 223-267.
3. We need not here discuss whether the social laws of Deuteronomy were mere utopian models or—as I think—describe obligations which had a basis in reality and which came into effect to some extent at least in the history of Israel. For a recent view, see Crüsemann, "Damit er dich segne," pp. 96-103.
4. Ernst, pp. 265-266.
5. Böckle and Höver, p. 96.

6. Huber, p. 202.

7. Braulik, "Abfolge der Gesetze."

8. Crüsemann, *Bewahrung der Freiheit*, p. 80.

9. See Braulik, *Sage, was du glaubst*, pp. 26-27, 29-30; and "Gesetz als Evangelium," pp. 137-140.

10. Verses 6:24-25, concerning Israel's relation to its social order, are structured by the enclitic personal pronoun *-nû*, repeated seven times. Braulik, *Sage, was du glaubst*, p. 139 note 38.

11. Braulik, *Sage, was du glaubst*, pp. 137-140.

12. Concerning the sabbath, see e.g. Negretti, pp. 121-124; Lohfink, "Sabbatruhe."

13. Deut 6:21 does relate Israel's bondage in Egypt to the exodus brought about by YHWH. The credo we have just discussed thus becomes very closely related to the sabbath commandment and to the social laws which follow. But—apart from differences in syntax and wording—this verse is narrative. Cf. 15:15 and 24:18, where, however (because of the context), the redemption through YHWH is mentioned.

14. See Hossfeld, pp. 38-57. I cannot, however, agree with the conclusions the author draws from his observations.

15. If only the free man were addressed, this would mean that his wife, alone of all the people in the household, either had to work on the sabbath or was always, even on weekdays, exempt from work. In both cases, it would also follow that the free woman is excluded from all lists of the addressees of the deuteronomic laws in which she is not explicitly mentioned. In that case, she would not, for instance, travel to Jerusalem in order to participate in the sacrifice and the feast at the principal sanctuary (cf. 12:18; 16:11, 14). All this is extremely unlikely, not least when we consider Deuteronomy's inclination towards the emancipation of women (see Weinfeld, *Deuteronomic School*, p. 291-293). At that time, women had the right to own property and could even sell themselves as debt slaves (15:12) in order to keep themselves and their families alive in case of extreme distress. Therefore the sabbath commandment must be understood to concern the work and rest of the free woman as well as of the free man—contrary to Schenker, p. 332.

16. Concerning this matter, see primarily Cardellini, pp. 269-276, 337-343.

17. On the level of the final redaction of Deuteronomy, the manumission in the seventh year is to be understood as an application of the sabbath commandment—see Braulik, "Abfolge der Gesetze," p. 259.

18. Cardellini, pp. 276-279.

19. Exod 3:8; 5:23; 6:6; 18:4, 8-10; Judg 6:9; 1 Sam 10:18. In Deuteronomy, *nṣl* (hi.) is found in 23:15, in the context of the camp law, which immediately precedes the law concerning the runaway slave.

20. Cf. 1 Sam 22:2; 25:10.

21. The expression is linked to the "alien" in Deut (16:11); 26:11; 28:43 and applies particularly to him.

22. Within the redaction of Deuteronomy which relates the individual laws to the commandments of the Decalogue, the passage 23:16-17 belongs to the transitional stage between the sixth commandment, which concerns sexual and family life, and the seventh commandment, which determines questions of property (Braulik, "Abfolge der Gesetze," p. 260). The slave thus finds his or her place between family and property. More particularly, 23:16-17 constitutes the first "commentary" on the prohibition of theft. This implies that, for Deuteronomy, "You shall not steal" means, above all, that the freedom of an escaped *'ebed* is to be guaranteed.

23. Hossfeld, p. 48.

24. See chapters 2 and 3 in the present volume, esp. pp. 52-60.

25. See Perlitt, "Ein einzig Volk"; Braulik, *Deuteronomium 1-16, 17*, pp. 16-17.

26. I should like to point out in passing that Deuteronomy knows not only human rights, but also animal rights (5:14; 22:1-3, 4, 6-7; 25:4) and even tree rights (20:19-20), which are intended to preserve the environment from being damaged and exploited.

27. See for instance Pesch, *Bergpredigt*.

Chapter 7. The Development of the Doctrine of Justification

1. Zimmerli, "Gesetz," p. 276.
2. Braulik, "Gesetz als Evangelium."
3. Köckert.
4. Hofius.
5. Hofius, p. 103 note 115.
6. The essential literature on this subject can be found in the two articles mentioned in notes 2 and 3 above. A detailed discussion of Köckert's arguments must be left for a later publication.
7. Lohfink, "Kerygmata."
8. Lohfink, "Kerygmata," pp. 92-96.
9. See chapter 4 in the present volume.

10. Concerning this explanation, see Lohfink, "Dtn 12:1 und Gen 15:18" and Lohfink, "ḥuqqîm."

11. Lohfink, "Kerygmata," pp. 98-99.

12. Lohfink, "Kerygmata," pp. 99-100.

13. 4:1-40 also explains the validity of the deuteronomic laws, which was obviously in dispute among the exiles. Neither exile nor return is made dependent on the observance or non-observance of these laws. According to 4:1, Moses teaches the statutes and ordinances (*ḥuqqîm ûmišpaṭîm*) outside the land, but Israel is obligated only to learn and to teach them. This is enough to assure that the people continue to live and that YHWH will give them the land to take possession of. The laws are to be kept "within the land" (*b^{e}qereb hā'āreṣ*), according to 4:5. If they are kept there, 4:40 promises that all will be well (*yṭb*) with Israel and that it may remain in the land. At the beginning of the deuteronomic parenesis, 4:1 anticipates the wording of 12:1. 4:5 even explains in more detail the validity of the laws as defined in 12:1. Both verses, however, demand more than 12:1, that the exiles know "the statutes and ordinances" (as the Decalogue - 4:10). Thus the communities in exile could survive, in the hope of being able to return one day.

Chapter 8. The Rejection of the Goddess Asherah in Israel

1. This has recently been affirmed by Wacker, "Jahwe und Aschera," p. 15.

2. This is the view of, for instance, Schroer, *Bilder*, p. 41.

3. The Old Testament uses the term "A/asherah" in order to refer both to the goddess and to her cult symbol, a tree stylized as a wooden pole. This has recently been pointed out by Day, "Asherah in the Hebrew Bible," pp. 397-406. That one cannot separate the goddess and her cult object was recently emphasized by Winter, pp. 555-560. M. Smith, *Early History of God*, pp. 80-94, attempts to demonstrate that YHWH and Asherah may have become merged in the early period of the judges. After that, all that remained was the symbol of Asherah, the wooden pole. This pole no longer had any relation to the goddess who had given it its name, but fulfilled various functions in the YHWH cult. However, under deuteronomic influence, this "asherah" was subjected to criticism. Its name became associated with the goddess Astarte. The thought that the "asherah" was "responsible" for fertility and healing gave rise to objections and its mantic use was rejected by the prophets. According to Smith, it is rather unlikely that Asherah was an Israelite goddess during the

monarchic period. This, however, remains conceivable if one evaluates the biblical and extrabiblical text material differently.

4. Olyan, *Asherah and the Cult of Yahweh*, pp. 3-22. However, Olyan has a totally uncritical attitude towards the "Deuteronomic History." He does not distinguish between sources and redaction(s). Neither does he reflect on problems of stratification or dating.

5. Olyan is, however, aware of the fact that most authors understand Asherah to have been the consort of Baal in the Iron Age, and no longer of El, as she was in the Bronze Age (*Asherah and the Cult of Yahweh*, p. 6 note 16 and pp. 38-61).

6. Olyan, *Asherah and the Cult of Yahweh*, p. 3.

7. Olyan, *Asherah and the Cult of Yahweh*, pp. 4, 72-73.

8. Holladay.

9. Regarding the theory of religious organization in typical Syro-Palestinian nation-states in the Iron II period and the archaeological verification in the Davidic-Salomonic kingdoms, see Holladay, pp. 266-280. Holladay formulates the following general "theorem" (p. 267): "Corporate religious expression in a typical Iron-II Syro-Palestinian nation-state should have operated on several different levels, each with its own place in the social order and each with its own set of material affects."

10. See Holladay, pp. 275-280.

11. The lower part of the body of these figurines is not developed but has the form of a small pillar. The breasts, on the other hand, are strongly emphasized. Often, the goddess/woman holds her breasts with her hands. See Engle, *Pillar Figurines*. Winter (pp. 107-109) has recently described the two fundamental types of the "naked woman" and the more recent sites where these figurines have been found.

12. Holladay, pp. 267-268.

13. Winter, p. 131.

14. Patai (pp. 29-52) was the first to identify the goddess as Asherah. Hestrin, p. 222 considers that the pillar represents the trunk of a tree—the asherah. Together with the full breasts, it symbolizes the mother goddess who gives life and nourishment. Winter, p. 557, criticizes the interpretation of the pillar figurines as *'šrym*. However, his argumentation remains caught up in false alternatives. What Tigay says ("Onomastic and Epigraphic Evidence," p. 192-193 and note 116) about the "Astarte figurines" falls behind the present state of research. According to Tigay, the figurines simply represented what women most wanted and attempted to obtain by magical means, and the fact that Israelite personal names, unlike Phoenician ones, do not contain the names of goddesses also militates against the idea that the figurines represent a goddess. See below for a discussion of this view.

15. Thus for instance Rose, p. 186. However, Rose thinks (pp. 184-186) that the pillar figurines which he distinguishes from a Canaanite "Astarte type" and regards as belonging to an "Asherah type," were diffused over the narrower area of Israel, especially over the southern part of Palestine, through all phases of settlement up to the monarchic period. According to Rose, it is unlikely that the worship of Asherah was limited to the Canaanite population. In any case, the figurines were not found only among the uneducated, more "primitive" lower classes, but also—as is shown for instance by the excavations of Ramat Raḥel—also within the precincts of the royal palace.

16. Holladay, pp. 278-280.

17. Holladay, p. 280; further pp. 257-258, 259-260, 274-275.

18. Margalit, "Meaning and Significance," p. 276-277.

19. Dever, p. 165; Lemaire, "Inscriptions de Khirbet el-Qôm," p. 603.

20. F.M. Cross, according to a reference in Dever, p. 165 note 53.

21. See the recent contributions by Hadley, "Khirbet el-Qom Inscription," bibliography; and Margalit, "Inscription and Drawing," pp. 372-373.

22. The reading *'ᵃšerâ* has been contested by Mittmann, "Grabinschrift." On the other hand, Margalit ("Inscription and Drawing," p. 371) even interprets certain incisions under the first four lines as the outline of a rudimentary tree, followed by *l'šrth* and *wl'(š)rth* in two further lines. The name of the goddess would be indicated by the cultic symbol. Concerning the tree of life on Pithos A from Kuntillet ‘Ajrud, see below.

23. Koch, "Aschera als Himmelskönigin," p. 99.

24. For instance against Lemaire, "Who or What," p. 5l. According to McCarter, p. 149, *'ᵃšerat yahweh* means "‘the Sign/Mark of Yahweh’ or perhaps even ‘the Effective/Active Presence of Yahweh.’" The asherah, as the presence of YHWH, which was in some sense "available" in the cult was worshiped as a "hypostatic personality."

25. Regarding this interpretation, see Hadley, "Khirbet el-Qom Inscription," pp. 56-57. On pp. 58-59, Hadley rejects the interpretation of *l'šrth* as a vocative *l* and *'ᵃšerata* with a double feminization instead of an enclitic personal pronoun. This interpretation is proposed by Zevit in "Khirbet el-Qom Inscription," p. 45. Weippert ("Synkretismus und Monotheismus," p. 171 note 40) holds that the personal suffix in the 3rd masculine singular in *'šrth* constitutes no obstacle to interpreting **'šrh* as the name of a goddess. Since there are designations of deities such as "Anath of Bethel" and "Aštar of Kamoš," one can hardly deny that it is grammatically possible to replace the divine name in the genitive case by a possessive (genitive) suffix: *'šrth* = **'šrt* YHWH, "YHWH's Asherah."

26. Lemaire, "Who or What," p. 44.

27. The most recent summary of the discussion of the most important texts and drawings on the two pithoi, as well as convincing solutions of the problems are offered by Hadley, "Two Pithoi," pp. 180-211. In what follows, I shall therefore dispense with further instances from the less recent literature.

28. Hadley, "Two Pithoi," pp. 184, 207-208. Coogan, pp. 118-119 emphasizes that this "microcosm of the cosmopolitan reality which Israel was" was multifunctional and had an important function in the cult.

29. Hadley, "Two Pithoi," pp. 182-187.

30. However, further observations made by Hadley ("Two Pithoi," pp. 187-188) again render the reading "YHWH of Teman" uncertain.

31. This has recently been stressed by Margalit in "Meaning and Significance," p. 276. See also Weippert, "Präskript," pp. 210-211.

32. Lemaire, "Date et origine," p. 139.

33. Margalit has recently ("Meaning and Significance," pp. 275, 288-289) pointed out that these two figurines are bovine, whereas the Egyptian Bes invariably is leonine.

34. Hadley, "Two Pithoi," pp. 189-196, 207. Recently, Margalit ("Meaning and Significance," pp. 288-291) has found that the smaller size, the breasts and the position of the figure on the right, slightly behind the larger figure in the foreground, are intended to represent feminine traits. The differences in head-dress also suggest that one figure is female, the other male. The "'loop' suspended between the legs of both figures is almost certainly an animal tail rather than a phallus" (p. 288). See further "Meaning and Significance," pp. 277, 295.

35. Hadley, "Two Pithoi," pp. 196-207; Margalit, "Meaning and Significance," pp. 289-291. Schroer, *Bilder*, p. 37, assumes an associative affinity between inscriptions and drawings and a larger cultic connotation of Asherah (and of her power to bless) on the potsherds.

36. Hadley, "Two Pithoi," pp. 204-205. Half a dozen stamp seals, representing suckling goats, are also from Palestine; see Keel, *Böcklein*, pp. 114-115. The motif is the "incarnation" of a numinous power, but does not refer to one particular goddess (p. 142). The suckling mother animal is found in the Palestine glyptic as early as the Late Bronze IIB period, and fairly frequently after that (Shuval, pp. 105-111).

37. Schroer, *Bilder*, pp. 38-39, Hestrin, pp. 214-215, 221. Hadley is more reserved in her judgment ("Two Pithoi," p. 205).

38. Meshel, *Kuntillet 'Ajrud.*

39. Beck, pp. 43-47.

40. Holladay, p. 259.

41. Gitin, "Olive-Oil Suppliers," p. 41 and p. 59 note 18; and "Artifacts, News, Notes, and Reports," p. 232.

42. Gitin, "Olive-Oil Suppliers," p. 59 note 18.

43. Gitin, "Olive-Oil Suppliers."

44. Ibid.

45. Schroer, "Zweiggöttin."

46. According to Schroer, *Bilder*, p. 39, this cultic stand, excavated by P.W. Lapp, may depict YHWH and Asherah together.

47. Schroer, "Zweiggöttin," pp. 212-215, 218.

48. Jaroš, pp. 207-210; Schroer, *Bilder*, p. 34 notes 63-64. Altogether, there are eleven seals which are relevant for Israel. They are nearly all from the Iron IIA/B period. According to verbal information from Christoph Uehlinger, the scaraboids Schroer mentions ("Zweiggöttin," p. 212, illustrations 25 and 26 on p. 213) do not belong to the twig goddess type. They represent the Asherah of the official national cultus.

49. Concerning the seal amulets, see Keel, "Glyptik," p. 416 (one possible exception is mentioned). Only the stand from Taanach which has already been mentioned (note 46 above) shows the naked goddess as ruler of the animals, holding two lions in the lowest register, whereas two registers higher up we find a tree with goats, again flanked by two lions.

50. Against Schroer, "Zweiggöttin," pp. 212-214, according to whom this type of image was frequently found in the eighth and seventh centuries BCE. However, Schroer substantiates this affirmation only by a scaraboid from Samaria and a potsherd from En-Gedi, which have no specific relation to the twig goddess. (Information from Christoph Uehlinger.)

51. Tigay, *No Other Gods*. De Moor, *Rise of Yahwism*, pp. 10-41, analyzes the biblical theophoric personal names and place names from the ninth century to David.

52. Tigay, *No Other Gods*. There are seventy-seven other names which are not taken into account in his statistics, since it remains uncertain which deity they refer to. They have the theophoric element *'ēl*, "god" or "El" and *'ēlî*, "my god" (*No Other Gods*, p. 12). The Old Testament knows 466 persons from preexilic times with theophoric names. 89 percent of these names are yahwistic, 11 percent are pagan. In the periods of the separate kingdoms and of late Judah, covered by epigraphic finds, the relation in the Bible is 96 percent to 4 percent (*No Other Gods*, pp. 17-18).

53. Tigay, *No Other Gods*, pp. 65-68. Fowler, pp. 60-63 lists fourteen occurrences of Baal in extrabiblical names, 11 of which were found on ostraca from Samaria and two on Phoenician seals.

54. This fact cannot be explained by pointing out that the names in the corpus are for the most part male. For in West Semitic onomastica, names of goddesses are found as elements both in male and female names. Also, many female Israelite names have YHWH or *'ēlî* as a theophoric element (Tigay, *No Other Gods*, p. 14). According to Fowler, p. 313, "titles of female deities are totally lacking in Hebrew." She also affirms that "there is no instance in the Hebrew onomasticon when close relationship between a female name-bearer and the deity is expressed."

55. Olyan, *Asherah and the Cult of Yahweh*, pp. 35-37. In Ugarit, for instance, there is no theophoric name containing Astarte as an element and only a single one with Asherah, although both these goddesses were fairly important in the official cultus, as is shown by myths, lists of sacrifices and registers of deities (Tigay, "Onomastic and Epigraphic Evidence," p. 20).

56. It is characteristic that no male deity in terracotta, metal or stone has yet been found in an indisputably Iron Age context—apart from a small bronze figurine from Stratum XI in Hazor (eleventh century), possibly representing El or the enthroned Baal. Other anthropomorphic pictorial representations of gods are equally rare. We only know one (or possibly two) drawing(s) incised on a 9 cm. high miniature altar in limestone from the Canaanite free town of Gezer (Stratum VIII, second half of the tenth century) with the warlike "smiting" god Reshef; further a limestone scarab from Achseb, also with a smiting god. See Keel and Uehlinger, *Göttinnen*.

57. Concerning the Chronicles, see Frevel.

58. Regarding Exod 34:13 and Judg 6:25-32, see, for instance Halbe, *Privilegrecht*, pp. 110-119. Whether the elimination of the asherahs in Exod 34:13b originally belonged to the list of destruction precepts is left undecided by Halbe. In any case, from the factual as well as from the linguistic point of view, it could be predeuteronomic.

59. Concerning Jer 17:2; Isa 17:8; 27:9; and Mic 5:13, see Olyan, *Asherah and the Cult of Yahweh*, pp. 14-17.

60. The question of whether or not these texts are authentic need not be discussed in this context. Even if they do not have the historical Hosea as their author, but were, for instance, edited by his disciples in Judah after the fall of Samaria, they would presumably still be older than Deuteronomy. And this date is sufficient for our argument.

61. Andersen and Freedman, p. 650.

62. See Kinet, *Ba'al und Jahwe*, pp. 85-87, 90-91, 209-212.

63. Hos 9:10 is about the sins in Baal-Peor; according to Andersen and Freedman, this is probably also the case for 13:1. Verse 11:2, which has "baals" in the plural, puts Baal in a different historical perspective.

64. See for instance Jeremias, "Hosea/Hoseabuch," pp. 591-592.

65. Against Olyan, *Asherah and the Cult of Yahweh*, pp. 7, 21. He rejects the idea that there is a reference to Asherah in 4:12 and 14:9ab, but his arguments are convincing only for the first passage. For 14:9, see note 81 below.

66. Lohfink, "Schilde."

67. The plural *ʿaṣabbîm*, like other similar expressions in Hosea is probably a kind of imitation of *ʾelōhîm* and refers to a single deity – Andersen and Freedman, p. 649 – not, however, to Baal (in spite of what Andersen and Freedman think, p. 378).

68. This translation of the text-critically problematic Masoretic Text follows Lohfink, "Schilde." In translating the text, Lohfink follows Nyberg, pp. 32-36. As Lohfink explains, it is decisive for the interpretation of the text that the two (usually emended) feminine singular suffixes in *māginnêhā* (4:18) and *ʾôtāh* (4:19) must refer to a feminine being. This being is the object of *ʾāhᵃbû hēbû*, which is formulated as a relative clause without a relative pronoun: the love (her, of whom it is true that) *qâlôn māginnêhā*, "her shields are ignominy" (4:18). Probably the writer was thinking of a type of image where the love goddess wore shields as an ornament. Lohfink has summarized a number of references to goddesses and their cult symbols where shields play a part (in "Schilde").

69. This fully corresponds to the rest of his polemic against the gods, where only Baal is named – and we do not even know for certain that, in that period, Baal was actually the name of a god. See Andersen and Freedman, pp. 649-650 for a list of Hosea's references to gods.

70. See the extensive discussion of possible image types in Lohfink, "Schilde."

71. The phrase *znh mittaḥat* with its implied sexual metaphor is not found elsewhere in the Old Testament. Compare the contrast in the phrase *znh mēʿal*, "is promiscuous away from his God," found only in Hos 9:1. (Concerning *znh*, see Bird "To Play the Harlot.")

72. It is probably not a question of boundless promiscuity during the festivals (against Balz-Cochois, pp. 151-152), but of a single act: a young married woman had intercourse for the first time with a stranger in the sanctuary in order to obtain fertility as a blessing from the deity in return for this opening of the womb. This initiation rite probably took place between the legal marriage (betrothal) and the husband's taking his bride into his home (wedding). Verses 4:13-14 make the heads of the families, not the husbands responsible in speaking only of "your daughters" and "your daughters-in-law," never of "your wives." In spite of Rudolph's objections in "Präparierte Jungfrauen," this is probably the best explanation of what is said in chapter 4, although it does not necessarily

explain the biography of Gomer in chapters 1-3. See Rost, p. 57; Wolff, *Hosea*, pp. 108-109 and 114. That this custom had to do with the worship of Anath/Astarte is also assumed by, for instance, Jeremias, *Der Prophet Hosea*, p. 71.

73. That Hosea also regards the female temple employees as victims of male transgressions seems to me to contradict the view that the prophet does not care about "women as such, but about women in their particular biological status as (potential) mothers, without whom Israel cannot survive"—against Wacker, "Frau-Sexus-Macht," p. 113.

74. Wacker, "Frau-Sexus-Macht," p. 108 note 21 agrees with this.

75. Andersen and Freedman, pp. 555-559.

76. In disagreement with Andersen and Freedman, p. 558, I translate 10:7 as follows: "Samaria has been annihilated, its king is like a broken twig on the water." The term *qeṣep*, only here used for "piece of wood" or "broken twig" presumably means the wooden core of *'eglôt*. Did Hosea choose this word in order to make an implicit reference to the "wooden pole" or "twig" which symbolized the goddess?

77. See Feuillet. However, 14:9 cannot be resolved as a dialogue between Ephraim and YHWH, with the speaker changing twice. For according to the MT, verse 9a constitutes a question asked by YHWH, not by Ephraim—in disagreement with van der Woude, pp. 483-485.

78. *lî* must not be emended to *lô* in accordance with the LXX and then be made to refer to Ephraim. The structure of 14:9 constitutes a stylistic argument for maintaining the MT; *('eprayim) mah-lî* and *mimmenî (pery^{e}kā)* correspond to each other. Today, there is epigraphic and iconographic evidence which substantiates the affirmation in the MT, contrary to what Rudolph affirms in Hosea, pp. 249.

79. Concerning the translation, see note 83 below.

80. Concerning the translation, see Thomas, pp. 395-396.

81. In spite of what Tångberg says (pp. 83-85), this translation of *b^{e}rôš* is preferable, since the juniper, unlike the fir, has edible fruit and the following stich speaks of fruit.

82. Regarding the palindromic structure of 14:9, see Yee, pp. 139-140.

83. The term is nowhere found as frequently as in Hosea. Verses 8:4-6 and 13:2 combine *'^{a}ṣabbîm* with the "calf." Such a reference is—evidently for factual reasons—lacking in 4:17 and 14:9. Since 4:17-18 is about "(the goddess) whose shields are ignominy," one can assume that the "idol" in 14:9 refers to this goddess.

84. There is no need to have recourse to Wellhausen's conjecture "I am his Anath and his Asherah" (*Kleinen Propheten*, p. 134). Besides, Wellhausen regards only Anath as a goddess, seeing Asherah merely as a

sacred pole. According to Day, "Asherah in the Hebrew Bible," pp. 404-406 (in more detail in Day, "Inner Scriptural Interpretation," pp. 314-316), Isa 26:13 - 27:11 was probably inspired by Hos 13:4 - 14:10. There are eight correspondences between the two pericopes and, with a single exception, they come in the same order. Isa 27:9 is dependent on Hos 14:9. Whereas the "full fruit" of the removal of Jacob's sin implies that no Asherim are erected (Isa 27:9), Ephraim's fruit comes from YHWH and not from the idol, that is, from the goddess (Hos 14:9). The interpretation in Isa 27:9 need not have hit on the original meaning of 14:9, but we cannot exclude the possibility that this, the oldest interpretation, was correct about the reference to Asherah. Emmerson, p. 5, also assumes a deliberate play on words. That *wa'ašûrennû* in Hos 14:9 alludes to *'aššûr* in verse 4 is unlikely both because of the context and because of the possibility of a parallel word play between *'ānîtî* and Anath. Since one cannot expect any allusion to the goddess Anath in a Hebrew text from the eighth century—by then she had long been superseded by Astarte—Margalit ("Meaning and Significance," p. 293) changes Wellhausen's emendation **'ntw* to **'(w)ntw*, deriving from *'nh*, "respond (sexually)," cf. Hos 2:17. This emendation also receives support from Margalit's etymological interpretation of "asherah" as "wife, consort," perhaps better rendered as "mate, partner." However, one can dispute the conjecture as well as the etymology.

85. Jacob, p. 97, goes so far as to affirm "YHWH absorbera Anat et Ashera. Il prend sur lui le rite assumé jusque là par les divinités de la fécondité; il sera lui-même l'arbre saint." The k^e, "like, as" in the comparison speaks against this view. Margalit, "Meaning and Significance," p. 294-295, also goes too far in his interpretation when he excludes a female partner for YHWH with the following statement: "YHWH is an androgynous fertility deity providing both halves of the sexual act needed to ensure fertility and fruition. He is a unity of 'Baal and Asherah,' 'husband-and-wife' in dialectical fusion, a theological hendiadys of law and love."

86. This possibility is not taken into account by Olyan, *Asherah and the Cult of Yahweh*, p. 21. Neither does he consider the possibility that *'aṣabbîm* might refer to a goddess. Hence his line of argument against the anti-(Anath-and-) Asherah polemic of 14:9 is not cogent.

87. Emmerson, p. 50. Perhaps this daring image of YHWH, unique in the Old Testament, also refers to trees under which, according to 4:12-13, people attempted to ensure fertility through sexual rites (cf. 14:8). Wolff, *Hosea*, p. 307, however, simply takes it to refer to the tree of life known from ancient Near Eastern mythology.

88. Koch, "Aschera als Himmelskönigin," pp. 100-107.

89. Koch, "Aschera als Himmelskönigin," p. 107. Perhaps the queen of heaven, worshiped in Jerusalem in the early sixth century (Jer 7:17-18; 44:15-27), should be equated with Asherah. This is Koch's view ("Aschera als Himmelskönigin," pp. 107-109), in disagreement with Olyan, "Identity of the Queen of Heaven," pp. 161-174, who considers it much more likely that she ought to be identified with Astarte. Ackerman, pp. 109-124, characterizes the Queen of Heaven as a syncretistic goddess who had assimilated aspects of the West Semitic Astarte and of the East Semitic Ishtar. Finally, it is disputed whether the "image of lust" *(sēmel haqqin'â)*, which according to Ezek 8:3-5 stood near the northern gate of the temple, was an Asherah statue which Jehoiakin had had reerected after Josiah's death. See Schroer, *Bilder*, pp. 25-28 and Koch, "Aschera als Himmelskönigin," pp. 111-112.

90. Cf. Spieckermann, pp. 212-221, esp. pp. 214-215.

91. Spieckermann, pp. 213-214.

92. Information about this may be found in Lohfink, "2 Kön. 22-23," pp. 27-28 (et bibli.). See also Lohfink, "Cult Reform."

93. See for instance W. Schmidt, "Jahwe," pp. 442-445.

94. Rost, p. 59, and following him Wolff, *Hosea*, p. 109, understand Deut 22:13-21 (the law concerning a man who charges his wife with not having been a virgin at the time of her marriage) as a legal reaction in imitation of Hosea. Deut 23:18-19 is directed against sacral prostitution with female prostitutes (condemned in Hos 4:14b), but also against recourse to male prostitutes. Whether this prostitution was part of a fertility ritual or constituted a source of profit for the temple (thus Toorn, p. 203) need not be discussed here.

95. See chapter 2 in the present volume.

96. See Lohfink, "Glaube."

97. Concerning *pesel* in the sense of "cultic image," see Dohmen, pp. 46-47.

98. The passages are redactionally related. Deut 12:3 takes up the precepts of 7:5 and 25. Deut 16:21-22 takes up the two laws, 12:2-3 and 12:29-31 which constitute the frame for the sacrificial order, 12:4-28 at the beginning of the laws governing worship. See Braulik, *Deuteronomischen Gesetze*, p. 47.

99. Spieckermann, p. 216. However, it is hardly possible to discover a hidden allusion to the Assyrian pantheon (p. 217).

100. In Deut 7:5 and 12:3, however, the verbs *gd'* pi. and *śrp* are associated alternately with *'ᵃšērîm* and *pᵉsilîm*, whereas the verbs used in connection with the altars and *maṣṣēbôt* remain the same. This usage may suggest a more specific relation between asherahs and idols.

101. Regarding the origin and translation of *šeger*, Müller, "Inschrift von Dēr 'āllā," pp. 64-65.

102. Baumgartner, p. 851.

103. Moawiyah and van der Kooij, pp. 27-28. Weippert, "Balaam Text," p. 176. See also Müller, "Inschrift von Dēr 'āllā," pp. 214 and note 3 and p. 230. It is not, however, certain whether *šgr* is a goddess or a god (p. 230 note 106).

104. Müller, "עַשְׁתֹּרֶת, *'štrt*," *TWAT* 6:461.

105. Delcor, pp. 8-10. Probably *šgr*, too, is a fertility deity (p. 14).

106. Plöger, pp. 170-173 concludes from the missing relative pronoun that the phrase "the increase of your cattle and the lambing of your sheep" in 28:4b and 18b, probably does not belong to the old formula of blessings and curses used in worship (28:3-6* and 16-19*—see *Untersuchungen*, pp. 141-144), but is a deuteronomistic addition. For the same reason, the phrase was probably added later to 7:13. 28:51 is secondary. Nor has Deuteronomy, in these passages, taken up an old cultic text, nor is the formula so late that it has lost its polemic character.

107. Müller, "Inschrift von Dēr 'āllā," p. 230 note 102 thinks that, in these passages of Deuteronomy, there was an "ad hoc demythologization of the names of deities, making them appellatives"; cf. Delcor, p. 14.

108. Keel, "Glyptik," p. 116.

109. This thesis is explained and substantiated more fully in Braulik, "Haben in Israel."

110. Braulik, *Deuteronomium 1-16, 17*, pp. 16-17. Further Perlitt, "Ein einzig Volk."

111. Lohfink, "Deuteronomische Gesetz."

112. Cf. Weinfeld, *Deuteronomic School*, pp. 291-293. Women and men are explicitly mentioned as subjects of the following legal precepts: Deut 15:12-18; 17:2-7; 21:18-21; 22:5 (22:22, 23-24); 23:18, 19; 29:9-10, 17; 31:12,. The equality of men and women among the upper classes is illustrated by 28:53-57. 5:16 and 27:16 are valid for the father as well as for the mother. Both sons and daughters are concerned with 7:3; 12:31; 13:7; 18:10. Sabbath rest and participation in sacrifices and feasts are legally assured to them as well as to male and female slaves. Presumably the laws concerning aliens and orphans are valid for both sexes, although no differentiation is made. According to 32:18, YHWH has "begotten" and "borne" Israel; he is Israel's mother as well as father. Correspondingly, 32:19 speaks of Israel as "his sons and daughters."

113. It is only in the two (probably latest) insertions in Deuteronomy that access to YHWH's altar is reserved for priests and Levites. According to 12:27, lay people had access to the altar in order to bring burnt offerings and sacrifices. Whereas 26:10 stipulated that the peasant should

set the basket with the first fruits "before YHWH," the secondary verse 4 (Kreuzer, pp. 150-156) states that the priest serving in the temple is to receive it and set it "before the altar of YHWH." According to 33:10b, an insertion in the saying concerning Levi (Gunneweg, p. 41), the Levites set the burnt offerings—which are of no importance in the rest of Deuteronomy—on the altar. In what follows, we can leave these limiting facts out of account.

114. See p. 51-52 in the present volume.

115. Lohfink, "Opfer und Säkularisierung"; Braulik, "Politische Kraft."

116. This is maintained by Bird in "Place of Women," p. 411. However, she also realizes that deuteronomic legislation aimed at bringing women more fully and directly into the religious assembly and that the community was redefined as a "body of lay men and women" (ibid.).

117. For the larger context of the following observations, see chapters 2 and 3 in the present volume.

118. Seitz, p. 191 note 288.

119. This is *a fortiori* true of the sabbath, since such an interpretation would mean that the free woman and housewife, alone in the entire household had to work. However, it is quite as improbable that the family mother is not mentioned in the sabbath commandment (5:14) because she was "not considered as belonging to the family work pool"—in disagreement with Schenker, p. 196. This ad hoc interpretation of the sabbath commandment provides no explanation for other instances in the sequence. Besides, the interpretation is erroneous. Women most certainly worked. Indeed, according to Deuteronomy, women could even sell themselves as slaves (15:12) in order to save themselves and their families from total destitution. In this context, a collection of seals from preexilic times (eighth to sixth century) may be of interest. Avigad has drawn attention to them in "Contribution of Hebrew Seals," pp. 205-206. These seals belonged to Israelite women and show the equal social status of women as regards the right to enter into valid contracts.

120. Cf. George Adam Smith, *Deuteronomy*, p. 167: "Wives are not mentioned here, for they are included in those to whom the law is addressed, a significant fact."

121. Bird, "Translating Sexist Language," pp. 92-93, speaking of the law concerning Hebrew slaves in Deut 15:12-18, points out that the precepts in verses 12 and 17 are explicitly extended to concern "a Hebrew woman" or "a female slave." Do not these specifications oblige us to conclude that in those Old Testament legal texts "where unambiguous extension of a case to both men and women is intended, explicitly inclusive language is used" (p. 93)? But there is a particular reason for the explicit mention of women in this law and this is quite compatible with

letting "you" imply women inclusively in normal cases. In the actual case, the legal tradition had been added to and therefore, had women not been explicitly mentioned in this passage, the "you" would automatically have been interpreted as referring to men only. We possess the older form of this deuteronomic law, namely Exod 21:2-11. The Book of the Covenant treats men in the first part (Exod 21:2-6) and women in the second (Exod 21:7-11). The deuteronomic law concerning the emancipation of slaves (Deut 15:12-18) corresponds only to the first part; the second part has no counterpart in Deuteronomy. Instead, Deuteronomy extends the stipulations concerning men who have sold themselves into slavery (Exod 21:2-6) to cover women as well. Since previous laws had expressed themselves differently, Deuteronomy, for the sake of juridical clarity, had to mention the "Hebrew woman" explicitly. Hence the reference to the "Hebrew woman" and the "female slave" do not allow us to infer that the masculine singular in legal texts was normally used exclusively, that is, that it referred only to men. The masculine forms in the sacrificial laws of Deuteronomy may quite well have an inclusive meaning. That they did in fact include women follows from the above analysis of how the lists of participants functioned.

122. 16:16-17 still partly mirrors predeuteronomic legislation (cf. verse 16 with Exod 23:15b, 17; 34:20b, 23). This passage demands that, at these festivals, "all your males" come to the central sanctuary, but not "empty-handed." In practice, this meant that they offered the sacrifice. The preceding deuteronomic festival laws in 16:11 and 14, however, stipulate that, at the Feast of Weeks and the Feast of Booths, "you, your son and daughter, your male and female slaves, the Levites, aliens, orphans and widows" are to rejoice before YHWH. The freewill offering demanded by 16:10 for the Feast of Weeks is brought by either the man or the woman, either of whom is the "you" addressed by the law.

123. These redactio-historical questions are not discussed by Winter, in his analysis of the status of women at the festivals (pp. 29-32). In the context of Exod 34:23; 23:17 he restricts himself in practice to the obligation in Deut 16:16, which—as is suggested by 16:14 may "not have excluded women entirely from being present," but "apparently excluded them from any form of active participation, and especially from offering sacrifices."

124. Cf. Bird in "Place of Women," p. 408.

125. Holladay, p. 294 note 126.

126. Here there is no mention of, perhaps even a denial of what, according to Bird in "Place of Women," p. 401, determined the place of women in the cultus elsewhere in the Old Testament: "(1) the periodic impurity of women during their reproductive years; (2) the legal subordination of women within the family, which places a woman under the male authority of father, husband or brother, together with a corresponding subordination in the public sphere in which the community is represented by its male members; and (3) an understanding of women's primary work and social duty as family-centered reproductive work in the role of wife-mother."

Chapter 9. Deuteronomy and the Commemorative Culture of Israel

1. Assmann, p. 212. Concerning Deuteronomy, see pp. 212-228.
2. Assmann, pp. 48-59 distinguishes between two forms of collective remembrance: communicative remembrance and cultural remembrance. Communicative remembrance is related to the immediate past; it is a kind of "generation remembrance" and constitutes a framework of personally guaranteed and communicated experience. It encompasses the biblical three or four generations and reaches a critical threshold after forty years. It works through the mode of a biographical memory and is dependent on social interaction. Cultural remembrance, which works with foundational memory and is part of a type of institutionalized mnemonics is different. This form of remembrance commemorates the earliest times, the "absolute" past in symbolic focussing points such as the exodus, the conquest and settlement, or the exile. It is transmitted by special tradition bearers, has a sacral element and is often commemorated liturgically at feasts.
3. Assmann, p. 213.
4. Assmann, pp. 213-214.
5. Assmann, p. 206.
6. This is the title of a section in Assmann, p. 112.
7. Lohfink, "Glaube," p. 153.

8. These instances are found in 4:1, 5, 10 (bis), 14; 5:1, 31; 6:1; 11:19; 14:23; 17:19; 18:9; 20:18; 31:12, 13, 19, 22. Other verbs such as יסר pi. (4:36; 8:5 (bis); 21:18; 22:18), ירא III hi. (17:10, 11; 24:8; 33:10) or ידע hi. (4:9; 8:3) play only a subsidiary part. The linguistic rules followed by Deuteronomy in the use of these verbs cannot by elucidated in this article. Only in the Psalms does למד occur more frequently (twenty-seven times), but it is difficult to compare the Psalms with Deuteronomy. Of these twenty-seven instances, thirteen must be discounted, since they occur in Psalm 119, a psalm influenced by Deuteronomy.

9. The archaeological and epigraphic evidence is not taken into account. See Jamieson-Drake, *Scribes and Schools*.

10. This is the subtitle of Lohfink's "Glaube."

11. The theme of teaching and learning in Deuteronomy should be treated in other contexts as well, for instance in connection with specific literary didactic methods. Lohfink (*Hauptgebot*, pp. 261-285) has made an important contribution, which to a great extent has remained unnoticed. He explains the "parenetic process" in Deuteronomy 5-11, "where all linguistic strata contribute to the real assertion (Lohfink, "Glaube," p. 261; see also Fischer and Lohfink, p. 69, n. 42).

12. Concerning the subsequent history of this "textbook," see Lohfink, "'d(w)t," pp. 92-93.

13. Lohfink, "ḥuqqîm," pp. 229, 238-239; and "'d(w)t," p. 89.

14. Couroyer, "'édût."

15. Lohfink, "'d(w)t," p. 92.

16. Lohfink, "2 Kön 23,3 und Dtn 6,17," pp. 41-42.

17. Fischer and Lohfink, p. 67.

18. Only on this assumption can we understand the regulations of 31:12 to summon "men and women, children and old people, and also the aliens" to the recital of the Torah at the Feast of Booths every seventh year, למען ישמעו ולמען ילמדו ויראו את-יהוה אלהיכם. Regarding the inclusive masculine verb forms in 6:7, see Lohfink, "Glaube," p. 262, n. 24.

19. Strictly speaking, the recital of the deuteronomic law is not limited to "transmitting it to the following generations" (this should be specified since it is not clear from Fischer and Lohfink, p. 63). In 6:7, the recitation is paratactically associated with שננתם לבניך; the dative object is not repeated. On the other hand, the variant in 11:19a:

ולמדתם אתם את בניכם לדבר בם

syntactically refers "reciting" unambiguously to teaching the children.

20. Assmann, p. 218.

21. Assmann, pp. 218-219.

22. The arguments to the contrary presented by Achenbach, pp. 105-108 on the basis of certain other passages are not cogent.

23. Lohfink, "Jahwegesetz."
24. Lohfink, "Jahwegesetz," p. 391.
25. Lohfink, "Jahwegesetz," p. 387.
26. Lohfink, "Kerygmata," pp. 132-137.
27. Lohfink, "ḥuqqîm," pp. 235.
28. Lohfink, "ḥuqqîm," pp. 235-237. Against Achenbach, p. 108 (cf. p. 111), who above all because of the resemblances to 30:11-14 (or 30:1-10) assumes a late date for 6:6-9. He does not even consider the possibility that 30:11-14 could be dependent on 6:6-9. The differences between the two texts hardly become clear. He does not mention that 6:6-9 and 30:11-14 form a kind of frame, one text occurring at the beginning, the other at the end of the promulgation of the law (cf. the love commandment in 6:5, to which the later 30:6 refers). The "sapiential metaphors" (p. 108) and the "fluctuation between metaphorical speech and concrete stipulations" (p. 112) are probably much less frequent than Achenbach thinks—see the article ("Worte") by Fischer and Lohfink (Achenbach apparently does not know of this article). Yet the perpetual recitation in Deuteronomy, like other analogous stipulations, is not an instance of rubristic casuistry, but has a theological purpose—see p. 81 and note 55 on p. 234 in the present volume. A late date cannot be substantiated in this way. That "the manifold—and therefore non-specific—ways in which the law is referred to here (6:6-9)" is a "characteristic feature of the late strata of Deuteronomy" (Achenbach, p. 112) is not demonstrated.
29. Regarding the meaning of שׁנן, see Fischer and Lohfink, p. 63; cf. Achenbach, pp. 111-112 and note 181.
30. This is clear even from the fact that when 11:19b, 20 quote 6:7b, 9, there is a change in number. See Braulik, *Deuteronomium 1-16, 17*, p. 90; Fischer and Lohfink, pp. 64-65; Achenbach, p. 391.
31. The play on words with the rather unusual דבר ב for "recite" in 6:7 could have determined the choice or the formulation of the expression used for "law."
32. Achenbach (p. 106) justly remarks on the special position of דברים in 6:6. The expression may certainly refer to "the law as a whole, including the parenesis," but not to "all that was to be said on the day of promulgation (היום)"—against Achenbach. Achenbach discovers "a certain parallel to the formulation" of 6:6-9 in the framework of the Song of Moses (32:44, 45-47) and, from this resemblance, determines the conceptual content of הדברים האלה in 6:6 as well as the date of 6:6-9. But in 32:45 at the end of the speech(es) of Moses, כל-הדברים האלה is a verbal reminiscence of 1:1 (Perlitt, "Priesterschrift," p. 64). Finally, the promulgatory sentence formulated with מעיד and the unique (to Deutero-

nomy) צוה pi. for the transmission by the parents in 32:46 cannot be compared with 6:6. These dissimilarities prohibit us from concluding "a fairly late date for the origins" of 6:6 (Achenbach) merely because of the late deuteronomistic verses 32:45-47.

33. Lohfink, "Kerygmata," p. 134.

34. Lohfink, *Hauptgebot*, pp. 154-157.

35. With G and against the text-critically probably secondary ועדתיו—see Lohfink, "2 Kön 23,3 und Dtn 6,17."

36. Lohfink, "'d(w)t," p. 89.

37. See Lohfink, "2 Kön 23,3 und Dtn 6,17."

38. The phrase עשׂה הטוב והישׁר בעיני יהוה occurs only twice in Deuteronomy, in 6:18a and 12:28b. In both passages, it is associated with the final determination למען ייטב לך. The two sentences are slightly expanded in 12:28b. In Deuteronomy, only verses 12:28a and 6:6 speak of הדברים האלה אשׁר אנכי מצוך. Perhaps 12:28 once terminated the oldest part of the centralization law. Do these texts, then, form a kind of inclusion?

39. Lohfink, "Kerygmata," p. 139 and Braulik, "Gesetz als Evangelium," pp. 142-144.

40. 6:20-25 was probably not part of the Josianic Book of the Covenant, since it associates the land and the law and uses the double expression חקים ומשׁפטים if, that is, this expression is original. It may have been added in connection with the "Deuteronomistic Conquest narrative," with 5:31 and 6:1, or have been added to 16:17 later (cf. Lohfink, "'d(w)t," p. 90.

41. Like 6:6-9, this catechismal instruction in the family was added at the beginning of החקים והמשׁטים. This credo, together with the second "brief credal formula" in Deuteronomy, the deuteronomistic "brief historical credo" in 26:5-10 (Lohfink, "Kleinen geschichtlichen Credo," p. 281-282), forms a framework for the parenesis and the individual laws. In connection with these texts, Lohfink, "Glaube," p. 156, speaks of a "situation oriented" and "situation reflecting" learning of the faith. Later (?), 6:6-9 together with the parallel 11:18-21 becomes a frame for the parenesis in chapters 6-11 and is taken up at the end of the Mosaic proclamation in 30:11-14.

42. Lohfink, "Glaube," pp. 154-156 and 153.

43. See chapter 2 in the present volume and Braulik, "Politische Kraft."

44. Regarding the apposition of this double phrase, see Lohfink, "ḥuqqîm," p. 230.

45. The prolongation of 6:1 need not be secondary—Lohfink, "ḥuqqîm," p. 237. On the other hand, Achenbach, pp. 61-62) considers 6:2 a secondary literary prolongation of 6:1.

46. Outside Deuteronomy, YHWH may certainly be the subject of למד pi. This occurs particularly frequently in the Psalms, for instance in Pss 18:35; 25:4, 9; 71:17 etc.; with a word meaning "law" as object for instance in Ps 119:12, 26, 64 etc. In the whole Old Testament, למד qal is never associated with God.

47. Cf. Lohfink, "ḥuqqîm," p. 240.

48. Cf. Wolff, *Hosea*, p. 123.

49. In order to be more precise than Lohfink, *Hauptgebot*, p. 66. Elsewhere in Deuteronomy 5, the object of שמע את is always קול, with the exception of 5:27, which has כל, (5:23, 25, 26, 28a, 28b), not the law as in 5:1 (and still in 4:6; 7:12; 12:28). 5:1 is the only instance in Deuteronomy where שמע את plus a term meaning "law" is found together with ישׂראל.

50. In 5:27, the phrase שׁמע את, characteristic of Deuteronomy 5, is united to כל, to all that YHWH says (דבר pi.) to Moses and that Moses is to recount (דבר pi.). Only in 6:3 do we find שמע ישׂראל together with the double phrase שמר לעשׂת for observance of the law.

51. Lohfink (*Hauptgebot*, pp. 66-68 and 15-16) has discovered the literary relation between 5:27 and 6:3, as well as the concentric structure at the boundary between the two chapters.

52. Thus, for instance, Seitz, p. 41; Achenbach, pp. 61-62.

53. Lohfink, "Kerygmata," p. 133.

54. Also occurs in 31:28 and with קרא as a promulgatory verb in 31:11. In 31:30 and 32:44, the phrase refers to the Song of Moses.

55. Only in 6:6 is היום part of the Mosaic promulgation clause.

56. Fischer and Lohfink, pp. 64-65.

57. Verse 18a "learn by heart" (A)
Verse 18b "sign on one's body" (B)
Verse 19 "teach" (C)
Verse 20 "sign on the buildings" (B´)
Verse 21 "reference to the blessing" (A´)

The framework and the center are related to each other: the notion of learning at the beginning is taken up by the notion of teaching in the center; the reference to the blessing at the end takes up the motif of children in the center. See Fischer and Lohfink, pp. 64-65.

58. Compare with שׂימו לבבכם לכל־הדברים (32:46) at the end of the development of the transmission theme, where the parents are said to be obliged (צוה pi.) to transmit what they have heard; elsewhere this is characteristic of the promulgation by YHWH or by Moses.

59. Braulik, *Deuteronomium 1-16, 17*, p. 90.

60. Fischer and Lohfink, p. 65.

61. Concerning this linguistic pattern, characteristic of Deuteronomy, see Lohfink, *Hauptgebot*, pp. 90-97. As elsewhere in Deuteronomy, it functions as a framework or a way of structuring the text.

62. In contrast to 11:21, 11:9a also speaks of וזרעם. For a long life in the land, it uses the very common expression האריך ימים. The phrase ימי השמים על-הארץ occurs only in 11:21 (in Deuteronomy).

63. According to Lohfink ("Gott im Deuteronomium," p. 38 note 45 and pp. 43-44, including note 57) the text which we here have in revised form, is older, but was not introduced into Deuteronomy until the exile. It was extended through 10:16, 19; 11:8b; and in 11:16 another preamble to the curses was substituted for the old one. However, one cannot—as Achenbach, p. 390 thinks—conclude from the linguistic affinity between 11:21 and 4:40 (recognized to be a late deuteronomistic text) that our text, too, must be dated late. The essential formulations in the two verses differ: the phrase רבה ימים and the comparison with the "days in which the heavens are above the earth" are found only in 11:21 in the entire book of Deuteronomy. The assurance that "all will be well with you" is missing in 11:21. In 4:40, on the other hand, the important theological topic of the oath to the fathers to give them the land (11:21) is missing.

64. This has recently been maintained by Schäfer-Lichtenberger, *Josua*, pp. 69-85.

65. Fischer and Lohfink, pp. 68-70.

66. Against Buchholz, pp. 17-21. See also the bibliography for Lohfink's review of this work.

67. Lohfink, review of Buchholz, "Die Ältesten."

68. Assmann, p. 220, refers to the pilgrimage festivals as "festivals of collective commemoration." According to the Old Testament festival calendar, this designation does not (yet) fit the Feast of Weeks; 16:12a does not give the context of the feast, but the motivation for the socially explosive participation of male and female slaves (Hardmeier, pp. 142-143). The yearly Feast of Booths can only be included under the (probable) supposition that at this feast the first fruits were offered and the "brief historical credo" with its recapitulation of history was recited (26:1-11).

69. K. Baltzer, *Bundesformular*, pp. 91-95, esp. p. 91; Weinfeld, *Deuteronomic School*, pp. 64-65.

70. The formulation is from Lohfink, "Glaube," p. 158. For what follows, pp. 158-159.

71. Lohfink, "Fabel."

72. Lohfink, "Glaube," p. 159.

73. Lohfink, "Glaube," p. 159. Lohfink presumes the original situation of the assembly at Horeb. So do Fischer and Lohfink (pp. 68-70) for the law on the king and the recitation of the Torah at the Feast of Booths (17:19 and 31:12-13 respectively). I myself have also formerly defended this view in various publications.

74. 31:12G, on the other hand (presumably as a way of adapting to 31:13 and other passages in Deuteronomy which combine למד and ירא) has ἵνα μάθωσιν φοβεῖσθαι, that is, the *lectio facilior*.

75. Against Becker, *Gottesfurcht*, p. 105 and Fischer and Lohfink, p. 69. They are right in emphasizing the paratactic relation of the two verbs in 31:12, through which they differ from the infinitive construction in 31:13 and from the other instances where verbs are combined, in 4:10; 14:23; 17:19. Fischer and Lohfink (p. 69 note 69) also consider the possibility of a "rhythmically conditioned variant which does not imply any difference in meaning." However, text-pragmatically speaking, למד qal cannot refer to "learning the law" (Becker) or "learning by heart" (Lohfink; cf. the German *Einheitsübersetzung* of the Bible).

76. Should the דברים refer only to the parenesis and the individual commandments, the blessings and curses would remain when the תורה is recited. But even in this case, repeating them would be enough, since on other occasions the blessings and curses need not be recited by heart.

77. Fischer and Lohfink, p. 68.

78. Fischer and Lohfink, p. 69. For the rest, the deuteronomic text with its linguistic form already aims at such a mediation through mystical unity." Lohfink has demonstrated this for chapters 5-11 in *Hauptgebot*, p. 69 note 42).

79. Lohfink, "Glaube," p. 159.

80. Fischer and Lohfink, p. 69.

81. Lohfink, *Hauptgebot*, p. 68.

82. Braulik, "Gesetz als Evangelium," pp. 54-61.

83. Schäfer-Lichtenberger, *Josua*, pp. 52-106.

84. See Braulik, "Gesetz als Evangelium," pp. 39-45.

85. See for instance, Merendino, p. 227; Mayes, p. 296; Lohfink, "חרם," p. 212 regards 20:18 as an exilic addition to the law on war.

86. In Deuteronomy, the plural תועבת is—apart from the Song of Moses (32:16 "abomination," "abominable things")—found only in the law on prophets (18:9, 12) and in the law on war (20:18).

87. Braulik, "Gesetz als Evangelium," p. 37.

88. Lohfink, "Glaube," p. 160 translates 31:21aβ: "his descendants will not forget it, but will recite it regularly."

89. Assmann, p. 220.

90. See Braulik, *Deuteronomium 1-16, 17*, pp. 224-226.

91. Lohfink, "Glaube," p. 160.

92. Cf. לא תשכח מפי זרעו in 31:21 with פן-תשכח in 4:9. See Assmann, pp. 222-225.

93. See the recent work by Knapp, passim.

94. More detail in chapter 1 of the present volume.

95. See, for instance, Braulik, "Stratigraphie" and "Einrahmung."

96. Lohfink, "ḥuqqîm," pp. 255-256.

97. Von Rad, *Deuteronomium*, p. 36; English translation, p. 49.

98. Assmann, p. 222.

99. Braulik, *Mittel*, passim.

100. For what follows, see pp. 5-7 in the present volume. However, today I would no longer affirm that "in the latest strata of the book, the didactic objectives gain in importance" or that למד "appears to have obtained its decisive role only in the context of the new theological orientations" (contrary to what I affirmed on pp. 5-6 above).

101. Cf. 4:1 מלמד with 5:1, where the root is lacking and the rhetorically emphasized למדתי in 4:5 with ללמד in 6:1.

102. In comparison with שמע ישראל את in 5:1, שמע אל in 4:1 (standing out against ישראל) is rhetorically emphasized and less rigid semantically.

103. Lohfink, "ḥuqqîm," p. 241.

104. Braulik, "Gesetz als Evangelium," p. 11.

105. Against Becker, *Gottesfurcht*, pp. 104-105. Even G and V understand אשר in the final sense. Cf. Also 4:40aβ, where there is also a final אשר in place of the customary למען.

106. In this context, verse 36 speaks of יסר, but possibly relates the education to the auditory and visual aspects of the theophany.

Abbreviations

Abbreviations used in the bibliography are in accordance with the standards set forth in the *Journal of Biblical Literature* 107(1988):583-596. Other abbreviations are as follows:

AASF.B	Annales Academiae Scientiarum Fennicae
AO	Der Alte Orient
AssB	Assyriologische Bibliothek
ATSAT	Arbeiten zu Text und Sprache im Alten Testament
BAW.AO	Bibliothek der Alten Welt. Der Alte Orient
BET	Beiträge zur biblischen Exegese und Theologie
BHBib	Bibliotheca Hispana Biblica
BN	*Biblische Notizen*
BOT	Boeken van het Oude Testament
BTF	*Bangalore Theological Forum*
Conc(D)	*Concilium. Einsiedeln*
CThM.BW	Calwer Theologische Monographien. Reihe A, Bibelwissenschaft
CV	*Communio viatorum*
EHS.T	Europäische Hochschulschriften. Reihe 23, Theologie
FAT	Forschungen zum Alten Testament
FZPhTh	*Freiburger Zeitschrift für Philosophie und Theologie*
HBS	Herders Biblische Studien
HTB	Harper torchbook
IKaZ	*Internationale katholische Zeitschrift*
JBTh	*Jahrbuch für Biblische Theologie*
JLW	*Jahrbuch für Liturgiewissenschaft*
KHC	Kurzer Hand-Commentar zum Alten Testament
Klio.B	Klio.Beiheft
KT	Kaiser-Traktate
KTB/BiKo	Kohlhammer-Taschenbücher/Biblische Konfrontationen
KuKi	*Kunst und Kirche*
LebZeug	*Lebendiges Zeugnis*

LuM	Liturgie und Mönchtum
MAOG	Mitteilungen der Altorientalischen Gesellschaft
MThS.H	Münchener Theologische Studien. Historische Abteilung
NCBC	New century Bible commentary
NEB.AT	Neue Echter Bibel. Kommentar zum AT
NHThG	*Neues Handbuch theologischer Grundbegriffe*
NStB	Neukirchener Studienbücher
NTG	Neue theologische Grundrisse
POS	Pretoria oriental series
RM	Religionen der Menschheit
SBAB	Stuttgarter Biblische Aufsatzbände
SJOT	*Scandinavian Journal of the Old Testament 24*
SDIO	Studia et documenta ad iura Orientis antiqui pertinentia
SEL	*Studi Epigrafici e Linguistici sul Vicino Oriente Antico*
SKC	Serie Kamper cahiers
SKK.AT	Stuttgarter Kleiner Kommentar - Altes Testament
ST(M)	Studium Theologie. München
StZ	*Stimmen der Zeit*
TBLNT	*Theologisches Begriffslexikon zum Neuen Testament*
THAT	*Theologisches Handwörterbuch zum Alten Testament*
ThG(B)	*Theologie der Gegenwart. Bergen-Enkheim*
ThJb(L)	*Theologisches Jahrbuch. Leipzig*
ThW	Theologische Wissenschaft
TOTC	Tyndale Old Testament commentaries
TUAT	*Texte aus der Umwelt des Alten Testaments*
TzZ	Theologie zur Zeit
UB.T	Urban-Taschenbücher
WB	Die Welt der Bibel
WBTh	Wiener Beiträge zur Theologie
WuD	*Wort und Dienst*
ZZ	Zwischen den Zeiten

Bibliography

Achenbach, Reinhard, *Israel zwischen Verheißung und Gebot: Literarkritische Untersuchungen zu Deuteronomium 5-11* (EHS.T 422; Frankfurt a.M. et al.: P. Lang, 1991).

Ackerman, Susan, "'And the Women Knead Dough': The Worship of the Queen of Heaven in Sixth-Century Judah," *Gender and Difference in Ancient Israel* (ed. P.L. Day; Minneapolis: Fortress Press, 1989) 109-124.

Aharoni, Yohanan, "Arad: Its Inscriptions and Temple," *BA* 31 (1968) 2-32.

Albertz, Rainer, *Persönliche Frömmigkeit und offizielle Religion: Religionsinterner Pluralismus in Israel und Babylon* (CThM.BW 9; Stuttgart: Calwer, 1978).

Altmann, Peter, *Erwählungstheologie und Universalismus im Alten Testament* (BZAW 92; Berlin: Töpelmann, 1964).

Amirtam, S., "To Be Near and Far Away from Yahweh: The Witness of the Individual Psalms of Lament to the Concept of the Presence of God," *BTF* 2 (1968) 31-55.

Ammermann, Maurus, *Die religiöse Freude in den Schriften des Alten Bundes* (Rome: Libreria Herder, 1942).

Andersen, Francis I. and David Noel Freedman, *Hosea: A New Translation with Introduction and Commentary* (AB 24; Garden City, NY: Doubleday, 1980).

Assmann, Jan, *Das kulturelle Gedächtnis: Schrift, Erinnerung und politische Identität in frühen Hochkulturen* (Munich: Beck, 1992).

Auerbach, Elias, "Die Feste im alten Israel," *VT* 8 (1958) 1-18.

Avigad, Nahman, "The Contribution of Hebrew Seals to an Understanding of Israelite Religion and Society," *Ancient Israelite Religion: Essays in Honor of Frank Moore Cross* (eds. P.D. Miller, P.D. Hanson and S.D. McBride; Philadelphia: Fortress Press, 1987) 195-208.

Bächli, Otto, *Israel und die Völker: Eine Studie zum Deuteronomium* (ATANT 41; Zurich: Zwingli Verlag, 1962).

Backherms, Robert E., *Religious Joy in General in the New Testament and Its Sources in Particular* (Fribourg/CH: St. Paul's Press, 1963).

Bade, William F., "Der Monojahwismus des Deuteronomiums," *ZAW* 30 (1910) 81-90.

Balscheit, Bruno, *Alter und Aufkommen des Monotheismus in der israelitischen Religion* (BZAW 69; Berlin: Töpelmann, 1938).

Baltzer, Dieter, *Ezechiel und Deuterojesaja: Berührungen in der Heilserwartung der beiden großen Exilspropheten* (BZAW 121; Berlin and New York: de Gruyter, 1971).

Baltzer, Klaus, *Das Bundesformular* (WMANT 4; Neukirchen: Neukirchener Verlag, 1960; 2nd ed. 1964).

Balz-Cochois, Helgard, *Gomer: Der Höhenkult Israels im Selbstverständnis der Volksfrömmigkeit: Untersuchungen zu Hosea 4,1-5,7* (EHS.T 191; Frankfurt a.M. and Bern: P. Lang, 1982).

Barth, Christoph, " גִּילָה / גיל II-V," *TWAT* (eds. G.J. Botterweck and H. Ringgren; Stuttgart et al.: Kohlhammer, 1973) 1:1013-1018.

Barth, Hermann, *Die Jesaja-Worte in der Josiazeit: Israel und Assur als Thema einer produktiven Neuinterpretation der Jesajaüberlieferung* (WMANT 48; Neukirchen-Vluyn: Neukirchener Verlag, 1977).

Barth, Karl, *Die kirchliche Dogmatik 3/4: Die Lehre von der Schöpfung* (3rd ed.; Zurich: EVZ, 1969).

Baumgartner, Walter et al., *HALAT* 1-4 (Leyden et al.: Brill, 1967-1990).

Beck, Pirhiya, "The Drawings from Horvat Teiman (Kuntillet 'Ajrud)," *Tel Aviv* 9 (1982) 3-68.

Becker, Joachim, *Gottesfurcht im Alten Testament* (AnBib 25; Rome: Pontificio Instituto Biblico, 1965).

____ *Messiaserwartung im Alten Testament* (SBS 83; Stuttgart: Kath. Bibelwerk, 1977).

Berg, Werner, "Die Eifersucht Gottes – ein problematischer Zug des alttestamentlichen Gottesbildes?," *BZ NF* 23 (1979) 197-211.

Bertholet, Alfred, *Deuteronomium* (KHC 5; Freiburg i.Br., Leipzig and Tübingen: Mohr, 1899).

Beyreuther, Erich, "Freude," *TBLNT* (ed. L. Coenen et al.; Wuppertal: Brockhaus, 1967) 1:379-388.

Bird, Phyllis, "Translating Sexist Language as a Theological and Cultural Problem," *USQR* 42 (1988) 89-95.

____ "The Place of Women in the Israelite Cultus," *Ancient Israelite Religion: Essays in Honor of Frank Moore Cross* (eds. P.D. Miller, P.D. Hanson and S.D. McBride; Philadelphia: Fortress Press, 1987) 397-419.

____ "'To Play the Harlot': An Inquiry into an Old Testament Metaphor," *Gender and Difference in Ancient Israel* (ed. P.L. Day; Minneapolis: Fortress Press, 1989) 75-94.

Boecker, Hans Jochen, *Recht und Gesetz im Alten Testament und im Alten Orient* (NStB 10; Neukirchen-Vluyn: Neukirchener Verlag, 1976).

Böckle, Franz and Gerhard Höver, "Menschenrechte / Menschenwürde," *NHThG* (ed. P. Eicher; Munich: Kösel, 1985) 3:95-104.

Böhl, Franz Marius Theodor de Liagre, *Der babylonische Fürstenspiegel* (MAOG 11/3; Leipzig: Harrassowitz, 1937).

Bogaert, Pierre Maurice, "Les trois rédactions conservées et la forme originale de l'envoi du Cantique de Moïse (Dt 32,43)," *Das Deuteronomium: Entstehung, Gestalt und Botschaft* (ed. N. Lohfink; BETL 68; Leuven: University Press, 1985) 329-340.

Borger, Rykle, "Assyrische Staatsverträge: Der Vertrag Assurbanipals mit dem Stamm Qedar," *TUAT 1: Rechts- und Wirtschaftsurkunden / Historisch-chronologische Texte* (ed. O. Kaiser; Gütersloh: Mohn, 1985) 177.

Boston, James R., "The Wisdom Influence Upon the Song of Moses," *JBL* 87 (1968) 198-202.

Botterweck, G. Johannes, "יָדַע *jāḏa'*," *TWAT* (eds. G.J. Botterweck and H. Ringgren; Stuttgart et al.: Kohlhammer, 1982) 3:479-512. – English translation: *TDOT* (Grand Rapids, MI: 1974), 5:448-481.

Braulik, Georg, "Die Abfolge der Gesetze in Deuteronomium 12-26 und der Dekalog," *Das Deuteronomium: Entstehung, Gestalt und Botschaft* (ed. N. Lohfink; BETL 68; Leuven: University Press, 1985) 252-272. [Reprinted in: id., *Studien*, 231-255.]

____ "Die Ablehnung der Göttin Aschera in Israel: War sie erst deuteronomistisch, diente sie der Unterdrückung der Frauen?," *Der eine Gott und die Göttin: Gottesvorstellungen des biblischen Israel im Horizont feministischer Theologie* (ed. Marie-Theres Wacker and Erich Zenger; QD 135; Freiburg: Herder, 1991) 106-136.

____ "Aufbrechen von geprägten Wortverbindungen und Zusammenfassen von stereotypen Ausdrücken in der alttestamentlichen Kunstprosa," *Semitics* 1 (1970) 7-11.

____ "Die Ausdrücke für »Gesetz« im Buch Deuteronomium," *Bib* 51 (1970) 39-66. [Reprinted in: id., *Studien*, 11-38.]

____ *Deuteronomium 1-16,17* (NEB.AT 15; Würzburg: Echter, 1986).

____ *Deuteronomium II: 16,18-34,12* (NEB.AT 28; Würzburg: Echter, 1992).

____ "Das Deuteronomium und die Geburt des Monotheismus," *Gott, der einzige: Zur Entstehung des Monotheismus in Israel* (ed. E. Haag; QD 104; Freiburg i.Br.: Herder, 1985) 115-159. [Reprinted in: id., *Studien*, 257-300.]

____ "Das Deuteronomium und die Gedächtniskultur Israels: Redaktionsgeschichtliche Beobachtungen zur Verwendung von למד," *Biblische Theologie und gesellschaftlicher Wandel.* Für Norbert Lohfink (ed. G. Braulik; Vienna: Herder, 1993) 9-31.

____ "Das Deuteronomium und die Menschenrechte," *TQ* 166 (1986) 8-24. [Reprinted in id., *Studien*, 301-324.]

___ "Die Entstehung der Rechtfertigungslehre in den Bearbeitungsschichten des Buches Deuteronomium: Ein Beitrag zur Klärung der Voraussetzungen paulinischer Theologie," *TP* 64 (1989) 321-333.

___ "Eucharistie – Fest der Gemeinde: Bibeltheologische Überlegungen," *Ordensnachrichten* 23 (1984) 127-138.

___ "Die Freude des Festes: Das Kultverständnis des Deuteronomium – die älteste biblische Festtheorie," *Leiturgia – Koinonia – Diakonia: Festschrift für Kardinal Franz König zum 75. Geburtstag* (ed. R. Schulte; Vienna: Herder, 1980) 127-179. [In a slightly expanded version reprinted in: *ThJb(L) 1983* (ed. W. Ernst et al.; Leipzig: St. Benno-Verlag, 1983) 13-54. – Reprinted in: id., *Studien*, 161-218.]

___ "Die Funktion von Siebenergruppierungen im Endtext des Deuteronomiums," *Ein Gott, eine Offenbarung: Beiträge zur biblischen Exegese, Theologie und Spiritualität. Festschrift für Notker Füglister zum 60. Geburtstag* (ed. F.V. Reiterer; Würzburg: Echter, 1991) 37-50.

___ "Gesetz als Evangelium: Rechtfertigung und Begnadigung nach der deuteronomischen Tora," *ZTK* 79 (1982) 127-160. [Reprinted in: id., *Studien*, 123-160.]

___ *Die deuteronomischen Gesetze und der Dekalog: Studien zum Aufbau von Deuteronomium 12-26* (SBS 145; Stuttgart: Kath. Bibelwerk, 1991).

___ "Die gesellschaftliche Innenseite der Kirche: Das Deuteronomium," *BK* 43 (1988) 134-139.

___ "Haben in Israel auch Frauen geopfert?: Beobachtungen am Deuteronomium," *Zur Aktualität des Alten Testaments: Festschrift für Georg Sauer zum 65. Geburtstag* (eds. S. Kreuzer and K. Lüthi; Frankfurt a.M. et al.: P. Lang, 1991) 19-28.

___ "Zur deuteronomistischen Konzeption von Freiheit und Frieden," *Congress Volume Salamanca 1983* (ed. J.A. Emerton; VTSup 36; Leyden: Brill, 1985) 29-39. [Reprinted in id., *Studien*, 219-230.]

___ "Die politische Kraft des Festes: Biblische Aussagen," *Liturgie zwischen Mystik und Politik: Österreichische Pastoraltagung 27. bis 29. Dezember 1990* (eds. H. Erharter and H.-M. Rauter; Vienna: Herder, 1991) 65-79.

___ "Leidensgedächtnisfeier und Freudenfest: »Volksliturgie« nach dem deuteronomischen Festkalender (Dtn 16,1-17)," *TP* 56 (1981) 335-357. [Reprinted in: id., *Studien*, 95-121.]

___ "Literarkritik und die Einrahmung von Gemälden: Zur literarkritischen und redaktionsgeschichtlichen Analyse von Dtn 4,1-6,3 und 29,1-30,10 durch D. Knapp," *RB* 96 (1989) 266-286.

___ "Literarkritik und archäologische Stratigraphie: Zu S. Mittmanns Analyse von Deuteronomium 4,1-40," *Bib* 59 (1978) 351-383.

___ "Menuchah – Die Ruhe Gottes und des Volkes im Lande," *BK* 23 (1968) 75-78.

____ *Die Mittel deuteronomischer Rhetorik: Erhoben aus Deuteronomium 4,1-40* (AnBib 68; Rome: Biblical Institute Press, 1978).

____ "Pascha – von der alttestamentlichen Feier zum neutestamentlichen Fest," *BK* 36 (1981) 159-165.

____ "[Review:] *Der einzige Gott: Die Geburt des biblischen Monotheismus* (ed. B. Lang; Munich: Kösel, 1981)," *TRev* 80 (1984) 11-15.

____ *Sage, was du glaubst: Das älteste Credo der Bibel – Impuls in neuester Zeit* (Stuttgart: Kath. Bibelwerk, 1979).

____ "Spuren einer Neubearbeitung des deuteronomistischen Geschichtswerkes in 1 Kön 8,52-53.59-60," *Bib* 52 (1971) 20-33. [Reprinted in id., *Studien*, 39-52.]

____ *Studien zur Theologie des Deuteronomiums* (SBAB 2; Stuttgart: Kath. Bibelwerk, 1988).

____ *Das Testament des Mose – Das Buch Deuteronomium* (SKK.AT 4; Stuttgart: Kath. Bibelwerk, 1976; 2nd ed. 1993).

____ "Weisheit, Gottesnähe und Gesetz – Zum Kerygma von Deuteronomium 4,5-8," *Studien zum Pentateuch: Walter Kornfeld zum 60. Geburtstag* (ed. G. Braulik; Vienna: Herder, 1977) 165-195. [Reprinted in: id., *Studien*, 53-93.]

Broide, Israel, *The Speeches in Deuteronomy, Their Style and Rhetoric Devices* (Typewritten doctoral dissertation [in modern Hebrew]; Tel Aviv: 1970).

Buchholz, Joachim, *Die Ältesten Israels im Deuteronomium* (GTA 36; Göttingen: Vandenhoeck & Ruprecht, 1988).

Buis, Pierre, "Un traité d'Assurbanipal," *VT* 28 (1978) 469-472.

Caloz, Masséo, "Exode, xiii, 3-16 et son rapport au Deutéronome," *RB* 75 (1968) 5-62; Pl. I-II.

Campbell, Anthony F., "An Historical Prologue in a Seventh-Century Treaty," *Bib* 50 (1969) 534-535.

Cardellini, Innocenzo, *Die biblischen »Sklaven«-Gesetze im Lichte des keilschriftlichen Sklavenrechts: Ein Beitrag zur Tradition, Überlieferung und Redaktion der alttestamentlichen Rechtstexte* (BBB 55; Bonn: Hanstein, 1981).

Carrillo Alday, Salvador, *El Cántico de Moisés (Dt 32)* (BHBib 3; Madrid: Instituto »Francisco Suarez«, 1970).

Casel, Odo, "Art und Sinn der christlichen Osterfeier," *JLW* 14 (1938) 1-78.

Castellino, Giorgio, "Urnammu: Three Religious Texts," *ZA* 53 (1959) 106-132.

Causse, Antonin, *Du groupe ethnique à la communauté religieuse: Le problème sociologique de la religion d'Israël* (EHPhR 33; Paris: Alcan, 1937).

____ "L'idéal politique et social du Deutéronome: La fraternité d'Israël," *RHPR* 13 (1933) 289-323.

Cazelles, Henri, "Sur un rituel du Deutéronome (*Deut.* XXVI, 14)," *RB* 55 (1948) 54-71.

Cholewiński, Alfred, *Heiligkeitsgesetz und Deuteronomium: Eine vergleichende Studie* (AnBib 66; Rome: Biblical Institute Press, 1976).

Cogan, Morton, *Imperialism and Religion: Assyria, Judah and Israel in the Eighth and Seventh Centuries B.C.E.* (SBLMS 19; Missoula, MT: SBL and Scholars Press, 1974).

Coogan, Michael David, "Canaanite Origins and Lineage: Reflections on the Religion of Ancient Israel," *Ancient Israelite Religion: Essays in Honor of Frank Moore Cross* (eds. P.D. Miller, P.D. Hanson and S.D. McBride; Philadelphia: Fortress Press, 1987) 115-124.

Couroyer, Bernard, "*'édût*: stipulation de traité ou enseignement?," *RB* 95 (1988) 321-331.

Cox, Harvey, *The Feast of Fools* (Cambridge, MA: Harvard University Press, 1969).

Craig, James Alexander, *Assyrian and Babylonian Religious Texts Being Prayers, Oracles, Hymns &c. Copied From the Original Tablets Preserved in the British Museum and Autographed* 1 (AssB 13; Leipzig: Hinrichs, 1895).

Crenshaw, James L., "Method in Determining Wisdom Influence Upon 'Historical' Literature," *JBL* 88 (1969) 129-142.

Cross, Frank Moore, "אֵל," *TWAT* (eds. G.J. Botterweck and H. Ringgren; Stuttgart et al.: Kohlhammer, 1973) 1:259-279. – English translation: *TDOT* (Grand Rapids, MI: 1974), 1:242-261.

____ "The Themes of the Book of Kings and the Structure of the Deuteronomistic History," id., *Canaanite Myth and Hebrew Epic: Essays in the History of the Religion of Israel* (4th ed.; Cambridge, MA: Harvard University Press, 1980) 274-289.

Crüsemann, Frank, *Bewahrung der Freiheit: Das Thema des Dekalogs in sozialgeschichtlicher Perspektive* (KT 78; Munich: Kaiser, 1983).

____ *Studien zur Formgeschichte von Hymnus und Danklied in Israel* (WMANT 32; Neukirchen-Vluyn: Neukirchener Verlag, 1969).

____ "»... damit er dich segne in allem Tun deiner Hand ...« (Dtn 14,29): Die Produktionsverhältnisse der späten Königszeit, dargestellt am Ostrakon von Meṣad Ḥashavjahu, und die Sozialgesetzgebung des Deuteronomiums," *Mitarbeiter der Schöpfung: Bibel und Arbeitswelt* (eds. L. and W. Schottroff; Munich: Kaiser, 1983) 72-103.

Day, John, "Asherah in the Hebrew Bible and Northwest Semitic Literature," *JBL* 105 (1986) 385-408.

____ "A Case of Inner Scriptural Interpretation: The Dependence of Isaiah XXVI. 13-XXVII. 11 on Hosea XIII. 4-XIV. 10 (Eng. 9) and Its Relevance to Some Theories of the Redaction of the Isaiah Apocalypse," *JTS NS* 31 (1980) 309-319.

Deissler, Alfons, "Das Priestertum im Alten Testament: Ein Blick vom Alten zum Neuen Bund," *Der priesterliche Dienst 1: Ursprung und Frühgeschichte* (QD 46; Freiburg i.Br.: Herder, 1970) 9-80.

____ *Psalm 119 (118) und seine Theologie: Ein Beitrag zur Erforschung der anthologischen Stilgattung im Alten Testament* (MThS.H 11; Munich: Zink, 1955).

Delcor, Mathias, "Astarté et la fécondité des troupeaux en Deut. 7,13 et parallèles," *UF* 6 (eds. K. Bergerhof, M. Dietrich and O. Loretz; Kevelaer and Neukirchen-Vluyn: Butzon & Bercker and Neukirchener Verlag, 1974) 7-14.

Deller, Karlheinz and Simo Parpola, "Ein Vertrag Assurbanipals mit dem arabischen Stamm Qedar," *Or NS* 37 (1968) 464-466.

Derousseaux, Louis, *La crainte de Dieu dans l'Ancien Testament: Royauté, Alliance, Sagesse dans les royaumes d'Israël et de Juda. Recherches d'exégèse et d'histoire sur la racine* yârê' (LD 63; Paris: du Cerf, 1970).

Dever, William G., "Iron Age Epigraphic Material from the Area of Khirbet el-Kôm," *HUCA* 40-41 (1969/70) 139-204.

Diepold, Peter, *Israels Land* (BWANT 95; Stuttgart et al.: Kohlhammer, 1972).

Dietrich, Walter, *Israel und Kanaan: Vom Ringen zweier Gesellschaftssysteme* (SBS 94; Stuttgart: Kath. Bibelwerk, 1979).

Dohmen, Christoph, *Das Bilderverbot: Seine Entstehung und seine Entwicklung im Alten Testament* (BBB 62; 2nd ed.; Frankfurt a.M.: Hain, 1987).

Driver, Godfrey Rolles and John Charles Miles, *The Babylonian Laws 1: Legal Commentary* (Oxford: Clarendon Press, 1952).

____ *The Babylonian Laws 2: Transliterated Text, Translation, Philological Notes, Glossary* (Oxford: Clarendon Press, 1955).

Driver, Samuel Rolles, *A Critical and Exegetical Commentary on Deuteronomy* (ICC; 3rd ed.; Edinburgh: Clark, 1902).

Dus, Jan, "Der ferne Gott und das nahe Gebot: Eine Studie zum Deuteronomium," *CV* 7 (1964) 193-200.

Ebeling, Erich, *Quellen zur Kenntnis der babylonischen Religion* 1 (MVAG 23/1; Leipzig: Hinrichs, 1918).

Ebeling, Gerhard, "Die Notwendigkeit des christlichen Gottesdienstes," *ZTK* 67 (1970) 232-249.

Eilers, Wilhelm, *Die Gesetzesstele Chammurabis: Gesetze um die Wende des dritten vorchristlichen Jahrtausends* (AO 31/4; Leipzig: Hinrichs, 1932).

Einheitsübersetzung der Heiligen Schrift: Die Bibel. Gesamtausgabe (ed. on behalf of the bishops of Germany et al.; Stuttgart: Kath. Bibelwerk, 1980).

Eissfeldt, Otto, *Erstlinge und Zehnten im Alten Testament: Ein Beitrag zur Geschichte des israelitisch-jüdischen Kultus* (BWANT 22; Leipzig: Hinrichs, 1917).

___ "Jahve und Baal," id., *Kleine Schriften* (eds. R. Sellheim and F. Maass; Tübingen: Mohr, 1962) 1:1-12.

___ "»Mein Gott« im Alten Testament," id., *Kleine Schriften* (eds. R. Sellheim and F. Maass; Tübingen: Mohr, 1966) 3:35-47.

Elliger, Karl, *Deuterojesaja 1: Jesaja 40,1-45,7* (BKAT 11/1; Neukirchen-Vluyn: Neukirchener Verlag, 1978).

___ *Leviticus* (HAT 1/4; Tübingen: Mohr, 1966).

Emerton, John Adney, "New Light on Israelite Religion: The Implications of the Inscriptions from Kuntillet 'Ajrud," *ZAW* 94 (1982) 2-20.

___ "Priests and Levites in Deuteronomy," *VT* 12 (1962) 129-138.

Emmerson, Grace I., *Hosea: An Israelite Prophet in Judean Perspective* (JSOTSup 28; Sheffield: JSOT Press, 1984).

Engel, Helmut, "Abschied von den frühisraelitischen Nomaden und der Jahweamphiktyonie: Bericht über den Zusammenbruch eines wissenschaftlichen Konsensus," *BK* 38 (1983) 43-46.

___ "Grundlinien neuerer Hypothesen über die Entstehung und Gestalt der vorstaatlichen israelitischen Stämmegesellschaft," *BK* 38 (1983) 50-53.

Engle, James Robert, *Pillar Figurines of Iron Age Israel and Asherah / Asherim* (Ph.D. University of Pittsburgh, 1979; Ann Arbor, MI: Xerox University Microfilm, 1981).

Ernst, Wilhelm, "Ursprung und Entwicklung der Menschenrechte in Geschichte und Gegenwart," *Greg* 65 (1984) 231-270.

Falkenstein, Adam and Mariano San Nicolò, "Das Gesetzbuch Lipit-Ištars von Isin," *Or NS* 19 (1950) 103-118.

Falkenstein, Adam and Wolfram von Soden, *Sumerische und akkadische Hymnen und Gebete* (BAW.AO; Zurich and Stuttgart: Artemis, 1953).

Fensham, F. Charles, "Widow, Orphan, and the Poor in Ancient Near Eastern Legal and Wisdom Literature," *JNES* 21 (1961) 129-139.

Feuillet, André, "»S'asseoir à l'ombre« de l'époux (*Os.*, XIV, 8ª et *Cant.*, II, 3)," *RB* 78 (1971) 391-405.

Finkelstein, Jakob S., "The Laws of Ur-Nammu," *JCS* 22 (1968/69) 66-82.

Fischer, Georg and Norbert Lohfink, "»Diese Worte sollst du summen«: Dtn 6,7 *wᵉdibbartā bām* – ein verlorener Schlüssel zur meditativen Kultur in Israel," *TP* 62 (1987) 59-72.

Floss, Johannes Peter, *Jahwe dienen – Göttern dienen: Terminologische, literarische und semantische Untersuchung einer theologischen Aussage zum Gottesverhältnis im Alten Testament* (BBB 45; Cologne and Bonn: Hanstein, 1975).

Fohrer, Georg, "Die wiederentdeckte kanaanäische Religion," id., *Studien zur alttestamentlichen Theologie und Geschichte (1949-1966)* (BZAW 115; Berlin: de Gruyter, 1969) 3-12.

____ "Die Weisheit im Alten Testament," id., *Studien zur alttestamentlichen Theologie und Geschichte (1949-1966)* (BZAW 115; Berlin: de Gruyter, 1969) 242-274.

Fowler, Jeaneane D., *Theophoric Personal Names in Ancient Hebrew: A Comparative Study* (JSOTSup 49; Sheffield: JSOT Press, 1988).

Frankowski, Janusz, "Requies, bonum promissum populi Dei in VT et in Judaismo (Hebr. 3,7-4,11)," *VD* 43 (1965) 124-149, 225-240.

Frevel, Christian, "Die Elimination der Göttin aus dem Weltbild des Chronisten," *ZAW* 103 (1991) 263-271.

Füglister, Notker, *Die Heilsbedeutung des Pascha* (SANT 8; Munich: Kösel, 1963).

Gadamer, Hans-Georg, "Die Kunst des Feierns," *Was der Mensch braucht: Anregungen für eine neue Kunst zu leben* (ed. H.J. Schultz; Stuttgart: Kreuz Verlag, 1977) 61-70.

Galling, Kurt, "Der Beichtspiegel: Eine gattungsgeschichtliche Studie," *ZAW* 47 (1929) 125-130.

Gaster, Theodor H., *Thespis: Ritual, Myth and Drama in the Ancient Near East* (HTB 1281; New York: Harper, 1966).

Gese, Hartmut, "Die Religionen Altsyriens," Hartmut Gese, Maria Höfner and Kurt Rudolph, *Die Religionen Altsyriens, Altarabiens und der Mandäer* (RM 10/2; Stuttgart et al.: Kohlhammer, 1970) 1-232.

Gesenius, Wilhelm and Frants Buhl, *Hebräisches und aramäisches Handwörterbuch über das Alte Testament* (17th ed.; Leipzig: Vogel, 1921).

Gitin, Seymour, "Artifacts, News, Notes, and Reports from the Institutes: Cultic Inscriptions Found in Ekron," *BA* 53 (1990) 232.

____ "Ekron of the Philistines II: Olive-Oil Suppliers to the World," *BARev* 18/2 (1990) 33-42, 59.

Golomb, Egon, "Kirchenstruktur und Brüderlichkeit heute," *Koinonia: Kirche und Brüderlichkeit: Weihnachts-Seelsorgertagung 27.-29. Dezember 1967* (eds. E. Hesse and E. Erharter; Vienna: Herder, 1968) 47-65.

Görg, Manfred, *Gott-König-Reden in Israel und Ägypten* (BWANT 105; Stuttgart et al.: Kohlhammer, 1975).

Gregory the Great, "Moralia," *PL* 75.

Gross, Walter, *Bileam: Literar- und formkritische Untersuchung der Prosa in Num 22-24* (SANT 38; Munich: Kösel, 1974).

___ "Die Herausführungsformel – Zum Verhältnis von Formel und Syntax," *ZAW* 86 (1974) 425-453.

___ *Verbform und Funktion: wayyiqṭol für die Gegenwart. Ein Beitrag zur Syntax poetischer althebräischer Texte* (ATAT 1; St. Ottilien: Eos, 1976).

Guardini, Romano, "Der Kultakt und die gegenwärtige Aufgabe liturgischer Bildung (a letter)" id., *Liturgie und liturgische Bildung* (Würzburg: Werkbund-Verlag, 1966) 9-18.

Gulin, E.G., *Die Freude im Neuen Testament 1: Jesus, Urgemeinde, Paulus* (AASF.B 26; Helsinki: 1932).

Gunneweg, Antonius H.J., *Leviten und Priester: Hauptlinien der Traditionsbildung und Geschichte des israelitisch-jüdischen Kultpersonals* (FRLANT 89; Göttingen: Vandenhoeck & Ruprecht 1965).

Haag, Herbert, "Kult II: Im AT," *LTK* (2nd ed.; eds. J. Höfer and K. Rahner; Freiburg i.Br.: Herder, 1961) 6:660-662.

___ "Das Mazzenfest des Hiskia," *Wort und Geschichte: Festschrift für Karl Elliger zum 70. Geburtstag* (eds. H. Gese and H.P. Rüger; AOAT 18; Kevelaer and Neukirchen-Vluyn: Butzon & Bercker and Neukirchener Verlag, 1973) 87-94. [Reprinted in: id., *Das Buch des Bundes: Aufsätze zur Bibel und zu ihrer Welt* (ed. B. Lang; Düsseldorf: Patmos, 1980) 216-225.]

___ "... und du sollst fröhlich sein!," *BK* 33 (1978) 38-43.

Haase, Richard, *Die keilschriftlichen Rechtssammlungen in deutscher Übersetzung* (Wiesbaden: Harrassowitz, 1963).

Hadley, Judith M., "Some Drawings and Inscriptions on Two Pithoi from Kuntillet 'Ajrud," *VT* 37 (1987) 180-213.

___ "The Khirbet el-Qom Inscription," *VT* 37 (1987) 50-62.

Haecker, Theodor, *Tag- und Nachtbücher 1939-1945* (Olten: Walter, 1946).

Halbe, Jörn, "Erwägungen zu Ursprung und Wesen des Massotfestes," *ZAW* 87 (1975) 324-346.

___ "Gemeinschaft, die Welt unterbricht: Grundfragen und -inhalte deuteronomischer Theologie und Überlieferungsbildung im Lichte der Ursprungsbedingungen alttestamentlichen Rechts," *Das Deuteronomium: Entstehung, Gestalt und Botschaft* (ed. N. Lohfink; BETL 68; Leuven: University Press, 1985) 55-75.

___ "Passa-Massot im deuteronomischen Festkalender: *Komposition, Entstehung und Programm von Dtn 16 1-8*," *ZAW* 87 (1975) 147-168.

___ *Das Privilegrecht Jahwes Ex 34,10-26: Gestalt und Wesen, Herkunft und Wirken in vordeuteronomischer Zeit* (FRLANT 114; Göttingen: Vandenhoeck & Ruprecht, 1975).

Haran, Menahem, *Temples and Temple-Service in Ancient Israel: An Inquiry into the Character of Cult Phenomena and the Historical Setting of the Priestly School* (Oxford: Clarendon Press, 1978).

Hardmeier, Christof, "Die Erinnerung an die Knechtschaft in Ägypten: Sozialanthropologische Aspekte des Erinnerns in der hebräischen Bibel," *Was ist der Mensch ...?: Beiträge zur Anthropologie des Alten Testaments. Hans Walter Wolff zum 80. Geburtstag* (eds. F. Crüsemann, C. Hardmeier and R. Kessler; Munich: Kaiser, 1992) 133-152.

Hartmann, Benedikt, "Monotheismus in Mesopotamien?," *Monotheismus im Alten Israel und seiner Umwelt* (ed. O. Keel; BibB 14; Fribourg/CH: Schweizerisches Kath. Bibelwerk, 1980) 49-81.

Harvey, Dorothea Ward, "Rejoice Not, O Israel!," *Israel's Prophetic Heritage: Essays in Honor of James Muilenburg* (eds. B.W. Anderson and W. Harrelson; New York: Harper & Brothers, 1962) 116-127.

Hempel, Johannes, *Das Ethos des Alten Testaments* (BZAW 67; 2nd ed.; Berlin: Töpelmann, 1964).

Herrmann, Siegfried, "Die konstruktive Restauration: Das Deuteronomium als Mitte biblischer Theologie," *Probleme biblischer Theologie: Gerhard von Rad zum 70. Geburtstag* (ed. H.W. Wolff; Munich: Kaiser, 1971) 155-170.

Hestrin, Ruth, "The Lachish Ewer and the 'Asherah," *IEJ* 37 (1987) 212-223.

Hidal, Sten, "Some Reflections on Deuteronomy 32," *ASTI* 11 (1977/78) 15-21.

Höffken, Peter, "Eine Bemerkung zum religionsgeschichtlichen Hintergrund von Dtn 6,4," *BZ NF* 28 (1984) 88-93.

Hoffmann, David, *Das Buch Deuteronomium: Übersetzt und erklärt 1. Deut. I-XXI,9* (Berlin: Poppelauer, 1913).

Hoffmann, Hans-Detlev, *Reform und Reformen: Untersuchungen zu einem Grundthema der deuteronomistischen Geschichtsschreibung* (ATANT 66; Zurich: TVZ, 1980).

Hofius, Otfried, "»Rechtfertigung des Gottlosen« als Thema biblischer Theologie," *JBTh 2: Der eine Gott der beiden Testamente* (eds. I. Baldermann et al.; Neukirchen-Vluyn: Neukirchener Verlag, 1987) 79-105.

Holladay, John S., "Religion in Israel and Judah Under the Monarchy: An Explicitly Archaeological Approach," *Ancient Israelite Religion: Essays in Honor of Frank Moore Cross* (eds. P.D. Miller, P.D. Hanson and S.D. McBride; Philadelphia: Fortress Press, 1987) 249-299.

Hölscher, Gustav, "Komposition und Ursprung des Deuteronomiums," *ZAW* 40 (1922) 161-255.

Horst, Friedrich, *Das Privilegrecht Jahwes: Rechtsgeschichtliche Untersuchungen zum Deuteronomium* (FRLANT 45; Göttingen: Vandenhoeck & Ruprecht, 1930). [Reprinted in: id., *Gottes Recht: Gesammelte Studien zum Recht im Alten Testament. Aus Anlaß der Vollendung seines 65. Lebensjahres* (ed. H.W. Wolff; TB 12; Munich: Kaiser, 1961) 17-154.]

Hossfeld, Frank-Lothar, *Der Dekalog: Seine späten Fassungen, die originale Komposition und seine Vorstufen* (OBO 45; Freiburg/CH and Göttingen: Universitätsverlag and Vandenhoeck & Ruprecht, 1982).

Huber, Wolfgang, "Menschenrechte: Ein Begriff und seine Geschichte," *Conc(D)* 15 (1979) 199-204.

Hulst, Alexander Reinhard, "De Betekenis van het Woord *m*[e]*nûḥâ*," *Schrift en uitleg: Studies van ond-leerlingen, collega's en vrienden aangeboden aan Prof. Dr. W.H. Gispen ter gelegenheid van zijn vijfentwintigjarig ambtsjubileum als hoogleraar aan de Vrije Universiteit te Amsterdam en ter gelegenheid van het bereiken van de zeventigjarige leeftijd* (eds. D.S. Attema et al.; Kampen: Kok, 1970) 62-78.

____ *Het karakter van den cultus in Deuteronomium* (Wageningen: Veenman & Zonen, 1938).

____ "עַם / גּוֹי *'am / gôj* Volk," *THAT* (eds. E. Jenni and C. Westermann; Munich and Zurich: Kaiser and TVZ, 1976) 2.290-325.

Humbert, Paul, "»Laetari et exultare« dans le vocabulaire religieux de l'Ancien Testament (Essai d'analyse des termes *Sâmaḥ* et *Gîl*)," *RHPR* 22 (1942) 185-214. [Reprinted in: id., *Opuscules d'un Hébraïsant* (Neuchâtel: Secrétariat de l'université, 1958) 119-145.]

Hvidberg, Flemming Friis, *Weeping and Laughter in the Old Testament: A Study of Canaanite-Israelite Religion* (Copenhagen and Leyden : Busck and Brill, 1962).

Ishida, Tomoo, *The Royal Dynasties in Ancient Israel: A Study on the Formation and Development of Royal-Dynastic Ideology* (BZAW 142; Berlin and New York: de Gruyter, 1977).

Jacob, Edmond, "Osée," Edmond Jacob, Carl-A. Keller and Samuel Amsler, *Osée, Joël, Abdias, Jonas, Amos* (CAT 11a; Neuchâtel: Derachaux & Niestlé, 1965) 7-98.

Jacobs, Paul Frederick, *An Examination of the Motif 'Life as Result or Reward' in the Book of Deuteronomy* (Theological Dissertation Union Theol. Sem. Richmond, VA, 1973; Ann Arbor, MI: Xerox Univ. Microfilms, 1975).

Jacobsen, Thorkild, "Mesopotamien," *Frühlicht des Geistes: Wandlungen des Weltbildes im Alten Orient* (eds. H. Frankfort et al.; UB 9; Stuttgart: Kohlhammer, 1954) 136-241.

Jamieson-Drake, David W., *Scribes and Schools in Monarchic Judah: A Socio-Archeological Approach* (JSOTSup 109 and SWBAS 9; Sheffield: Almond Press, 1991).

Janssen, Enno, *Juda in der Exilszeit: Ein Beitrag zur Frage der Entstehung des Judentums* (FRLANT 69; Göttingen: Vandenhoeck & Ruprecht, 1956).

Jaroš, Karl, "Die Motive der Heiligen Bäume und der Schlange in Gen 2-3," *ZAW* 92 (1980) 204-215.

Jeremias, Jörg, "Hosea / Hoseabuch," *TRE* (ed. G. Müller; Berlin and New York: de Gruyter, 1986) 15:586-598.
___ *Der Prophet Hosea: Übersetzt und erklärt* (ATD 24/1; Göttingen: Vandenhoeck & Ruprecht, 1983).
___ *Theophanie: Die Geschichte einer alttestamentlichen Gattung* (WMANT 10; 2nd ed.; Neukirchen-Vluyn: Neukirchener Verlag, 1977).
John Chrysostom, "De sancta pentecoste Hom. 1," *PG* 50, 453-464.
Johannes, Gottfried, *Unvergleichlichkeitsformulierungen im Alten Testament* (Dissertation; Mainz: 1968).
Jongeling, Bastian, "Le particule רַק," *Syntax and Meaning: Studies in Hebrew Syntax and Biblical Exegesis* (ed. A.S. van der Woude; OTS 18; Leyden: Brill, 1973) 97-107.
Joüon, Paul, *Grammaire de l'Hébreu biblique* (2nd ed.; Rome: Institut Biblique Pontifical, 1947).
Jüngling, Hans-Winfried, "Die egalitäre Gesellschaft der Stämme Jahwes: Bericht über eine Hypothese zum vorstaatlichen Israel," *BK* 38 (1983) 59-64.
Kaiser, Otto, *Der Prophet Jesaja: Kapitel 13-39. Übersetzt und erklärt* (ATD 18; Göttingen: Vandenhoeck & Ruprecht, 1973).
___ "Die alttestamentliche Exegese," Gottfried Adam, Otto Kaiser and Werner Georg Kümmel, *Einführung in die exegetischen Methoden* (ST[M] 1; München: Kaiser and Grünewald, 1975) 9-60.
Kaiser, Walter C., "The Promise Theme and the Theology of the Rest," *BSac* 130/518 (1973) 135-150.
Kapp, A., "Ein Lied auf Enlilbāni von Isin," *ZA* 51 (1955) 76-87.
Kasper, Walter, "Von der Humanität und Spiritualität der christlichen Freude: Advent – Philipper 4,4-9," id., *Gottes Zeit für Menschen: Besinnungen zum Kirchenjahr* (Freiburg i.Br. et al.: Herder, 1978) 18-32.
Keel, Othmar, *Das Böcklein in der Milch seiner Mutter und Verwandtes: Im Lichte eines altorientalischen Bildmotivs* (OBO 33; Freiburg/CH and Göttingen: Universitätsverlag and Vandenhoeck & Ruprecht, 1980).
___ "Gedanken zur Beschäftigung mit dem Monotheismus," *Der Monotheismus im Alten Israel und seiner Umwelt* (ed. O. Keel; BibB 14; Fribourg/CH: Schweizerisches Kath. Bibelwerk, 1980) 11-30.
___ "Früheisenzeitliche Glyptik in Palästina / Israel: Mit einem Beitrag von H. Keel-Leu," Othmar Keel, Menakhem Shuval and Christoph Uehlinger, *Studien zu den Stempelsiegeln aus Palästina / Israel 3: Die Frühe Eisenzeit. Ein Workshop* (OBO 100; Freiburg/CH and Göttingen: Universitätsverlag and Vandenhoeck & Ruprecht, 1990) 331-421.
Keel, Othmar and Christoph Uehlinger, *Göttinnen, Götter und Gottessymbole: Neue Erkenntnisse zur Religionsgeschichte Kanaans und Israels aufgrund bislang unerschlossener ikonographischer Quellen* (QD 134; Freiburg i.Br. et al.: Herder, 1992).

Kinet, Dirk, *Ba'al und Jahwe: Ein Beitrag zur Theologie des Hoseabuches* (EHS.T 87; Frankfurt a.M. and Bern: P. and H. Lang, 1977).

____ "Theologische Reflexion im ugaritischen Ba'al-Zyklus," *BZ NF* 22 (1978) 236-244.

Klauser, Theodor, "Fest," *RAC* (ed. T. Klauser; Stuttgart: Hiersemann, 1969) 7:747-766.

Knapp, Dietrich, *Deuteronomium 4: Literarische Analyse und theologische Interpretation* (GTA 35; Göttingen: Vandenhoeck & Ruprecht, 1987).

Knierim, Rolf, "Offenbarung im Alten Testament," *Probleme biblischer Theologie: Gerhard von Rad zum 70. Geburtstag* (ed. H.W. Wolff; Munich: Kaiser, 1971) 206-235.

Koch, Klaus, "Aschera als Himmelskönigin in Jerusalem," *UF* 20 (eds. K. Bergerhof, M. Dietrich and O. Loretz; Kevelaer and Neukirchen-Vluyn: Butzon & Bercker and Neukirchener Verlag, 1988) 97-120.

____ "צדק *ṣdq* gemeinschaftstreu / heilvoll sein," *THAT* (eds. E. Jenni and C. Westermann; Munich and Zurich: Kaiser and TVZ, 1976) 2:507-530.

Köckert, Matthias, "Das nahe Wort: Zum entscheidenden Wandel des Gesetzesverständnisses im Alten Testament," *TP* 60 (1985) 496-519.

Köhler, Ludwig, *Theologie des Alten Testaments* (NTG; 4th ed.; Tübingen: Mohr, 1966).

König, Franz Kardinal, "Ein weltlicher Gottesdienst?," id., *Die Stunde der Welt* (Graz et al.: Styria, 1971) 80-85.

Kornfeld, Walter, "Fruchtbarkeitskulte im Alten Testament," *Dienst an der Lehre: Studien zur heutigen Philosophie und Theologie* (ed. Kath.-Theol. Fakultät der Universität Wien; Festschrift für Franz Kardinal König zum 60. Geburtstag; WBTh 10; Vienna: Herder, 1965) 109-117.

Kramer, Samuel Noah and Adam Falkenstein, "Ur-Nammu Law Code," *Or NS* 23 (1954) 40-51.

Kraus, Fritz Rudolf, "Ein zentrales Problem des altmesopotamischen Rechts: Was ist der Codex Hammu-rabi?," *Genava NS* 8 (1960) 283-296.

Kraus, Hans Joachim, "Zum Gesetzesverständnis der nachprophetischen Zeit," id., *Biblisch-theologische Aufsätze* (Neukirchen-Vluyn: Neukirchener Verlag, 1972) 179-194.

____ *Gottesdienst in Israel: Grundriß einer Geschichte des alttestamentlichen Gottesdienstes* (2nd ed.; Munich: Kaiser, 1962).

____ *Psalms 2 (Psalms 60-150)* (Augsburg: Minneapolis, 1989).

Kreuzer, Siegfried, *Die Frühgeschichte Israels in Bekenntnis und Verkündigung des Alten Testaments* (BZAW 178; Berlin and New York: de Gruyter, 1989).

Kutsch, Ernst, "Erwägungen zur Geschichte der Passafeier und des Massotfestes," *ZTK* 55 (1958) 1-35.

Laaf, Peter, "חג שבעות, das Wochenfest," *Bausteine biblischer Theologie: Festgabe für Georg J. Botterweck zum 60. Geburtstag dargebracht von seinen Schülern* (ed. H.-J. Fabry; BBB 50; Cologne and Bonn: Hanstein, 1977) 169-183.

Labuschagne, Casper Jeremiah, *The Incomparability of Yahweh in the Old Testament* (POS 5; Leyden: Brill, 1966).

____ "נתן *ntn* geben," *THAT* (eds. E. Jenni and C. Westermann; Munich and Zurich: Kaiser and TVZ, 1976) 2:117-141.

Landsberger, Benno, "Die babylonischen Termini für Gesetz und Recht," *Symbolae ad iura Orientis Antiqui pertinentes Paulo Koschaker dedicatae* (eds. J. Friedrich et al.; SDIO 2; Leyden: Brill, 1939) 219-234.

Lang, Bernhard, "Neues über die Geschichte des Monotheismus," *TQ* 163 (1983) 54-58.

____ "Die Jahwe-allein-Bewegung," *Der einzige Gott: Die Geburt des biblischen Monotheismus* (ed. B. Lang; Munich: Kösel, 1981) 47-83, 130-134, 142-145.

____ "The Yahweh-Alone Movement and Jewish Monotheism," id., *Monotheism and the Prophetic Minority: An Essay in Biblical History and Sociology* (SWBA 1; Sheffield: 1983) 13-56.

Lemaire, André, "Date et origine des inscriptions hébraïques et phéniciennes de Kuntillet ʻAjrud," *SEL* 1 (1984) 131-143.

____ "Les inscriptions de Khirbet el-Qôm et l'Ashérah de Yhwh," *RB* 84 (1977) 595-608.

____ "Who or What Was Yahweh's Asherah?: Startling New Inscriptions from Two Different Sites Reopen the Debate About the Meaning of Asherah," *BARev* 10/6 (1984) 42-51.

Lessing, Gotthold Ephraim, "Von der Erziehung des Menschengeschlechts," *Lessings Werke in fünf Bänden* 5 (ed. Forschungs- und Gedenkstätte der klassischen deutschen Literatur in Weimar; 6th ed.; Berlin: Aufbau Verlag, 1982).

Lindars, Barnabas, "Torah in Deuteronomy," *Words and Meanings: Essays Presented to David Winton Thomas* (eds. P.R. Ackroyd and B. Lindars; Cambridge: University Press, 1968) 117-136.

Lindblom, Johannes, "Wisdom in the Old Testament Prophets," *Wisdom in Israel and in the Ancient Near East: Presented to Professor Harold Henry Rowley in Celebration of His Sixty-Fifth Birthday, 24 March 1955* (eds. M. Noth and D.W. Thomas; VTSup 3; Leyden: Brill, 1955) 192-204.

Lohfink, Norbert, "Die Ältesten Israels und der Bund: Zum Zusammenhang von Dtn 5,23; 26,17-19; 27,1.9f und 31,9," *BN* 67 (1993) 26-42.

——— "Beobachtungen zur Geschichte des Ausdrucks עם יהוה," *Probleme biblischer Theologie: Gerhard von Rad zum 70. Geburtstag* (ed. H.W. Wolff; Munich: Kaiser, 1971) 275-305. [Reprinted in: id., *Theologie*, 99-132.]

——— "חָרַם *ḥāram* / חֵרֶם *ḥērem*," *TWAT* (eds. G.J. Botterweck and H. Ringgren; Stuttgart et al.: Kohlhammer, 1982) 3:192-213.

——— "Die *ḥuqqîm ûmišpāṭîm* im Buch Deuteronomium und ihre Neubegrenzung durch Dtn 12,1," *Bib* 70 (1989) 1-30. [Reprinted in: id., *Studien II*, 229-256.]

——— "Zum »kleinen geschichtlichen Credo« Dtn 26,5-9," *TP* 46 (1971) 19-39. [Reprinted in: id., *Studien I*, 263-290.]

——— "The Cult Reform of Josiah of Judah: 2 Kings 22-23 as a Source for the History of Israelite Religion," *Ancient Israelite Religion: Essays in Honor of Frank Moore Cross* (eds. P.D. Miller, P.D. Hanson and S.D. McBride; Philadelphia: Fortress Press, 1987) 459-475.

——— "Darstellungskunst und Theologie in Dtn 1,6-3,29," *Bib* 41 (1960) 105-134. [Reprinted in: id., *Studien I*, 15-44.]

——— "Das Deuteronomium: Jahwegesetz oder Mosegesetz? Die Subjektzuordnung bei Wörtern für »Gesetz« im Dtn und in der dtn Literatur," *TP* 65 (1990) 387-391.

——— "Zur neueren Diskussion über 2 Kön 22-23," *Das Deuteronomium: Entstehung, Gestalt und Botschaft* (ed. N. Lohfink; BETL 68; Leuven: University Press, 1985) 24-48. [Reprinted in: id., *Studien II*, 179-207.]

——— "Dtn 12,1 und Gen 15,18: Das dem Samen Abrahams geschenkte Land als der Geltungsbereich der deuteronomischen Gesetze," *Die Väter Israels: Beiträge zur Theologie der Patriarchenüberlieferungen im Alten Testament. Festschrift für Josef Scharbert zum 70. Geburtstag* (ed. M. Görg; Stuttgart: Kath. Bibelwerk, 1989) 183-210. [Reprinted in: id., *Studien II*, 257-285.]

——— "Dtn 26,17-19 und die »Bundesformel«," *ZKT* 91 (1969) 517-553. [Reprinted in: id., *Studien I*, 211-261.]

——— "*ʿed(w)t* im Deuteronomium und in den Königsbüchern," *BZ NF* 35 (1991) 86-93.

——— "Zur Fabel des Deuteronomiums," *Bundesdokument und Gesetz: Studien zum Deuteronomium* (ed. G. Braulik; HBS 4; Freiburg i.Br. et al.: Herder, 1995).

——— *Unsere neuen Fragen und das Alte Testament: Wiederentdeckte Lebensweisung* (Herder TB 1594; Freiburg i.Br. et al.: Herder Tb Verlag, 1989).

——— "Freizeit: Arbeitswoche und Sabbat im Alten Testament, insbesondere in der Priesterlichen Geschichtserzählung," id., *Wörter*, 190-208. [Reprinted in: id., *Fragen*, 75-97.]

——— "Die segmentären Gesellschaften Afrikas als neue Analogie für das vorstaatliche Israel," *BK* 38 (1983) 55-58.

____ "Das deuteronomische Gesetz in der Endgestalt – Entwurf einer Gesellschaft ohne marginale Gruppen," *BN* 51 (1990) 25-40.

____ "Gewaltenteilung: Die Ämtergesetze des Deuteronomiums als gewaltenteiliger Verfassungsentwurf und das katholische Kirchenrecht," id., *Wörter*, 57-75. [Reprinted in: id., *Fragen*, 52-74.]

____ "Der Glaube und die nächste Generation," id., *Das Jüdische am Christentum: Die verlorene Dimension* (Freiburg i.Br. et al.: Herder, 1987) 144-166, 260-263.

____ "Gott: Polytheistisches und monotheistisches Sprechen von Gott im Alten Testament," id., *Wörter*, 127-144. [Reprinted in: id., *Fragen*, 98-118.]

____ "Gott im Buch Deuteronomium," *La notion biblique de Dieu: Le Dieu de la Bible et le Dieu des philosophes* (ed. J. Coppens; BETL 41; Gembloux and Leuven: Duculot and University Press, 1976) 101-126. [Reprinted in: id., *Studien II*, 25-53.]

____ "Gottesvolk: Alttestamentliches zu einem Zentralbegriff im konziliaren Wortfeuerwerk," id., *Wörter*, 111-126. [Reprinted in: id., *Fragen*, 33-51.]

____ *Das Hauptgebot: Eine Untersuchung literarischer Einleitungsfragen zu Dtn 5-11* (AnBib 20; Rome: Biblical Institute Press, 1963).

____ *Höre Israel!: Auslegung von Texten aus dem Buch Deuteronomium* (WB 18; Düsseldorf: Patmos, 1965).

____ "Kerygmata des deuteronomistischen Geschichtswerks," *Die Botschaft und die Boten: Festschrift für Hans Walter Wolff zum 70. Geburtstag* (eds. J. Jeremias and L. Perlitt; Neukirchen-Vluyn: Neukirchener Verlag, 1981) 87-100. [Reprinted in: id., *Studien II*, 125-142.]

____ "2 Kön 23,3 und Dtn 6,17," *Bib* 71 (1990) 34-42.

____ "Opfer und Säkularisierung im Deuteronomium," *Studien zu Opfer und Kult im Alten Testament mit einer Bibliographie 1969-1991 zum Opfer in der Bibel* (ed. A. Schenker; FAT 3; Tübingen: Mohr, 1992) 15-43.

____ "Pluralismus: Theologie als Antwort auf Plausibilitätskrisen in aufkommenden pluralistischen Situationen, erörtert am Beispiel des deuteronomischen Gesetzes," id., *Wörter*, 24-43.

____ "[Review:] Buchholz, Joachim, *Die Ältesten Israels im Deuteronomium* (GTA 36; Göttingen: Vandenhoeck & Ruprecht, 1988)," *TRev* 89 (1993) 192-195.

____ "Die Sabbatruhe und die Freizeit," *StZ* 194 (1976) 395-407.

____ "»Die, deren Schilde eine Schande sind« (Hos 4,18): Hat Jahwe im Hoseabuch eine göttliche Gegenspielerin?," (unpublished).

____ "Die Sicherung der Wirksamkeit des Gotteswortes durch das Prinzip der Schriftlichkeit der Tora und das Prinzip der Gewaltenteilung nach den Ämtergesetzen des Buches Deuteronomium (Dt 16,18-18,22)," *Testimonium Veritati: Festschrift Wilhelm Kempf* (ed. H. Wolter; FTS 7; Frankfurt a.M.: Knecht, 1971) 143-155. [Reprinted in: id., *Studien I*, 305-325.]

____ *Studien zum Deuteronomium und zur deuteronomistischen Literatur I* (SBAB 8; Stuttgart: Kath. Bibelwerk, 1990).

____ *Studien zum Deuteronomium und zur deuteronomistischen Literatur II* (SBAB 12; Stuttgart: Kath. Bibelwerk, 1991).

____ *Studien zur biblischen Theologie* (SBAB 16; Stuttgart: Kath. Bibelwerk, 1993).

____ "Das Alte Testament und sein Monotheismus," *Der eine Gott und der dreieine Gott: Das Gottesverständnis bei Christen, Juden und Muslimen* (ed. K. Rahner; Schriftenreihe der Katholischen Akademie der Erzdiözese Freiburg i.Br.; Munich and Zurich: Schnell & Steiner, 1983) 28-47. [Reprinted in: id., *Theologie*, 133-151.]

____ "Gesellschaftlicher Wandel und das Antlitz des wahren Gottes: Zu den Leitkategorien einer Geschichte Israels," *Dynamik im Wort: Lehre von der Bibel, Leben aus der Bibel. Festschrift aus Anlaß des 50jährigen Bestehens des Katholischen Bibelwerkes in Deutschland (1933-1983)* (ed. Kath. Bibelwerk; Stuttgart: Kath. Bibelwerk, 1983) 119-131. [Reprinted in: id., *Theologie*, 64-77.]

____ *Unsere großen Wörter: Das Alte Testament zu Themen dieser Jahre* (Freiburg i.Br. et al.: Herder, 1977).

____ "Zur deuteronomischen Zentralisationsformel," *Bib* 65 (1984) 297-329. [Reprinted in: id., *Studien II*, 147-177.]

Lohfink, Norbert and J. Bergman, "אֶחָד," *TWAT* (eds. G.J. Botterweck and H. Ringgren; Stuttgart et al.: Kohlhammer, 1973) 1:210-218. – English translation: *TDOT* (Grand Rapids: 1974), 1:193-201.

Luyten, Jos, "Primeval and Eschatological Overtones in the Song of Moses (Dt 32,1-43)," *Das Deuteronomium: Entstehung, Gestalt und Botschaft* (ed. N. Lohfink; BETL 68; Leuven: University Press, 1985) 341-347.

Maag, Victor, "Erwägungen zur deuteronomischen Kultzentralisation," id., *Kultur, Kulturkontakt und Religion: Gesammelte Studien zur allgemeinen und alttestamentlichen Religionsgeschichte. Zum 70. Geburtstag* (eds. H.H. Schmidt and O.H. Steck; Göttingen and Zurich: Vandenhoeck & Ruprecht, 1980) 90-98.

Macholz, Georg Christian, *Israel und das Land: Vorarbeiten zu einem Vergleich zwischen Priesterschrift und deuteronomistischem Geschichtswerk* (Typewritten habilitation; Heidelberg: 1969).

Malfroy, Jean, "Sagesse et Loi dans le Deutéronome," *VT* 15 (1965) 49-65.

Mansfeld, G., *Der Ruf zur Freude im Alten Testament* (Typewritten Doctoral Dissertation; Heidelberg: 1965).

Marböck, Johannes, "Gesetz und Weisheit: Zum Verständnis des Gesetzes bei Jesus Ben Sira," *BZ NF* 20 (1976) 1-21.

Margalit, Baruch, "The Meaning and Significance of Asherah," *VT* 40 (1990) 264-297.

____ "Some Observations on the Inscription and Drawing from Khirbet el-Qôm," *VT* 39 (1989) 371-378.

Martin, Gerhard Marcel, *Fest und Alltag: Bausteine zu einer Theorie des Festes* (UB.T 604; Stuttgart et al.: Kohlhammer, 1973).

Martini, Carlo Maria, "L'esclusione dalla comunità del popolo di Dio e il nuovo Israele secondo Atti 3,23," *Bib* 50 (1969) 1-14.

May, Herbert Gordon, "The Fertility Cult in Hosea," *AJSL* 48 (1932) 73-98.

Mayer, Rudolf, "Monotheismus in Israel und in der Religion Zarathustras," *BZ NF* 1 (1957) 23-58.

Mayes, Andrew David Hastings, *Deuteronomy* (NCBC; Grand Rapids and London; Eerdmans, Marshall, Morgan & Scott, 1981).

McBride, S. Dean, *The Deuteronomic Name Theology* (Typewritten Ph.D. Harvard University; Cambridge, MA: 1969).

McCarter, P. Kyle, "Aspects of the Religion of the Israelite Monarchy: Biblical and Epigraphic Data," *Ancient Israelite Religion: Essays in Honor of Frank Moore Cross* (eds. P.D. Miller, P.D. Hanson and S.D. McBride; Philadelphia: Fortress Press, 1987) 137-155.

McKane, William, *Prophets and Wise Men* (SBT 44; 2nd impr.; London: SCM Press, 1966).

McKay, John W., "The Date of Passover and Its Significance," *ZAW* 84 (1972) 435-447.

____ *Religion in Judah Under the Assyrians 732-609 BC* (SBT 2/26; London: SCM Press, 1973).

Menes, Abram, *Die vorexilischen Gesetze Israels im Zusammenhang seiner kulturgeschichtlichen Entwicklung: Vorarbeiten zur Geschichte Israels 1* (BZAW 50; Giessen: Töpelmann, 1928).

Merendino, Rosario Pius, *Das deuteronomische Gesetz: Eine literarkritische, gattungs- und überlieferungsgeschichtliche Untersuchung zu Dt 12-26* (BBB 31; Bonn: Hanstein, 1969).

Meshel, Zeev, *Kuntillet 'Ajrud: A Religious Centre from the Time of the Judean Monarchy on the Border of Sinai* (Israel Museum Catalogue 175; Jerusalem: Israel Museum, 1978).

Metzger, Martin, "Himmlische und irdische Wohnstatt Jahwes," *UF* 2 (eds. K. Bergerhof, M. Dietrich and O. Loretz; Kevelaer and Neukirchen-Vluyn: Butzon & Bercker and Neukirchener Verlag, 1970) 139-158.

Miller, Patrick D., *The Divine Warrior in Early Israel* (HSM 5; Harvard, MA: Harvard University Press, 1973).

Mittmann, Siegfried, *Deuteronomium 11-63 literarkritisch und traditionsgeschichtlich untersucht* (BZAW 139; Berlin and New York: de Gruyter, 1975).

____ "Die Grabinschrift des Sängers Uriahu," *ZDPV* 97 (1981) 139-152.

Moawiyah, Ibrahim M. and Gerrit van der Kooij, "The Archeology of Deir 'Alla Phase IX," *The Balaam Text From Deir 'Alla Re-evaluated: Proceedings of the International Symposium Held at Leiden 21-24 August 1989* (eds. J. Hoftijzer and G. van der Kooij; Leyden: Brill, 1991) 16-29.

Moltmann, Jürgen, *Neuer Lebensstil: Schritte zur Gemeinde* (Munich: Kaiser, 1977).

Moor, Johannes C. de, *The Rise of Yahwism: The Roots of Israelite Monotheism* (BETL 91; Leuven: University Press, 1990).

____ *New Year with Canaanites and Israelites 1: Description* (SKC 21; Kampen: Kok, 1972).

Moore, Brian Robert, *The Scribal Contribution to Dt 4:1-40* (Diss. Notre Dame 1976; Ann Arbor: Xerox Univ. Microfilms, 1977).

Morenz, Siegfried, *Ägyptische Religion* (RM 8; Stuttgart: Kohlhammer, 1960).

Morgan Donn Farley, *The So-Called Cultic Calendars in the Pentateuch: A Morphological and Typological Study* (Claremont Graduate School Ph.D. 1974; Ann Arbor, MI: Xerox Univ. Microfilms, 1980).

Mosis, Rudolf, "גָּדַל II-III," *TWAT* (eds. G.J. Botterweck and H. Ringgren; Stuttgart et al.: Kohlhammer, 1973) 1:928-956. – English translation: *TDOT* (Grand Rapids: 1975) 2:391-416.

Mühl, Max, *Untersuchungen zur altorientalischen und althellenischen Gesetzgebung* (Klio.B 29; Aalen: Scientia Verlag, 1963 [reprint from 1933]).

Mühlen, Heribert, *Entsakralisierung: Ein epochales Schlagwort in seiner Bedeutung für die Zukunft der christlichen Kirchen* (Paderborn: Schöningh, 1971).

Müller, Hans-Peter, "Die aramäische Inschrift von Deir 'Allā und die älteren Bileamsprüche," *ZAW* 94 (1982) 214-244.

____ "עשתרת, *'štrt*," *TWAT* (eds. H.-.J. Fabry and H. Ringgren; Stuttgart et al.: Kohlhammer, 1989) 6:453-463.

____ "Einige alttestamentliche Probleme zur aramäischen Inschrift von Dēr 'Allā," *ZDPV* 94 (1978) 56-67.

Murphy, Roland E., "Assumptions and Problems in Old Testament Wisdom Research," *CBQ* 29 (1967) 101-112 [= (407)-(418)].

Nebeling, Gerhard, *Die Schichten des deuteronomischen Gesetzeskorpus: Eine traditions- und redaktionsgeschichtliche Analyse von Dt 12-26* (Typewritten Theological Dissertation; Münster: 1970).

Negretti, Nicola, *Il settimo giorno: Indagine critico-teologica delle tradizioni presacerdotali e sacerdotali circa il sabato biblico* (AnBib 55; Rome: Biblical Institute Press, 1973).

Nelson, Richard Donald, *The Redactional Duality of the Deuteronomistic History* (Theological Dissertation Union Theol. Sem. Richmond, VA, 1973; Ann Arbor: Xerox Univ. Microfilms, 1975).

____ *The Double Redaction of the Deuteronomistic History* (JSOTSup 18; Sheffield: JSOT Press, 1981).

Neuenzeit, Paul, "Die Gemeinde Jesu als gottesdienstliche Versammlung," *Liturgie der Gemeinde: Weihnachts-Seelsorgertagung 28.-30. Dezember 1965* (eds. E. Hesse and H. Erharter; Vienna: Herder, 1966) 11-24.

Neunheuser, Burkhard, "Mysterium Paschale: Das österliche Mysterium in der Konzilskonstitution »Über die heilige Liturgie«," *Österliches Mysterium: Das Pascha-Mysterium – Grundmotiv der Liturgie-Konstitution* (LuM 36; Maria Laach: Ars liturgica, 1965) 12-36.

____ "Vom Sinn der Feier," *Gott feiern: Theologische Anregung und geistliche Vertiefung zur Feier von Messe und Stundengebet* (ed. J.G. Plöger; Freiburg i.Br. et al.: Herder, 1980) 17-28.

Nicholson, Ernest, "The Centralisation of the Cult in Deuteronomy," *VT* 13 (1963) 380-389.

Nicolsky, Nicolaj M., "Pascha im Kulte des jerusalemischen Tempels," *ZAW* 45 (1927) 171-190.

Nielsen, Eduard, "»Weil Jahwe unser Gott ein Jahwe ist« (Dtn 6,4f.)," *Beiträge zur Alttestamentlichen Theologie: Festschrift für Walther Zimmerli zum 70. Geburtstag* (eds. H. Donner, R. Hanhart and R. Smend; Göttingen: Vandenhoeck & Ruprecht, 1977) 288-301. [Reprinted in: id., *Law, History and Tradition: Selected Essays* (Kopenhagen: Gads Forlag, 1983) 106-118.]

Noth, Martin, *Überlieferungsgeschichtliche Studien: Die sammelnden und bearbeitenden Geschichtswerke im Alten Testament* (3rd ed.; Tübingen: Niemeyer, 1967).

____ *Könige* (BKAT 9/1; Neukirchen-Vluyn: Neukirchener Verlag, 1968).

____ "Die Bewährung von Salomos »göttlicher Weisheit«," id., *Gesammelte Studien zum Alten Testament* II (TBü 39; Munich: Kaiser, 1969) 99-112.

Nötscher, Friedrich, *»Das Angesicht Gottes schauen« nach biblischer und babylonischer Auffassung* (Würzburg: Becker, 1924).

Nyberg, Henrik Samuel, *Studien zum Hoseabuch: Zugleich ein Beitrag zur Klärung des Problems der alttestamentlichen Textkritik* (UUÅ 1935:6; Uppsala: Lundequistska Bokhandeln, 1935).

Oettli, Samuel, *Das Gesetz Hammurabis und die Thora Israels: Eine religions- und rechtsgeschichtliche Parallele* (Leipzig: Hinrichs, 1903).

Olyan, Saul M., *Asherah and the Cult of Yahweh in Israel* (SBLMS 34; Atlanta: Scholars Press, 1988).

____ "Some Observations Concerning the Identity of the Queen of Heaven," *UF* 19 (eds. K. Bergerhof, M. Dietrich and O. Loretz; Kevelaer and Neukirchen-Vluyn: Butzon & Bercker and Neukirchener Verlag, 1987) 161-174.

Otto, Eckart, *Das Mazzotfest in Gilgal* (BWANT 107; Stuttgart et al.: Kohlhammer, 1975).

Otto, Eckart and Tim Schramm, *Fest und Freude* (KTB/BiKon 1003; Stuttgart et al.: Kohlhammer, 1977).

Panikulam, George, *Koinōnia in the New Testament: A Dynamic Expression of Christian Life* (AnBib 85; Rome: Biblical Institute Press, 1979).

Patai, Raphael, *The Hebrew Goddess* (New York: Ktav, 1967; 2nd ed. 1981).

Perlitt, Lothar, "Anklage und Freispruch Gottes: Theologische Motive in der Zeit des Exils," *ZTK* 69 (1972) 290-303. [Reprinted in: id., *Deuteronomium-Studien*, 20-31.]

___ *Bundestheologie im Alten Testament* (WMANT 36; Neukirchen-Vluyn: Neukirchener Verlag, 1969).

___ *Deuteronomium-Studien* (FAT 8; Tübingen: Mohr, 1994).

___ "»Ein einzig Volk von Brüdern«: Zur deuteronomischen Herkunft der biblischen Bezeichnung »Bruder«," *Kirche: Festschrift für Günther Bornkamm zum 75. Geburtstag* (eds. D. Lührmann and G. Strecker; Tübingen: Mohr, 1980) 27-52. [Reprinted in: id., *Deuteronomium-Studien*, 50-73.]

___ "Priesterschrift im Deuteronomium?," *ZAW* 100Sup (1988) 65-88.

Pesch, Rudolf, *Bergpredigt und Menschenrechte: Symposium und Akademie 30 Jahre Menschenrechte am 23. November 1978* (Vienna: Österreichisches Pastoralinstitut: 1979).

Peter, Michał, "Dtn 6,4 – ein monotheistischer Text?, *BZ NF* 24 (1980) 252-262.

Pettazoni, Raffaele, *Der allwissende Gott: Zur Geschichte der Gottesidee* (Fischer Bücherei 319; Frankfurt a.M.: Fischer, 1960).

Pieper, Josef, *Zustimmung zur Welt: Eine Theorie des Festes* (Munich: Kösel, 1963).

Ploeg, Johannes Petrus Maria van der, "Slavery in the Old Testament," *Congress Volume Uppsala 1971* (eds. G.W. Anderson et al.; VTSup 22; Leyden: Brill, 1972) 72-87.

Plöger, Josef G., *Literarkritische, formgeschichtliche und stilkritische Untersuchungen zum Deuteronomium* (BBB 26; Bonn: Hanstein, 1967).

Pritchard, James B., *ANET* (2nd ed.; Princeton: Princeton University Press, 1955).

Proksch, Otto, *Jesaja I: Kapitel 1-39* (KAT 9/1; Leipzig: Scholl, 1930).

Prümm, Karl, "Griechen," *Religionswissenschaftliches Wörterbuch: Die Grundbegriffe* (ed. F. König; Freiburg i.Br.: Herder, 1956) 316-325.

___ *Religionsgeschichtliches Handbuch für den Raum der altchristlichen Umwelt: Hellenistisch-römische Geistesströmungen und Kulte mit Beachtung des Eigenlebens der Provinzen* (Freiburg i.Br.: Herder, 1943).

Rad, Gerhard von, *Das fünfte Buch Mose: Deuteronomium. Übersetzt und erklärt* (ATD 8; Göttingen: Vandenhoeck & Ruprecht, 1964; 4th ed. 1983). – English translation: *Deuteronomy* (OTL; London: SCM Press, 1966; 7th impr. 1988).

____ "Das Gottesvolk im Deuteronomium," id., *Gesammelte Studien zum Alten Testament* II (ed. R. Smend; TBü 48; Munich: Kaiser, 1973) 9-108. [Reprint of: id., *Das Gottesvolk im Deuteronomium* (BWANT 47; Stuttgart: Kohlhammer, 1929).]

____ "Josephsgeschichte und ältere Chokma," id., *Gesammelte Studien zum Alten Testament* (TBü 8; 3rd ed.; Munich: Kaiser, 1965) 272-280.

____ "Es ist noch eine Ruhe vorhanden dem Volke Gottes: Eine biblische Begriffsuntersuchung," *ZZ* 11 (1933) 104-111. [Reprinted in: id., *Gesammelte Studien zum Alten Testament* (TBü 8; 3rd ed. Munich: Kaiser, 1965) 101-108.]

____ *Old Testament Theology 1: The Theology of Israel's Historical Traditions* (New York: 1962). – German original: *Theologie des Alten Testaments 1: Die Theologie der geschichtlichen Überlieferungen Israels* (Munich: Kaiser, 5th ed. 1966; 6th ed. 1969).

Rahner, Karl, "Zur Theologie des Gottesdienstes," *TQ* 159 (1979) 162-169.

Ratzinger, Joseph Kardinal, "Zur Frage nach der Struktur der liturgischen Feier," *IKaZ* 7 (1978) 488-497.

Reicke, Bo, *Diakonie: Festfreude und Zelos in Verbindung mit der altchristlichen Agapenfeier* (UUÅ 1951:5; Uppsala and Wiesbaden: Lundequistska Bokhandeln and Harrassowitz, 1951).

Reifenberg, H., "Von der Freude der Feier: Aspekte und Anregungen zu einem wesentlichen Grundzug des Gottesdienstes," *Gott feiern: Theologische Anregung und geistliche Vertiefung zur Feier von Messe und Stundengebet* (ed. J.G. Plöger; Freiburg i.Br. et al.: Herder, 1980) 52-60.

Reindl, Joseph, *Das Angesicht Gottes im Sprachgebrauch des Alten Testaments* (ETS 25; Leipzig: St. Benno-Verlag, 1970).

Rendtorff, Rolf, "Die Erwählung Israels als Thema der deuteronomischen Theologie," *Die Botschaft und die Boten: Festschrift für Hans Walter Wolff zum 70. Geburtstag* (eds. J. Jeremias and L. Perlitt; Neukirchen-Vluyn: Neukirchener Verlag, 1981) 75-86.

____ *Studien zur Geschichte des Opfers im Alten Israel* (WMANT 24; Neukirchen-Vluyn: Neukirchener Verlag, 1967).

Renger, Johannes, "Hammurapis Stele »König der Gerechtigkeit«: Zur Frage von Recht und Gesetz in der altbabylonischen Zeit," *WO* 8 (1975/76) 228-235.

Reventlow, Henning Graf, "Die Völker als Jahwes Zeugen bei Ezechiel," *ZAW* 71 (1959) 33-43.

Richter, Wolfgang, *Grundlagen einer althebräischen Grammatik: A. Grundfragen einer sprachwissenschaftlichen Grammatik – B. Die Beschreibungsebenen – I. Das Wort (Morphologie)* (ATSAT 8; St. Ottilien: Eos, 1978).

Ringgren, Helmer, "אֱלֹהִים," *TWAT* (eds. G. Botterweck and H. Ringgren; Stuttgart et al.: Kohlhammer, 1973) 1:285-305. – English translation: *TDOT* (Grand Rapids, MI: 1975) 1:267-284.

Rombold, Günter, "Die existentielle Bedeutung des Festes," *Diakonia* 10 (1979) 11-16.

Rose, Martin, *Der Ausschließlichkeitsanspruch Jahwes: Deuteronomische Schultheologie und die Volksfrömmigkeit in der späten Königszeit* (BWANT 106; Stuttgart et al.: Kohlhammer, 1975).

Rössler, Erich, *Jahwe und die Götter im Pentateuch und im deuteronomistischen Geschichtswerk* (Dissertation; Bonn: 1966).

Rost, Leonhard, "Erwägungen zu Hosea 4,13f.," id., *Das kleine Credo und andere Studien zum Alten Testament* (Heidelberg: Quelle & Meyer, 1965) 53-64.

Roth, Wolfgang, "The Deuteronomic Rest Theology: A Redaction-Critical Study," *Papers of the Chicago Society of Biblical Research* (eds. R.G. Boiling et al.; Chicago: Chicago Society of Biblical Research, 1976) 21:5-14.

Rücker, Heribert, *Die Begründungen der Weisungen Jahwes im Pentateuch* (ETS 30; Leipzig: St. Benno-Verlag, 1973).

Rudolph, Wilhelm, *Hosea* (KAT 13/1; Gütersloh: Mohn, 1966).

___ "Präparierte Jungfrauen? (Zu Hosea 1)," *ZAW* 75 (1963) 65-73.

Ruppert, Lothar, *Die Josephserzählung der Genesis: Ein Beitrag zur Theologie der Pentateuchquellen* (SANT 11; Munich: Kösel, 1965).

Ruprecht, E., "שׂמח *śmḥ* sich freuen," *THAT* (eds. E. Jenni and C. Westermann; Munich and Zurich: Kaiser and TVZ, 1976) 2:828-835.

Sauer, Georg, "Israels Feste und ihr Verhältnis zum Jahweglauben," *Studien zum Pentateuch: Walter Kornfeld zum 60. Geburtstag* (ed. G. Braulik; Vienna et al.: Herder, 1977) 135-141.

Schäfer-Lichtenberger, Christa, *Josua und Salomo: Eine Studie zu Autorität und Legitimität des Nachfolgers im Alten Testament* (VTSup 58; Leyden: Brill, 1995).

___ *Stadt und Eidgenossenschaft im Alten Testament: Eine Auseinandersetzung mit Max Webers Studie »Das antike Judentum«* (BZAW 156; Berlin and New York: de Gruyter, 1983).

Scharbert, Josef, "Formgeschichte und Exegese von Ex 34,6f und seiner Parallelen," *Bib* 38 (1957) 130-150.

___ *Heilsmittler im Alten Testament und im alten Orient* (QD 23/24: Freiburg i.Br. et al.: Herder, 1964).

Schenker, Adrian, "Der Monotheismus im ersten Gebot, die Stellung der Frau im Sabbatgebot und zwei andere Sachfragen zum Dekalog," *FZPhTh* 32 (1985) 323-341. [Reprinted in: id., *Text und Sinn im Alten Testament: Textgeschichtliche und bibeltheologische Studien* (OBO 103; Freiburg/CH and Göttingen: Universitätsverlag and Vandenhoeck & Ruprecht, 1991) 187-205.]

Schmidt, Johannes Michael, "Vergegenwärtigung und Überlieferung: Bemerkungen zu ihrem Verständnis im dtn.-dtr. Überlieferungsbereich," *EvT* 30 (1970) 169-200.

Schmidt, Martin, *Prophet und Tempel: Eine Studie zum Problem der Gottesnähe im Alten Testament* (Zurich: Evangelischer Verlag, 1948).

Schmidt, Werner H., "»Jahwe und ...«: Anmerkungen zur sog. Monotheismus-Debatte," *Die Hebräische Bibel und ihre zweifache Nachgeschichte: Festschrift für Rolf Rendtorff zum 65. Geburtstag* (eds. E. Blum, C. Macholz and E.W. Stegemann; Neukirchen-Vluyn: Neukirchener Verlag, 1990) 435-447.

Schmökel, Hartmut, *Hammurabi von Babylon: Die Errichtung eines Reiches* (Libelli 330; Darmstadt: Wissenschaftliche Buchgesellschaft, 1971).

Schottroff, Willy, *»Gedenken« im Alten Orient und im Alten Testament: Die Wurzel zākar im semitischen Sprachkreis* (WMANT 15; Neukirchen-Vluyn: Neukirchener Verlag, 1964).

Schreiner, Josef, "Exodus 12,21-23 und das israelitische Pascha," *Studien zum Pentateuch: Walter Kornfeld zum 60. Geburtstag* (ed. G. Braulik; Vienna et al.: Herder, 1977) 69-90.

Schroer, Silvia, *In Israel gab es Bilder: Nachrichten von darstellender Kunst im Alten Testament* (OBO 74; Freiburg/CH and Göttingen: Universitätsverlag and Vandenhoeck & Ruprecht, 1987).

____ "Die Zweiggöttin in Palästina / Israel: Von der Mittelbronze II B-Zeit bis zu Jesus Sirach," *Jerusalem: Texte – Bilder – Steine. Im Namen von Mitgliedern und Freunden des Biblischen Instituts der Universität Freiburg Schweiz zum 100. Geburtstag von Hildi + Othmar Keel-Leu* (NTOA 6; Freiburg/CH and Göttingen: Universitätsverlag and Vandenhoeck & Ruprecht, 1987) 201-225.

Schulte, Raphael, "Zum christlichen Verständnis von Religion und Kult," *TPQ* 115 (1967) 34-44.

Schultz, Hans Jürgen, (ed.), *Was der Mensch braucht: Anregungen für eine neue Kunst zu leben* (Stuttgart: Kreuz-Verlag, 1977).

Schulz, Waltraud, *Stilkritische Untersuchungen zur deuteronomistischen Literatur* (typewritten doctoral dissertation; Tübingen: 1974).

Schwantes, Milton, *Das Recht der Armen* (BET 4; Frankfurt a.M. et al.: P. Lang, 1977).

Seeligmann, Isac Leo, "Erkenntnis Gottes und historisches Bewußtsein im alten Israel," *Beiträge zur Alttestamentlichen Theologie: Festschrift für Walther Zimmerli zum 70. Geburtstag* (eds. H. Donner, R. Hanhart and R. Smend; Göttingen: Vandenhoeck & Ruprecht, 1977) 415-445.

Seitz, Gottfried, *Redaktionsgeschichtliche Studien zum Deuteronomium* (BWANT 93; Stuttgart et al.: Kohlhammer, 1971).

Sehmsdorf, Eberhard, "Studien zur Redaktionsgeschichte von Jes 55-66 (I) (Jes 65 16b-25 66 1-4 56 1-8)," *ZAW* 84 (1972) 517-562.

Shuval, Menakhem, "A Catalogue of Early Iron Stamp Seals from Israel," Othmar Keel, Menakhem Shuval and Christoph Uehlinger, *Studien zu den Stempelsiegeln aus Palästina / Israel 3: Die Frühe Eisenzeit. Ein Workshop* (OBO 100; Freiburg/CH and Göttingen: Universitätsverlag and Vandenhoeck & Ruprecht, 1990) 67-161.

Smend, Rudolf, *Die Entstehung des Alten Testaments* (ThW 1; 4th ed.; Stuttgart et al.: Kohlhammer, 1989).

____ "Essen und Trinken – ein Stück Weltlichkeit des Alten Testaments," *Beiträge zur Alttestamentlichen Theologie: Festschrift für Walther Zimmerli zum 70. Geburtstag* (eds. H. Donner, R. Hanhart and R. Smend; Göttingen: Vandenhoeck & Ruprecht, 1977) 446-459.

Smith, George Adam, *The Book of Deuteronomy* (The Cambridge Bible; Cambridge: University Press, 1918).

Smith, Mark S., *The Early History of God: Yahweh and the Other Deities in Ancient Israel* (San Francisco: Harper & Row, 1990).

Soden, Wolfram von, *AHW* 2 (Wiesbaden: Harrassowitz, 1972).

____ "Religion und Sittlichkeit nach den Anschauungen der Babylonier," *ZDMG* 89 (1935) 143-169.

Spieckermann, Hermann, *Juda unter Assur in der Sargonidenzeit* (FRLANT 129; Göttingen: Vandenhoeck & Ruprecht, 1982).

Splett, Jörg, "Der Mensch und die Freude," *ThG(B)* 21 (1978) 93-101.

____ "Was bedeutet mir Weihnachten?: Im Blick auf das 'schönste Fest' Gedanken zu Feier und Fest überhaupt," *LebZeug* 34/4 (1979) 6-15.

Stamm, Johann Jakob, *Die akkadische Namengebung* (2nd ed.; Darmstadt: Wissenschaftliche Buchgesellschaft, 1968).

Steuernagel, Carl, *Das Deuteronomium* (HAT 1/3/1; 2nd ed.; Göttingen: Vandenhoeck & Ruprecht, 1923).

Stolz, Fritz, "נוח *nūaḥ* ruhen," *THAT* (eds. E. Jenni and C. Westermann; Munich and Zurich: Kaiser and TVZ, 1976) 2:43-46.

____ "Jahwes Unvergleichlichkeit und Unergründlichkeit: Aspekte der Entwicklung zum alttestamentlichen Monotheismus," *WuD* 14 (1977) 9-24.

____ *Strukturen und Figuren im Kult von Jerusalem: Studien zur altorientalischen, vor- und frühisraelitischen Religion* (BZAW 118; Berlin: de Gruyter, 1970).

Tångberg, K. Arvid, "'I Am Like an Evergreen Fir; From Me Comes Your Fruit': Notes On Meaning and Symbolism in Hosea 14,9b (MT)," *SJOT* 2 (1989) 81-93.

Thomas Aquinas, *Opuscula Theologica 2: De re spirituali* (Turin and Rome: Marietti, 1954).

Thomas, David Winton, "Some Observations on the Hebrew Word רַעֲנָן," *Hebräische Wortforschung: Festschrift zum 80. Geburtstag von Walter Baumgartner* (ed. B. Hartmann et al.; VTSup 16; Leyden: Brill, 1967) 387-397.

Thomassin, L. de, *Traité des festes d l'Église: Traités historiques et dogmatiques* 2 (Paris: 1683).

Thompson, John Alexander, *Deuteronomy: An Introduction and Commentary* (TOTC; London: Inter-Varsity, 1974).

Tigay, Jeffrey H., *You Shall Have No Other Gods: Israelite Religion in the Light of Hebrew Inscriptions* (HSM 31; Atlanta, GA: Scholars Press, 1986).

____ "Israelite Religion: The Onomastic and Epigraphic Evidence," *Ancient Israelite Religion: Essays in Honor of Frank Moore Cross* (eds. P.D. Miller, P.D. Hanson and S.D. McBride; Philadelphia: Fortress Press, 1987) 157-194.

Toit, Andreas B. du, *Der Aspekt der Freude im urchristlichen Abendmahl* (Winterthur: Keller, 1965).

Toorn, Karel van der, "Female Prostitution in Payment of Vows in Ancient Israel," *JBL* 108 (1989) 193-205.

Vanoni, Gottfried, "Der Geist und der Buchstabe: Überlegungen zum Verhältnis der Testamente und Beobachtungen zu Dtn 30,1-10," *BN* 14 (1981) 65-98.

de Vaux, Roland, "»Le lieu que Yahvé a choisi pour y établir son nom«," *Das ferne und nahe Wort: Festschrift Leonhard Rost zur Vollendung seines 70. Lebensjahres am 30. November 1966 gewidmet* (ed. F. Maass; BZAW 105; Berlin: Töpelmann, 1967) 219-228.

Viganò, Lorenzo, *Nomi e titoli di YHWH alla luce del semitico del Nord-ovest* (BibOr 31; Rome: Biblical Institute Press, 1976).

Volkwein, Bruno, *Textkritische Untersuchungen zu Dtn 32,1-43* (typewritten doctoral dissertation; Rome: Pont. Ist. Bib., 1973).

Volp, Rainer, "Plädoyer fürs Fest," *KuKi* 34 (1971) 57-61.

Vorländer, Hermann, *Die Vorstellungen vom persönlichen Gott im Alten Orient und im Alten Testament* (AOAT 23; Kevelaer and Neukirchen-Vluyn: Butzon & Bercker and Neukirchener Verlag, 1975).

____ "Der Monotheismus Israels als Antwort auf die Krise des Exils," *Der einzige Gott: Die Geburt des biblischen Monotheismus* (ed. B. Lang; Munich: Kösel, 1981) 84-113, 134-139, 145-48.

Wacker, Marie-Theres, "Frau – Sexus – Macht: Eine feministisch-theologische Relecture des Hoseabuches," ead., *Der Gott der Männer und der Frauen* (TzZ 2; Düsseldorf: Patmos, 1987) 101-125.

___ "Jahwe und Aschera: Feministisch-theologische Überlegungen zu einem Götterkampf," (unpublished lecture ms; 1990) 15.

Wambacq, Benjamin Nestor, "Les Maṣṣôt," *Bib* 61 (1980) 31-54.

Weinfeld, Moshe, "Cult Centralisation in Israel in the Light of a Neo-Babylonian Analogy," *JNES* 23 (1964) 202-212.

___ *Deuteronomy and the Deuteronomic School* (Oxford: Clarendon Press, 1972; 2nd ed. 1990).

___ "The Worship of Molech and of the Queen of Heaven and Its Background," *UF* 4 (eds. K. Bergerhof, M. Dietrich and O. Loretz; Kevelaer and Neukirchen-Vluyn: Butzon & Bercker and Neukirchener Verlag, 1972) 133-154.

Weippert, Manfred, "The Balaam Text from Deir 'Alla and the Study of the Old Testament," *The Balaam Text From Deir 'Alla Re-evaluated: Proceedings of the International Symposium Held at Leiden 21-24 August 1989* (eds. J. Hoftijzer and G. van der Kooij; Leyden: Brill, 1991) 151-184.

___ "Zum Präskript der hebräischen Briefe von Arad," *VT* 25 (1975) 202-212.

___ "Synkretismus und Monotheismus: Religionsinterne Konfliktbewältigung im alten Israel," *Kultur und Konflikt* (eds. J. Assmann and D. Harth; edition suhrkamp 1612; Frankfurt a.M.: Suhrkamp, 1990) 143-179.

Weiser, Alfons, "ἀγαλλιάω / ἀγαλλίασις," *EWNT* (eds. H. Balz and G. Schneider; Stuttgart et al.: Kohlhammer, 1980; 2nd ed. 1992) 1:17-19.

Wellhausen, Julius, *Die kleinen Propheten: Übersetzt und erklärt* (4th ed.; Berlin: de Gruyter, 1963).

Westermann, Claus, " גיל *gîl* jauchzen," *THAT* (eds. E. Jenni and C. Westermann; Munich and Zurich: Kaiser and TVZ, 1971) 1:415-418.

___ *Der Segen in der Bibel und im Handeln der Kirche* (Munich: Kaiser, 1968).

Whybray, Roger Norman, *The Intellectual Tradition in the Old Testament* (BZAW 135; Berlin and New York: de Gruyter, 1974).

Wijngaards, Johannes N.M., *Deuteronomium uit de grondtekst vertaald en uitgelegd* (BOT 2/3; Roermond: Romen & Zonen, 1971).

Wildberger, Hans, *Jesaja I: Jesaja 1-12* (BKAT 10/1; Neukirchen-Vluyn: Neukirchener Verlag, 1972).

___ "Der Monotheismus Deuterojesajas," id., *Jahwe und sein Volk: Gesammelte Aufsätze zum Alten Testament. Zu seinem 70. Geburtstag am 2. Januar 1980* (eds. H.H. Schmid and O.H. Steck; TBü 66; Munich: Kaiser, 1979) 249-273.

____ "Die Neuinterpretation des Erwählungsglaubens Israels in der Krise der Exilszeit: Überlegungen zum Gebrauch von *bāḥar*," *Wort – Gebot – Glaube: Beiträge zur Theologie des Alten Testaments. Walther Eichrodt zum 80. Geburtstag* (ed. H.J. Stoebe; ATANT 59; Zurich: Zwingli Verlag, 1970) 307-324.

Winter, Urs, *Frau und Göttin: Exegetische und ikonographische Studien zum weiblichen Gottesbild im Alten Israel und in dessen Umwelt* (OBO 53; 2nd ed.; Freiburg/CH and Göttingen: Universitätsverlag and Vandenhoeck & Ruprecht, 1987).

Wiseman, Donald J., "The Laws of Hammurapi Again," *JSS* 7 (1962) 161-172.

Wolff, Hans Walter, *Anthropologie des Alten Testaments* (Munich: Kaiser, 1973).

____ *Dodekapropheton 1: Hosea* (BKAT 14/1; Neukirchen-Vluyn: Neukirchener Verlag, 4th ed. 1990).

____ "Das Geschichtsverständnis der alttestamentlichen Prophetie," id., *Gesammelte Studien zum Alten Testament* (TBü 22; 2nd ed.; Munich: Kaiser, 1973) 289-307.

____ "Das Kerygma des Jahwisten," id., *Gesammelte Studien zum Alten Testament* (TBü 22; 2nd ed.; Munich: Kaiser, 1973) 345-373.

Worden, Thomas, "The Literary Influence of the Ugaritic Fertility Myth on the Old Testament," *VT* 3 (1953) 273-297.

Woude, Adam Simon van der, "Bemerkungen zu einigen umstrittenen Stellen im Zwölfprophetenbuch," *Mélanges bibliques et orientaux en l'honneur de M. Henri Cazelles* (eds. A. Caquot and M. Delcor; AOAT 212; Kevelaer and Neukirchen-Vluyn: Butzon & Bercker and Neukirchener Verlag, 1981) 483-499.

Würthwein, Ernst, "Der Sinn des Gesetzes im Alten Testament," id., *Wort und Existenz: Studien zum Alten Testament* (Göttingen: Vandenhoeck & Ruprecht, 1970) 39-54.

Yee, Gale A., *Composition and Tradition in the Book of Hosea: A Redaction Critical Investigation* (SBLDS 102; Atlanta: Scholars Press, 1987).

Zeilinger, Franz, *Das Passionsbrot Israels: Deutungsgeschichtliche Untersuchung zum ungesäuerten Brot im Alten Testament* (typewritten dissertation; Graz: 1963).

Zenger, Erich, "Die späte Weisheit und das Gesetz," *Literatur und Religion des Frühjudentums: Eine Einführung* (eds. J. Maier and J. Schreiner; Würzburg and Gütersloh: Echter and Mohn, 1973) 43-56.

Zevit, Ziony, "A Phoenician Inscription and Biblical Covenant Theology," *IEJ* 27 (1977) 110-118.

____ "The Khirbet el-Qôm Inscription Mentioning a Goddess," *BASOR* 255 (1984) 39-47.

Zimmerli, Walther, "Erkenntnis Gottes nach dem Buche Ezechiel," id., *Gottes Offenbarung: Gesammelte Aufsätze zum Alten Testament* (TBü 19; Munich: Kaiser, 1963) 41-119.

—— "Das Gesetz im Alten Testament," id., *Gottes Offenbarung: Gesammelte Aufsätze zum Alten Testament* (TBü 19; Munich: Kaiser, 1963) 249-276.

—— "Der Wahrheitserweis Jahwes nach der Botschaft der beiden Exilspropheten," id., *Studien zur alttestamentlichen Theologie und Prophetie: Gesammelte Aufsätze* 2 (TBü 51; Munich: Kaiser, 1974) 192-212.

Zorell, Franciscus, *Lexicon Hebraicum et Aramaicum Veteris Testamenti* (Rome: Institutum Biblicum, 1968).